Race in gram

ORIENTALISTS, PROPAGANDISTS, AND *ILUSTRADOS*

anthropology

pedagogy

epistemology

epistemology

orthography

lexicography

VICISSITUDES

Samscrit

infidel

trope

thematic

Hellenist

philology

Orientalists, Propagandists, and *Ilustrados*

. . . .

Filipino Scholarship and the End of Spanish Colonialism

Megan C. Thomas

University of Minnesota Press
Minneapolis
London

Portions of chapter 4 have been previously published as "'K' Is for De-Kolonization: Anti-Colonial Nationalism and Orthographic Reform," *Comparative Studies in Society and History* 49 (2007).

Published by the University of Minnesota Press
111 Third Avenue South, Suite 290
Minneapolis, MN 55401-2520
http://www.upress.umn.edu

Library of Congress Cataloging-in-Publication Data

Thomas, Megan C. (Megan Christine).
Orientalists, propagandists, and *ilustrados* : Filipino scholarship and the end of Spanish colonialism / Megan C. Thomas.
 Includes bibliographical references and index.
 ISBN 978-0-8166-7190-8 (hc : alk. paper)—ISBN 978-0-8166-7197-7 (pb : alk. paper)
 1. Ethnology—Philippines. 2. Ethnohistory—Philippines. 3. Philippine literature—19th century—History and criticism. 4. Orientalism—Philippines—History. 5. Philippines—Colonization. 6. Philippines—Historiography. 7. Spain—Foreign relations—Philippines. 8. Philippines—Foreign relations—Spain. 9. Spain—Colonies—Asia. I. Title.
 GN671.P5T47 2012
 305.8009599—dc23   2011031792

Printed in the United States of America on acid-free paper

The University of Minnesota is an equal-opportunity educator and employer.

20 19 18 17 16 15 14 13 12   10 9 8 7 6 5 4 3 2 1

Contents

Acknowledgments

THIS PROJECT has been long enough in the making, and aided by so many people in ways big and small, that I cannot possibly adequately acknowledge all my debts. In my dissertation and in earlier publications, I thank many who by all rights should be named again here, too, but for brevity's sake I mention here only those whose help came later or was most significant.

Ben Anderson first interested me in the nineteenth-century Philippines, and his support and guidance over the years have been incredible. He has remained willing to advise, read drafts, and give priceless comments long after I left Cornell, but perhaps that should come as no surprise, since he has always shared generously his knowledge and time (and his irrepressible sense of humor). Paul Kramer is the other person to whom this project owes the most. A chance meeting in Rizal Library's Filipiniana reading room led first to conversations and then to wonderfully helpful comments on conference papers, chapters, and finally the entire book (more than once). His guiding hand has been invaluable both intellectually and professionally, and despite thorough testing, I have yet to find any limit to his generosity.

I am particularly grateful for the generous assistance I received from those at many institutions in Manila: the Ateneo de Manila University's Institute of Philippine Culture and Rizal Library (especially the staffs of the Filipiniana, American, Pardo de Tavera, and microfilm collections), the archives of the University of Santo Tomas, the National Archives, the National Library, the Lopez Museum, and the library of the University of the Philippines–Diliman.

This work began at Cornell University, where the Southeast Asia Program, Government Department, and Olin and Kroch Libraries were indispensable. The University of California's Pacific Rim Research Program funded further research in Manila, and UC Santa Cruz's Academic

Senate Committee on Research supported research in Madrid's National Library. Sabbatical from UC Santa Cruz and the generosity of the Newberry Library's staff (especially Jim Grossman and Diane Dillon of the Newberry's Office of Research) allowed me to stretch out the benefits of a short-term fellowship at the Newberry Library, and the library's photoduplication department generously and quickly provided the book's images. The book has benefited enormously from others' labor. Some commented on the entire manuscript or performed another act of heroic assistance, some sparked thoughts in key conversations, and some supported in other ways, but I'm grateful to all and wish I could have incorporated more of the collective wisdom I received: Andrew Abalahin, Judith Aissen, Myrna Alejo, Mark Anderson, Jody Blanco, Denver Brunsman, Susan Buck-Morss, Richard Chu, Jim Clifford, Chris Connery, Michael Cullinane, Deirdre de la Cruz, Shelly Errington, Alice Fahs, Katherine Gordy, Debbie Gould, Derek Hall, Eva-Lotta Hedman, Gail Hershatter, Courtney Johnson, Isaac Kramnick, Smita Lahiri, Gina Langhout, Kim Lau, Ada Loredo, Roy Loredo, Lourdes Martínez-Echazábal, Dean Mathiowetz, Kirstie McClure, Robert Meister, Helen Mendoza, Helene Moglen, Resil Mojares, Radhika Mongia, Jeanne Morefield, Rosalind Morris, Ambeth Ocampo, Vince Rafael, Raquel Reyes, Maria Elena Rivera-Beckstrom, Lloyd Rudolph, Abby Salacata, Sanjay Seth, Vanita Seth, Noel Inocencio Valencia, Dan Vukovich; the institutions and people of the venues where I have presented this work, including the University of Wisconsin–Madison Center for Southeast Asian Studies, Whitman College's Politics Department, the Newberry Library Fellow's Seminar and Colloquium, the UCLA Political Theory Seminar, the UCSC Center for Cultural Studies colloquium, and annual meetings of the American Ethnological Society (Toronto, 2007) and the Association for Asian Studies (San Diego, 2004; Atlanta, 2008); and the good people of Popular Education for People's Empowerment. I am grateful for translation advice from Gabriela Andrea Frank (German), Cora Gorman Malone (Spanish), and Thomas Genova (Spanish); Tom meticulously combed through notes, quotations, and translations more than once, and his corrections and inquiries led to critical revisions. Maria Theresa Savella's miraculous Tagalog instruction gave me access to the most fun part of my work. Finally, Jason Weidemann at the University of Minnesota Press has been wonderfully supportive and patiently shepherded the manuscript through its more recent metamorphoses. None of these people are responsible for the errors in fact and interpretation that surely remain.

Finishing would have been unimaginable without the support of my growing family—Alice Thomas, Bruce Thomas, Lise Thomas, Valerie Thomas, Chloe Thomas-Green, Collin Thomas-Green, Cora Turk-Thomas, and Ben Turk—and my best friends and scholarly companions Derek, Vanita, Dean, Kate, and of course my sweetheart Mark. Because profuse thanks are standard in this kind of situation, the mountain that I owe Mark would never actually be fully visible to anyone aside from him and me, no matter how I put it. In limited words, thank you.

Worldly Colonials

Ilustrado Thought and Historiography

Revolutionary Cause

We will begin at the end of the story. In October of 1896, during the "insurrection" that would become known as the Philippine Revolution, a teacher at one of Manila's top schools wrote a letter in defense of his school and its faculty. Jesuit Father Miguel Saderra Mata recounted a rumored charge against the Ateneo Municipal: "In Madrid they were saying 'that the principal cause of the insurrection in the Philippines was the Jesuit fathers, for giving to the youth of the Archipelago . . . an education that was cosmopolitan . . . and not Spanish . . . like that of other religious orders.'"[1] In his frustrated reply, he defended the Jesuit fathers against the accusations by portraying their school as a model of Spanish patriotism. The Ateneo's courses were "cosmopolitan" only in the sense that they were "capable of being taught in all parts of the world," and the school pursued its curriculum precisely "in order to accomplish one of the goals of the founding of the Ateneo, that is, that Filipinos do not go abroad (which, in my opinion, is not very cosmopolitan)."[2] Father Saderra Mata then suggested that perhaps another of Manila's schools, the Dominican University of Santo Tomás, was responsible for the Revolution's outbreak: "The record shows that more than a few alumni have left the University [of the Dominicans] on account of problems with the professors . . . and have gone to study outside of the Philippines, where they learned separatist ideas."[3] To illustrate the point, he named, "e.g., Rizal," referring to José Rizal Mercado y Alonzo (1861–96), the son of a well-to-do agricultural family from the Tagalog-speaking province of Laguna, a family that, like many of a rising agricultural business class, was officially "native" but historically Chinese mestizo.[4] Rizal had left the islands to pursue his education in Spain, where he trained as an ophthalmologist, studied broadly, traveled widely in Europe, and wrote prolifically: newspaper articles, two political novels, and scholarly works on the history, ethnology, and folklore of the Philippines, for which he earned the admiration of many but the suspicion of the most powerful. He would be executed in Manila at the end of 1896 on trumped-up charges of "subversion" (*filibusterismo*) and complicity with the revolutionaries.

The Dominicans, likely the source of the rumor to which Saderra Mata was responding, also pointed fingers of blame for the Revolution outside the archipelago. The Dominican prior provincial, Father Bartolomé Alvaréz de Manzano, wrote confidentially to the Spanish minister of *ultramar* (lit. "overseas minister," or colonial minister) in August 1897, accusing the scholarly works of Rizal and other young Filipinos of inciting the revolution. Rizal's "*Notes* to the Morga [an account of early Spanish presence in the Philippines] and his articles and pamphlets . . . caused such great excitement among many of the educated of the country . . . such writings were no more than conscious preparation for obtaining the independence of the archipelago."[5] Alvaréz likewise singled out the historical works of Pedro Alejandro Paterno (1858–1911), the scion of a prominent mestizo (Tagalog-Chinese) family of Manila who had pursued his education in Spain (as many other young men of means would later do), where he had written, among other things, about religions and cultures of the pre-Hispanic Philippines. The Dominican wrote that Paterno's works had, "emphasizing the value of the ancient Tagalog civilization, spread the same ideas as Rizal in his notes to the Morga, and sought to demonstrate how very little the inhabitants of these islands owed to Spain and to the Church."[6] And whom did the Dominican ultimately blame for these "real agents of the Philippine revolution"?[7] They had been "[i]nfluenced by that cultivated Europe, and encouraged [*halagados*] by several of our men of science and prominent politicians of Madrid," for until these young men had returned from "that cultivated but unhinged Europe . . . trying to 'open their [Filipinos'] eyes and initiate them into progress and modern culture,'" the Philippines had "remained peaceful and prosperous for three centuries, without dreaming of utopian independences, of so-called individual rights, of political suffrage, of redeeming liberties, or that they were equal to the Europeans."[8]

There is good reason to be suspicious of these words and of the vision of history that they paint where revolutionary action in the Philippines is caused by European ideas via the thoughts and writings of a few elite

Filipinos. Neither Jesuits nor Dominicans could imagine that the revolutionary *Katipunan*, the secret plebeian organization whose discovery by officials in August of 1896 had sparked the revolution, could possibly have acted without the instigation of more educated elite leaders. But the finger of blame (or credit, if you will) points more distantly to Europe, as if even the thought of Filipino elites acting autonomously as historical agents was too much to bear. The fathers' accusations also reflect struggles between the Church and secular forces in Europe: both Jesuits and Dominicans defend themselves and their schools from the charge of being bad influences on Filipino elites by arguing that the source of those bad influences were peninsular enemies of the Church—men of science and prominent politicians. Though they agreed on little else, they concurred that the ultimate responsibility for the revolutionary sons of the Philippines lay outside the islands—in secular Europe—and so outside their sphere of influence.

As easily as these Catholic charges can be dismissed for their clear bias and self-interest, they reveal a truth: Some young Filipino authors in the 1880s and early 1890s found certain ideas, models, and principles "from Europe" to be both available and attractive to them as they thought about their place in the world and as they rewrote the narratives in which they saw themselves and their homeland figured. In producing these writings, they did lay scholarly intellectual foundations for a nationalist challenge to Spanish authority.[9] The extraordinary flowering of scholarly writing about the peoples and history of the Philippines, written by young Filipinos in the years preceding the Philippine Revolution, is the subject of this book.

The book examines this single but significant example of the political lives of scholarly fields. It seeks to explain how young colonial subjects could produce such scholarship, what appeal these scholarly pursuits held for them, and what political significance the writings had for their contemporaries. These writings show that the political meanings of scholarly and intellectual traditions are shaped by their content and methods, though not wholly determined by them.

These young Filipinos drew on a set of scholarly practices—linguistics (philology), folklore, ethnology—that were part of European Orientalism and nineteenth-century racial sciences and, in turn, associated with European colonial pretensions. This study treats the ways those scholarly practices traveled outside Europe and were sometimes put to anticolonial ends. When seen at this distance, the contours of the story look similar to those outlined by Partha Chatterjee's Indian nationalists. In Chatterjee's telling, Indian nationalist thought first had to accept the terms and form of colonizing knowledge before revaluing those terms, thus changing the valence of the forms of knowledge, and finally transforming the forms themselves.[10] As we will see in the Philippine case, colonial subjects also constructed conceptions of history and society using knowledges often associated with colonial projects.

In the case of the Philippines, however, these "European" knowledges were largely absent from the colonizer's repertoire and traveled to "the colony" on the colonized's terms. Here, the intellectual history of the Philippines is distinctly unlike that of India. Part of why this is so has to do with the particularities of the Spanish colonial and intellectual worlds, and the unusual position these young educated Filipinos occupied in the cosmopolitan scholarly world of the 1880s and early 1890s. These Filipinos' writings were among the first Spanish-language writings in these genres to treat the Philippines, and some of them were significant contributions to Spanish-language scholarship in these areas more generally, which tended to be dominated by English, French, and German authors. These young colonial subjects positioned themselves as modern scholars and intellectuals in a broader field in which their colonizers, the Spanish, often lagged behind.[11] The intellectual practices that we associate with colonialism, then, were here importantly not *of* the colonizer before these colonial subjects took them up. Instead, they represented a world that Rizal described as the "free sphere of scientific facts," a world that recognized no political boundaries or authority, but only the authority of reason and evidence.[12]

Young Filipinos were confident that they could travel in these scholarly worlds in part because Manila's Jesuit and Dominican schools gave them both the institutional and intellectual requisites to do so. With degrees from the Jesuit and Dominican institutions, and attendant grasps of the languages, literatures, and subjects represented in their curricula, they were able to travel beyond the physical confines of the colony, enrolling in universities in Spain and beyond. They also traveled intellectually beyond the confines of the Catholic curricula to a wider world of scholarship. Though consummate outsiders—colonial subjects of the backward Spanish empire—they entered some of the most current European scholarly spaces.

Though the peculiarities of the Philippine case help to explain why it departs from Chatterjee's Indian model, this book further argues that to understand why Orientalism and newer nineteenth-century racial sciences were politically malleable—subject to multiple political uses and effects—we have to look at particular features of those scholarly practices themselves. The specific contours of Orientalism and nineteenth-century racial sciences made them troublesome but also indispensable for their Filipino practitioners. Particular practices (e.g., ethnology, folklore, philology, history) have distinct sets of possibilities and constraints, as illustrated by the distinct trajectories they followed in the nineteenth-century Philippines. By tracing the particular possibilities of each scholarly genre and refusing to treat Orientalism as a homogeneous discourse, I show both the anticolonial possibilities and political constraints of such scholarship.

Some political uses of similar scholarship have long been recognized. We know that nineteenth-century European nationalisms, for example, were bolstered by the "energetic activities" of "lexicographers, philologists, grammarians, folklorists, publicists, and composers," whose work promoted the idea of the tangibility, grandeur, and antiquity of *individual* linguistically based nations but also the idea that each of these nations was part of a world filled with other nations, each of similar type yet unique in content.[13] It was not only the humanistic sciences but also emerging social sciences of the nineteenth century that became associated with nationalist thought and whose studies promoted both individual nations specifically as well as the general idea of nations as the natural units dividing the human world. To the previously given list of nineteenth-century nation-makers, then, we might add not only poets, novelists, and philosophers but also historians, numismatists, archeologists, ethnographers, and ethnologists. These scholars studied the seemingly endless variety of humanity and its products—coins, buildings, tools, jewelry, customs, or clothing—and organized this variety into the cubbyholes of nations or peoples, each with its own particular content. Such studies collectively portrayed a world divided into nations or peoples, each with its own qualities but similar in type; they related to each other horizontally.

However, many of these nation-making social sciences employed narratives, languages, and tropes that were at odds with the idea of a world divided into nations of roughly equal *status*. For example, while it is clear that folklore studies were often integral parts of emerging intellectual nationalisms, less attention has been paid to, or explanation given of, how these folklore studies saw peoples organized *hierarchically* as well as horizontally: some beliefs are more advanced than others, more modern than others, better than others. These contradictory tendencies—to organize peoples hierarchically as well as horizontally—were common to practices of ethnology, history, and linguistics as well: some peoples, histories, or languages were more advanced than others. Any particular political use of such scholarly practices, then, depended in part on whether it avoided, incidentally employed, or indeed actively promoted its vertical organizational logics as well as horizontal ones. Vertical logics provided particular dilemmas for marginally European or extra-European nationalisms, which could rarely claim their people to be at the pinnacle of such hierarchically organized schemes.

These scholarly genres had emerged out of a set of interests, assumptions, and techniques of an older conglomeration of studies associated with the tradition of Orientalism that had blossomed in the late eighteenth and early nineteenth centuries. In the late nineteenth century, these practices were in the midst of transformation, incorporating new premises, questions, methods, and data brought by nineteenth-century scientific developments of evolutionary biology, political-economic developments of industrialism and nationalism, and the imperatives of a Europe hungry for land, markets, plantations, and coaling stations. Many of these newer practices imagined "race" to be the unit of their scientific investigation of human history, and so these "human sciences" can also be thought of as "racial sciences." Some of these scholarly practices would, in their travels between different languages, politics, and institutions, eventually settle in the early twentieth century into a set of subdisciplines of "anthropology." But in the 1880s, these practices—philology, ethnology, ethnography, and folklore—were in the midst of transformation; their premises were shifting, and their relationships with each other, and with a broader scholarly and political world, were still plastic. As part of the broader traditions of "Orientalism" and "anthropology," these scholarly practices have often been associated with the politics of colonization, but they have not always been so.[14]

It is one of these "not always" moments that we will examine here, not merely as an interesting exception. What we will find in this iteration is that these same scholarly disciplines lent themselves to quite different political ends than those of furthering colonial rule, in part because of their methods, data, presumptions, and even languages. Filipino scholars were only in some senses on the margins of European scholarship, and we will find in their citations, correspondences, and intellectual and political affiliations reminders that the disciplines were in flux and that it is from among countless possible scholarly worlds that history has stumbled toward the present. By examining this admittedly exceptional moment, we can see with more clarity how specific and, to a certain degree, how arbitrary are the political associations, disciplinary conventions, methodological presumptions, and scholarly affiliations of these fields, as they eventually were reified by early twentieth-century academia.

These contentions disrupt two commonly held models of the politics of knowledge in the colonial world. First, Orientalism and nineteenth-century racial sciences are often treated as if they are politically homogenous and overdetermined—that is, that they necessarily value Europe (and White) over civilizational and racial "others." Second, where scholars have noted Orientalism and anthropological sciences in the service of anticolonial nationalism, they argue that the tools of the colonizer have been appropriated by the colonized. The writings I treat show that neither of these models clearly stands. Orientalist and racial sciences can be used for liberatory projects as well as repressive ones; they are subject to the particular political and historical context in which they are deployed, and also to manipulation by their practitioners.

The aim here is neither to deny the colonial histories that these knowledges have had in other times and places nor to deny colonial possibilities and tendencies even in this case. Instead, I trace some alternative political paths that these knowledges took—paths often only briefly winding through the metropole en route to the colony—to delineate what made those paths possible.

Finally, this book shows that the category of "nationalist thought" may obscure as much as it illuminates. I look at how these writings held the potential to validate a Filipino nation opposed to Spanish rule, but I also look at what other kinds of communities these writings sketched and produced. It would be difficult to see the variety of the kinds of communities imagined if we presumed at the outset that the aim of these authors was "the nation" or that their writings are examples of "nationalist thought." Further, the category of "nationalist thought" is not self-evident. Does "nationalist thought" comprise the thoughts articulated by those who conceive of themselves as being members of a nation, or does it more specifically refer to arguments defending or promoting the nation as the basic political unit? Does "nationalist thought" defend nationalism as a general principle, or does it champion the existence, value, and political destiny of a *particular* nation? Is thought that conceives of a people sharing a language, culture, or history necessarily "nationalist," and, conversely, must nationalist thought be articulated via the word "nation," or can nationalist thought be expressed in terms of "people," "culture," or "race"?

Another set of questions arises about political self-sovereignty as a presumptive aim of nationalism. Does nationalism always take sovereignty to lie at the level of the "nation"? What, then, to do with thought in which self-sovereignty as such is rarely articulated as a principle? What other kinds of political futures might "peoples," "cultures," or "races" be thought to have? Sometimes the label "nationalist" can be familiar and convenient enough that it loses specificity. The problem is not so much with the label itself but with the tendency to leap too quickly over the question of content—of what does any given nationalism consist?—to the presumptive end of all nationalisms in the self-sovereign nation-state. Not only is the shortest path between two points sometimes crooked, to paraphrase Chatterjee, but the path itself splits into and merges with others along the way.[15] The shortest path between two points may be crooked precisely because the second point is not the only possible destination. This book treats its subjects as points along intersecting paths, exploring paths less well traveled, paths that may lead to places other than the nation.

To consider any subject primarily or self-evidently as "nationalist" might too quickly elide significant differences and hide more particular or salient political circumstances and aspirations. For example, campaigns to have the Philippines treated as a Spanish province, or critiques of extraordinary political power of the Catholic Church in the islands, should be seen neither as imperfect or incipient nationalism nor as incompatible with it. These political discourses had their own trajectories and possible outcomes other than an independent nation-state. To understand how they intersected with, but are not reducible to, thought that presumes the inevitability of the nation-state, first we have to investigate how "the nation" but also other forms of collectivities were thought.

Ilustrados, Propagandistas, and Philippine Historiography

This book focuses particularly on writings of José Rizal, Pedro Paterno, T. H. Pardo de Tavera (1857–1925), Isabelo de los Reyes y Florentino (1864–1938), Mariano Ponce (1863–1918), Pedro Serrano Laktaw (1853–1928), and their Bohemian supporter Ferdinand Blumentritt (1853–1913). I focus on their scholarly writings but read them with reference to some of the political writings they and others contributed to newspapers in the Spanish peninsula and the Philippines. Most of these young men were politically active during the tumultuous years surrounding the Revolution of 1896, and some of their texts have become icons of the birth of Philippine nationalism. But approaching these writings as collectively "nationalist" may hinder more than help to understand how these texts were formulated, to what kinds of ideas and politics they were responding, and to what possible futures they aimed.

Even an abbreviated list of titles may serve to briefly introduce the scope of this work: *Contribution to the Study of Ancient Alphabets of the Philippines* (1884); *Sanskrit in the Tagalog Language* (1887); *Filipino Folk-Lore* (1889, two volumes); *The History of Ilocos* (1890, two volumes, the first "Pre-Historical" and the second "Historical"); *The History of the Philippines* (1890, "Pre-Historic Epoch" with later volumes planned but not published); and, referring to specific peoples of the Philippines, "The Tinguian" (1887), *The Itas* (1890), and *The Ancient Tagalog Civilization* (1887, later retitled *The Ancient Civilization of the Philippines*). Many of these titles appeared in whole or in part first as a series of newspaper articles in Manila; others were published in their entirety first in Spain or elsewhere in Europe.

Each of the individuals that contributed to this movement requires his own introduction, but as I attempt here to document a collective intellectual-political moment, I begin with the broad features that describe their group. All were from Catholic families; all but Blumentritt—setting aside for the moment this obvious biographical outlier—were born in the Philippines to families who had maneuvered up economically during agricultural and commercial transformations facilitated by the opening of ports to foreign commerce beginning in 1834.[16] For a variety of reasons, families officially designated as "Chinese mestizo" were often well positioned to take advantage of this economic development. While Chinese mestizos had originally descended from migrating Chinese fathers and local mothers, they spoke the local language, were Catholic, and were in many respects culturally indistinct from wealthier "natives" (*indios*), another official category that encompassed the Catholic, lowland peoples who were largely integrated into the Spanish colonial state.[17] By the late nineteenth century, tax laws had become more favorable for "natives," and as a consequence—and perhaps facilitated by intermarriage—some "mestizo" families changed their official status to "native." It was from this

increasingly indistinct mestizo-cum-native rising class that these young
men often came, though Pardo de Tavera's family, also of some mixed
parentage and tied to local elites, was officially "creole" (*criollo*)—also
referred to as "Philippine[-born] Spaniard" (*español filipino*)—and his
family (unusually) spoke Castilian as a first language. Though originally
from different provinces, they all received a strikingly classical education
in Manila's Catholic institutions of higher education, many first at the
Jesuit Ateneo and many also at the University of Santo Tomás, which
served them both as entrance to universities of Europe and as sources
for their own political and philosophical writings. Castilian was the common language in which this polyglot group—mostly, but not all, Tagalog
speakers—corresponded, studied, and published.[18] Their advanced education drew them together, distinguished them from other "natives," and
has been identified as having enabled both their scholarly writings as well
as their political aspirations; thus they are often collectively referred to as
the *ilustrados* (which can be translated as "educated" or "enlightened").[19]

Some of these authors wrote pieces on politics and policy that formed
part of a careful and often circumspect conversation about the possibilities of political reform under Spanish rule, and of revolt against it. As a
group of "propagandists"—named for the "Propaganda Committee"
in Manila that supported their efforts to publicize Philippine political
issues in the Spanish peninsula and distributed clandestine publications
in the islands—some of these young men wrote newspaper articles (even
published their own newspapers) and pursued political alliances in the
peninsula that aimed to secure rights for Filipinos as Spanish citizens and
political reforms that would make government and education in the Philippines more like they were in the peninsula. Filipino propagandists built
a case for their homeland to be treated as a province equal in its legal status
to other Spanish provinces, basing this in part on the precedent set by the
liberal constitution of 1812 that had sought to stem the flow of independence through the Americas by granting representation in the Cortes to
those provinces, including the Philippines (hitherto a distant administrative outpost of New Spain). The propagandists understood all too well
that the Philippines was in practice a colony, but they appealed to historical precedent and standing laws to argue that sons of the Philippines, like
those of peninsular Spain, were Spanish citizens.[20] Their best-known project is the newspaper *La solidaridad*, published first in Barcelona and then
Madrid (1889–95), but as I have argued elsewhere, this paper should be

seen in the context of others published in the Philippines in the 1880s and 1890s that also strove to promote progressive change.[21]

One of *La solidaridad*'s main refrains, and a common theme of many of the propagandists' other writings, was the hold of the Church, and friar orders in particular, over education and government in the islands. In the late nineteenth century, nowhere in the world were so many people under the sway of friar orders as they were in the Philippines. As *La solidaridad* complained, exaggerating for effect by referring to "uncivilized" peoples of the Cordillera mountains of the Philippines (*igórrotes*, or "Igorots") and using the derogatory Spanish term for "native" (*Indio*), "[f]rankly, we are humiliated—though we might be Igorots and *Indios*—when we are governed by the people that Europe has thrown out as representatives of obscurantism."[22] The Church and its representatives—in particular, the friar orders—had both official standing and power in the administration unequalled anywhere else, as well as unofficial sway over policy and practice at both local and higher levels. But it had appeared, at least briefly, that it would not always be so. The vicissitudes of peninsular politics had insular consequences, and the 1868 liberal revolution in Spain had seemed to bring the possibility for significant change in the Philippines with a brief but remarkable era of reform in Manila ushered in by Captain-General Carlos María de la Torre y Nava Cerrada, who, as Benedict Anderson has put it, "horrified much of the Peninsular colonial elite by inviting creoles and mestizos into his palace to drink to 'Liberty'" when he took up his post.[23] The brief years of de la Torre's administration left a legacy not so much of long-lasting change but of the unforgettable taste of its promise: under de la Torre, press censorship was relaxed and the overseas ministry decreed significant educational reforms, including that the Dominican "Royal and Pontifical University of the College of Santo Tomás of Manila" was to become the "University of the Philippines," the existing rector being demoted to the position of dean of the faculty of theology and replaced by a civil government appointee.[24] These and other attempts at secularization in the Philippines were cut off by the arrival in 1871 of the new conservative Captain-General Rafael de Izquierdo y Gutierrez, and an otherwise minor military mutiny in 1872 became the occasion for the persecution of liberals and those who had pushed for secularization. In the aftermath, three (secular) priests were executed—one of whom was housing Rizal's older brother—and many prominent liberals were exiled, including Pardo de

Tavera's guardian and uncle, Paterno's father, and others who would later collaborate with the younger generation of educated, insular liberals.[25]

Those of the younger generation were both products and critics of the Catholic education and administration of the islands. These young men, many of whom traveled to Europe for educational or political opportunities, were quick to point out the anachronistic circumstances of their homeland, in part in order to promote a different possibility: that the Philippines be administered not as a Spanish colony with laws distinct from those applied to Spain but as a Spanish province where, as was the case in the rest of Spain, friars and friar orders had no particular privileges, where educational institutions were supervised by the secular state, and where, at least in theory, the laws enacted by a representative government were impartially enforced. As evidence for their arguments, they exhibited the pitfalls and regressive qualities of what they sometimes called the "friarocracy" or "friar-rule" (*frialocracía*) of the Philippines, and the failures of the Dominican university.[26] And if these reforms were not forthcoming, what might become of the islands? They wrote in a time when independence from Spain was an imaginable possibility but not a clearly desirable one, and Spain's loss of the Americas was sometimes cited in these discussions. Though the descent of Latin American republics into *caudillismo* prevented them from serving as positive examples, the independence of the former Spanish colonies was held out to demonstrate the dangerous consequences of misrule, and the revolutionary upheavals in Cuba presented a more contemporary example of a future possibility.[27]

The writings of the *ilustrados* illustrate a problem common to studies of nationalist and anticolonial thought: To what extent is nationalism or anticolonialism articulated in these texts? Given the predominance of the nation as a point of reference in the twentieth century and the fact of the present-day nation-state of the Philippines, the *ilustrados* appear as proto-nationalist figures, and their writings appear to articulate (albeit sometimes imperfectly) the existence and legitimacy of the Filipino nation and so to anticipate the Philippine Revolution. But the *ilustrados'* aims (and indeed those of various moments of the Revolution) may not have been either clearly "nationalist" or even clearly "anticolonial."[28] What were the fault lines within this "nationalist" movement? What kind of "nation" was enacted or promoted?

The propaganda efforts, reformist though the arguments usually were, are generally treated as early instances of Filipino nationalist sentiments and thoughts. Philippine historiography has long attended to how the work of propagandists and prominent ilustrados (José Rizal in particular) relates to the Revolution of 1896 and the First Philippine Republic. One might even say that this historiographical attention is glimpsed in an early form in the near-hysteria of contemporary conservative Spanish and Catholic reactions, as Alvaréz's letter, which introduced this chapter, demonstrates. Though scholarship has long treated the propagandists and *ilustrados* as proto-nationalists, the same scholarship has also raised questions about the degree to which various *ilustrados* aimed for revolution versus reform, and whether they sought self-sovereignty for the Philippines or full rights as "Spanish" citizens for some Filipinos.

Agents of U.S. colonization in the early twentieth century preferred to see the propaganda movement as an expression of Filipino nationalism that was not so much anticolonial as anti-*Spanish*.[29] In the later twentieth century, however, Filipino historians reevaluated the history of the revolution and the place of the propagandists, Rizal in particular, in it.[30] As Reynaldo Ileto has characterized the problem identified by prominent historians, "they pose the disturbing question: Why is our national hero not the leader of our revolution?"[31] For Teodoro Agoncillo, Rizal was as if a tragically indecisive Hamlet who could not bring himself to commit the violence against Spain that the Filipino nation demanded. More generally, in Agoncillo's telling, the *ilustrados* were self-interested elites, and the propagandists were at best tragically incomplete prefigurative voices of the collective will (that would later coalesce around the revolutionary Katipunan and its leader Bonifacio).[32] Renato Constantino painted the early propaganda movement as an example of incomplete reformism (with the exception of Del Pilar who he argued would have supported the Revolution) yet also necessary for articulating the revolutionary inclination of the people in terms of the Filipino nation. The masses' Revolution, he wrote, was given its particular form of articulation by *ilustrados*, but was also later co-opted by elite leaders.[33]

Because these historians emphasized the popular nature of the Revolution and its goal as political independence, they considered *ilustrados'* scholarly writings less important than the propagandists' overtly political writings. The same emphasis can be found even in the first major book-length study of the propagandists as a whole, Father John Schumacher's 1973 *Propaganda Movement*.[34] Schumacher traces intellectual influences and the social and political contexts of his sources, but his overall framing

emphasizes their place in a political movement that ends with nationalism. He ends by evaluating the successes and failures of the movement: he
judges that the work of advocating full political assimilation of the Filipinos with Spain was itself a failure, but only if misunderstood as a true goal
of the propagandists. Instead, the propagandists' efforts toward assimilation had to be understood as "much more a strategy or a first step than
an ultimate goal," which was "nationalist development."[35] As Schumacher
characterized it, the propaganda campaign was the intellectual project
that made possible the Revolution by inspiring its leaders, through whom
"these ideas would percolate down to the masses of the people."[36] Though
Schumacher describes significant differences among the propagandists'
chosen strategies, he presents an overall picture of unity in the movement's aim.[37] That unity is achieved in part via his focus on overtly political
strategies and arguments rather than scholarly writings.

More recent scholarship has approached the scholarly work of *ilustrados* and political projects of propagandists in ways that highlight variation
and explore inconsistencies within *ilustrado* writings. Resil Mojares's
Brains of the Nation centers on scholarly writings rather than political projects, though it treats the relation between the two.[38] The work illuminates
the writings of Pedro Paterno, Pardo de Tavera, and Isabelo de los Reyes,
treated respectively in three intellectual-biographical sections, unmatched
in breadth or depth. These sections are framed by larger discussions about
the politics of knowledge that distinguish the origin and originality of the
works of these figures as well as later studies that they anticipated. Mojares
shows that *ilustrados'* writings are neither contained by the propaganda
movement nor centered in Europe. Pardo de Tavera and Paterno only
loosely affiliated themselves with propagandist politics, and de los Reyes
was oriented toward Ilocos and located in Manila, rather than Europe
(where Schumacher's propagandist movement was centered). My work
likewise centers on scholarly writings, while relating them to political
projects. I organize the work around questions of how particular scholarly
disciplines, conventions, and genres in *ilustrado* writings presented opportunities but also inscribed limits for political thinking.

Anderson's recent work also shows that what had been thought of as
a relatively compact propaganda movement was intensely global and
diverse.[39] In Anderson's treatment, the figures and writings of the canonical Rizal, on the one hand, and the relatively marginalized de los Reyes, on
the other, move in their thoughts, writings, inspirations, and connections

through diverse geographical, political, and intellectual worlds. In Anderson's reading, political models, intellectual frameworks, and aesthetic conventions circulate readily through the cosmopolitan worlds that individuals inhabited. As Anderson's and Mojares's works show, the biographies of these figures reveal the surprising connections and creations possible among those who travel between and among peripheries and centers, intellectual traditions, and political strategies and visions. Anderson and Mojares, along with Filomeno Aguilar and Paul Kramer, highlight how *ilustrado* scholarship often looked for its models not to Spain (the "motherland," or the "colonizer") but instead to Berlin, London, Paris, Leiden, and elsewhere where modern sciences were most advanced.[40] *Ilustrado* cosmopolitanism underscores that national thinking requires comparative, global thinking, and always pictures the world, not just the local.[41]

The emphasis on *ilustrado* cosmopolitanism in recent work is complemented by renewed attention to the knotty problem of Spanish-ness in *ilustrado* thought and propagandist politics. Vicente Rafael's recent work revisits *ilustrado* and propagandist writings as efforts to usurp friars' authority in order to become the (Castilian-bilingual) agent of transmission between metropole and masses.[42] Rafael locates an origin of Filipino nationalism in the Filipino intelligentsia's ambivalent relationship to Castilian and in their possession of "the power of translation—the capacity to cross boundaries and put diverse groups in contact with one another."[43] Precisely by reconsidering the status of Castilian in Filipino nationalism—Castilian as a language, but also as an object of fascination and a technology for transmission—Rafael illuminates the significance of the Castilian-Spanish world in *ilustrado* texts. While nationalism has for him an "originary cosmopolitanism," the "foreign" relationships at the heart of Filipino nationalism are largely contained within the Spanish world.[44]

The cosmopolitan worlds and the Castilian-Spanish worlds of the *ilustrados* and propagandists are not mutually exclusive interpretive frames. Both approaches require rethinking categories of colonizer/colonized that have long animated works on nationalist thought and movements in the colonial world. These elites neither form Frantz Fanon's middle class that betrays the national masses by mimicking the colonizer nor rework the tools of the colonizer's knowledge (in this case, late Spanish colonialism).[45] They entered scholarly discourse from the margins of a marginal empire, inserting themselves in disciplines that had little part in the political subjection of their homeland.

The *ilustrados*' works can only be partially illuminated by focusing on whether they advocate reform or revolution, or whether they exemplify anticolonial nationalism or assimilationism. Starting with these oppositions makes it is more difficult to see the terms with which these authors thought and wrote. Take, for example, the word "Filipino." In 1880, *filipino* could mean "Philippine-born Spaniard," or it could more broadly refer to someone or something "of the Philippines," as an adjective that could stand in for a noun in the Spanish language. But at that time there was no "Filipino" ethno-national identity such as that indicated by this word today. By the end of the decade, however, "Filipino" would come to be used in a new, seemingly proto-national sense.[46] How the word was transformed is one of the stories that this book traces, but also seeks to recover other articulations of commonality whose meanings might since have been left behind, for these writings use a variety of different terms to articulate the groups with which they were concerned. "Nation" is but one among many types of collectivity that is articulated ("race," "people," "civilization," for example). Further, different but overlapping adjectives specify instances of these generic types (such as "Filipino" but also "Malay," "Spanish," "Tagalog," or even the ambiguous "indigenous" [*indígena*]). In none of these writings does the "Filipino nation" clearly predominate as a protagonist or subject.

Rather than treat the different communities invoked in these writings —sometimes overlapping, sometimes distinct—as imperfect versions of nationality, some coming closer and others remaining further from the concept of "nation" that would come to predominate, the present work aims to take the terms in which these authors wrote as the starting points from which to understand the collectivities whose boundaries and internal commonalities they sought to identify. The aim, then, is to trace not *how* "people," "race," or "civilization" became disciplined as ideas, either conforming to "the nation" or falling away, but instead the aim is to understand what exactly was signified by these collectivities.

Another aim is to understand *why* these particular categories of collectivity seemed viable and significant. Here, it is important to consider the genres in which these works were written. Scholarly genres themselves carried vocabularies, presumptions, categories, and conventions, which determined what kinds of community they could articulate. *Ilustrados* both engaged in and transformed the generic conventions of folklore, philology, ethnology, and history. By virtue of engaging in them, these authors took on some of the conventions, vocabularies, and methods of the genres. These conventions, vocabularies, and methods made it possible to think in terms of some kinds of social groupings and political arrangements, not only defining limits to the space in which authors could maneuver, but also producing certain forms of thought.

By focusing on different scholarly methods and genres, I show how Filipinos drew on and spoke to worlds within the Philippines, in Spain, and in German-, French-, and English-speaking Europe. In the case of ethnological sciences, for example, Filipinos drew on an international body of scholarship, and on local knowledge, to recast questions of race and civilization as they had been figured in Spanish-language literature. In the emerging practice of folklore, Filipinos hewed more closely to Spanish models, but in doing so they could both distinguish Filipinos from, and also incorporate them into, a world of Spanish folklore that had political analogues. In the world of linguistics, Filipinos drew on international scholarship of French and German provenance to develop a "Filipino" orthography around which both controversy and political opportunity emerged. In all these cases, Filipino authors wrote about their homeland, entering international scholarly worlds, and pressing against the limits of Spanish national-colonial politics.

These young men were concerned with calling attention to the failings and limitations of Spanish-Catholic administration and education in the Philippines. Because of this, they would seldom see or praise the unusual opportunities that these institutions enabled, in comparison with those of other parts of the colonial world. For the Dominican University of Santo Tomás was not only the oldest university in Asia; it was also, until 1857 in Calcutta, the only in which "natives" were taught, and it had no comparable peer anywhere in Southeast Asia during the nineteenth century.[47] The Dominicans of the university, caught between their commitment to Thomistic philosophy and pressures to modernize the curriculum, had to admit subjects and curricula whose teachers were not always Dominican.[48] These young men were armed with scholarly languages (Latin, Greek, and often French), versed in the classics, and living in a world where science and technology progressed by leaps and bounds (some watched the Eiffel Tower being built!). They emerged from their classrooms in Manila able to encounter scientific worlds that their education had hardly begun to touch.

The Plan of the Work

Rizal dedicated his 1890 critical annotation of a rare account of the early years of Spanish conquest (Morga, orig. published 1609) to "*los filipinos*," with the following words:

> In [the 1887 novel] *Noli me Tángere* I began the sketch of the present state of our *patria* [motherland or fatherland]: the effect that my study produced made me understand, before proceeding to develop other successive pictures before your eyes, the necessity of first revealing the past, in order to be able to better judge the present and measure the path traversed during three centuries.... If [this] book succeeds in awakening in you the consciousness of our past, erased from memory, and in correcting that which has been falsified and slandered, then I will not have worked in vain, and with this foundation, as small as it may be, we will all be able to dedicate ourselves to studying the future.[49]

Though Rizal's words cannot speak for every author or text, the relationships that he drew between the past and the future and between politics and scholarship are ones that we will see repeated in many of the chapters that follow.

To appreciate the significance of the Filipinos' scholarly writings and understand the particularities of the immediate scholarship to which they spoke, we will first back up and broadly consider the shifting grounds of Orientalism and anthropology. Both Orientalism and anthropology have treated, at their core, the tension between ideas of the universality of "Man" and the specificity of peoples, whether understood as "races," "nations," or another kind of grouping. Those tensions have enabled the colonial histories of both Orientalism and anthropology; they also enabled some kinds of nationalist sentiments and could issue challenges to an ideology that would justify colonial rule. In the next chapter, I begin with the promise that Orientalism held for some nationalist thinkers, paying particular attention to the case of India. Then I turn to how specific tools of Orientalism were, or were not, available to these young men of the late nineteenth-century Philippines. Finally, I consider how a new set of methods and questions, brought by the younger sciences that would become anthropology, helped these young men to deal with the gaps left by Orientalism's methods.

Then I turn to the reconstruction of the distant past—the "pre-history" of the Philippines, in the language of the day. The second chapter argues that ethnology as a discipline was both an available and in a sense a necessary way to work through the racial diversity that marked the Philippines off from other places and also that marked divisions among different peoples of the Philippines. While ethnology's focus on the historical relationships between human groups made it an ideal vehicle for theorizing the origins of peoples of the Philippines, the presence of contemporary "primitives" was treated in different ways by different authors. Some authors sought to distance the great ancients from contemporary primitives; others represented their contemporaries as living ancestors. Regardless of how racial and civilizational difference were approached in these works, the problems of relative civilization could not be avoided.

The book then turns from ethnology proper—or the general work of theorizing the relationships between different peoples—to one of the more particular disciplines in which that work was done. Chapter 3 begins by showing how folklore was used to theorize the pre-Hispanic unity of different peoples of the Philippines. At the same time, the nature of folklore's data—the contemporary practices of people—lent it to social and political criticism, and so this chapter reads specific sections of folkloric writings for their critical qualities. Further, the chapter argues that unlike other disciplines considered here, the folklore writings of the Philippines followed relatively closely, and even could be considered part of, Spanish folklore, though this could signify a challenge to Spanish authority as much as recognition of it. Finally, the chapter considers the authorial voices of Filipino folklorists, and how they navigated between an intimate relationship with their subjects and the distant and objective voice of the scientist or documentarian.

Chapter 4 traces how linguistic studies, which began as philology and as one technique with which to approach the ethnological puzzle of the Philippines, developed into a movement for orthographic reform to Filipino languages (most significantly, Tagalog). The chapter traces the controversy that erupted in the Manila press when the new orthography was adopted and evaluates the political significance of the orthography: it masked the Spanish origins of Tagalog words. Such a specific application of a scholarly study was unusual among the sciences under study here; however, the vehemence with which it was taken up (and also opposed) shows the high political stakes of such scholarship.

Finally, the fifth chapter considers historical works that sought to reevaluate the history of Spanish colonization in the Philippines. While this practice of political history would not generally be considered part of the group of disciplines that were emerging as anthropology, some of the same methods and data derived from folklore and ethnology were used to reevaluate Spanish colonial history as a history of decline. These histories, however, also employed an Orientalist narrative in which an earlier golden era of Philippine history was seen to be in present-day decline and in need of revival. This narrative incorporated the pre-Hispanic era, and also an early era of more noble Spanish actions in the islands, as the pasts that contrasted with the unjust and hypocritical present. Overall, these histories suggested that Spanish rule in the islands was fragile, always subject to the peoples' cooperation, and that the future of the noble past might not lay in the institutions of the Spanish colonial state but in the hands of the people themselves.

The conclusion returns to some salient points of comparison between this body of scholarship and similar scholarly projects produced in other parts of the world in which colonial or imperial rule was being contested. In comparison with scholarly efforts in British South Asia, in German-speaking Europe, and along Europe's western and eastern peripheries, this scholarship of the Philippines is in some respects exceptional. However, we find that elsewhere, too, the Orientalist and anthropological projects of the nineteenth and early twentieth centuries not only condoned forms of colonialism but could be used to challenge them. They were the languages through which peoples and nations could be articulated.

One of the challenges of entering this world and reading these documents is that they invoke political and intellectual worlds that are now, if still legible, usually held apart from each other by disciplinary convention. While on the one hand, the *ilustrados* were very much focused on a particular world of late nineteenth-century politics and life in the Philippines, they were also relentlessly cosmopolitan and immersed in scholarly worlds and connections only remnants of which have survived in any kind of common historical knowledge. These texts make references to a wide variety of peoples, places, ideas, and events, many of which are unlikely to be familiar to a contemporary reader, and some of which are likely to elude even many broadly read specialists. The references are both wide ranging and also particular: references are made to now-obscure authors and persons of the French intellectual world, the administration of the Spanish colonial Philippines, the Catholic curriculum's versions of ancient Greece and Rome, and German anthropological associations; to political structures and events of nineteenth-century Spain, the Philippines, and Germany, of the sixteenth- and seventeenth-century Spanish Philippines and Americas, and of ancient Greece and Rome; to concepts particular to Ilocano, Tagalog, Spanish, or German languages and cultures, and in the languages of Latin, German, Spanish, French, Ilocano, Tagalog, and Visayan. These lists are representative but hardly exhaustive. The proliferation of references, their diversity and their particularity, can stand in the way of the contemporary reader as she tries to make meaning from the words on the page. I provide historical contextualization to help her through the forest of references, whose density might threaten to obscure a view of its larger significance.

But the density of this forest itself has significant historical and theoretical consequence, in particular for those who study how ideas travel across barriers of geography, language, culture, politics, and class. The density of references from such seemingly disparate and discrete worlds reveals an extraordinary and seemingly specific set of interconnections of the late nineteenth century. It is one of the arguments of this book that though the interconnectedness and cosmopolitanism of this late nineteenth-century outpost of a dying empire might have been particular in its content and unique in its breadth, it was not exceptional in its form. In late colonial Bengal, for example, "[e]ven the most determinedly nationalist forms of cultural discourse . . . took form within the profoundly transnational context of the circulation of ideological norms."[50] The contexts in which these texts need to be read, then, are local and global, linguistic and ideological, political and historical.

Students of intellectual history need to attend not only to the ideas that resonate with the contemporary world but also to those that do not, not only to the references to works whose reputation has been deeply engraved in intellectual history by repeated tracings, but also to those whose names were only lightly etched on its surface before they were forgotten. The extraordinary range of references in the works we will consider, and the myriad ways that they are invoked and put to work, shows how broad are the possibilities of making meaning and, to some extent, how arbitrary is the selection of meanings that survive any particular moment or travel outside of any particular context.

Intellectual work always takes place in political, social, linguistic, economic, and historical contexts that constitute its conditions of possibility.

As students of political, intellectual, and social history, we have to take care not to confuse our own prejudices and limitations with those of our subjects.[51] This book attempts to reconstruct possible meanings, possible ideas, and possible futures past, most of which have lost their potency and faded from view. Far from being inevitable or natural, ideas that emerged as part of this moment and have survived in some form in the present were at one time foreign, obscure, and novel, and others that seemed to have a secure position are now foreign, obscure, or obsolete.

CHAPTER 1

Locating Orientalism and the Anthropological Sciences

The Limits of Postcolonial Critiques

Orientalism's Histories

A general enthusiasm for things Oriental swept through German, French, and English intellectual worlds in the eighteenth and nineteenth centuries "like a rapid-fire series of explosions," driven largely by European scholars' linguistic "discovery" of the relationship between Sanskrit and European languages.[1] Early European studies of non-European languages had been carried out by Catholic missionaries and emerged out of the biblical tradition that sought to identify the language of God, and its descendents, among the languages of man on earth. The advent of modern Orientalist studies, however, marked a decisive shift in which the languages and literatures of Asia were for the first time approached by European scholars "totally independent of the biblical and classical traditions." The new approach marked the beginning of both the "history *of* languages and history *through* languages," as Raymond Schwab has remarked of A. H. Anquetil-Duperron's pioneering translation of the *Zend Avesta*.[2] This and other studies by scholars such as William Jones (founder of the Asiatic Society of Calcutta), Wilhelm von Humboldt, Eugène Burnouf, and Franz Bopp established a method of studying languages' affiliations to each other through comparing their writing systems, vocabularies, and grammars (a practice known as comparative philology). By the 1830s, comparative philology had been thoroughly established in England, France (the *École des Langues Orientales* [School of Oriental Languages] was established in revolutionary Paris in 1794), and Germany (whose practitioners included Jacob Grimm).

While philology was at the heart of Orientalist studies, the texts on which those studies were based also became the basis for interdisciplinary, wide-ranging excitement about the laws, literature, history, poetry, and philosophy of the Orient. The intellectual excitement surrounding Orientalist studies became pervasive enough that contemporaries dubbed it an "Oriental Renaissance," as Victor Hugo did in 1829 when he wrote that "[t]oday, for a thousand reasons, all of which foster progress, the Orient is of more concern than it has ever been before. Never before have oriental studies been explored so deeply. In the century of Louis XIV one was a Hellenist: today one is an Orientalist. This is a great step forward."[3] Scholars such as Friedrich Schlegel and, later in the nineteenth century, Max Müller were particularly fascinated by ancient Indian civilizations and texts. Through comparative study of these texts, Europe discovered that its own past was related to an ancient world in India, a world far older than any previously linked to European civilization. With this discovery, the world became "truly round," in Schwab's words.[4] The shift that Hugo described, from Hellenism to Orientalism, reflected a new understanding of the origins of European civilization.

Orientalist interventions, beginning in the eighteenth century, argued that Greece and Rome were not "original" civilizations but instead borrowed ideas from earlier knowledges and societies. It was precisely the "discovery" of the relationship between European and Indian languages that prompted the flurry of scholarship tracing the relationship between Europe and ancient India, in which Greece and Rome figured not as the progenitors of Europe but instead as earlier descendants of a common intellectual inheritance, an earlier and more original version of which was to be found in ancient Indian texts. "Western" philosophy, mythology, science, and poetry were reconceived as not having originated with Greece and Rome but as having temporarily made those places home on their westward travel from more ancient Eastern origins.[5]

This chapter traces the sometimes conflicting political histories and significance of Orientalism's methodological and thematic qualities as well as those of the related and younger anthropological sciences.[6] Orientalism and the anthropological sciences employed methods, tropes, and themes whose particular features made them more or less available and useful to Filipino intellectuals. In order to better understand the specificities and significance of the Filipino case, the chapter begins by identifying the special significance that India has held in Orientalist (and subsequently postcolonial) scholarship, noting features of the Indian case that make it unique rather than a generalizable model. The chapter then turns to

Orientalism's tools and presumptions. Two specific features of Orientalism are significant both in European Orientalist studies (of India, especially) and for subsequent Indian and Filipino political-intellectual projects: first, Orientalism's focus on authoritative texts, and second, its narrative of historical decline from ancient greatness. Though these features were shared across European Orientalism and its Indian and Filipino appropriations, they worked differently in each case. Orientalism as a scholarly form was, in the nineteenth century, joined by a newer set of methods and presumptions of the emerging anthropological sciences. While both Orientalism and the newer anthropological sciences treated similar questions about the macrohistorical relationships between human societies, the newer sciences had distinct presumptions and methods that shaped the possibilities of their use in and for the Philippines: first, they treated specifically textless societies, and second, they conceived of human history as being a story of "races" in relation to each other. These features, too, were taken up in particular ways by Indian intellectuals and their Filipino counterparts. Both Orientalism and the anthropological sciences have had richer and more contested political histories than some late twentieth-century critiques of these practices allow.

The chapter ends by describing some of the peculiarities of the late nineteenth-century scholarly world of the Philippines: its higher educational institutions, the unusual contours of Spanish Orientalism, and the dearth of Spanish scholarship about the Philippine islands and peoples. Throughout the chapter, scholarship about and of India appears as a point of comparison. India is a particularly compelling comparative site; it was central to Orientalism, it had rich nineteenth- and early twentieth-century intellectual and nationalist movements, and its history and historiography have largely driven postcolonial studies. Despite the significant differences between the political structures of the Philippines and India, and between the scholarly traditions in the two places, the comparison illuminates the particularities, and also generalities, of the Philippine case.

From the moment that Orientalists "discovered" the relationship between Sanskrit and European languages, Orientalist scholarship challenged Europe's self-perceptions. In this, India played a significant role: ancient India signified a challenge to European originality. India's role here is unique in the history of secular thought in Europe. During the Renaissance, Greece and Rome displaced biblical antiquity as the "original" moment from which secular European thought itself derived. Since then,

Greece had been the "original" civilization that had dominated the European intellectual-historical imagination. It was not the venerable age of the Greek and Roman civilizations but rather the belief that those civilizations were original, completely new in themselves, that excited Niccolo Machiavelli and that left him puzzling over how to duplicate originality.[7] It was the purported originality of Greece and Rome, in other words, that made these civilizations the antiquity to which modern Europe traced its origins. Only ancient India threatened to displace Greece and Rome in Europe's imagination, when the Oriental Renaissance aimed to debunk what it saw as a myth of Greek originality (and so, by extension, the idea of the uniqueness of modern European culture and its distinction from the rest of the world). India's antiquity demanded to be compared with that of Greece and Rome, and had profound philosophical systems expressed in complex languages that were newly recognized as related to European languages.[8]

Yet some of this same Orientalism held Asia and more particularly India to be naturally home to imitation, inaction, contemplation, and repetition; this characterization resonated with a broader discourse that associated Europe with originality and action, in contrast to the imitative and passive East. Johann Gottfried Herder, for example, objected to judging one era by the standards of another (as each era and each nation had its own genius), yet the particular values he found in the Orient were those of benevolent paternalism, submission, and obedience.[9] Herder's Orient was beautiful and admirable, but it was still the child of humanity, and thus it was a small step from there to G. W. F. Hegel's philosophy of history in which each nation's particular genius was ranked hierarchically with regards to others', and the Orient—India in particular—was both prior and inferior to Europe.[10] Müller, referring more specifically to Indian texts, drew a stark contrast between the ancient northern "Greek, Roman, German, Celt, and Slave [sic]," who developed "the active, combative, and political" side of human nature, and the ancient Indians, who characterized "the passive, meditative, and philosophical" side.[11] He allowed that the contrast might be valued in different terms: "Of course we should call [their] notions of life dreamy, unreal, unpractical, but may not they look upon our notions of life as short-sighted [and] fussy...?" But the content of the contrast was not in question: the "active" was associated with "us" and "passive" with "them."[12] Even among Orientalist authors for whom India's status as European ancestor was most important and who debunked the myth of Greek originality, one still finds a contrast drawn between Europe (active, original) and India (passive, imitation). This contrast has been a subject of late twentieth- and twenty-first-century scholars.

Edward Said calls "Orientalism" both a broader discourse that associated originality with Europe and imitation with the East, and the scholarly and aesthetic works about "the Orient" (and India in particular) that so captured intellectual Europe's attention in the eighteenth and nineteenth centuries. Said first studied the political implications of Orientalism's logics and brought them to the attention of both the scholarly world and a broader public; subsequent work has both taken up and taken issue with key premises of Said's study and the conclusion he reaches.[13] In Said's analysis, Orientalism is not just a field of study that takes Asian languages, literatures, peoples, religions, and histories as its objects; Orientalism is an approach to its subject matter, a broader Anglo-European cultural chauvinism and racism, and the political institutions that have supported Western colonialism and imperialism in the East. Orientalism, for Said, must be understood to be all of these things simultaneously; it is the interconnections between epistemological, political, and aesthetic forms of oppression. Though Said makes important connections between politics and scholarship in part by encompassing such a broad variety of intellectual and political movements in what he calls "Orientalism," significant specificities get lost in this generalizing move. Distinguishing between general cultural chauvinism, on the one hand, and a scholarly movement, on the other, can help us to see how "originality" resonates with earlier Orientalist formulations and how it has come to be a preoccupation of contemporary scholarship.

Said implicates Orientalism in colonialism (and vice versa), and while this relationship has been complicated by critics' detailed analyses, Said's approach to Orientalism as epistemological-political-aesthetic endures as a compelling framework. The present study seeks to contribute to the literature that corrects Said's overreaching thesis while still attending to the political concerns that drive his work. By noting how Orientalism is a differentiated and varied discourse, I follow in the lead of others who have both built on and criticized Said as well as some who worked earlier or contemporaneously.[14] Orientalism was not always or even primarily a tool of or cause for European domination, and sometimes was used precisely against such domination. Orientalism's particular methods, presumptions, and vocabularies were useful for valorizing its subjects and contributed to narratives that challenged colonial rule. These features of Orientalism's history ought to be neither a surprise nor a particular reason to doubt the agency of colonial subjects who employed it.

For Said, Orientalism marked Europe as action, in contrast with an Orient that was fundamentally inactive, passive, unoriginal, and so incapable of agency. This very formulation of Orientalism—itself a political intervention—has been problematized by scholars who, sympathetic to Said's concern to trouble a complacent hegemony, emphasized both the historical fact and theoretical significance of the agency of Orientalism's purported subjects. Many scholars have taken up the task of revealing how Orientalist knowledge was not solely the product of European scholars; the reality of Asian intellectuals' contributions has gone unrecognized both by their European contemporaries and beneficiaries, and by later scholars who would critique Orientalism as a *European* discipline.[15]

A different strain of thought has taken up Said's critique of the epistemological power of colonialism, attending to how the epistemologies of colonial rule constructed colonial subjects as mimics, or secondary to the European original, and how this figure pervaded and haunted nationalist thought and historiography. Scholars such as Partha Chatterjee and Homi Bhabha embrace the problem of agency posed by indigenous appropriation (or imitation, borrowing, or mimicry) of colonial formations. For Chatterjee, colonial subjects' borrowing and appropriation of Orientalist frameworks becomes a step in the dialectical development of nationalist thought that truly overcomes colonial logics.[16] The initial act of appropriation, then, is derivative, but part of a larger story of originality. For Bhabha, the act of imitation becomes less something that colonial subjects *do* than a principle of colonial discourse that is fundamentally ambivalent: it is a "strategy of authority in colonial discourse" that is "erratic, eccentric," raising questions about the bases of its own authority.[17] Dipesh Chakrabarty's formulation of the impossible dilemma of postcolonial history fully articulates the anxiety about originality, and its lack, that has troubled postcolonial criticism.[18] As Chakrabarty explains, "the Enlightenment's story of the struggle of 'science-rationalism' versus 'faith-religion' can be repeated in India only as an example of bad translation," because the poles of that dichotomy in India "do not repeat the history of [the corresponding] European categor[ies] of thought."[19]

Many studies of intellectual production in colonial and postcolonial contexts evince a preoccupation with originality, mimicry, and derivation.[20] This is neither a new concern nor, strictly speaking, limited to works that center on India: Franz Fanon's anxiety about and criticism of the colonial bourgeoisie was based in its fundamentally imitative, and so unrevolutionary, quality. Unlike a real bourgeoisie, the colonial bourgeoisie had no revolutionary role and was merely a colonial mimic, a mark of the extension and decadence of colonial capital. The colonial bourgeoisie, then, was incapable of action and unoriginal: it only hampered the formation of a true national (revolutionary) consciousness and culture.[21] Much of the scholarship that has centered the themes of originality, mimicry, and derivation as problems of colonial and postcolonial intellectual production, however, derives from considering the contours of Indian histories.

Is derivation a colonial and postcolonial problem more generally, or is it better understood as a problem that resonates in particular ways in the Indian context? As numerous examples show, appropriation has worked against colonialism in India and elsewhere where intellectuals claimed for themselves the patrimony of such ideals as "liberty" and "equality" to end oppressive rule perpetuated by metropolitan institutions that claimed the same principles.[22] But such appropriation is not always considered to imply a lack of agency or originality. When Ada Ferrer argues that "anti-colonial arguments, of necessity, engaged colonial ones," she suggests that the fact of derivation itself—in this case, the way that nineteenth-century Cuban arguments derived from "European" ones—ought not to be taken as a sign of inferiority or of fundamental lack.[23] These argumentative anticolonialisms ought not to be seen as always already dominated by colonialist arguments, even if they derive from European discourses.

More generally, we should recognize that whether the context is colonial or not, intellectual borrowings ought not to be confused with validations of a political order. To engage in a discourse is not necessarily to be dominated by it (or, alternatively, to be dominated by those who have used that discourse before). As Andrew Sartori has recently argued, "surely there is no moment in intellectual history that is not derivative in some fundamental sense. How would one formulate an argument or an analysis without drawing from a preexisting repertoire of concepts? As such, there seems no prima facie reason to treat an act of intellectual appropriation as substantially different from an act of conceptual innovation."[24] Whether colonial subjects or metropolitan aristocrats, authors' products reflect the conventions of the genres in which they write, which is why genres are recognizable. A piece's innovation and originality are only distinguishable to the degree that the piece can be understood in relation to others. Any thought must be uttered in terms at least somewhat familiar in order to be heard, or even thinkable, and no knowledge springs sui generis from a brain untainted with language or modes of thinking.

The problem of derivation and originality might be better understood, instead, as *especially* troubling in the Indian context because of the particular resonances of Orientalism there. As we have seen, it was precisely ancient India's newly discovered "originality" that inspired European Orientalist research and theories of India's relationship to, but distinction from, Europe. Other scholars tell us that nineteenth-century Indian intellectuals confronted the problem of originality (and its corollary, action) in their writings. Chatterjee argues that what he calls the early moment of nationalist thought, exemplified by the writings of Bankimchandra Chattopadhyay (1838–94), "accepts and adopts the same essentialist conception based on the distinction between 'the East' and 'the West'" and adopts a framework that is "exactly the reverse of that of Orientalism. That is to say, the 'object' in nationalist thought is still the Oriental, who retains the essentialist character depicted in Orientalist discourse. Only he is not passive. . . . He is seen to possess a 'subjectivity' which he can himself 'make.' . . . His subjectivity, he thinks, is active, autonomous, and sovereign."[25] Likewise, Gyan Prakash writes that nationalist historiography "transformed the object of knowledge—India—from passive to active, from inert to sovereign, capable of relating to History and Reason."[26] The preoccupation with action and originality in this Indian intellectual moment—or at least in scholarship about it—may reflect the specificities of India in the Orientalist imagination as much as it does a logic of nationalist thought under colonial rule.

Considerations of how thought in the colonial world derived from colonial knowledge, or appropriated it, have often been less than specific about precisely what is appropriated. The discourse that was most interestingly appropriated by Indian colonial intellectuals was not an overly broad "Western rationalism" or "post-Enlightenment rationalist thought."[27] Questions have been rightly raised about identifying such a broad intellectual trend to be "of Europe" or, even more specifically, "of the colonizer," when post-Enlightenment European thought varies widely and includes thought critical of rationalism.[28] Indeed, recent work on nationalist thought in turn-of-the-century Bengal shows that German idealism, in particular, was attractive for more than one strain of Indian nationalist thought and that its use "should not really strike us as so surprising, given Hinduism's longstanding positioning by German philosophers and Orientalists as the ancestor of modern idealism."[29] It would be worth exploring how the *idea* that "rationality" and "rationalism" were products of or belonged to Europe became hegemonic in colonial India, if indeed it did. (Chakrabarty's formulation is that it was precisely in the *colony* that it became "hyper-rationalism," not the same thing as European rationalism.)[30] But more to the point for this study, the more specific European discourse that was appropriated by Indian intellectuals was a strain of Orientalism in which ideas about India, in particular, played a central role.

What is less clear is whether Indian intellectuals' engagement with the colonizer's discourse of "Orientalism" is a generalizable model, and this is more relevant for the purposes of comparison. Indian colonial intellectuals confronted colonial chauvinism, but they also had at their disposal a narrative, championed by some English intellectuals and scholarship, that held India to be the home of a great ancient civilization from which the European was derived. These conditions made it attractive for Indian intellectuals to engage in discourse "of" the colonizer. Much of Western Europe—not just the English—had been fascinated by the idea of ancient India. This raises the question of whether the discourse taken up by Indian intellectuals was indeed of the "colonizer," properly speaking.

In the Philippines, intellectuals took up some of the same scholarly discourses, but these were not, for the most part, of *their* colonizers. Instead, particular features of those discourses were available for use in the Philippines, but not in the same ways that they were in India. The Philippines had never been conceived of as home to a great ancient civilization from which Europe had derived. The search for its precolonial history, then, did not follow the narratives of "the colonizer," but did use narratives of Orientalism and anthropological sciences, engaging with their premises and models. This engagement is better understood as one version among the many possible, than as derivation of a European colonizing original.[31]

The specificities of the Philippine case help us to identify specificities of the Indian one, and these reveal further problems with the colonized-colonizer schema for understanding elite thought in the colonial world and its preoccupation with derivation as a problem of intellectual history.[32] Derivation and originality have distinct meaning for and resonance in the Indian case and are not best understood as endemic to a generalized colonial or postcolonial condition. Colonial intellectuals sometimes were actively seeking academic discourses "of Europe," rather than responding to their imposition via institutions of colonial rule, and the status of these discourses as property of "the colonizer" was not always secure. Before proceeding to the Philippine case, it will be helpful to consider how key Orientalist tropes could be subject to reappropriation toward anticolonial ends in the Indian and Bengali contexts.

Scholars of nineteenth-century Bengali intellectuals have analyzed how Orientalism's characterizations of cultures, religions, and languages of Asia became material for the recuperation of indigenous "past glory, necessarily idealized, but often based on the results of serious research by European and Indian scholars."[33] Orientalist research was a foundation on which nationalists "adopted the heritage of Hindu culture as the focus of its identity and gloried in the Hindu past," though they did so with an eye toward a future that would only partially resemble that past.[34] Later nationalist historians "saw the origin of the modern nation in that same ancient India [of the Orientalists]; and for such historians, the old Orientalist scholarship's sympathetic remarks on the India of the texts . . . became objective and authoritative statements that affirmed India's great past."[35] Such reappropriation of Orientalist veneration is illustrated by Mahatma Gandhi's quotations of Schlegel (*On the Language and Wisdom of the Indians* [1808] and *Lectures on Literature, Ancient and Modern* [1815]) and Müller (*India: What Can It Teach Us?* [1818]) in appendices to his *Hind Swaraj*.[36] The tools and focus of Orientalism—specifically, its focus on language and texts and the search for authenticity through those texts—were useful for revaluing Orientalism's dichotomies and so served these colonial intellectuals' purposes.[37]

In Orientalism's classic moments, the focus on ancient texts worked in part to establish the authority of the (European) Orientalist over that of the "native" keepers of the text. That is, the existence of a written text, and knowledge of the language in which it was written, allowed the (European) scholar to interpret its significance without reference to the readings or interpretations of any indigenous scholarly or priestly institutions or authorities.[38] Thus Orientalism's focus on ancient texts performed work analogous to Protestantism's emphasis on the Bible: access to the text itself allowed for traditional institutional authority to be usurped. Further, the particularly ancient quality of the texts on which the Orientalists lavished their attentions was important in part because it confirmed their authenticity. For Schlegel, Müller, or Jones, for example, the more ancient the text, the closer it was to the true, untainted original, unpolluted by the decay of the latter-day Orient, with the perversions of the Persian (read: Muslim) translation or the influence of Dravidian (read: dark-skinned) cultural practices.[39] The theme of Oriental decay emphasized both the greatness of the ancient and the need to rescue it from the present-day Orientals, which simultaneously authorized European scholarly work and political rule.

The Orientalist narrative of decay was answered by colonial Indian scholars who used modern science to study the past with an eye toward the future.[40] As one would expect, there was more than one approach to the problem—and opportunities—of Orientalism's narrative of decay for nationalist thought in India. Orientalism's focus on ancient texts could work in ways that destabilized Europe's authority by helping to identify, reify, and canonize the texts understood to be foundational for a nation, civilization, or people. Even the theme of Oriental decay could be turned into a call for revival of the ancient greatness of the past.[41] In calling attention to both the antiquity and the accomplishments of these texts, Orientalists also called attention to the complexity of the political and religious structures in which they were produced. Such structures suggested a past golden age, to which colonial subjects could point as evidence of future possibilities.

Orientalism's tools were not equally available to all colonial subjects in all parts of "the Orient." In particular, the circumstances of the Philippines presented a different set of opportunities and obstacles for local Orientalist work. Hindu intellectuals in colonial India imagined their nation's history as one of decline from ancient greatness, in part because this narrative had been established in post-Enlightenment terms by (especially British and German) Orientalists.

Such an imagined history of decline for the Philippines was unavailable to the *ilustrados* and propagandists, for the deep pasts of their people were text-less, thought to be among those without history. The distant civilizations of precolonial societies in the Philippines were difficult to study precisely for the lack of surviving "original" texts. Though many Filipino languages had their own scripts before the Spaniards arrived, no documents survived from the precolonial era, and the earliest textual sources were chronicles written mostly by friars in the early years of Spanish conquest. Textual sources for Orientalist research, then, were not great ancient texts of the pre-Hispanic Philippines but sixteenth- and seventeenth-century Spanish chronicles that these young scholars combed—with a critical eye—for data about the peoples of the Islands at the moment the Spaniards arrived.

The lack of ancient textual documents itself threatened to consign pre-Hispanic societies of the Philippines to the heap of the premodern and primitive, because to ascend to the pedestal of the "classical," an ancient society needs to be able to show evidence of its grandeur, usually in the form of texts. For this reason, Filipinos faced challenges different from their predecessors and peers elsewhere who worked to selectively appropriate a "classical" pagan past into the story of a present and future nation or civilization. For example, pagan Greece and Rome had a place in the history of the glorious Catholic civilization that might have been familiar enough to these classically educated young men to serve as a model for them. Similar work had been undertaken by Spanish American creoles a century earlier, eager to appropriate the glorious indigenous past for a new creole political identity rooted in the Americas.[42] As we have seen, nationalists in South Asia could draw on significant sources that documented civilizations in India that long predated British rule or even presence. And while even neighboring Java contained rich materials—temples, statues, chronicles, and literary traditions—with which its precolonial history might be studied, "in the Philippines," as T. H. Pardo de Tavera lamented, "we have neither monuments, nor statues, nor literature that tell us anything."[43] Lacking temples, inscriptions, or texts, Pardo de Tavera and his compatriot scholars turned to methodological tools that could mine other materials for historical gems.

Those theories, methods, and sources of data that the *ilustrados* used can be loosely grouped into two intellectual and scholarly traditions: one, the Orientalist tradition of philology, and the other, a newer set of concerns, methods, and theories now associated with the predecessors of physical, archeological, and cultural anthropology. Orientalist philology used the data of languages—words, grammars, writing systems—to trace origins and influence between languages, and so, it was presumed, between the past and present peoples who used them. Thus peoples of the past and their migrations, relationships, admixtures, and conquests could be studied via the evidence of their language that survived into the present, whether in the form of written texts or living oral language.[44] Facing a contemporary linguistic reality of extraordinary diversity, scholars of the Philippines used Orientalist linguistic tools, relying on the living spoken languages and the few surviving accounts of pre-Hispanic writing systems, to show commonalities between the languages, positing a common origin. All the authors whose works we will study drew to some extent on these linguistic techniques.

They also used another set of scholarly tools: that of comparative ethnology, folklore, mythology, and what they generally referred to as the study of "pre-history," or the history of human societies before (or without) surviving textual records.[45] The newer anthropological sciences provided methods by which these authors could "discover" and interpret evidence of the pre-Hispanic past in the present, even in the absence of textual sources. Their sources were, besides linguistic data (drawing from the older philological Orientalist tradition), surviving physical artifacts of past human societies, the comparative physiology of past and present human bodies, and what we might now call "cultural" data drawn from contemporary societies, including practices and beliefs of dress and adornment, courtship and marriage, pregnancy, birth, child rearing, death, government, medicine, and agriculture, as well as traditional or popular stories, children's tales, rhymes, songs, and games.

These methods, which were later associated with a four-field "anthropology," were generally used to study the "primitive"—that is, the unlettered, the textless. As George Stocking has put it, peoples "without written languages and historical records" were "generally excluded from [most] human scientific disciplines," and these peoples were the provenance of anthropological study.[46] Inseparable from the question of method, then, were the presumed unities of those studied by most human sciences in contrast with those studied by anthropology: other human sciences studied "Europeans," while anthropology treated the "others," or "peoples who were long stigmatized as 'savages.'"[47]

In the overlapping anthropological practices of ethnology and the study of "pre-history," both physical and cultural data about the varieties of mankind were gathered, not only to document human diversity or tabulate similarities and differences among different groups, but also to theorize how different groups were related to each other as the different branches of the human family tree. All these data could be plotted in order to reveal, it was thought, where a people had come from ("originally"), what other peoples they were related to, and thus the history and filiation of peoples of mankind. This was a practice of global genealogy that, like Orientalist philology, relied on a method of comparison.[48] Its most basic analytical unit was a category of human grouping often referred to as "race."

This practice of global genealogy had roots in theories that both pre-dated and competed with theories of human history as described by evolution. Though progressivist conceptions of human history were in vogue before Charles Darwin's 1859 *Origin of Species*, the significance of Darwin's work on the direction, language, and implications of humanistic sciences cannot be overestimated. Some of these earlier theories of human development, and of the historical relationship between different groups, had been the result of the startling developments in Orientalist philology that showed a relationship between Indian and European languages and therefore, it was thought, people. Before the evolution of human groups was conceived of in terms of biological races, the evolution of language was understood to reflect the evolution of human groups in more civilizational terms. The anthropological sciences generally took over from Orientalism an attention to the relationship between different peoples in macrolevel world history, and shifted the terms of this study from one of comparative civilizations to one that increasingly focused on racial difference organized into a hierarchy that also was conceived along a timeline.

Whether monogenist or polygenist, diffusionist or evolutionist, nineteenth-century anthropological sciences could never belong wholly to the present or the past: they were sciences of seeing the past in the present and the present in the past. In this respect, all of their methods aimed to reveal the history of human races through time, and here "race" should be understood to encompass understandings of both physical and cultural properties that were supposed to distinguish one people from another. What might be puzzling for contemporary readers is that cultural and linguistic properties were thought to be neither more nor less "racial" than physical ones. Furthermore, many of those practicing these sciences believed that neither did biology determine culture nor did physiology dictate behavior, though some racially inclined (and racist) theorists disagreed. While among those who practiced this kind of racial science were many who believed intellectual aptitude to be a "racial" quality (whether or not they thought it to be biologically determined), there were others who did not, and who thought that intellectual aptitude corresponded in no way to racial groupings. To speak of the history of human groups in time, one used the language of race.

Ethnology—the study of human groups' filiations with each other—was in some sense initially a branch of philology, which later developed different methodological tools, including archaeology, (and for our purposes importantly) ethnography, mythology, and folklore. In this tradition, "ethnology" and "ethnography" had related and overlapping meanings. Loosely speaking, "ethnography" was the study of a particular group, and "ethnology" was the more theoretical practice of ascertaining relationships between peoples through comparison. In British and later English-language anthropology, the distinction between the practice of ethnography and ethnology was sometimes more specific: "ethnography" referred to gathering data "in the field" and writing it up, whereas "ethnology" considered that data comparatively in order to theorize the relationships between peoples, and the history of man. As historians of the discipline have shown, fieldwork was not practiced by trained anthropologists until relatively late, and instead ethnographic data was gathered largely from accounts of naturalists and missionaries and analyzed back at home (in Europe) by those theoretically equipped to determine its ethnological import.[49] When Isabelo de los Reyes in 1887 described his piece "The Tinguian" as being a work of ethnography, he was being modest; the scholar who translated this work into German for publication in Vienna judged that the piece "reveals the erudition and competence of the author in ethnological matters," which is to say his erudition and competence in the more theoretical, loftier science of ethnology, which was generally the provenance of Europeans only.[50]

Both in India and in the Philippines, the local elite's confidence in the future that awaited them under colonial rule diminished in part because they increasingly experienced racism in the mid to late nineteenth century.[51] The modern knowledges appropriated by both Indians and Filipinos, however, included the racialized sciences that searched for origins and filiations among the human family. Orientalism's Aryan model of history, which held that an ancient race of Northerners had split into two branches (one in Europe and one in the Indian subcontinent), each of which conquered the (darker) Southern population that it encountered—a model first formulated by Schlegel, developed by Müller, and encouraged by the new comparative sciences of philology and mythology—proved to be surprisingly versatile and useful for ever more racialized theories of the history of human groupings.[52] As Vasant Kaiwar has helpfully explained, the model has been able to support fascist political projects that gained control of the state, both in twentieth-century Germany and more recently in India.[53] We can only understand why the content of Orientalism and of these two nationalist movements could be so similar, if we set aside a rigid and ahistorical sense of the politics of certain scholarly presumptions and methods, and instead attend to their particular instantiations in different political and historical contexts.

Late nineteenth-century *ilustrados* carved out their own spaces between Orientalism and the newer anthropological sciences. In considering how they did so, we will see that this intellectual-political moment had more than one possible future; it anticipated present-day political critiques of both Orientalism and anthropology, but these possibilities by no means eclipsed a more open sense of what such scholarly work might accomplish.[54] Before turning to how ethnology, folklore, linguistics, and history each articulated certain aspirations and critiques in the Philippine context, this chapter outlines some of the parameters in which late nineteenth-century Filipinos worked: university education in the Philippines, Spanish Orientalism's lacunae, and the keenly felt inadequacy—among educated Spaniards and Filipinos alike—of Spanish knowledge about this part of the Spanish empire.

Patriotism and the Languages of Scholarship

While the methods and data of Orientalist and emerging anthropological sciences were useful for considering the history of peoples without history, how did it come to be that they were taken up by these Spanish colonial subjects, and what political significance did this have? The differences between the educational systems of India and the Philippines, and the particularities of Spanish scholarly trajectories, positioned Filipinos to take up these "modern" knowledges in a way that was not available to their Indian counterparts. The status and ownership of "modern" education was an issue among both Indian nationalists and Filipino *ilustrados*. Nineteenth-century India was home to some scholarly institutions that predated British colonialism. The institutions of Indian scholarship had been transformed when they were incorporated into British scholarship and the colonial state; in turn, Indian scholarship had transformed British scholarship and colonial institutions.[55] Such interactions between "Indian" and "British" scholarly institutions were quite distinct, however, from the introduction of "modern" education in India. When English-style universities were established in 1857 in Calcutta, Bombay, and Madras, their new style of education sparked debates among nationalists who disagreed about what kind of education was appropriate and valuable, and in what ways this "modern" education might threaten existing indigenous institutions of learning and knowledge, and their achievements.[56]

Debates in these terms could not have taken place in nineteenth-century Manila, where Spanish-Catholic education was long established (University of Santo Tomás, founded 1611) and the only form of institutionalized advanced education; unlike India, the Philippines had no competing "indigenous" institutions. In some respects, however, the propagandists' struggle to push their colonial administration to offer more and better modern higher education sounds similar to their Indian counterparts' efforts. The propagandists denounced what they characterized as a backward scholastic Dominican university, hostile to modern secular sciences and pedagogy, in much the same terms that some Indians, embracing the value of "modern" education, criticized the English system as not being modern enough, "describing Indian universities as 'bad imitations' of the (already imperfect) English originals."[57] The premodern that the Filipinos were battling against—Catholic scholasticism—was a different premodern from the "traditional" educational institutions of India that the "modern" British-style universities displaced and transformed, and in the Filipinos' case, the premodern (Catholic scholasticism), along with its most vociferous defenders, was located in the institutions of the colonizer. In these arguments, it was the colonial government—or at least some of its institutions, the friar orders—that was stuck in the past and that hindered the Philippines from progressing to its own modern future.

But the Indian comparison reminds us also that there had been an earlier and distinct moment in the Philippines, a brief period when a modern Philippines, as part of a greater Spanish world, had seemed a possibility. Tapan Raychaudhuri describes how nationalist consciousness in India "rejoiced that India was part of a glorious, world-wide empire and nurtured hopes of a steady progress under Britain's providential guidance. The contradiction between pride in the Hindu identity and faith in a regime seen to be identified with the most vicious critics of the cherished culture was apparently not obvious in the early phases of nationalism."[58] A similar kind of faith—or at least hope—had been apparent in Manila in the toast to liberty in the governor-general's palace under an earlier liberal administration. In the name of this hope, the propagandists' newspaper *La solidaridad* continued to protest its patriotism and ally itself with what it took to be a modern and liberal republican Spanish politics.[59]

After the more repressive swing of post-Cavite (1872) politics in the Philippines and what was perceived by *ilustrados* and propagandists as the increasing influence of the friar orders, the "apparent contradiction" about which Raychaudhuri writes was less sustainable.[60] While one might argue that in Indian nationalist consciousness "concerns for the improvement of 'society' and a burgeoning pride in the inherited culture" could coexist "with a total acceptance of colonial rule," such coexistence was more difficult—though not impossible—for elites in the late nineteenth-century Philippines, given that the glory days of Spanish empire were long over.[61]

Modern knowledges were available to Filipinos without the liability of having been pioneered by the colonizers; and indeed, to acquire them was in a way to highlight Spanish deficiency both as moderns and as colonizers. With the important exception of folklore, Spain lagged far behind its European neighbors in these Orientalist-cum-anthropological sciences, particularly regarding work on the Philippines. These young men's interest in their homeland put them in touch with a world of scholarship in which, in some cases, they became the Spanish-language representatives.[62]

The embarrassment of Spain's scholarly delay is nicely captured by peninsular scholar Francisco García Ayuso who, though not at all concerned with the Philippines, outlined the dire situation of his *patria's* (motherland's or fatherland's) neglect of Orientalist studies. In the introduction to his Spanish-language Arabic grammar textbook published in 1871, he explained that in Munich he had studied Oriental languages, "some unknown and others little cultivated in my beloved *patria*," and that he wrote the book because "it seemed to me embarrassing that we had to go to foreign [universities] in order to study one of the languages most related to our history and literature."[63] The same patriotism had earlier inspired him to publish *The Study of Philology with Regard to Sanskrit* (also 1871) in which he aimed to introduce his countrymen to "the various and sublime aims" of the "new" and "most important" science of philology, a science mostly unknown in Spain.[64] García Ayuso enthused that in the wake of its "discovery" of Sanskrit, philology, "from a purely *humanistic* study, has been elevated to a *science*, and now occupies a distinguished place in scientific-literary circles. Outstanding geniuses such as Herder, Hervas, Humboldt, Schlegel, Bopp, Grimm and Burnouf" had contributed to this "glorious result" from the study of Sanskrit, which had enabled "*general and comparative philology*."[65] These wonderful achievements, however, could not be claimed by his *patria*; they were the fruits of "universities of cultivated Europe" and "supported by the majority of European governments" but not by Spain.[66] García Ayuso's own scholarship aimed to help Spain catch up with its more cultured neighbors, by promoting Spanish studies of Sanskrit and philology: "If with this little work I can provoke the love of philological studies and of the supremely beautiful language of India to be aroused among the young men of letters of my beloved *patria*, I will consider my time and work well spent."[67] Though he implicitly admonished the government and universities of Spain for their failure, the reproach was a gentle one, expressed to inspire and encourage his *patria* and compatriot scholars.

Spanish Orientalism, fraught with anxieties of inferiority, provides fertile ground for exploring conflicting loyalties in scholarly practice. García Ayuso could not devote himself to the scholarly pursuits of philology without recognizing that philological science's bragging rights might seem to come at the expense of his *patria*. In his introductory essays, García Ayuso found his Spanishness, and the Spanishness of his scholarly writings, something that warranted comment, precisely for the lack of Spanish achievements in the field in which he worked. It might have occurred to a German, French, or English Orientalist scholar to note the achievements of his compatriots in the field and take the occasion to verbally pin a medal of honor on the collective national chest, but for the Spaniard, the national record was a source of anxiety and had to be addressed. The sole Spaniard in his list of distinguished philologists, Lorenzo Hervás y Panduro, had written much of his work from Jesuit exile in Rome, and while his work had been used by some of the most famous early German Orientalists—something García Ayuso emphasized—it had not inspired similarly talented Spaniards.[68] Though García Ayuso's own works were pioneering for Spanish Orientalism, they were by no means on the cutting edge of the cosmopolitan scholarly practice.[69] Even by the end of the century, Spanish Orientalist literature was largely in translation, and Spanish scholars had yet to contribute significantly to the international field.[70]

Spain also lagged behind in other nineteenth-century scholarly fields, and of particular interest here are those thought useful for colonial rule. This was also a source of anxiety for Spaniards concerned with national scholarly pride, but at a more practical level it concerned those who worried that Spain was losing her hold on her few remaining colonies. In 1870, Segismundo Moret y Prendergast, the liberal Spanish minister of *ultramar* (colonial minister), lamented that in Spain there was a "total ignorance of everything that has to do with the Philippine Archipelago, an ignorance that reigns not only in public opinion, but in official realms," and that the archipelago was "better known in foreign lands than in our own."[71] Moret planned to help develop Spain's colonial knowledges by awarding prizes to works that he thought would help advance and diffuse useful scholarly knowledge about the Philippines and colonization. These prizes were to be awarded to works related to "the description, history, and institutions of the Islands, the means of developing their colonization and the examination of the institutions and systems employed in the rule of England's and Holland's possessions in India [and the East Indies]."[72] The minister's aim was less to contribute to original scientific research than to combat widespread ignorance by "populariz[ing] necessary knowledges and disseminat[ing] books that might contribute to this end."[73] Another of Moret's proposals was to establish three new chairs at the Central University of Madrid in relevant and hitherto-neglected fields. The first chair would be in "the Tagalog language and its principle dialects"; the second proposed chair would be in "the history and civilization of English and Dutch possessions in Asia and Oceania[;] their indigenous peoples' customs, habits, religion, literature, political and religious institutions, etc.; [and] European institutions in all their aspects, and a critical examination of the same"; and the third chair would be in "the history and civilization of the Philippine Islands[;] the indigenous peoples' customs and habits[,] religious and political institutions etc.; [and] Spanish legislation and institutions, their examination and critique."[74] Moret wanted Spain to imitate the successes of the English and Dutch, both in colonial policy and in the academic practices that supported it.

The dearth of Spanish knowledge about the Philippines and resulting Spanish ineptitude in matters of colonial government were also concerns for the peninsular author José Montero y Vidal who noted that "[e]very single German knows more about the Philippines than many of us [Spaniards]; and do not think that we refer only to the uneducated, but also to persons whose erudition is well known."[75] In the area of anthropology, in particular, Spanish scholarship was judged by its own practitioners to be deficient, for as Paul Kramer tells us, "Spanish physical anthropologist Manuel Antón lamented that 'not even a single insignificant fact' could be presented regarding the islands' anthropology. While Spain's Museum of Natural History had only 'a few dozen crania and some photographs,' those of Paris and Dresden had 'thousands of specimens of Philippine anthropology.'"[76]

Peninsular Spaniards were not the only ones to point out the deficiency of Spanish scholarship about the Philippines. Pardo de Tavera complained in 1884 that "Philippine ethnography, which owes so much today to Germans and Austrians, has received so little contribution from Spanish pens that it seems to be a question of more interest to the former than to the latter."[77] Pardo de Tavera referred here to a group of scholars of whom the foremost European authority on the Philippines was Ferdinand Blumentritt. A Bohemian schoolteacher, and amateur but highly respected ethnographer and historian, Blumentritt's interest in the Spanish colonial world grew out of a childhood fascination with the books and artifacts of his great-aunt's house, which had come from her husband's *patria* of Peru. Perhaps the family story that his father descended from a governor-general of the Philippines encouraged Blumentritt's particular interest in that westernmost Oriental outpost of the Spanish empire.[78] The quintessential armchair scholar, who never visited the Philippines, Blumentritt synthesized data gathered by others and analyzed the theories proposed by them. He enthusiastically welcomed and promoted serious study by young Filipinos of their homeland, encouraging them in their studies, introducing them to scientific circles, citing their works, and translating them into German. Blumentritt became a close friend of a few of these Filipinos and a steadfast supporter of their campaigns to win political reforms. Though he was among the most outspoken critics of peninsular racism toward Filipinos, he wrote in highly racialized terms.

Blumentritt's work partook of a Continental practice of anthropology dominated by questions of biology and racial descent for which the Philippines held particular interest. The physically, culturally, and linguistically diverse peoples of the Philippines were thought to belong to or descend from two or three different major pre-Hispanic racial groups (Malay, Negroid, Mongoloid), but precisely which groups belonged to which races or mixtures of them, and how and when they came to the islands, was the subject of dispute. The Philippines, then, was thought to contain data that could potentially yield significant progress in the quest to unlock secrets of human racial affinity and diversity. During the late nineteenth century the Philippines received intense attention among a few influential European ethnologists such as Rudolf Virchow, perhaps the most important figure in nineteenth-century German anthropology, and A. B. Meyer, the director of the famed ethnographic museum of Dresden.[79] These two gathered their data in part via the ethnographic collections acquired by other ethnographer-naturalist travelers such as Hans Meyer and Alexander Schadenberg (who contributed their own analyses on the ethnographic question); those collections included items of clothing, tools, weapons, and of course skulls.[80] This German interest in the racial puzzle of the Philippines was a context for the joking exchange between José Rizal and Virchow when they met at a meeting of the Geographic Society of Berlin in January of 1887. Afterward, Rizal related to a friend that "the scholar told me [Rizal] jestingly that he wished to study me 'ethnographically'" and that he (Rizal) had gracefully quipped in reply, "'yes,' for the love of science, and [I] promised to bring another example (my compatriot)."[81] The example—or specimen—is what is telling here; the joke depended on the presumed distance between "native" of the Philippines and "scholar," for it positioned Rizal as a physical specimen (like a living version of the many skulls and other body parts that had traveled to Virchow's labs via the crates of German gentleman-scholars) as well as a guest of the society (he later became a member). De los Reyes, too, via Blumentritt, engaged this tradition, and in more than one respect he is a contemporary of Virchow's student, Franz Boas, the patriarch of American anthropology who is credited with pioneering "fieldwork" as a method, for he was the first prominent, theoretically minded, and scholarly ethnologist to gather data from the field himself. Yet two years before Boas began his fieldwork, de los Reyes told the reader of his ethnographic piece on the Tinguian that "I myself in 1881 took much care in gathering [the information] as precisely as possible in Abra, where I think the characteristics of the original [primitive] Tinguian are preserved better than in some settlements of Ilocos."[82] His and others' appeals to having firsthand knowledge and using it in the name of science complicated the highly racialized approach of the Continental anthropologists, even while engaging its premises.

The scholarly attention that these European ethnographers paid to the Philippines—even in its most racialized forms—was for many of these young Filipino writers a welcome contrast to the dearth of serious scholarship from Spain.[83] While Spaniards had written historical works on the Philippines, Pardo de Tavera commented, their "favored occupation has been to relate politico-religious events," and their works were "laden with miraculous events and stories of divine punishments."[84] By the 1880s, Spaniards had yet to produce a significant body of contemporary knowledge about the Philippines, and had not engaged the newly emerging anthropological sciences for which the Philippines held such importance.

Kramer has analyzed how *ilustrados*' ethnographic writings were part of a strategy of proving their civilization, and their fitness to rule, via demonstrating their mastery of this colonial science.[85] To engage in these sciences was to engage in the latest European scholarship and also to demonstrate one's superiority to peninsulars in these fields useful for colonial rule. Yet not all sciences were created equal, and not all were used in the same way to the same ends. The study of folklore, for example, was uncharacteristically well developed in mid-1880s Spain, and so its practice in the Philippines in some ways complemented, and in some ways competed with, Spanish scholarship.

Overall, we will find that the scholarly voices of these young Filipinos varied significantly. Some bragged, some apologized, some challenged, and others offered laurels. Some seemed to write for a European audience, others Spanish peninsular, others Filipino, and often a combination of all of these. In every case, however, we see a working through of the tension between "native" authority and scholarly objectivity and an appropriation of scholarly tools for political ends. Their works resonate with political and scholarly problems that exceed those specifically addressed. The following chapter explores how three Filipino intellectuals took up the challenges and possibilities offered by ethnological sciences of race and Catholic discourses of civilization.

CHAPTER 2

The Uses of Ethnology

Thinking Filipino with "Race" and "Civilization"

IN 1887, EVARISTO AGUIRRE WROTE from Madrid to José Rizal, who was then traveling elsewhere in Europe, about the embarrassing behavior of one of the other prominent young Filipinos living in the Spanish capital. Pedro Paterno had, Aguirre complained, resurrected the title of "Maguinoo," an ancient Tagalog title of nobility that the friar chronicles documented but that was neither officially recognized nor commonly used by the late nineteenth-century elite. Adorning himself with this title, Paterno had taken on outward signs of royalty that his chagrined compatriot considered both pretentious and ridiculous:

> The "Maguinoo" [pronounced mah-ghee-no-o] says that this is
> a . . . high *filipino* title that belongs to his family; and on the body of
> his coach, the harnesses of his horses, his traveling cloak, his business card, and other things, has a coat of arms painted, worked in
> silver, embroidered, and lithographed. . . . [The coat of arms looks]
> like this:
> A sun, as if half French and half Japanese, and above it a *salakot* crowned with a ducal or royal crown, that has a bird on its
> crest, and beneath, tied by the chin-strap—that is, the ties of the
> *salakot*—[are] two machetes. This [behavior] is putting on airs,
> and acting a fool [*Esto se llama lucirse y hacer el tonto también*].[1]

Aguirre mocked Paterno for claiming nobility and cloaking himself, literally, with its sign. The sign on Paterno's carriage, cloak, and card—all the trappings that would announce him on the streets and in the foyers of high society—was one that Aguirre thought could be recognized by all as a crude counterfeit, for the model was a European coat of arms and

Paterno's creative version (Figure 2.1) was a hodgepodge of generic com-
ponents, some European, some Filipino substitutes, and some not clearly
identifiable as either: the *salakot* (a wide hat, usually worn by peasants but
here in a style sometimes worn by petty officials) in place of a European
helmet; the *bolos* (machetes) where swords might be used as supports;
a bird of indeterminate species; the sun, which Aguirre thought suffered
from a confused identity ("half French and half Japanese"); and the crown
derived from European, not Philippine, models. Aguirre wrote with some
relief that Paterno was "*unique* in such sublime extravagances."[2]

Paterno expressed his royal aspirations in more scholarly trappings as
well, and some of them inspired similarly derisive reactions. The same year
that Aguirre complained of his pretensions, Paterno published *Ancient*

*Figure 2.1 Pedro Paterno's coat of arms, described by Aguirre to Rizal. The image appears
on the title page of Paterno's* Antigua civilización tagálog. *Photo courtesy of the Newberry
Library, Chicago. Call # Ayer 1251.P29 1887.*

Tagalog Civilization, a book extolling the accomplishments of the civilization of its title.[3] The book was not particularly well received among fellow
ilustrados and scholars. Rizal, for example, warned Ferdinand Blumentritt
to "pay no attention to what Paterno says . . . in his work. P. A. Paterno is
[here the manuscript has a scribble] I can't find a word for it, but only a
sign like this: [another scribble]."[4] Paterno was probably more concerned,
however, with his image among Madrid's elite. *Ancient Tagalog Civilization* was published the same year as Madrid's Philippine Exposition, and
Paterno might have hoped that both the exhibition and his book—the
title page of which (Figure 2.2) included a reproduction of the coat of
arms belonging to its author, the "Maguinóo Paterno"—would raise his
profile as Tagalog prince in fashionable circles.[5] But the buzz surrounding the exposition largely centered on a living display of Filipinos, many
of them members of ethnolinguistic groups on the political margins of
the Philippines, who were supposed to represent their "type" or "race."[6] It
seems that notoriety of the "primitive" peoples dominated Madrileño perceptions of the Philippines. Paterno might have written *Ancient Tagalog
Civilization* hoping that the exposition's hype would highlight the newly
revealed sophistication of the ancient Tagalog culture, and its modern-day
heir and prince, in his own person. Instead, Paterno's ancient civilization
was upstaged by contemporary "primitives."

Members of the Filipino colony of Madrid—as they referred to
themselves—responded to this part of the exhibition with indignation
that expressed both humanitarian protest as well as their anxieties about
racial and cultural status.[7] On the one hand, many of their writings, both
public and private, reveal outrage over the inhumanity of the display, both
in principle for displaying humans as artifacts and in practice for the conditions in which these individuals were forced to live (and as a result of
which, several died). Graciano López Jaena, in particular, wrote articles
for the Madrid press complaining that these people's housing was unsani-
tary and cold and that they were effectively prisoners in their compound.
At the same time, López Jaena's articles called attention to the discrepancy
between the "civilized" Philippines and those who represented the country at the exposition, and argued that it was the former that should have
been included as planners of the exhibition, not the latter as specimens
in it.[8] Those *ilustrado* reactions reveal at least as much concern about the
bad image of the Philippines that they feared these "uncivilized" people
would project to the "civilized" world, as they revealed concern for the

LA ANTIGUA

CIVILIZACIÓN TAGÁLOG

(APUNTES)

POR

PEDRO ALEXANDRO MOLO AGUSTÍN PATERNO Y DE VERA IGNACIO

MAGUINÓO PATERNO

DOCTOR EN JURISPRUDENCIA

MADRID
TIPOGRAFÍA DE MANUEL G. HERNÁNDEZ
IMPRESOR DE LA REAL CASA
Libertad, 16 duplicado
1887

Figure 2.2 Title page of Paterno's Ancient Tagalog Civilization. Photo courtesy of the Newberry Library, Chicago. Call # Ayer 1251.P29 1887.

people themselves.[9] The display of such "primitives" undermined the propagandists' claims that Filipinos should be recognized as politically equal to peninsulars. Further, some of the Filipinos living in Madrid found that Madrileños equated them with the "uncivilized" people on display, and this heightened their sense of alienation from the racist society in which they sought recognition.[10] They were dismayed and outraged that the Philippines was being presented as a primitive and exotic colony, rather than as a part of the modern world.

Paterno's pretensions, the exhibition, and the Filipino colony's reactions to both illustrate some of the consequences of the combined focus on racial origins, on the one hand, and civilizational progress, on the other, that underwrote much of the scholarship in whose idiom Filipinos wrote about pre-Hispanic history. In their attention to reconstructing an era that predated the imposition of foreign rule, *ilustrados'* efforts were like those of nineteenth-century intellectuals of other would-be nations emerging from other established empires. Greeks, Armenians, Croats, Serbs, Slovenes, Magyars, Romanians, Czechs, Germans, Poles, and others were emerging from the Prussian, Austrian, Russian, and Ottoman empires, often bolstering their national claims with writings that documented the nation's existence before its imperial subjugation.[11] Those writings would typically stress elements of that people's culture or history that distinguished it from those who ruled over it or from neighboring peoples, such as the practice of religion, the written or oral literature of a language, or the legitimacy of an earlier political regime. In a parallel way, some intellectuals in nineteenth-century South Asia highlighted the pre-British (and also often pre-Mughal) Hindu past, invoking the authority of textual and scholarly traditions even while often reforming them.[12]

For young educated elites of the Philippines, such stories were available only in modified form. The polities that preceded Spanish rule in the Philippines were numerous and small scale, its many native tongues diverse. For the same reasons, however, the Philippines was of obvious interest to ethnological sciences. The diversity of the peoples of the Philippines— diverse languages, practices, and physiologies—made it a rich resource for studying historical relationships among human groupings. Emerging ethnological sciences, in turn, provided tools, presumptions, and even sometimes political associations that were of interest to these young educated elites.

This chapter investigates how ethnological ideas were employed in scholarly discourse about the Philippines in the 1880s and early 1890s, focusing on T. H. Pardo de Tavera's *Sanskrit in the Tagalog Language*, Pedro Paterno's *Ancient Tagalog Civilization* and *The Itas*, and the "prehistory" section of Isabelo de los Reyes's *History of Ilocos*.[13] It examines these works in the context of, and in comparison with, other ethnological works from which they drew and to which they spoke. The methods and presumptions of ethnological sciences worked to find commonalities across some of the numerous ethnolinguistic boundaries in the Philippines, commonalities that suggested the existence of a cohesive "people" that predated and was independent of their Spanish civilization and so was proto-notional, as some *ilustrado* writings demonstrate. However, *ilustrado* writings reveal even more strongly that ethnological sciences were sometimes laden with a hierarchical politics that reinforced established narratives of civilization, even while translating those narratives into new terms. Whereas established narratives of "civilization" conceived its limits along the lines of universal religion, in the idiom of ethnological sciences the same exclusions and inclusions were reimagined along lines of plural ethnicities, peoples, or "races."

The methods of ethnological sciences were able to recover and reconstruct elements of what appeared to be a pre-Hispanic history and culture, making it possible to see value in what had hitherto appeared as a dark past. This idea of a unified pre-Hispanic past of diverse contemporary peoples was expressed in part through the language of race, a language that naturalized commonalities, as well as difference. Race discourse "has a great ability to circulate, a great aptitude for metamorphosis, or a sort of strategic polyvalence," by which it can be and has been taken up in quite markedly divergent and often opposed political projects.[14] As we will see, the different nuances of "race" and of related conceptions of "people," "civilization," and "culture" reveal how various were the meanings and associations of "race" at this time, and more particularly, how these variations contained both opportunities as well as challenges for those who wrote about the Philippines.

While the idea that "race" marks difference and hierarchy is more familiar in a twenty-first-century idiom, we need to understand, too, how it marked commonalities and equivalence in order to see its use and operation in this case. On the one hand, "race" as a category, like "people" or "nation," could have what Anthony Milner has described in the context of colonial Malaya as "egalitarian overtones," in that "concern about the condition of the race is a concern not for an aristocratic elite but rather an entire community."[15] In this mode of thinking, members of a race were of equal status in relation to that race, in a way that members of a nation were in principle of equal status with respect to that nation. As Milner argues, the formal equivalence of members of a "race" was reflected in how "race" concerned "the interests of the common people" and "possesse[d] no necessary hierarchical implications."[16] In this sense, the history of races was a kind of effort at history from below: the subject was collective and common, not individual or exceptional. This history of races, as divisions of human groupings, was the science of ethnology.

Of course, ideas about "race" were not universally democratic, as is well known. The vocabulary of race was often employed with a grammar of hierarchy, according to which some races were taken to be more advanced than others. Borders that marked racial difference could be drawn *around* the Philippines but also within it, marking some peoples of the Philippines as more advanced than others. The hierarchical grammar that was often employed with the vocabulary of race worked both for and against these intellectuals in their efforts to authorize the common and advanced civilization of some peoples of the Philippines. On the one hand, some elite Filipinos could claim rights and status for a broader multilingual group on the basis that this "people" or "race" was distinct from but approaching the level of advanced European peoples, and distinct from and leaving behind others deemed more barbaric. Yet employing the vocabulary of race with the grammar of hierarchy brought liabilities as well, for the *ilustrados* were sometimes on the receiving end of racial discrimination and deprecation, and their claims to advancement were not always accepted by those invested in racialized thinking.[17]

A third set of questions revolves around the term "Filipino" and the story of the transformation of its meaning from "of the Philippines" to a conception of a people with a common past, present, and political future. A grouping of "Filipino" emerges in some of the ethnological works of *ilustrados* that deal most explicitly with ethnology and race. "Filipino" was not the only or even predominant grouping of these texts, but its meaning was changing and its content contested. We know that before the 1880s the term *filipino*, when used in a sense more narrow than the general adjectival "of the Philippines," referred specifically to people of Spanish parentage born in the Philippines (equivalent with the term used across the Spanish colonial world, *criollo*). Thus it was a political distinction as much as it was racial, for it identified those in the insular polity who had certain privileges and obligations, distinct from those of the *peninsular* (Spanish, born in the peninsula); the *indio* or *indígena* ("native" of the Philippines, which could be any of many different ethnolinguistic groups); the *mestizo* (of mixed parentage, sometimes Spanish and native, but more often *mestizo chino* or *mestizo de sangley*, Spanish and Chinese); the *chino* or *sangley* (Chinese); and, on the edges of Spanish sovereignty, the *moro* (Muslim) and the *infiel* ("infidel," often referred to in groupings of "tribes," referring to ethnolinguistic groups generally living outside of Spanish sovereignty and that were neither Christian, Muslim, nor Chinese).[18]

By the late 1880s and 1890s, the meaning of "Filipino" was changing. First, it came to be used in a "metropolitan sense" as a way to refer rather simply to "people from the Philippines," regardless of their location in colonial law and society.[19] That sense emerged both from peninsular Spaniards' failure to distinguish between *mestizo* or *indio*, for example, and also from the young men who, when called *filipino* by others, took on that collective identity, both because the distinctions that separated them in colonial society became less meaningful to them when they found themselves collectively alone across the oceans, and also because in this metropolitan context they referred to themselves as those around them did. So, as Rizal wrote to a friend, "we call ourselves simply *filipinos*" when in Madrid.[20]

However, some of these same people—Paterno and Pardo de Tavera in particular—were also beginning to think in more ethnological terms when they employed "Filipino" in scholarly writings of the 1880s. In fact it is these authors from the Philippines who first use "Filipino" in an ethnological sense. To be sure, they draw on German and French scholarly ideas that identify peoples in terms of such ethnological categories, but no previous scholars had used "Filipino" in particular to mark an ethnological grouping. In *ilustrado* writings, the ethnological sense of "Filipino" transcended some linguistic divisions but also either clearly excluded, or only ambiguously and marginally included, those who were "of the Philippines" and also Chinese, mestizo, Muslim, or "infidel." To the extent that "Filipino" emerged in *ilustrado* scholarly works via the science of ethnology, it was in its origin also a term that denoted race, with all its attendant political ambivalence.[21]

The idea of "Filipino," then, has origins as both an ethnological *and* a political term. It first emerged in this post-creole sense during the 1880s both through elites' common experience of pilgrimage and exile and through their engagements with the scholarly world of ethnology. It was based both on assertions of natural existence and on the contextual lived experience of exile. That it would come to have a broader political meaning for people in the Philippines—for Filipinos, beyond these few elites—is not explained in these pages. However, to make political claims in the name of the "Filipino nation" depended on establishing that that nation was natural. "Filipino," as a *national* category, was a new concept, yet in its inception, it conjured its own distant past. This work was already done in scholarly terms by these *ilustrado* writings, when "Filipino" came to be widely accepted in its modern political sense.

But the meaning of "Filipino" was far from apparent or fixed in these early *ilustrado* writings. This chapter investigates a few different examples, then, of how "race," "civilization," "people," "culture," and "nation" were configured in writings about the pre-Hispanic Philippines and how they were used to draw boundaries and fill in the shapes they outlined. These terms were widely and variously used because in Europe, too—not just in the colonies—emperors ruled over different "peoples" in the name of "civilization." So while the terms had particular resonances in and for the Philippines, their slipperiness in that context is also part of a more general story of how these terms were overlapping and in flux.

People, Nation, Race

To begin to understand what some of these contested terms meant in the writings of *ilustrados*, consider how Rizal clarified the meanings of the Spanish words for "race," "tribe," and "nation" for Blumentritt in 1886. Rizal was responding to Blumentritt's query about how to translate the German word for "tribe" (*Stamm*) and whether "race" (in Spanish, *raza*) would be an appropriate translation. Rizal replied, "I looked up the word 'race' in my Dominguez dictionary [of the Spanish language] and I believe its meaning is not [the same as the German word for] 'tribe' [*Stamm*]."[22] He went on to explain two related but distinct meanings for the Spanish word for "race." First, he referred to a conception of races as the most basic types of humans: "We call 'races' the Caucasian, Mongolian, Malayan, and the Black," which were considered the most general types, and any more particular group was thought to be traceable to one of them, or a combination.[23] Scholars who subscribed to such a racial typology might disagree over whether the races descended from a single source or from different sources (monogenism versus poligenism), and they might disagree about which races were the most basic and which were derivative. For example, some thought "Malay" or "Malayan" was not one of these basic races but was instead the result of a mixture of "Mongolian" and "Black." Most scholars held that there were at least three races, and some held that there were five or more. Despite these scholarly arguments, the existence of such discrete types was widely accepted, and the work of ethnology was in part to trace the origins of any of the world's present peoples back to one or more of these original types.[24] This work was known as investigating the "filiation," or blood relationships, between human groups across space and time, after the manner of a great family tree for all of humankind. Though traits that we might call "cultural" (language, for example) could be relevant to making such large-scale racial distinctions, physiological traits were often invoked as the distinctive ones at this level of racial organization. In this usage, most Christian groups in the Philippines were considered to be primarily of the "Malayan race," which distinguished them from other peoples in the Philippines who had ancestry either of the "Mongolian race" (Chinese) or of the "Black race" (peoples in the Philippines who were referred to generically, in the Spanish of the time, as *negritos*, meaning literally "little Blacks").[25]

But Rizal went on to clarify that Spanish also used the word "race" in a different way, to indicate subdivisions of these more general categorizations: "We also use [in Spanish] this word ['race' or *raza*] to refer to peoples [*Völker*] which are significantly large [in population], around half a million souls, which you call [in German] 'nations,' but we don't call peoples that are not independent 'nations' e.g. the Tagalog or Visayan 'race' but not the Tagalog or Visayan 'nation,' on the other hand, the Spanish 'race' and 'nation.'"[26] Rizal's distinction emphasized the political significance of these terms in the Spanish context: not all *razas* were also politically independent *naciones*. But more to the point, these smaller-unit *razas* (whether Tagalog, Visayan, or Spanish) were of course much more numerous than what were supposed to be the original discrete physiological types from which they were thought to have been derived (the Tagalog and Visayan *razas*, for example, were considered different branches of the more general "Malayan" *raza*.) This sense of "race" carried with it a stronger conception of shared habits or customs, for Rizal noted that it was like the German *Volk* that carried with it a sense of being a "people."

What we might call cultural traits—language, moral systems, beliefs about the supernatural, medical practices, oral literature, celebrations, and ceremonies—were taken as data that could indicate origin, just as physiological data was supposed to do.[27]

Rizal went on to explain the Spanish distinction between "race" and "tribe" as one of further subdivision: "Tribe [*Tribu*] is smaller than race, and means something like a division of race. For example, the Jewish race, the tribe of Judah, of Levi, etc. . . . and one always gives this name in relation to a trunk from which the tribes [branches] originate: e.g. the tribe of Judah, of Levi, of Dan, in relation to the father Jacob."[28] Rizal also clarified that "tribe" could have a more particular political meaning, however; for it "is the most common name that the Spaniards give people who are neither numerous, nor have a government, nor great importance," and this meaning accords with how the "infidel tribes" were referred to in the Philippines.[29] Rizal concluded his report to Blumentritt by writing that "nothing else comes to mind for [the German word for] 'tribe' [*Stamm*]," after having ruled out two other possibilities: "'Clan' [*Clan*] is adopted in Spanish now, but only in its first and original meaning, as a group of several families in Scotland. 'Caste' [*Casta*] seems to me more political than ethnographic, and in this respect I give this noun no great worth."[30] It was a distinction both physical and cultural—the ethnographic distinction—that Rizal was trying to help Blumentritt capture.

Though Rizal uses examples from the Philippines, he does not give "Filipino" as an example of any of these terms—"race," "nation," "people," or "tribe"—as the word had not yet come to have any of these meanings clearly. Further, we see already in Rizal's letter that these generic terms for human groupings could have biological, cultural, or political meanings, and sometimes a confusing combination of these. We have also noted that references to the "Malayans" of the Philippines were usually clearly meant to distinguish these peoples from "Negritos" or "Chinese" and to refer to one of the basic racial types to which all peoples of the earth were supposed to belong. We will see that this general category, "Malay" or "Malayan," was sometimes used ambiguously in the writings of ethnologists and *ilustrados* and that the two definitions of "race" that we have identified—one a larger and more general category of what were presumed to be irreducible differences, and the other a more specific and numerous category in which culture was more significant—were not always held apart. Shared cultural qualities among "Malayan" peoples of the Philippines suggested a common origin in the larger "Malayan race," but they also indicated a more significantly emotive bond that could allow a "race" to approach the German sense of "nation" or "people" (*Volk*).

"Malay" or "Malayan" was, however, a troublesome way to denote affiliations among peoples of the Philippines, and between those and others. "Malay" clearly excluded Negritos and Chinese. However, it did not distinguish Christians from Muslims in the Philippines nor did it distinguish between those peoples of the Philippines and peoples of the Malay peninsula. The "Malay" category seems to cut off peoples in the Dutch East Indies in favor of an association with those to the west of the Malayan peninsula. We will encounter significant disagreement about whether and how peoples to the south were related to those in the Philippines, which reflects anxieties about the ways that "race" could cross old "civilizational" boundaries between Christian and Muslim. Those possible crossings were usually cut off in *ilustrado* writings.

In different writings, we will see sometimes awkward connections and distinctions drawn among "Malayan," "Filipino," "native" (*indígena*), *indio*, and terms that specify more particular ethnolinguistic groups like Tagalog, Ilocano, Visayan, and so on. Any of these groupings may be referred to as a *raza*, *pueblo*, *civilización*, or even *nación*. We have already seen how Rizal delineated some of the ambiguities of *raza* and *nación*. *Pueblo*, which could mean simply "town," "township," or "townsfolk," more commonly in these writings meant "a people," specifically in the sense of a large-scale group, similar to the Spanish *raza* or *nación* or German *Volk*.[31] Both *pueblo* and *nación* can be translated into English as "nation." *Pueblo* was often used in *ilustrado* writings with this sense of "a people," perhaps to selectively bridge certain ethnolinguistic divides while maintaining others. *Nación* was less often used, perhaps because, as Rizal wrote, it usually indicated political independence.

Civilización had a different kind of meaning, one that indicated a relatively high level of refinement and sophistication, in contrast to *rudeza natural* (natural rough manners).[32] We see "civilization" used in *ilustrado* texts in a plural sense (Tagalog civilization, Hindu civilization, and so on), and so we will witness here how a newer conception of the term emerged. This kind of plural usage was only first accepted by the conservative Royal Spanish Academy in 1925. Before then, "civilization" was, according to the academy, strictly singular: a person or a people could partake in or acquire it, but there were not many different civilizations. It was precisely this quality of "civilization," its pretense to universality, that made it useful for empires within Europe, and those that extended beyond Europe, because in the name of civilization (a common civilization because universal) a diverse set of peoples could be ruled over. This sense of civilization is both catholic (in that it could accommodate anyone, in principle, who is willing and able to become civilized) and also Catholic (in that such a universal mission describes the Church's characteristic holding-together of a broad array of cultures, political structures, languages, and practices). We will see in some *ilustrado* writings that "civilization" was used *both* to indicate a certain level of sophistication or advancement—the version that is not specific because, in principle, it is universal—and also in a plural sense in which each civilization can have its own specific content (like "culture"). This combination—of the singular-universal and plural-specific senses of "civilization"—allowed for some peoples of the Philippines to be elevated over others.[33]

Finally, we should note here that the word for "culture" (*cultura*) is noticeably absent. Like the Spanish *civilización, cultura* only took on a plural sense much later (in this case, officially in 1983), when it came to signify the "collection of modes of life and customs."[34] Before this, the word referred to what one could gain by cultivating one's intellectual faculties according to the collective wisdom of human knowledge. Though the German *Kultur* had a meaning much closer to how *ilustrados* sometimes used "civilization" during this period, the Spanish *cultura* never appeared in their texts, and its use in this sense was still far off.[35]

Ethnography and ethnology invited speculation about the relationship between the different peoples of the Philippines who were thought to be related—that is, the peoples (*razas, Völker*) or "races" who were thought to be part of the larger Malayan race that had made the islands their home and then, at some pre-Hispanic moment, split into different branches. As we will see, the term "Filipino" was offered to stand for that grouping, at moments and tentatively. However, the pre-Hispanic "Filipino" of *ilustrado* writings generally referred to those who shared a history of Spanish colonization, and so the term reproduced the inclusions and exclusions of Catholicism's "civilization," even though ethnological data could cut across such civilizational distinctions. More specifically, *ilustrado* ethnologists delineated not only distinctions between the Malayan peoples of the Philippines and those thought to be either wholly or significantly "Mongoloid" (Chinese) or "Black" (Negrito) but also sometimes points of connection.

Others peoples, such as Muslims in the south, were clearly excluded from the pre-Hispanic unity, even while their race was sometimes marked "Malayan." Some of these texts incorporate "Malayan" highland animists into the pre-Hispanic unity by portraying them as contemporary ancestors. Finally, the manifest fact of Chinese parentage among Christian "natives" is minimized in these writings, sometimes via imagining races or peoples as having originary moments rather than thinking in terms of ongoing processes of interrelation. While the main focus of this chapter is on *ilustrado* ethnographic writings, we must first consider how some of these different kinds of terms—those denoting race, religion, or civilizational or legal status—overlapped in other writings about Philippine ethnology.

"Race" and "Civilization" in Philippine Ethnology

Though earlier chroniclers had speculated about how the islands had come to be populated, *ilustrado* authors responded to the newer wave of interest in this question brought by ethnologists concerned with racial filiation. The Philippines' rich ethnographic diversity—diversity mapped on religious, linguistic, and physiological lines—provided both questions about human filiation and also the data with which they could be answered. How had the present-day peoples of the Philippines come to be where they were, looking, believing, practicing, dressing, and speaking as they did? What was the history, predating written records, of the movements, meetings, confrontations, combinations, dominations, expulsions, conversions, divisions, and flights of peoples to and among the islands? Both Christianity and Islam had arrived within the preceding several hundreds of years—relatively recently in terms of the history of human settlement in the area—so those variations were not as interesting to ethnologists as those that predated the arrival of the Spanish by unknown hundreds of years. Linguistic variation, variation in habits and customs not attributed to Christianity or Islam, and also variation in physiologies were the data that were thought to reveal that more distant era. Because the islands were so ethnographically diverse, they were thought to hold rich resources for studying complexities of human filiation. For the most part, it was not the Spanish who had exploited these resources.

Blumentritt was one of the figures who devoted significant attention to these questions and who attempted a serious scholarly appraisal of others' theories and data: his 1882 German-language *Toward an Ethnography of the*

Philippines was aimed toward the goal of a systematic, encyclopedic guide to ethnographic groups of the Philippines.[36] The organization of Blumentritt's text reflects his engagement with racial theories. The work identifies fifty-seven different groups, all but six of which are categorized as subgroups of the general racial category "Malay." The remainder are grouped in the general categories of "Negrito," "Chinese, Chinese Mestizos and Japanese," and finally, "Whites and other Population Groups" (*Weisse und andere Bevölkerungsbestandtheile*). This very neatly corresponds with the structure of the four most basic racial groups into which Blumentritt and others thought the world's peoples could be divided ("Malay," "Black," "Mongoloid," and "White"). Blumentritt outlined an ethnological puzzle in this work that fascinated many of his German-language colleagues: What was the parentage of the "Igorots"? "Igorot" was an imprecise term, as many who used it explained, that comprised a number of different non-Christian groups (*tribus infieles*) in the mountains of northern Luzon. The ethnological puzzle was whether they were properly speaking "Malay" or of a different race. Blumentritt answered this question via his version of a theory of racial migration that had come to dominate the field.[37]

This general theory of racial migration held that the diversity of the Philippines could in part be explained by discrete waves of past immigration. It had long been speculated that the dark-skinned "Negritos" of the Philippines represented an earlier era of human settlement, hailing from Australia or New Guinea, and that they had been pushed to the interior by later-arriving peoples from the Malay peninsula, whose descendents the Spanish found on the islands' shores and called *indios*. Such a narrative had by 1878 made it into the *Compendium of the History of the Philippines*, a textbook for use in the Ateneo, the Jesuit's secondary school in Manila, by Father Francisco Baranera who had even adopted the term "Malay" as an ethnographic, racial term to describe the later inhabitants.[38] The ethnologists, however, attempted to work out more precisely than did Baranera the origins and histories of the peoples of the Philippines, and Blumentritt and other scholars produced detailed versions of the theory of racial migration, citing and synthesizing as much ethnological data as they could gather. Ethnologists agreed that the first people to arrive on the islands were the "Negritos" and that they were followed by later waves of migration, which pushed the Negritos off the coasts, into the interiors, and up the interior mountains of the islands. However, scholars disagreed about whether there were two or more waves of migration and whether all the waves after the original Negrito were "Malay" or whether one or more were of another race.

In his 1882 *Toward an Ethnography*, Blumentritt held that there were three distinct waves but that both the second and third were Malay. Joseph Montano, a French scholar who had traveled to the region from 1879 to 1881, proposed in his 1885 *Report to the Minister of Public Education [of France] on a Scientific Mission to the Philippine Islands and Malaya* that there had been three waves of three distinct races.[39] The first wave brought "Negritos." A second wave of migration brought a race that he called "Indonesian," using a term and racial distinction proposed by a German ethnologist but whose validity was debated (the term was not taken up in any but ethnographic circles until much later).[40] Finally, the third wave brought "Malay." Descendents of each of these original migration waves, Montano reported, could be found in concentric circles in the Philippine islands: In his terms, "Negritos" had been pushed into the interior by the "Indonesians," and in turn, when the "Malay" arrived on the coasts, both earlier groups were pushed yet further inland. Blumentritt and Montano were among a much broader group of European scholars that attended to the Philippines, which included particularly prominent German scholars. Blumentritt dedicated his 1882 work to A. B. Meyer, the director of the Dresden ethnographic museum, who traveled to the region and published significant studies in the 1880s and 1890s. While in the Philippines, Meyer had collected skulls—mostly stolen—and sent them back to Virchow, who had used them to settle what was called the "Negrito question" (*Negritofrage*): whether the dark-skinned peoples of the Philippines and New Guinea were related to sub-Saharan Africans.[41] The ethnological data of the Philippines were worth studying, both for what they could say about the history of the peopling of the Philippines and also for what they could show about human filiation more generally. While the Philippines was of interest to German ethnologists for its valuable data that could serve in the study of scientific questions, such scholarly attention carried with it political significance in the context of the late nineteenth century.

The 1880s were a decade of turbulence and conflict in the Spanish empire, especially with regards to relations with Germany. German-language scholarship in the realms of anthropology far preceded Germany's political unification in 1871. By the beginning of the 1880s, the young nation-state of Germany was on the verge of engaging in overseas colonial ventures (1884). The Spanish empire, meanwhile, had been bleeding for years. When Germany challenged Spanish sovereignty in the Carolinas, the response was not only military and diplomatic but also epistemological and exhibitional: the 1887 Philippine Exposition of Madrid was supposed to demonstrate and literally exhibit Spanish mastery over its colony. Spain used the exhibition model to tie more tightly the strings of empire binding the islands with the peninsula, not just by confirming military or administrative sovereignty, but also by demonstrating Spain's competency to properly represent the islands in the terms of modern knowledges.[42] Though the exhibition attempted to solidify Spain's position as colonizer, its ethnological report shows that Spain's representatives only ambivalently embraced the terms of ethnological science.

The main ethnological writing that came out of the exposition was the report relating to the section on "Population."[43] The report, edited by the Dominican José María Ruíz, a professor at the University of Santo Tomás, was the work of the four friar orders and the Jesuits, testament to the involvement of the Catholic Church in educational institutions of the islands, in government administration, and in the organization of the exposition.[44] Much of the data about the "habits, customs, rituals," and "character" of peoples in the Philippines was gathered from parish priests, always peninsular Spaniards and members of religious orders.[45] These friars were, in a sense, being presented as the on-the-ground data gatherers of modern Spanish science—the Church's equivalent to the bureaucrat-ethnographers of other colonial empires, perhaps—with compiler Ruíz performing the theoretical and integrative work of the ethnological scholar. The friar orders, here, laid claim to modern scientific discourse, as articulated by Ruíz: "In an attempt to describe the variety of customs of the extensive islands of the Archipelago, with the diverse races and multiple mixings of them that have occurred, we will follow the most recent ethnographic studies."[46] In addition to using data from his fellow friars, he relied heavily on data gathered by secular agents of the state (e.g., Ramón Jordana y Morera, whose 1885 "Geographical and Natural-Historical Sketch of the Philippine Islands" had been extracted by Blumentritt for *Globus*).[47]

Though Ruíz and another contributor (the Jesuit Francisco Sánchez) referred to Montano's idea of three distinct races in the Philippines—Negrito, Indonesian, and Malay—the report's organization shows that Ruíz could not, or would not, fully integrate a racialized approach to human classification. Instead, the report is structured by classifications of religion, of what was understood as degrees of relative civilization, of legal category, and of social and economic class. Overall, for example, the report is divided into two sections. The first, "ethnology[,] classifies, describes, and locates races," while the second, "ethology," treats the different races' "religion, habits and customs."[48] One might expect the two sections to have parallel structures, but this is not the case. The first section, written by the Jesuit Sánchez, is predictably organized into three headings that correspond to Montano's racial groups of Negrito, Indonesian, and Malay. The second section, however, organizes the "races" into two major headings: "infidel tribes" and "Christian peoples." Only the "infidel tribes" are broken down into the racial subdivisions of Negrito, Indonesian, and Malay, with a small part of the "Malay" section devoted to "Moros," or Muslims.[49] In other words, the primary "racial" point of distinction, for Ruíz, was religious: Christians versus all others (including Muslims).

Though Ruíz treated (some) individual groups of "infidels" separately, those differences were for him relatively unimportant. As he wrote, "Although there are notable differences in the habits and customs of the different tribes of infidels of the Malayan race, they are all in agreement on their way of life, with little difference, and though it can not always be rightly called entirely savage, neither does it merit the label of rational and civilized."[50] This overall convergence of the pagan and Muslim peoples is duplicated where Ruíz treated the "Christian peoples," which he introduced by noting their difference from the "infidels":

> Having described the characteristics of the different races and infidel tribes that populate the Philippine Archipelago, we now proceed to indicate those of the peoples brought into [reducidos á, lit. "reduced to"] social and political life, which is to say the Christians, subjected to the Government of Spain.
> They are commonly called "indios filipinos," and are found spread among the coasts and plains, distinguished from each other by some minor differences in their clothing, habits, and customs according to the provinces in which they live and the dialect that is particular to them.[51]

Ruíz almost completely discarded the kind of ethnographic divisions that were commonly used—such as Tagalog, Ilocano, and so on, which he only briefly referred to as linguistic and possible physiological types—and instead described a generalized indio.[52] Thus, though he claimed to follow recent ethnographic studies organized along lines of race, in practice Ruíz's overarching classifications were between Christians and non-Christians, and he saw far more affiliations among the groups in each of those categories than he saw among the various peoples of any given racial group (e.g., "Malayan") that were thought to span those categories.

Where he did divide the category "Christians" into different peoples or types, he did so not according to "races" or ethnolinguistic groups but instead according to what he called "social classes": "peasant *indios*," "plebeian *indios*," "middle-class *indios*," "rich *indios*," "mestizos," "the Chinese," and "Spaniards" (in which he wrote of peninsulars and *filipino* Spaniards, in turn).[53] Civilization and class, in other words, were the significant differences among Christian peoples of the Philippines; race was a salient category before Christianity (i.e., among non-Christians), or to the extent that it dictated class, but not in and of itself. Once peoples were "reduced" (incorporated into the religious, civil, and political life of Christian and Spanish dominion) their "racial" or "filial" attributes became less relevant.

Ruíz's "Chinese" are oddly placed in this overarching "Christian" category, since, according to his own account, only some had converted to Catholicism. He dwells on the vices of the Chinese—their avarice, sexual perversions, and opium addiction—and laments that they played an indispensable commercial role in the islands.[54] It is their important position in commercial and urban life, not their religion, that places the Chinese in this section of Ruíz's study. The overlap between racial, legal, and class categories in Ruíz's text—and the effacement of racial difference among *indios*—reveals that the section on "Christians" was less about the science of ethnology than it was an opportunity to comment on the state of peoples of the Philippines, and their relative level of (Catholic) "civilization," and so to identify the proper work of colonial institutions such as governmental administration and education, and underscore the indispensability of the Church.

In some respects, we find similarly productive ambiguities in the racial, legal, and civilizational categorizations in the works of *ilustrado* ethnologists. These ambiguities can be productive in the sense that they allow for the terms that define certain categories, such as "Filipino," to accumulate new meanings. Pardo de Tavera, Paterno, and de los Reyes were each interested by the possibility that ethnological science held for discovering pre-Hispanic unity among different peoples of the islands, though they drew such entities in different ways and with differing political significance. In some *ilustrado* writings, we see racial origins linked to civilizational destinies; in others, race is divorced from destiny, and instead civilization is held out as something acquirable through *ilustración*—education, enlightenment.

Distinguished by Ancient Colonization: Pardo de Tavera's Filipinos

Trinidad Hermenegildo Pardo de Tavera was born in the Philippines in 1857 to a prominent *criollo* family (Philippine-born Spanish), though he had ancestry more mixed than this official status would indicate.[55] His father, who died when Trinidad was very young, and his uncle, who then became his guardian, were both prominent lawyers in Manila and had been appointed to significant positions in governmental administration. His uncle was also appointed to the law faculty of the University of Santo Tomás in 1868, the same year as the liberal revolution in Spain, and was among the prominent gentlemen of Manila to advocate liberal reforms in the islands. During the wave of repression in the early 1870s, his uncle was exiled from the Philippines on account of his liberal politics, and the entire Pardo family—uncle, aunt, Trinidad, his brother, sister, and mother—relocated to Paris. Trinidad, a student in Manila at the time of his uncle's deportation, finished his medical studies in Paris, earning his doctor of medicine degree in 1881. His scholarly interests were broad, and he took the opportunity to study Sanskrit and Malay at the famous Orientalist *École des Langues Orientales*. It was at the School of Oriental Languages, from which he obtained a diploma in 1885, that he learned Orientalist linguistic methods that he used to treat what he called "the ethnographic question" of the origins of and relationships between different peoples of the Philippines. His Orientalist and in particular philological methods—focusing on written alphabets—encouraged him to find an ancient "high civilization" and to locate the origins of that civilization in what he theorized to have been an ancient era of Hindu conquest, transposing to the Philippines a model of historical development and civilizational conquest that explained the rise and fall of ancient empires of India. This model divided the peoples of the Philippines into all those who had been colonized by Hindus and all others. Those who had been colonized by Hindus had therefore, he surmised, developed a more sophisticated level of civilization than their uncolonized brethren.

In Pardo de Tavera's linguistic writings—first in *Contribution to the Study of Ancient Filipino Alphabets* (1884) and then in *Sanskrit in the Tagalog Language* (1887)—he treated language and its elements, specifically alphabets and vocabulary, as evidence that could reveal historical events.[56] Quoting "the celebrated French Orientalist Rémusat," Pardo de Tavera wrote that "the language of a people is the most faithful mirror of its civilization, the most complete picture of the social revolutions that have marked its existence."[57] His first linguistic work focused specifically on peoples "of the Malayan race, called Indios [*de raza malaya llamados Indios*]" who "had their own alphabets and manner of writing" when the Spanish arrived.[58] Though no pre-Hispanic writings survived, Pardo de Tavera could use the alphabets themselves, as recorded in early friar chronicles, to study "the history of those islands, a history so neglected and so little known, despite or perhaps because much has been written about it, that it still remains to be studied and written."[59] Although the library shelf might be filled with histories of the Philippines by Spanish authors, these books were "generally laden with miraculous events and stories of divine punishments" and failed to treat the history of the peoples of the islands before the Spanish arrival, a history that could be uncovered through ethnographic data and methods.[60] Thus his linguistic writings took as their premise ethnographic categories, including those of race, but he specifically limited himself to the groups in the Philippines of the "Malayan race" that had their own alphabets, methodologically excluding from his view not only groups of other races (such as the "Negritos") but also those of the "Malayan race" whose languages did not have a documented pre-Hispanic alphabet.

He compiled twelve different alphabets from the sources at his disposal, which included both friar chronicles from the early years of Spanish colonization and works from more recent ethnologists and linguists who had worked with those older texts as sources. The alphabets that he compiled represented, he deduced, five different languages of the Philippines (Tagalog, Ilocano, Visayan, Pangasinan, and Pampangan [Kapampangan]). These alphabets, however, he understood not as distinct from each other but as variations of a single alphabet: "Immediately one can see that the difference that exists among these alphabets is not fundamental: it can be said that they are one and the same, their differences consisting in the manner of drawing them, as is the case with English, French, or Spanish writing."[61] While some of these alphabets appeared to have minor differences in the way that they drew characters, and some alphabets even appeared to have characters that were missing from others, he argued that the former differences were minor, and the latter "depended, as is easy to understand, on the phonetical exigencies of each [spoken] language," rather than on any differences between the alphabets as such.[62] "In sum," he was able to describe "the alphabet (or alphabets, if you like), adopted by the Filipinos [*los Filipinos*]," using linguistic evidence of commonality to refer to the peoples as one in the neologism "Filipinos."[63]

Yet precisely to whom did he refer with this appellation? The "Filipinos" in this work seem to have existed almost always but not exclusively in the past. Generally, he situated them in pre-Hispanic time, or as the people who the Spanish first encountered.[64] These "Filipinos" are ancestors about whom little is known, except that they were *there*, in what is now called the Philippines, and so were "of the Philippines." "Filipinos," in other words, serves as a kind of nonspecific placeholder for the ancient (collective) ancestors about whom little is properly known; and therefore, perhaps, no more specific or accurate name can be given. Pardo de Tavera closed the piece with thoughts that emphasized the distance between these people—ancient "Filipinos" who wrote in "Filipino" alphabets— and his own chronological contemporaries. These present-day "natives of the Philippines [*indígenas de Filipinas*] have [now] completely forgotten the characters with which their ancestors wrote, upon banana and palm leaves, their poems . . . and perhaps their chronicles and traditions."[65] To the contemporary natives, however, "those characters now say absolutely nothing, and they are even unaware that they may have existed."[66] This distinction between "Filipinos" (the ancients) and their present-day descendents is nearly consistently made in the piece, but there is an important exception that suggests that Pardo de Tavera's conception of "Filipinos" could indeed transcend historical time and include his contemporaries: in one place in the text, "Filipinos" act in the present as speakers who "confuse" (in the present tense) the sounds of "o" and "u," and "e" and "i."[67] Here, the meaning of "Filipinos" is more likely closer to "people from the Philippines" than it is to a sense of unified peoplehood. However, by demonstrating the unity of the ancient "Filipinos," he established a basis for their present-day descendents to be, in common, "Filipino."

Though Pardo de Tavera argued that the pre-Hispanic alphabets of the Philippines "are one and the same"[68] and though he casually referred to the speakers of the languages associated with those alphabets as all being "Filipino," he located the origins of those alphabets outside of the Philippines in ancient India. Other scholars had speculated that the alphabets of the Philippines had Indian origins and had traveled via neighboring islands of Oceania or the Malay peninsula. Pardo de Tavera argued that "the Indian origin of those alphabets can not be put in doubt," for "Filipino alphabets [*alphabetos Filipinos*] have a greater resemblance" to third-century BCE Pali inscriptions of India "than to any other alphabet of India or Oceania," derive "directly" from the Pali inscriptions, and "have conserved very faithfully their primitive [*primitiva* as in 'original'] form."[69] The significance of this thesis lies in its ability to unify different Malayan peoples of the Philippines while distancing them from other Malayan neighbors, both those of the mainland and those of islands lying farther to the south. These particular Malayans were "Filipinos," then, not just through the coincidence of having been encountered by the Spanish and named *indios* but because they shared a particular pre-Hispanic history.

More details of this pre-Hispanic history were forthcoming in *Sanskrit in the Tagalog Language*, where Pardo de Tavera took up the question of how the Indic alphabet had traveled to the Philippines.[70] In this work, which catalogued Tagalog words that he believed derived from Sanskrit, he theorized a past era of Hindu civilization in the Philippines, concluding that because of "the number and kind of words" of Sanskritic origin in Tagalog, the realms of "the military, religion, literature, industry and agriculture were at one time in the hands of the Hindus [*los hindus*], and that this race [*raza*] indeed ruled in the Philippines."[71] Drawing on conclusions from his earlier work on alphabets, Pardo de Tavera concluded that Hindus had dominated in those parts of the archipelago "in which today the most cultured [*cultas*] languages are spoken, like Tagalog, Visayan, Pampangan and Ilocano, and the greater refinement [*mayor cultura*] of these languages originates precisely from the influence of that race of Hindus on the Filipinos [*aquella raza de hindus sobre los filipinos*]"; for, from the language of the Hindus, Filipino languages had obtained words with which they could express "more elevated concepts" and "abstract ideas without using circumlocutions."[72] Pardo de Tavera delicately avoided extending his theory of cultural origins to conjecture about *racial* origins, for he wrote that since he was coming from "the linguistic point of view," he limited himself to noting only "those [historical consequences] which, seeming obvious to me, I could not pass over without mention, without being accused of negligence."[73] As we have seen from his writing elsewhere, he understood that his research spoke to ethnological and specifically "racial" questions, but he hesitated to draw a conclusion about racial origins on the basis of this linguistic data, focusing instead on the question of civilization.

That the civilization of the Hindus was admirable was beyond question, and Pardo de Tavera appealed to the Orientalist veneration of ancient Hindu civilization when he lauded the effects that it had brought both the Javanese and the ancient Tagalogs, noting that the Tagalog language "took new forms and acquired vigor under the influence of the Hindus [los hindus]."[74] Pardo de Tavera stressed that in adopting foreign elements, the culture of Tagalogs had not become less authentically Tagalog but instead had gained something through a process of cultural adaptation.

But what could be gained or borrowed depended on the content and context of the loaning language, and not all civilizations were created equal. In contrast to the laudatory effects of Sanskrit in Java or the Philippines, Pardo de Tavera alleged that the Chinese language added nothing of value to the Tagalog language or culture, for it was merely a language of trade. Noticeably derisive of Chinese culture and people, Pardo de Tavera remarked of the Chinese in the Philippines that they had contributed no words having to do with "religion, morals, political institutions, or social life. And this can be easily understood, since the Chinese man [el chino] came, to buy and sell, pure and simple, nothing more than to do business, without any thought of religious propaganda or introducing customs, which on the contrary he carefully hides as he does his religion, fearing that no other of [all] mankind should imitate and avail themselves of what his race [raza] holds solely for itself."[75] In shifting from the Chinese trader of the past who "came to buy and sell, pure and simple," to the contemporary who jealously guards "what his race holds solely for itself," Pardo de Tavera linked the contemporary Chinese of the Philippines to their ancestors, accentuating their difference from the Filipinos (in this case, Tagalog), while refusing the possibility of their cultural influence.

Pardo de Tavera's linguistic works, then, used the specificity of the general racial category of "Malay," in combination with methods that could identify "Sanskritic" linguistic origins, to theorize a particular grouping of "Filipinos" whose unity predated the arrival of the Spaniards and could be distinguished from other neighboring "Malayan" peoples. At the same time, this unity was broken internally along civilizational lines, according to which some "Filipinos" partook of the great ancient Hindu civilization, while others had missed out on this culturally beneficent subjugation. Though he framed his writings in terms of "the ethnological question" and employed racial categories, he also often used "race," "civilization," and "people" interchangeably. His "Filipinos" by assumption were racially part of the more general "Malayan" race, but what interested him more was the *civilization* that they had developed, in part through their shared history of subjection to a pre-Hispanic colonizer.

The core of his "Filipinos" was clearly delineated and excluded both the "Negroid" peoples of the Philippines as well as the avaricious Chinese. Its boundaries in the south, however, were less distinct. For it was precisely in the Muslim south where the racial lines of European ethnographers often blurred and where Pardo de Tavera's great ancient Hindus had been succeeded not by the glorious Catholic civilization of the Spanish but by the Islamic civilization of "the Arabs." He explained that while the Philippine archipelago had felt the influence of both the Arab and the Hindu civilizations, "she" had felt them only superficially, "as if she had wanted to keep herself a virgin not only to be able to adopt . . . the civilization of the Christian world, but also to be able to contribute to its further development in science, arts, industry and commerce."[76] And though Arabic and Persian words were significant in the languages of neighboring Malay peoples to the south and west, Pardo de Tavera noted that "the Spanish arrived on the island of Luzon just as Islamism [*el islamismo*] was beginning to be introduced there."[77] He thus dismissed any relevance of Islamic Malayans to his subject.

Pardo de Tavera limited his attention to certain groups, in part because his methodology used written language. He was interested in "the ethnographic question" more generally—or the question of the origins of and blood relationships between different peoples—and saw linguistic data as one way to approach that question. His linguistic data led him to identify connections between some groups in the Philippines as well as between these peoples and other conquerors, invaders, or infiltrators (e.g., Hindus, Arabs, Chinese, and Spanish). The Hindus and Spanish, in his reading, had a particularly beneficent influence on the Malayan "Filipinos" who they had conquered. Pardo de Tavera's writings did not, however, address the question of the relationship of these Malayan "Filipinos" to the peoples that were supposed to have predated their arrival in the islands: the "Negritos," whose dark skin and kinky hair provided German ethnologists with so much grist for the mill of ethnological theory.

The question of delineating this relationship drove Pedro Paterno's writing about the ancient history of the Philippines, in which he found a glorious Tagalog civilization that had usurped an earlier and more primitive culture but also had taken the best from it. Paterno's ethnological writings were both more ambitious and more fanciful than Pardo de Tavera's, but we will see that both authors charted successive eras of civilizations in the Philippines. Pardo de Tavera was little concerned with the categories of race per se, though he articulated his "prehistory" using then-current ethnological terms. Paterno's writings on "prehistorical" civilizations, on the other hand, would have been impossible without the vocabulary of race and some presumptions of racial ordering in history; the very logic of his history hinged on a tight relationship between a people's race—understood broadly in a physiological-cum-cultural way—and its historical actions. Paterno responded to a different kind of discourse about race, one that emphasized physical difference and correlated physical type with political destiny and civilizational achievement. Moreover, while Pardo de Tavera outlined a series of civilizations in the Philippines and clearly articulated the Spanish as the pinnacle of those, his series did not represent a clear upward progression. Pedro Paterno, on the other hand, adopted from European formulations of "universal" history a teleological model, in which each succeeding era improved upon the last. In producing that teleological history and distinguishing the great ancient society of the Tagalogs (to which he claimed to be a royal heir), he constructed a story of a race destined for greatness, whose strength lies not in its purity but precisely in its mixed origin.

Paterno's Ancient Tagalogs, Ancient Ita, and Contemporary Primitives

Pedro Paterno was born the same year as Pardo de Tavera to a similarly prominent family, though his family was Tagalog-Chinese mestizo rather than *español filipino*. While the Pardo de Taveras were known as lawyers, the Paternos were a business family with interests in shipping, retail, agriculture, and trade.[78] The young Paterno was educated at the esteemed Jesuit Ateneo of Manila before leaving for Madrid to pursue higher education, completing a law doctorate in 1880 at Madrid's Central University. Like Pardo de Tavera's, Paterno's family was caught in the repressions of the early 1870s; when Pedro was already in Spain, his father was deported for alleged conspiracy, though he returned to Manila in 1882. With the exception of one year's return to the Philippines and then a brief round-the-world tour, Paterno spent the 1870s through 1890s in Spain, practicing law, living well off of the pension his family sent to support him, and generally promoting himself in social circles to the exasperation of some of his compatriots.

Paterno's *Ancient Tagalog Civilization* (1887) and *The Itas* (1890) engaged in complicated and innovative appropriations of scholarly and theoretical discourses, combining ideas from quite distinct traditions in novel ways.[79] He used frameworks of "universal" history (invoking at least two different formulations: one Catholic and another secularized), borrowed from French debates about how the biological theory of evolution explains human society and politics, invoked Orientalist research (especially emphasizing spiritualist and mystical readings), and referenced social psychology. He brought these scholarly discourses into conversation with migration-wave theories of pre-Hispanic Philippine history, performing a complicated action of intellectual appropriation and innovation to theorize the relationship between peoples of the Philippines and their respective places in history.

Paterno confidently cited "the law of *progress*," confirmed by "*the Philosophy of History*," "*ethnological* theory," and "*geographical* theory" in support of his outline of Philippine—and Filipino—history.[80] He used the outlines of "universal" history, a concept and practice by which all of the world's peoples were placed within a grand historical schema that marked the rise and fall of successively advanced civilizations, to interpret ethnological data of Philippine history. Whereas the richly named "universal" history was typically written from a particular perspective quite clearly European (the writings of G. W. F. Hegel come to mind), Paterno sought to rewrite universal history to *include* the Philippines. His universal history sometimes sounded quite Catholic—as when he wrote that the study of Philippine "prehistory" could show "the progressive march of that Archipelago in the ways of Providence"—yet sometimes sounded secular.[81] In searching for the data of "prehistory," he wrote, "it is necessary, in addition to having refined them, to study them one and a hundred times, searching for their relations, similarities, and union amongst themselves or with those characteristic of other peoples, as the modern sciences demand; since in this mode those same data, etc. will rise to the heights where only Universal History is written, to the purest regions where only the spirit of Humanity lives and works. It matters a great deal to us that the Philippines is not excluded from the Universe."[82] While others might see in the Philippines valuable data for studying the history of human filiation, Paterno craved a history that was more normative, a history that described not just descent and relation but progress and advance.

He used the outlines of universal history, and explicitly racial theories, to ennoble and also manage a connection between the primitives and his own advanced contemporaries, especially focusing on the Ita (now generally called "Aeta," who are "Negrito" people of the highlands of Luzon) and Tagalogs.[83] Paterno placed the Ita at the center of Filipino *history*, though he distinctly differentiated *contemporary* Ita from "advanced" Filipinos, and predicted the Ita's future extinction. He treated the Tagalogs as having incorporated but also overcome the ancient Ita because as a "civilization" and "race," the former were inclined toward progress. The "Tagalog" for Paterno was characteristically *filipino* (as in "of the Philippines" but also ambiguously marked as the ontological center of a broader "Filipino" civilization-race, as addressed later in the chapter), and this greater Tagalog was both the culmination of pre-Hispanic Philippine history as well as the agent of future Philippine advance. Paterno told a story in which the Ita were racially and culturally both *other to* the Malayan peoples of the Philippines, and *of* them; the Tagalog people, in turn, were the epitome of the Malayan peoples of the Philippines, and inherently progressive.[84]

Writing in a speculative mode, Paterno conceived of three eras of Philippine history, characterized in turn by "the aborigines," "the Tagalog civilization," and finally "the Catholic civilization."[85] Though in general terms Paterno followed the widely accepted theory of migration waves, his telling was distinct. Paterno distinguished the Ita (first wave, Negrito) from the later Tagalog (second wave, Malay) by characterizing the latter as those who had first achieved an actual "civilization," while the former had only a historical era. For Paterno, inspired by French formulations, it was via civilization and culture that a race was superior or inferior, and so thrived or languished as a result.[86]

Paterno dedicated the bulk of *The Ancient Tagalog Civilization* to interpreting the secrets of the titular civilization, the second epoch of Philippine history. The Tagalog epoch—like the civilization—was a general one. While the "Tagalog civilization" was (not coincidentally) named for the ethnolinguistic group to which Paterno himself belonged, which was considered by many to be the most advanced in the Philippines, for Paterno it stood broadly for a civilization that he thought was common to different groups. Contrary to the practices of ethnological science, he did little to document the relationship between what might appear to be distinct groupings, and instead made broad claims about *the* Tagalog civilization, which had dominated the Philippines during this era.[87] Though he clearly excluded Negritos from this civilization (more on this later), he otherwise used it to unite the ancestors of Filipinos, notwithstanding manifest ethnological diversity; and so his ancient Tagalog civilization, though it might seem to have a more specific and narrow name, might have been more broad than Pardo's ancient "Filipinos" (who were primarily those colonized by the Hindus). The descendants of this ancient civilizational ancestry, however, were not always clearly identifiable: Paterno did not make clear precisely where the boundaries between those included and those excluded lie.

Most of his focus was on a rich and somewhat fanciful explication of that civilization and, in particular, its religion, which he called alternatively "Tagalism" (*Tagalismo*) or "Bathalism" (*Bathalismo*), the latter deriving from *Bathala*, the pre-Hispanic Tagalog divinity.[88] Arguing that pre-Hispanic Tagalog religion was neither animist, "spiritist," nor pantheist, he wrote that Bathalism was a religion on par with Catholicism, equally inspired by truth. He proved this by finding in Bathalism institutions, concepts, and figures that paralleled those of Catholicism, including the Catholic idea of God (*Bathala*) but also equivalents for Catholic saints, priests, cathedrals, heaven, hell, bishops, confession, friar orders, and even for the virgin mother.[89]

Paterno's attempts to show the equivalence between Catholicism and Bathalism (or Tagalism) went so far as to argue not just that Bathalism was as good as Catholicism; he said that Bathalism *was* Catholicism. Catholicism, he wrote, was present in the Philippines before the arrival of the Spaniards, albeit in a subtle, Oriental form.[90] Though he noted that Spaniards had, "with arms in hand, brought to us knowledge of the True God," he posited that the seeds of Catholicism had indeed already been planted in the Tagalogs.[91] In arguing that Bathalism looked like Catholicism, Paterno drew on similar arguments made by seventeenth- and eighteenth-century Jesuit missionaries in China who thought they found in Confucianism concepts similar to Catholicism's; some even saw evidence of ancient Christianity, of which contemporary practices were thought to be perversions.[92] These interpretations, meant to show the great potential for Jesuit success converting in their Asian territories, were strongly disputed by Dominicans and Franciscans. Whereas Jesuits had claimed to be uniquely positioned to bring Catholic truth to China, Paterno positioned himself as uniquely able to translate the ancient (Bathalist-Tagalog) concepts for his modern (Catholic-Tagalog) time.

But it was not only Catholicism that Paterno found in Philippine pre-history; he likewise associated other grand traditions with the Tagalog civilization, further ennobling it and placing it at the center of universal history. In fact he explained the presence of pre-Hispanic proto-Catholicism by amassing evidence of the influence of Catholicism in other Asian cultures, and the influence of other Asian cultures in the Philippines. So, for instance, he wrote sections on Brahma in the Tagalog civilization, Buddha in Tagalism, China in Tagalism, Christian doctrines in China before the Christian era, Persia in Tagalog, and Egypt in Tagalog.[93] His sources here were largely French, of the Orientalist tradition of which he partook, a tradition both scholarly and more broadly diffused in Parisian parlors. He positioned the Philippines, more specifically the pre-Hispanic Tagalog civilization, as a kind of missing link between the great civilizations of the West and the ancient ones of the East, and as the culmination of all of them.

The ancient Tagalog civilization in Paterno's 1887 work was central to the unfolding of the world's ancient history. By his later *The Itas* (1890), the ancient Tagalog civilization had taken on a distinctly racial character, and was thoroughly indigenized via a complicated historical relationship to the "first settlers" of the Philippines: the "primitive" and physiologically other Negritos, or Ita. For Paterno, the "aborigines" of the Philippines were the "*Aetas, Etas* or *Itas,* or as the Spanish call them, the *Negritos,*" who, of all "the diverse races that are found in the Archipelago," seemed to be "the first settlers of the country."[94] In the 1890 work, Paterno's version of the familiar migration-wave theory imagined the migrations as a series of cultural-civilizational interactions and transformations, in which each succeeding wave of immigrants gratefully and enthusiastically received the hospitality of those they encountered and in turn raised their level of civilization.[95] Before later migration waves arrived, the original Ita "lived happy in their fortunate islands . . . in their state, primitive though it may have been, but with a free and independent life."[96] The invading immigration waves disrupted the stasis, but not violently. The invaders "learned the language and the habits of the country on which they set foot, with enthusiasm and the desire to please"; they "solicited [its] women, and acquired family and friendships" with the result that they "quickly blend[ed] among the diverse established tribes"; and thus "a new race that was mixed in peace with the ancient settlers [*antiguos pobladores*]" was begat.[97] For Paterno, the Ita were racial and cultural ancestors of the Tagalog, which was itself a mixed race of the Ita and invading peoples.

In this story, the Ita's language, habits, customs, and so on were initially adopted by the invaders but were eventually overwhelmed by the latter's superiority. Indeed, the indigenous initially survived only because of the "characteristic tenacity of the women of the country" in whom "ancient habits [*antiguos usos*]" were deeply engrained.[98] Despite women's tenacity, however, progress (and so, implicitly, men) eventually prevailed, for "with time, as things seek their proper place [or natural level, *nivel natural*], the superior language [as well as beliefs, habits, and customs] . . . succeeded in absorbing the inferior."[99] Elsewhere, Paterno borrowed the exact language of a Jesuit textbook of Philippine history, which held that the aboriginal Ita had been "conquered by invaders of more robust constitution and endowed with a higher degree of culture."[100] Paterno's innovation was to explain this conquering not simply as the domination of one at the expense of the other but as a peaceful process engendering a new race: the Tagalog (more about this later). Contemporary Tagalogs' ancient Ita ancestors had been "vanquished . . . by culture [*cultura*]," giving way to the superior civilization and language, thus being incorporated (by cultural extermination) in the new progressive mixed race.[101] The Ita were the historical ancestors of both the ancient and contemporary Tagalogs; but what of contemporary Ita?

The ancient Ita also had a *distinct* contemporary legacy, for living Ita were the descendents of other ancient Ita, those who had "retreated, appealing to arms," and who, "vanquished . . . , took refuge in the harshness of the mountains."[102] This Ita people, "abhorring union or mixing with others, wastes its existence in the most degenerate isolation," making it unique among peoples of the Philippines.[103] By emphasizing the ancient and above all the *static* quality of contemporary Itas, Paterno excluded them from the contemporary Filipino-Christian civilization. In contrast to the dynamism of the mixed-race legacy, which had its apex in the Tagalog language and culture, "the pure Ita race [*la raza ita pura*] has remained resting in [its] path, and its language has remained stationary."[104] Contemporary Ita were *not* "the surviving remains of cultured ancestors [*antepasados cultos*], but rather peoples who have fallen behind [*pueblos rezagados*], who, because of particular circumstances, have remained arrested in one of those stages through which humanity passed in the infancy of its life, a ship of civilization that dropped anchor in the ocean of life, but has not moved backward."[105] Contemporary Ita were unlike the ancestral Ita, for the former had preserved their traditions and so remained stuck in the past, whereas the later had embraced progress brought by superior invaders. Contemporary Ita, like primitive Negrito peoples elsewhere in the world, represented an ailing, decaying body whose natural death approached:

> By continuous isolation during long centuries … [this people has]
> not felt the necessity of modifying its type of life, has not acquired
> the aptitude of transforming itself, has become accustomed to
> sloth, stasis, inaction, petrifaction, in other words, to not progress-
> ing in the moral order, to perishing in the physical order; it is a
> people that has nourished itself for a long time with a few unchang-
> ing and poor ideas, leaving it very weak, and now it is difficult for
> it to move, to work, to carry out any effort or regenerative project,
> and is therefore condemned to disappear before the peoples that
> know how to progress, that live, work, and march forward.[106]

The Ita were condemned not by their contemporaries (be they Tagalog or Spanish) but by their cultural inability to transform themselves, by their atrophy as a people.

This story, in which progress and evolution were conceptualized in terms of the use and disuse of organs and abilities, derives from the particularly Lamarckian version of evolutionary ideas (stressing environmental adaptation) that remained strong in France even among those who embraced Darwin's ideas (which stressed natural selection). Ideas of racial hierarchy were long established in France, but they had become complicated and internally contested over questions such as which kinds of markers were the significant "racial" ones (biological or cultural-civilizational) and whether racial "purity" was itself a benefit or liability.[107] In these debates, one of the most prominent and controversial figures was Vacher de Lapouge, who drew on Lamarckian ideas of adaptation in 1886 to predict the future extermination of entire races (since "superior races will substitute themselves by force for the human groups retarded in evolution") and advocated eugenics as a framework for thinking about the relative value of races and their struggle for existence.[108] For Paterno, the Ita were one of those inferior races doomed to extinction; the Tagalog, the superior, was capable of adaptation.

However, Paterno also drew from Lapouge's critics, such as Yves Guyot, to argue that racial purity was a liability rather than a source of strength.[109] For Paterno, the Ita's pure lineage made their culture static and explained their contemporary degeneracy and future obsolescence, for "it is known that races that do not mix degenerate in the course of time, and then disappear. On the contrary," mixed origins begat dynamism, for "those that mix—the *mestizo* races, like the Spanish, the French, the German, the English, in general 'those of the western countries of Europe'—that . . . 'are found to be so intermixed that none could claim an authentic genealogy'— [those races] live [to be] robust and powerful."[110] Quoting Guyot, he continued: "The most complicated organs are perfected through the accumulation of innumerable variations, slight though they may be; the same thing happens in social organisms. Heterogeneity is one of the causes of the strength of France, and the men that work to destroy it, take on not only an impossible task, but also a retrograde one. No doubt they seek to take us [back] to the static civilizations of Asia. It is a disgrace for the Chinese, the Arabs, and the sects inhabiting Indostan, to have conserved their hegemony."[111] Published just the previous year in French, Guyot's preface to *Problems of History* referred critically to Joseph-Arthur de Gobineau (who conceived of human history as a series of contests between races in which the victor was always diminished by mixing with the vanquished).[112] But Guyot also referenced the language of French controversies about whether racial "purity" was itself a good (Lapouge said yes, Guyot, no).[113] While Guyot *questioned* the idea that races had destinies (instead emphasizing adaptation via mixing), Paterno turned Guyot's words to *support* such a position (some peoples advance, and others decay), while connecting racial progress to openness to intermixture.

Yet Paterno, like Guyot, also drew on the classic Orientalist conception of Asian societies as "static," contrasting them with the dynamic "western countries of Europe," to pit one mode of racialized and racist thought against another. Here, the image of "static" Asian societies was used to cast aspersion on an ideal of racial purity. Paterno, in turn, used this quotation to distance the Ita, a static race, from the more dynamic or "intermixed" races of the Philippines, of which Tagalog was exemplary. Unlike their "disgraced" Oriental neighbors, Tagalogs had not "conserved their hegemony"—they were a "robust and powerful" race like the French, German, English, or Spanish. Tagalogs were, perhaps, the best of both worlds; they were distinguished ancients, but they were also robust and mixed.[114]

As we have seen, Paterno stressed the *difference* between the ancient ancestral Ita and contemporary Negritos. Yet he thought that the study of the latter could reveal something about the former, and so about the Tagalog's own past. It was important for contemporary advanced peoples to understand the contemporary primitive, for "the condition and customs of savage life [*vida salvaje*] are similar in many aspects . . . to those of our own ancestors in an age now very distant [and] the studies of stationary peoples illustrate and explain many customs and ideas, particularly those nebulous and occult, encrusted in the spirits of advanced peoples like fossils in rock."[115] The Ita were analogous to an inanimate specimen for the study of natural history, which could be studied "as a geological medal with the date rubbed out, buried among the evolutions of humanity, and its study will awaken us, as if it were the Prehistory of the Filipino people [*pueblo filipino*]."[116] The living Ita, then, were not exactly the "Prehistory of the Filipino people," but they were something *like* that: isolated elements of their "customs and ideas" remained buried deep in the "spirit" of advanced Tagalogs, the "Filipino people." Paterno used here a narrative of progress and the metaphors of archaeology both to lay claim to a past and also to affirm its distance from the present.

However, Paterno sometimes wrote in more relativistic terms about the ancient Ita's value. Though progress was the overall shape of history, every stage in that history had its own particular contribution (a conception common to Hegel and Johann Gottfried Herder). Like other "simple and first civilizations," Paterno wrote, the Ita had, like "all civilization[s] . . . something of value in itself, and always something new that is not found in any other."[117] For the sake of their contributions to human history as a whole, Paterno enjoined his reader to appreciate primitive peoples:

[F]ar from disdaining inferior civilizations in view of the superior ones, we look at them with interest and we study them with love, as new and original examples of human activity, following the steps of the learned naturalist, who does not disdain moss and lichen in view of the slender palm or the sturdy pine; since true History does not consist so much in the succession of facts, as in the manifestation of human activity, in the universality of the investigations, extending to all thought, all language, all tradition of man, or rather his beliefs, customs, laws, sciences, arts, letters, in all places and all times.[118]

Paterno employed here a plural conception of what we today might call "cultures" but he called "civilizations"—one that was not completely relativist but one that admitted both difference and equivalence. Paterno negotiated the difficult terrain on which he both claimed the Ita as ancestors and claimed the status of the civilizationally advanced, in part through adopting this model in which those who were advanced appreciated the contributions of primitive "others." His was a smaller-scale and more intimate version of the more general sort of claim that a European scholar might make to the patrimony of an earlier and "other" civilization, without for a moment risking taint by association; Paterno attempted to claim the more primitive Ita as the patrimony of the advanced Filipino people, simultaneously confirming their primitivism and their value, and underscoring both connection and distance. The Herderian task that Paterno encouraged his readers to undertake allowed the Ita to be viewed as distinctly primitive in comparison with the "Christian Civilization," but not for that reason worse. It simply belonged to another time and had to be judged accordingly: "in order to understand them . . . it is necessary for us to cast off all our customs and habits, and to approach [them] with no . . . preoccupations of any kind."[119] Highlighting the difficulty of the task, however, and the distance between "us" and "them," emphasized precisely the distance that separated him from these primitive ancestors.

The distance between the "us" and the "them," and the relativist bent of the model that he adopted, allowed Paterno to criticize "European civilization," ever so gently, in the voice of an imagined other. He reminded his reader that while "for those born in and accustomed to European civilization, there is nothing superior to it in any place or time; but on the other bank of the river . . . the fundamental laws change."[120] It was not just that "[t]he *Itas* have looked at Christian civilization through their own lenses; and under their color, our civilization has nothing admirable nor appealing," but also that, from their opposite riverbank, "the great European civilization appears as a deceitful siren. . . . Its morals are hypothetical; its justice . . . rests on brute force, and its theoretical preachings of liberty, progress and wellbeing produce only slavery, anarchy, and tribute [*tributo*, compulsory payments to a ruler]."[121] Paterno articulated these strident criticisms of "our civilization" by placing them in the mouths of those understood as primitive but toward whom the advanced could demonstrate sympathy. By demonstrating his ability to evaluate the "other" and to understand though not accept its point of view, he adopted the superiority of the truly "civilized."

Finally, the study of the Ita was valuable for the progress of the advanced peoples of the Philippines because it would help them recognize what they needed to change or leave behind. For the advanced Filipino peoples to fulfill their promise, they had to "know to adapt their ancient traditions [*antiguas tradiciones*] to Progress" and "succeed in harmonizing their ancient habits and customs [*antiguos usos y costumbres*] with new ideas."[122] The Philippines was well suited to this, not only because it had "the *faculty of adapting itself* to the new conditions of existence with which it is presented," but because—and here Paterno called on theories of racial strength through mixing—"ancient races [*razas antiguas*] are gathered in its bosom, like races rejuvenated by active and hardworking blood," which have a "powerful action of advance."[123] In order for those active agents to complete the natural progress against the "hereditary influences [of the ancient races] that work in the contrary sense," advanced peoples of the Philippines needed "knowledge of their traditions [*tradiciones*]; in obeying them and knowing when to get rid of them in time, when they have become useless or prejudicial, lies the secret of giving life and advance[ment] to that numerous people [*pueblo*]."[124] This art or skill, of knowing when to obey tradition and when to abandon it, was precisely what the people who had descended from the mixed race had demonstrated. Through study of their own primitive past, the advanced people of the Philippines could ensure that their trajectory continued upward, and ultimately they could arrive at the "brilliant, glorious future" to which they were "called."[125] The story of the Tagalog-Filipino people is one of historical and future triumph, with the present marked as a key and urgent moment in which the correct decisions must be made to hasten the (right) future.

It is tempting to attribute Paterno's praise for racial mixing to his own family's *mestizo* status. However, in his own writing he never referred to Chinese patrimony in the Philippines, the most prominent manifestation of *mestizaje* in contemporary Manila. Whether one reads this as a lack of interest or as studious avoidance of an uncomfortable subject, it is a notable absence. Yet to read *mestizaje* in Paterno's text too exclusively in contemporary Manila's terms would be reductive, for Paterno was also responding to and using French scholarly arguments that were infused with political significance, in addition to the outlines of "universal history" and its attendant validation of colonial rule.

Paterno took debates in French anthropology, sociology, and economics and used them to make an argument about the Tagalog "race," which accommodated the idea of Ita ancestry and overcame any sense of that primitive ("Negrito" or "Black") ancestry being a liability. Here, then, is an example of how "universal" principles (of natural selection and racial strength), articulated in and out of *local* political configurations (ideas of race and fitness in late nineteenth-century France), became available, precisely through their articulation as universal, to quite different and distinct *local* arguments (about race and fitness in the Philippines). While the model was the idea of the French as a race of mixed-race origins yet superior in civilization to its ancestors, France needed not be referred to in order for Paterno to use the model: the idea, stated in general terms, could be applied by Paterno to the Tagalogs.

What is significant about Paterno is that he embraced the concept of race-as-culture, that is, a version of how evolutionary biology was thought to apply to social and political life in which "race" was the unit of analysis, but it was a race's *cultural* features—its civilization—that were most meaningful. Those features were mutable and adaptable, yet they significantly belonged to a race.[126]

What impresses the reader about Paterno's writings is the eclectic combination of approaches, sources, and arguments. His writings harnessed the possibilities of various scholarly discourses—of race, history, civilization, and progress—in the service of promoting the Philippines, not necessarily against Spain but as a location of advancing history. Though self-aggrandizing in manner, his writings constructed a productively vague unity among some pre-Hispanic peoples of the Philippines. Paterno kept aloof from the more political arguments of *La solidaridad* and of the propagandists in Spain and was privately and even sometimes in print criticized by his peers for his fervid imagination, yet his writing about the glories of the pre-Hispanic Tagalog civilization was published in that periodical. It served as a kind of propaganda, which was both to promote the Filipino as scholar of his own country and to promote an idea of pre-Hispanic accomplishment.

Thus far, we have considered how two *ilustrados* reconstructed pre-Hispanic history in terms of a series of civilizations. Pardo de Tavera found the tools of linguistic research useful for uncovering that history and theorized an era of Hindu colonization hitherto unknown by modern scholars. In contrast, Paterno explained the succession of civilizational epochs as part of a greater law of historical progress, which he read back into the series of eras to reconstruct their value and meaning. Paterno's work, while it employed ethnological terms and followed an ethnological account of the history of the peopling of the islands, largely eschewed systematic analysis of linguistic, physiological, or cultural evidence to make his case. We will turn now to consider some of the writings of Isabelo de los Reyes. As we will see, his writings engaged more directly in some of the questions of ethnological research, and in particular, he was interested in finding in ethnographic data evidence of the filiation among the peoples of the Philippines—in other words, to posit a kind of unity among different groups. While he accepted some of the normative terms that Paterno had used to describe "primitive" peoples, he rejected the racial destiny that Paterno had accorded them.

Living Ancients? De los Reyes's Racial Ethnology against Racial Determinism

In contrast to Paterno and Pardo de Tavera, each of whom grew up in Manila and its environs, Isabelo de los Reyes was born in Vigan, a provincial port city on the northwestern coast of Luzon, and lived there until he was sixteen years old. He identified himself in his writings as Ilocano—one of the Christian, "advanced" peoples—though there is some indication that his family had been classified as Chinese mestizo.[127] His mother was a poet, and she apparently passed on to her son a love of writing. Isabelo moved from Vigan to Manila in 1880, enrolling in San Juan de Letran, and shortly thereafter began his extraordinary and prolific journalistic career.[128] In 1882 he began to publish works on the folklore and history of the Philippines in local newspapers; these caught the attention of Blumentritt. We will hear more about his folklore writings in the next chapter. Unlike many of the *ilustrados* who lived, studied, and wrote from Europe, de los Reyes did not leave the Philippines until he was deported after his arrest during the Revolution, and so he was distanced from many of the *ilustrados* by his Ilocano native tongue and birthplace, and his location in the islands. Though he often referred to Ilocos, not the Philippines, as his *patria*, in his work and writings he aimed to bridge divisions of language and educational class in native society in the Philippines.

De los Reyes's attention to race and racialized thinking stemmed partially from his general interest in the newly developing anthropological fields, and this interest grew out of his affectionate curiosity about the beliefs, rational or otherwise, of his countrymen. But his attention to ethnology's conception of race went beyond merely accepting it as the language in which folkloristic research could be written. Ethnology, for de los Reyes, was a way of thinking that held the potential of uniting peoples of the Philippines across divisions of language, geography, and civilization, according to a principle that predated Spanish arrival in the islands.[129] Ethnological race (or *raza*), in other words, held the promise of naturalizing a "people" of the Philippines. De los Reyes had already learned the ethnological language of racialized thinking by the time he wrote his piece "*The Tinguian*" in 1887, in which he considered his data in terms of what it could reveal about his subjects' racial origins. We can also see an increasing focus on race in the transition from his *Visayan Islands in the Age of the Conquest* (1889) to *The History of the Philippines, Part I: Pre-History* (1889) to *The History of Ilocos* (1890), each successive work containing more detail about the relationships between different pre-Hispanic peoples of the Philippines, drawn from ethnological works and data.[130]

The ethnography section of the volume on "Pre-History" of *The History of Ilocos* is almost identical to the chapters on "Filiation" in *Visayan Islands* and in *The History of the Philippines*, which indicates that, for de los Reyes, to study the question of the origin of one of these groups was to study the question of filiation of all of them. The version in *The History of Ilocos* contains some data particular to Ilocos that has no equivalent in the other two works, but for the most part he treated the same material in these three chapters and often simply changed particular phrases: "of the Visayas" became "of the Philippines" and then "of Ilocos," for example.[131] Though he did not think that the "Ilocanos," "Visayans," and "Filipinos" were all simply the same, the overlapping content of these three works reflects his conviction that "prehistory" traced the *common origin* of these peoples. More specifically, for de los Reyes, all "Malayan Filipinos" shared a common ancestry.

These chapters on filiation and ancestry followed Montano's 1885 *Report*, which, it will be remembered, had largely followed Blumentritt's theory of three migration waves except in that it theorized a racial distinction—"Indonesian" versus "Malay"—between the second and third waves. De los Reyes noted his disagreements with Montano's premises and conclusions and brought in data from other sources, but the organizing questions were the same: What were the distinct "races" that originally populated the Philippines? How were they represented by the present-day peoples of the islands and in what combinations?

De los Reyes doubted Montano's proposal that there was a distinct wave of "Indonesian" migration and even doubted that there was such a thing as a general "Indonesian" race. Explaining his skepticism, he noted that "there is no country called 'Indonesia,'" referring to the absence not of a state but of any geographic area known as such. "This ethnographic division is founded in new data and is not yet well confirmed. It is not adopted by the majority of ethnographers, and among its own supporters there is no unanimity about what races should belong to the Indonesians."[132] De los Reyes likely relied here on counsel of Blumentritt, with whom he corresponded and whose theory (of there being two root races of the Philippines, the Negrito and the Malay) he accepted. That Montano classified de los Reyes's own people, the Ilocanos, as a mix of "pure Malayans" and "Indonesians" helped condemn the legitimacy of the distinction.[133] If "Indonesian" was distinct from "Malay," the Ilocanos—as mixed descendents of both—were not quite "Malay" (i.e., their difference from other indios had biological roots associated with the Muslim south). However, if "Indonesian" was not a distinct race, then Ilocanos were "Malay." De los Reyes preferred to explain Ilocanos' difference from other indios with the theory that the former had, in fact, better preserved some ancient Malayan cultural traits.

He fully accepted, however, the distinction between "Malay" and "Negrito" races and, like others, believed that the "Negrito" or "Aeta" (Paterno's Ita) were "the aborigines" of the Philippines and were racially other to the "Malayans."[134] Though he referred to himself elsewhere as "brother of the Aetas of the forest [los selváticos aetas]" when modestly introducing himself in a piece of writing addressed to Spanish folklorists, here he described the Negritos or Aetas as having a "shy, misanthropic, and nomadic" character, and much of the evidence that he cited as revealing their origins and filiation was of the kind used by racialist physical anthropology, especially hair color and type.[135] He embraced highly racialized classifications of peoples and even accepted that one could describe the character of a people or race; this racial data, however, was significant for him insofar as it helped to reveal the origins of peoples and their historical relationships to each other. As we will see, he believed that character traits were not biologically given, but mutable.

De los Reyes then moved from treating the "Negrito" to the subject of "the Malayan race," focusing largely on whether the Malay "type" in the

Philippines had Chinese filiation. He argued vehemently against those (including Montano) who believed that the "Malay type" in the Philippines was often a mestizo (with Chinese ancestry).[136] For de los Reyes, it was only after the arrival of the Spaniards that Malay and Chinese mixed in any significant way; thus the peoples that the Spaniards encountered in the islands were neither Chinese nor of Chinese heritage. He aligned himself with those who traced the Malay presence in the Philippines to Bornean ancestry, citing a chronicler who had described a community in Borneo who spoke a language of the Philippines ("Pampango," or Kapampangan) and identified themselves as descendants of those who came from elsewhere. Apparently concerned that his readers might doubt this data, de los Reyes reassured them that "it is found to be confirmed by respectable modern ethnologists."[137]

Concluding his chapter on ethnography, he summed up his findings: in present-day Ilocos, there were to be found four racial "types," two of them at least relatively "pure" (Malay and Negrito) and two markedly "mixed." Noting each type and where examples of it were to be found, he attempted to understand contemporary complexity in general racial categories that specified origins. The "Malay" type, he wrote, was only "relatively pure, since the Malay type in the Philippines is actually disfigured by crossbreeding. Belonging in this category are the Ilocanos, almost all the Tinguians, the subjugated Igorots and the 'rebellious' ones of Abra."[138] The two mestizo types derived from Malay, mixed either with Chinese (clearly marked exogenous) or with Negrito: the first, the "markedly Malayo-Chinese mestizos, like the Chinese mestizos of Vigan, [and] the Igorots and Tinguians of southeast Ilocos Sur, who have Chinese-ified eyes," and the second, the "markedly Malayo-Negrito mestizos," found "not only among their close neighbors the Negritos, but also among the Ilocanos, especially in the North."[139] The final type (apparently the only truly pure one) was that of the "Negritos, neither more nor less than those of Mariveles."[140] Note that these racial "types" were not the equivalent of races in a cultural-civilizational sense—the Chinese mestizos of the old colonial town of Vigan could hardly be confused with the Tinguian of southeast Ilocos Sur, though both were for him Chinese mestizo "types." Racial purity itself had no particular value for de los Reyes but instead was noted in its presence or absence as a way to determine the origins of the peoples that were present when the Spanish arrived.

The Chinese were, for de los Reyes, decidedly not an "original" race in the Philippines. De los Reyes acknowledged that Chinese traded in the islands before the Spanish arrived but used racist logic in arguing that "the avaricious and selfish character of the Chinese [being] well known, it would be wrong to say that they had abandoned" the islands if they had ever settled there; therefore, because chronicles made no mention of Chinese settlements, they must never have existed, and so Chinese could not have mixed significantly with the locals before the Spanish arrived.[141] Thus the only two root races were the Malay and the Negrito. Establishing the relatively late arrival of Chinese filiation was significant in establishing the Malay core of both his own Ilocanos and also the Tinguian. Each of these groups played a key part in his theorization of the underlying unity of (many) peoples of the Philippines, both historically and in a progressive future.

It was the "Malayan race" that de los Reyes was most interested in and whose parameters he used to argue against ideas of innate racial ability. Like Pardo de Tavera's conception of the "Filipinos" (who had been ruled by Hindus in ancient times), de los Reyes believed that "Filipino-Malays" [malayos filipinos] constituted a large and multilingual group, united across the great linguistic divides and geographical distances of the archipelago: "The Ilocanos are of the same origin as the Tagalogs, Bicolanos and other civilized Filipinos, and I believe they are Malayan with Negrito blood."[142] De los Reyes attempted to demonstrate the underlying unity of these peoples through studying and comparing their habits, religious beliefs and practices, styles of dress, forms of government, practices surrounding pregnancy, birth, marriage, death, and so on. He argued that these practices all derived from a common origin, and thus collectively provided evidence of a single cultural and racial origin of the people who practiced them.

While he believed that "Filipino-Malays," as he often referred to them, were a distinct race, he noted the difficulty of using that as a term of reference. Musing about the possibility of adopting a broader sense of the word "Tagalog," he wrote,

Authors call "Tagalogs" only those that populate the central coasts of Luzon; but for those [people], this denomination [Tagalog] is common to all Filipino-Malays [malayos filipinos] including Ilocanos, Bicolanos, etc. And in truth this denomination would be more proper than that of "Indios" (because they are not from India), "indigenous" (because this word means "natives" and is applicable to any child of a resident), and "Filipinos" (because this word does not distinguish between races and can be given to a child of Europeans born in the Philippines, just as to an Aeta of Ilocos).[143]

This meaning of "Tagalog" would transcend linguistic differences but correctly, in his mind, delineate racial ones. The appealing utility of the term was precisely that it *was* a racial term, as opposed to the term "Filipino," which he noted was unable to mark race. "Tagalog" was a racial word that, unlike "Malay," was autochthonous to the Philippines; and so it included all Malays of the Philippines but excluded all those not racially Malay—most notably the (Negrito) Aetas and (White or Caucasian) Europeans, whom he names here, and as we will see, the (Mongoloid) Chinese. Indeed, this "Tagalog" might be quite similar to Paterno's generalized conception of "Tagalog," though Paterno never so directly addressed the latter's inclusions and exclusions.

De los Reyes described the *malayos filipinos* more inclusively than Pardo de Tavera did his ancient "Filipinos" and more inclusively also than some European ethnologists against whom he argued. For de los Reyes, *malayos filipinos* also included the Ilocanos' most immediate and only half-civilized neighbors, the Igorots and Tinguian, who some ethnologists believed to be of Chinese descent. On the contrary, de los Reyes believed that "the Tinguians and Igorots of Ilocos . . . are much closer to the Ilocanos than to another race, and therefore they are of the same origin."[144] His ethnography of the Tinguian focused largely on their racial filiation, and he aimed specifically "to refute the dominant opinion that the Tinguian are of the Mongoloid family."[145] Instead, for de los Reyes, it was clear that the Tinguian, "like the other Filipino-indigenous [*indígenas filipinos*], are, by filiation, Malay [*malayos*], according to what we are told by the kinship of languages, traditions, ethnography, and other ethnological proofs."[146]

The Tinguian and Igorot were racially Malay, and for de los Reyes this allowed for a unique relationship between them and their more "civilized" relatives: the Igorot and Tinguian could reveal what Ilocanos had been like in an earlier age. Earlier Ilocanos had worn their hair and groomed their teeth "like the Igorots."[147] Arguing that the Tinguian were "of the Malay race," he found ethnological evidence that they were related to Tagalogs and Ilocanos in similarities between the religious ideas of contemporary

Tinguian and the Bathalism of ancient natives: "The deity whom the Tinguian worship, respect, and fear is *Anito*, who according to Tinguian beliefs is like the ancient *Bathala meycapal* of the natives [*indígenas*],"[148] and he wrote that while "[t]he Tinguian maintains that he is a monotheist; . . . it is likely that, if not still to this day, in the past he rendered tribute to second-order deities, like the *anitos* of the ancient natives [*antiguos indígenas*] . . . [T]he Tinguian is very close to the ancient natives in their religious practices."[149] Put succinctly, "the Tinguian and the native are of the same race: the Malayan [*la malaya*]," and "[t]he civilized of Abra," he wrote, "were in the beginning Tinguian."[150]

For de los Reyes, the Tinguian were the "primitive" Malay type: *biologically* of the same family as the Ilocanos, Tagalogs, and Visayans but *civilizationally* distinct. As Paterno had treated the Ita, de los Reyes found these "primitives" to be like living ancestors of the more modern *malayos filipinos*. Quite unlike Paterno, however, de los Reyes used racial categories as a way to undermine ideas of innate racial civilization (or lack of it). Civilization was acquired, and the varying degrees of civilization evident among different branches of *malayos filipinos* provided the evidence:

> The insignificant differences that exist—between the relatively civilized Ilocano, the Tinguian that now wears pants and jacket, the subjugated Igorot that although still nearly naked has already lost his shy and cruel character, and the rebellious one with cannibalistic practices—these differences are effects of the places where they live and one sees that they are civilized or savage according to whether they are near or far from places frequented by Spanish or by civilized Ilocanos. Even among these latter, that have already acquired a considerable degree of culture, at times human sacrifice is practiced . . . , and in the beginning they were neither more nor less than the cannibals of Abra.[151]

Embracing the language of progress, de los Reyes argued against an idea of innate racial ability—or inability—by appealing precisely to the broad civilizational variety of a single race (his own). De los Reyes was unworried about the potential political liabilities of associating the civilized Ilocanos with their "savage" ancestors and brethren, and even imputed to his own "civilized Ilocanos" an occasional "savage" practice. What struck de los Reyes was the possibility—perhaps inevitability—of cultural change, a change that occurred not through racial mixture but through civilizational contact. Among the three authors we have considered, de los Reyes attended most closely to biological conceptions of race and racial difference, yet he used such evidence to argue for the possibility of a people acquiring civilization, and against ideas of innate racial ability.

As the following chapter shows, de los Reyes's conviction that civilization could be acquired was combined with his affection for the incredulous, superstitious peasant and the particularities of local culture. He delighted in detailing superstitious practices, perhaps even more lovingly because he believed that they were going to disappear. His writings on folklore and his indefatigable work publishing bilingual newspapers show both his confidence that common people could be educated and a conviction that they must be.

Thus far, we have seen how de los Reyes used racial categories to argue precisely that race need not dictate what a people could achieve. As we have briefly noted, however, his comments about Negritos and Chinese show less generosity toward those peoples' potential. Another group of peoples notably absent from de los Reyes's view are the Muslims in the south; while technically he thought that these peoples, too, were Malay, he did not include them in his studies. Such exclusion, while in part dictated by sources, was probably not coincidental. Blumentritt—with whom we began this chapter and with whom both Pardo de Tavera and de los Reyes corresponded—strove to compile what was known about these peoples and to add it to the ethnological map of the Philippines. As we turn briefly to Blumentritt's work, we see yet another way that the conflation of racial and civilizational terms could produce unities, as well as divisions, among the peoples of the Philippines.

Other Malayans: Blumentritt's *Moros*

Blumentritt's "Indigenous Races of the Philippines" (1890) updated his 1882 work *Toward an Ethnography*, emphasizing recent works that treated the southern and western parts of the archipelago: "Until now the islands of Luzon and the Visayas were the main object to which the studies of scholars and both domestic and foreign travelers were dedicated, without the islands of Mindanao and Paragua [Palawan] . . . drawing the attention of Philippinologists."[152] Exciting new data from the vast areas of Mindanao and Palawan, brought to light by new missionary activities of the tributions by the Frenchman Montano and the German ~~~enberg, confirmed for him that there were "only two ~~~us races in the Philippine archipelago, the Malay [*la malaya*] and ~~~he Negrito [*la negrita*]," in contrast to "*ethnographic fashions of the day*" (that distinguished "Indonesian" from "Malay").[153] What he wrote, however, about the peoples and races of significantly Muslim Mindanao and Palawan is instructive.

"Indigenous Races of the Philippines" is organized as a series of brief descriptive entries about individual peoples of the Philippines, alphabetically ordered by name.[154] Typically, the entries begin by identifying the racial origin of the people—whether Malay, Negrito, or a mix of these two. Sometimes, he identified a people's race by noting that it was a subtype of a larger general group (which was in its own entry racially identified, most as "Malay"). Among those general groups is "*moros*," the generic Spanish term for Muslim peoples of the Philippines, whom he designated as "Muslim Malayans."[155] Other such general groups were *indios* and "infidels" (*infieles*), whose subtypes he almost always presumed to be racially Malay, unless specified otherwise (as Negrito-mestizo, for example). Though nearly every entry in Blumentritt's piece is eventually traceable to a racial category (Negrito, Malay, or a mixture of these), he used the terms *moro*, *indio*, and "infidel" so commonly as general referents that they take on a racial sense themselves, as if ethnological branches of the greater "Malayan race." Their ethnological-racial sense is bolstered by some telling exceptions: while *indio* usually refers to Christian peoples, and "infidel" to pagan peoples, occasionally the phrase "infidel *indios*" or "savage *indios*" reveals that, for Blumentritt, *indio* indicated something besides just "Christian" (Figure 2.3).[156] The term *moro*, on the other hand, was never used with either "infidel" or *indio*. So while "infidel" and *indio* sometimes overlapped, *moro* was its own quite separate category. *Moros*, for Blumentritt, formed their own group—distinct from *indios*—within the larger Malayan race. *Moros* were distinct from all other peoples of the Philippines, whether Malayan or Negrito, Christian or pagan.[157]

Blumentritt followed, in effect, the medieval Spanish convention by which all Muslims were *moros*: after the Spaniards had driven the Moors (*moros*) from the peninsula in the fifteenth century, they traveled around the globe only to encounter them again in Magellan's islands. While it is not clear that any *moros* thought of themselves as such when Blumentritt rancherías de Zambales, Nueva Ecija, Bonguet, y Porac [?]. Son cristianos.

PANGUIANES (V. PUNGIANES).

PANIPUYES. Tribu de indios salvajes («igorrotes»). Sus rancherías deben existir en la parte occidental de Nueva Vizcaya ó Isabela de Luzón. Solamente Más y Buzeta–Bravo citan su nombre.
Variación del nombre: PANIPUTES.

PIDATAVOS. En las ilagas del pueblo moro de Libungán (delta del río grande de Mindanao) vive una tribu de salvajes de aquel nombre. No se conoce más.

PINTADOS †. Nombre que recibieron los visayas por los españoles por su costumbre de pintarse el cuerpo. Siglos XVI y XVII.

PUNGIANES. Tribu de mayoyaos.

QUIANGANES. Infieles sanguinarios pertenecientes á una rama de la raza malaya, que comprende los ifugaos, mayoyaos, filipanes, etc.
Habitan la comandancia de Quiangán.

QUIMPANGOS (V. GUIMBAJANOS).

QUINANES (V. GUINANES).

SAMALES. 1. Raza malaya que habita la isla Samal del seno de Dávao. Según el P. Gisbert S. J. proceden de moros, pero ahora, ó son infieles ó ya cristianizados.

SAMALES. 2. Moros que habitan las islas situadas entre el S. de Basilán y el E. de Joló.

SAMALES–LAÚT. Así se denominan los moros de la costa de la isla de Basilan. [P. Pablo Cavallería S. J.]

SAMBALES. Según algunos autores se llaman así los indígenas que pueblan el interior de la isla de Basilan. Se cree que son los aborígenes de la isla. No sé si existen aún ó si son idénticos con los moros yacanes. Según el Sr. D. Claudio Montero y Gay, son infieles.

SANGUILES. 1.) Hasta época reciente se entendían bajo esta denominación, los infieles que habitan la península que separa la bahía de Saranganí del seno de Dávao. Los PP. Jesuitas no encontraron allá ninguna raza infiel así llamada, tal vez Sanguil era un nombre colectivo dado á los bilanes, dulangues y manobos que viven en aquella península. El nombre puede derivarse del volcán Sanguil ó Saranganí.
2.) Moros sanguiles se llaman los moros cuyas rancherías están situadas desde el puerto de Craán hasta la punta Panguitan ó Tinaka [Mindanao S.].

SILIPANES. Infieles sanguinarios de una rama de la raza malaya, á la que pertenecen también los ifugaos, mayoyaos, quianganes, etc.
Su nombre se deriva de la ranchería Silipán (hasta 1880 pertenecía á Nueva Vizcaya].

SOLOG. Nombre holandés de Joló y joloanos.

SOULOUAN. Nombre francés de los joloanos.

SUBANOS (ó mejor SUBÁNON, «gente de río»). Raza malaya, ocupan casi toda la península de Sibuguey [Mindanao Ol]. Son infieles.

SUPLIS. Según los Sres. Barrantes y el autor anónimo de los Apuntes interesantes etc., es su/fin un dialecto igorrote

Figure 2.3 Some entries in Blumentritt's "Indigenous Races of the Philippines," in the Boletín de la Sociedad Geográfica (Madrid), 28 (1890): 36–37. Notice that groups identified as moros are not usually racially specified as Malayan (Samales meaning 2, Samales-laút, Sanguiles meaning 2); Samales meaning 1 is an exception that underscores the presumed distinction between Malayan and moros (they are Malayan—either infidel or Christian—who might have "come from" [proceden de] moros). Meanwhile, there are both "savage indios ('Igorots')," (Panuipuyes) and also "infidels" of the "Malayan race" (Subanos, Quianganes, Silipanes, the latter two also "bloodthirsty" [sanguinarios]). Photo courtesy of the Newberry Library, Chicago. Call # G 008.55.

wrote, the appellation "Moro" would become something close to an ethnic identity in the twentieth century.[158] In contrast with the *ilustrado* authors, Blumentritt included them in his account of Philippine races, noting their Malay-ness. What was less clear, however, in Blumentritt's work was whether they were *filipino*, as they were always marked as separate from *indio*. In a sense, Blumentritt's work highlights the core tensions in *ilustrado* works between a sense of *filipino-malay* as a biological-racial family, *filipino* as a cultural-racial grouping, and *filipino* as a type of (advanced) civilization.

Conclusion

Questions of race and civilization were particularly productive both for recovering the history of the pre-Hispanic Philippines and for some kinds of political claims, even at the same time that they haunted those claims to civilizational and political equality. Anthropological concepts and methods could provide a natural pre-Hispanic basis for unity among some peoples of the islands and rescue the pre-Hispanic Philippines from obscurity or from an image of disgraceful barbarity by picturing a common ancient society. For those seeking to promote the recognition of Filipinos' rights to political representation and legal equality with peninsular Spaniards, the methods of racialized sciences brought opportunities but also risks.

In racialized studies of human history, in principle every human society had its place in the great scheme that traversed both spatial and temporal dimensions. As has been the subject of much reflection, in many versions of these schemes, some peoples were thought to belong, properly speaking, to the past, rendering their present-day representatives as primitive or out of time.[159] To the extent that contemporary civilized peoples of the Philippines were the source of ethnological data for reconstructing the past, they were linked—perhaps too closely for political comfort—to those thought to be both historically prior and primitive. The risk, in other words, was that contemporary Filipinos would be seen as present-day incarnations of a primitive past rather than as moderns with ancient ancestors.

Sometimes contemporary "primitives" were specifically invoked as the modern-day equivalent of "civilized" Filipinos' ancestors. Here, these authors not only engaged in scholarly techniques of racial theorizing to try to reconstruct past societies of the Philippines; they also characterized as primitive the contemporary peoples from whom they considered their own to be distant. When explaining the distance between contemporary civilized Filipinos and their primitive "others," then, these authors often participated in prejudicial formulations of race and civilization, similar to those of which they complained when they were on the receiving end.[160] But the racial science of ethnology also traced a different kind of relationship between "civilized" and "primitive." Because it searched for common origins, it pointed toward connections between peoples—in particular, between non-Christian mountain tribes and lowland Christian Filipinos, as we have seen evidenced in de los Reyes's writings. Racial sciences, then, offered a double action—distinction from but also relation to. Racial sciences also employed different kinds of scales along which this double action could be measured or traced: sometimes the scale was of civilizational degree, sometimes of physiological-racial difference, sometimes of cultural-racial difference, and sometimes a combination of these. These combinations and contradictions can help explain how, despite the fact that the imagined core of the "Filipino" grouping remains roughly consistent, the meaning of its political boundaries can vary greatly.

We can read each of these authors' use of ethnological science against a background of his personal biography and the political projects with which he was associated. Pardo de Tavera, for example, was known particularly in later years for his assimilationist and collaborationist politics. Though he and Paterno both came from families that had been exiled as subversives following the Cavite mutiny of 1873, and though he was part of the Filipino colony of Madrid, he took pains to avoid associating himself with controversial propagandist politics.[161] He was optimistic, one might say, about the possible benefits of colonization, attributing some of the accomplishments and more sophisticated ideas of ancient Filipinos to Hindu colonization. Paterno, self-fashioned Tagalog prince but also Chinese mestizo, found opportunities in racialized theories of mestizo vigor. Promoting his own importance in a variety of political environments, he "had an untroubled view of his location betwixt colony and empire," as Mojares has put it, and was able to reconcile patriotism for Spain and the Philippines.[162] Likewise, he employed both racialized ethnological science and an older discourse of civilizations, showing both racial and cultural continuity between different eras of "civilization" in the Philippines, but also distinct moments of cultural-civilizational advance. De los Reyes had spent his early years in a provincial center rather than Manila, and he never left the Philippines during this period. In comparison with both Paterno and Pardo de Tavera, he was more interested in the relationship between Christian Filipinos and their highland non-Christian "broth-ers," and, while he, too, used ethnological theory to argue for a historical relationship between Christians and non-Christians of the Philippines, he also saw contemporary connections between the groups. Though his association with the institutions of the revolution is unclear, many of his writings during this period were clearly propagandist.[163]

These contexts are significant in considering why each of the authors might have made the choices that he did in taking up, molding, and expressing ethnological theory. However, this chapter, in considering these authors' works together, and against other ethnological writings, has shifted the weight of attention from each author's political involvements to the overarching question of what was understood by "race" and why it was a concept more easily adopted by each of these Filipino authors than it was for the Dominican whose account of the ethnology section of the 1887 exposition began our chapter. "Race" was a category each of these thinkers found useful; for them, "race" stood more for a possibility of drawing con-nections between different people of the Philippines—albeit unevenly and with exclusions—than it did for distinguishing between "Spaniards" and "Filipinos." This is not to say that a distinction between "Spaniard" and "Filipino" could not be made, was not understood, or was not often accompanied by prejudice and chauvinism. But the category of "race" held a good deal more promise for these Filipinos than the subsequent history of racism might allow us to understand. We see in this chapter a tension between different ways of categorizing peoples—by "race" and by "civilization"—and, while the latter could be accommodated easily within a Catholic framework, the former could not. The universalism of Catholicism's quest ran up against the pluralism enabled by a partially physiological sense of human difference.

Each author used contemporary sciences of man to highlight the civi-lizational potential of the populations he took to be at the center of the emerging ethnological category of "Filipino." A muddled discourse of race and civilization, haunted by their Eurocentric attributes, nonetheless facilitated the production of filial connections and marked differences and hierarchy among the Philippines' peoples.

CHAPTER 3

Practicing Folklore

Universal Science, Local Authenticity, and Political Critique

WRITING FROM HIS CORNER OF late nineteenth-century Bohemia, Ferdinand Blumentritt lamented that his age was bringing about the homogenization of human life via "progress, which tends to level all the races [*razas*] with its steamships, trains, commercial activity and the telegraph."[1] For Blumentritt, the object of "folkloric science" was to preserve cultural artifacts—including superstitions, legends, architecture, painting, clothes, and language—of both "civilized and savage peoples," from that inevitable "progress" whose relentless uniformity would devour them.[2] The aim was not necessarily to preserve folklore in *living* form—for that would be to deny progress itself—but instead to preserve for posterity *specimens* in the form of folkloric data. Like other European folklorists, Blumentritt articulated the urgency of collecting folklore by noting how quickly it was disappearing with the spread of industrialism.

The apt comparison in the Philippines, as both Blumentritt and Isabelo de los Reyes noted, was with the cultural transformations brought by Spanish colonialism and Catholic conversion. De los Reyes, however, emphasized that indigenous folklore had not been obliterated by centuries of Catholic missionary efforts but instead had been remarkably resilient. "As beliefs are not changed like a suit of clothes," he wrote, "the apostles of Christianity had to take years and centuries to banish the remains of the Malayan Mythology [*Mitología malaya*], which is still preserved in all of its purity among the mountainfolk, and relics of it remain still in the spirit of the most devoted [Catholic] Filipinos."[3] Living folklore in the Philippines was not in danger of immanent extinction, in his opinion. However, the study of folklore was still urgent, for "[t]his country [*país*] is in more need than European nations of someone or many who would record traditions, customs, fables, superstitions etc., so that learned men [*doctos*] can later make comparisons that would have as their object to scrutinize the thousand mysteries that the past of these peoples [*pueblos*] contain."[4] Folklore was a particularly precious resource for the Philippines, which had otherwise relatively few sources with which to reconstruct its own past, especially the pre-Hispanic Philippines and Filipino.

De los Reyes's folklore works in ways common to folklore projects elsewhere: it legitimizes an idea of a nation by seeking commonality and history in the practices and beliefs of the *Volk*, or the rural, the peasant, the figure supposedly untainted by modern cosmopolitan capitalism with its urban-metropolitan cores and provincial-colonial tentacles. De los Reyes, however, put folklore to the service of other projects. Most significantly, he used folklore's methodological focus on contemporary people's practices to comment on contemporary society and politics.

This chapter considers how folklore was written in the 1880s in the Philippines—what it was about, how and where it appeared, who took it up and for what ends, what kinds of data it used, and what and whose authority it invoked and established. Isabelo de los Reyes's writings on folklore have recently been the subject of much deserved attention to which this chapter contributes.[5] This chapter also considers the lesser-known second volume of the two-volume *El Folk-Lore Filipino*, which de los Reyes edited but to which other authors contributed.[6] Included in the collections are folktales; poems; riddles; beliefs about and practices of pregnancy, marriage, childbirth, food, agricultural techniques, and medicine; and religious beliefs and practices of both Catholic and pre-Hispanic origins. Much of that two-volume work was written by de los Reyes himself, and so he is rightly the central figure in the field of folklore and also the central figure of this chapter. Significantly, however, other authors contributed to the project of documenting folklore in the Philippines. Pedro Serrano Laktaw and Mariano Ponce, both avid propagandists and later contributors to *La solidaridad*, wrote pieces about folklore (of Pampanga and Bulacan, respectively) at de los Reyes's instigation, which were published in a Manila newspaper before appearing as part of this collection. Pedro Serrano Laktaw (1853–1928), a Tagalog-speaking Bulaqueño, moved to Manila at age fourteen to study, obtaining a teacher's certificate, and taught in elementary schools in Pampanga, Malolos, Bulacan, and Manila. In the late 1880s, he headed the Propaganda Committee of Manila, raising funds, writing, and helping to distribute clandestine pamphlets and other propagandists' literature.[7] Mariano Ponce (1863–1918) was, like Serrano

Laktaw, a native of Bulacan. He studied in Manila before leaving in 1887 for Spain to continue his studies, where he became a central figure in propagandistic work. His labors are evident in the pages of *La solidaridad*, and he also was a close friend of José Rizal, helping to distribute the latter's publications.[8] We know little about Pío Mondragón, apart from this work (on Tayabas). This chapter also considers Pedro Paterno's 1885 novel *Ninay* as well as a scholarly piece by José Rizal comparing a Tagalog folktale with a similar Japanese one, published in *Trübner's Record*, a London periodical with a masthead that declared it was "Devoted to the Literature of the East."[9]

These writings drew from a number of distinct genres and accomplished different kinds of work. First, we will see that much of this folklore was written in the ethnological terms that theorized relationships and filiation, complementing the themes and writings treated in the previous chapter. Folklore was used as a tool to recover knowledge about the pre-Hispanic peoples of the Philippines and establish their unity on the basis of shared pre-Hispanic cultural patrimony, one version of the nationalist bent of folklore studies elsewhere. The beliefs and practices of peoples of the Philippines were studied in comparison with each other and with those of Spain in order to disentangle pre-Hispanic cultural influences from Spanish ones. Ultimately, however, the pre-Hispanic was difficult to completely isolate, and much of the writing also shows great attention to Catholic syncretic practices and beliefs.

Folklore's methods and aims also lent it to concerns distinct from those of ethnological filiation. One of these was its penchant to collect data in the spirit of preservation—not so much to preserve living practices as to document practices being obliterated or changed via global transformations of colonialism and industrialism. In this vein, folklore was data to be preserved via documentation, rather like specimens, to be available to the science of what was called "universal folklore." De los Reyes's *El Folk-Lore Filipino* was, as Anderson has shown, startlingly up to date and pathbreaking as the work of a colonial subject that contributed to international scholarly circles.[10] To understand the innovations of his works and others', we will consider the practice and attributes of folklore in the peninsula and elsewhere.

Folklore scholarship appeared in the Philippines in the 1880s after having followed different paths from those of ethnology and linguistics. Unlike those sister disciplines in which Spanish scholars lagged far behind their German or French counterparts, folklore was enthusiastically embraced in Spain. Like Spanish folklore, some folklore of the Philippines took a newer ethnographic-scientific approach, and some followed an earlier literary *costumbrista* model, which was oriented more toward preserving or lauding practices than documenting them in the face of change or theorizing their transformation.

Folklore presumed commensurability, and this had particular significance in the Philippines; in the process of identifying Spanish origins, folklore studies highlighted the superstitious and backward nature of Spanish friars. Filipino folklore was compared to that of peoples from around the world, sometimes establishing the authority of the folklorist as capable of such cosmopolitan comparisons, sometimes establishing equivalency of Filipinos with peoples from the most "advanced" nations of the world. In this vein, some Filipino folklore emphasized, via comparison, the rich, lustrous "Oriental" patrimony of the Philippines' folklore. These folklore writings reveal discomfort with whether Filipino folklore revealed civilization, or its lack, among people of the Philippines.

By picking up the folklorist's pen, young colonial subjects followed the lead of peninsular scholars, and in some quite direct ways the lines of influence are traceable from colony to metropole. The two places, despite the unequal relationship between them, had shared reasons for finding in folklore a fruitful "national" science. In both Spain and the Philippines, folklore was an imperfect but precious tool that could root an idea of a nation when its boundaries were both politically and culturally ill defined. Despite many commonalities and direct lines of influence between peninsular and insular folklore, however, the Filipino practitioners produced material that only partially resembled the studies of the peninsula. In the Philippines, the pre-Hispanic (and pre-Catholic) was the obvious point of focus for folklore studies, and so these studies resonated with contested accounts of colonial rule's legacy and effects. Second, Filipino folklore could be read as a subsidiary of Spanish folklore but also as its equivalent, an ambiguity that underscored the politically ambiguous strategy of claiming rights for Filipinos as Spanish citizens by claiming parity between the Philippines and Spain.

The third significant difference between Filipino and Spanish folklore studies was that the "native informant" of Filipino folklore had to grapple with different parameters for establishing authority than did peninsular folklorists because he had to negotiate the position of being both a folklorist *and* a colonial subject. Filipinos characterized their relation to their subjects in different ways, in some cases establishing their authority on the basis of their proximity with "the folk" that they describe, and in other cases assuming a more distant perspective. Folklore's standards of authenticity put these young colonial subjects in an unusual position as folklorists, for their authority as folklorists depended on their proximity with and access to the "untainted" common people, yet their authority as colonial subjects writing in a cosmopolitan scholarly world also depended on their ability to distance themselves from their (backward) subjects.

And finally, especially in de los Reyes's writings, we will see that folklore studies in the Philippines differed from Spanish practice in that the former was quite pointedly a vehicle for criticism of contemporary society and politics. De los Reyes routinely found opportunities not only to document popular beliefs but also to satirically criticize the ineptitude and corruption of government officials. The data of folklore—that it treated contemporary events and beliefs—lent it to this use. These kinds of folklore writings were the most significantly innovative and politically engaged.

El Folk-Lore Filipino and *El Folk-Lore Español*

In the world of folklore scholarship, Spanish scholars were reasonably up to date, and Filipino folklore writing followed the Spanish literature far more closely than did Filipino ethnology or linguistics. What is notable about the story of folklore's translation from Spain to the Philippines is, in fact, how much could and did translate and how these translations challenged, rather than affirmed, the politically subordinate relationship of the Philippines to Spain. The extent of this debt has not been acknowledged. By exploring some of the ways in which the two projects reinforced and borrowed from each other, some of the different and even potentially conflicting work of folklore in the Philippines comes into focus.[11]

As other scholars have explained, folklore got its start in the Philippines when the Manila newspaper *La oceanía española* (*Spanish Oceania*) published an article "inviting its readers to contribute" to the project "Folk-Lore of the Philippines [*Folk-Lore de Filipinas*]."[12] De los Reyes responded with enthusiasm. By his own account, his interest in folklore predated his involvement in the project. He was raised in Vigan by servants from the countryside, "where everything is shadow and superstition," who told him "many fantastical and superstitious stories, and

I believed in them as in dogmas of faith."[13] William Henry Scott tells us that one of his schoolteachers (a friar) organized a competition among the schoolboys to collect superstitions in order to highlight their absurdity and error. De los Reyes easily won the competition, "presenting a list of superstitions longer than even all of those of my rivals put together," and so began one of the most remarkable folklore collections of the era, inadvertently stimulated by a friar's efforts to promote Catholic truth against local error.[14] De los Reyes's early interest in and intimate connection with superstitions, and his love of Ilocano poetry (inspired by his mother, herself a poet), flourished in the venue and structure of the study of folklore.[15] His newspaper articles were enthusiastically noted by Blumentritt, who would also translate some of his work into German and publish it in the journals *Ausland* (*Abroad*) and *Globus*. De los Reyes's folklore work was also enthusiastically received by peninsular folklorists Antonio Machado y Álvarez (1846–93) and Alejandro Guichot y Sierra; they had called for regionally based folklore studies (a call articulated in the *Spanish Oceania* article). The peninsular folklorists sent him "all the folkloric works that were published in Spain," which constituted a vibrant and somewhat eclectic practice of multilingual scholarship, arguably at the forefront of a newly defined field of study, an unusual position for Spanish scholars in the nineteenth century.[16] The relatively new study of folklore was taken up in Spain in part because it allowed for regional and local specificity, which as we will see was significant for the work of both *El Folk-Lore Español* and *El Folk-Lore Filipino*.

The emergence of folklore as a field of study and its connections to nationalist thought are generally considered to belong to the era of European, especially central European, nationalism. The roots of folklore studies are often understood to be found in German Romanticism, which turned to the German language, and the *Volk* who spoke its variants, as a source of wisdom and spirit to counter the cold rationality of some versions of Enlightenment thought, and the political domination of the French empire. But "folk-lore" as a term was an English coinage (William J. Thoms, 1846), and late nineteenth-century folklore aimed to scientifically study peoples and the past via comparison. Folklore became data that ethnology could use to study the remains of the past in the present.[17]

The study of "folklore" as such in Spain got its start when the Andalusian Machado learned in 1880 that the (first ever) Folk-Lore Society had been established in London in 1878. As his collaborator Guichot would later write, Machado "[i]mmediately got in touch with Mr. Gomme, the general secretary of [the Folk-Lore Society in London], and decided to plan to establish a *Folklore* association in Spain," promoting its study in Spain and beyond.[18] Machado himself had begun by collecting popular songs and publishing them in periodicals as early as the late 1860s, but it was a decade later, when he became the director of the "Popular Literature" section of a scholarly society, that his particularly *scientific* bent becomes apparent. Though the genre of popular literature might seem to lend itself to humanistic methods and aims, Machado was already, in 1879, making reference to E. B. Tylor, Herbert Spencer, and the Grimm brothers, as he explained the use of popular literature and its value for scientific knowledge of cultural survival.[19] Machado's work in this periodical was noticed at least as far away as Vienna, where it was praised in the scholarly *Ausland* as an "indispensable reference for those dedicated in Europe to the study of popular literature."[20] Folklore studies in Spain, then, at Machado's direction, followed major scientific trends of English and German scholarship, which adopted evolution and cultural survival as frameworks for understanding present-day rural and "primitive" peoples as living ancestors of more "advanced" societies.

At the same time, however, romanticism was another pole of Machado's work, reinforced by other collectors of Spanish folklore. Machado's great-uncle, Agustín Durán, had authored a five-volume collection of Castilian *romances* (ballads) and believed that "the emancipation of thought in literature is the dawning of independence and the most expressive indication of nationality."[21] Luis Montoto y Rautenstrauch (who contributed to one of the Spanish regional folklore projects, *El Folk-Lore Andaluz,* and who was along with Guichot more given to the literary and *costumbrista* traditions) later described Machado as a lover of nature, the countryside, and the common folk, and reported that Machado had advised him to "study the people [*pueblo*], who, without grammar and without rhetoric, speak better than you, because they express entirely their thought, without adulteration or chicanery; and they sing better than you do, because they say what they feel. The people, not the academies, are the true conservers of the language and the true national poet."[22] Such Herderian sentiments were quite at home among the more literary-romantic folklorists in Spain, whose humanistic interests and sometimes *costumbrista* style predated Machado's more scientific approach to folklore and constituted a counterweight to the scientific sensibility of *El Folk-lore Español* whose strength varied according to region.[23]

Costumbrismo, an earlier literary mode important in nineteenth-century Spain, prefigured some of folklore's forms and interests and came to be associated with the more literary-romantic strands of Spanish folklore practices. *Costumbrismo* of nineteenth-century Spain portrayed literary and visual portraits of people as "types" engaging in activities, set in places, and dressed in clothing taken to be quintessential or characteristic of that type. Nineteenth-century Spanish *costumbrismo* had two tendencies of particular interest for our purposes. First, Spanish *costumbrista* writers used the genre in part to defend their *patria* against the mischaracterizations of foreign observers.[24] Second, *costumbrismo* was also a genre that could convey critical satire of a society whose failures were only too apparent to one of its critical, yet sympathetic, members.[25] These features were characteristic, too, of the *costrumbrista* writings of peninsular Spaniards in Manila, which, as John Blanco has argued, constituted a kind of colonial *costumbrismo*.[26] In peninsular folklore circles, however, *costumbrismo* was associated with the literary-romantic, rather than the scientific, pole of folklore studies, and was oriented toward the recuperation of a pure past, rather than representing the complex contemporary world.[27]

For some Spanish folklorists, including Machado, the literary-romantic and scientific-evolutionary poles were reconcilable via the positivist and romantic philosophical-ethical movement of Krausism. Krausism, a particularly Spanish phenomenon, drew its inspiration from German idealist philosophy and sought the perfectibility of man through popular education and enlightenment.[28] Some of the earliest folklore in Spain had been published in the *Boletín de la Institución Libre de Enseñanza* (*Bulletin of the Free Institution of Teaching*), a Krausist venue in which appeared de los Reyes's contribution to the "international discussion to fix the true definition of *Folk-Lore*" and that continued to publish works of folklore after other venues ceased publication in the mid-1880s.[29] The Free Institution of Teaching was dedicated to furthering modern science and promoting education conceived of as popular and "free"—that is, breaking away from the structures, institutions, traditions, and restrictions of traditional university teaching.[30] From its inception, then, the study of folklore in Spain was part of a project to reconceive knowledge and modernize it and, at the same time, to spread it among the people via new routes and institutions. De los Reyes shared Machado's interest in promoting learning outside of the traditional

and elite institutions of higher education. He was among th
newspapermen of Manila during the 1880s and founded a r
gual newspapers with political and educational content, aimea ..
popular readership than that of the Spanish-language press.[31]

Though Machado never completely abandoned a romantic sensibility,
when he adopted the term "folk-lore" to describe his work his approach
became more methodical, comparative, and theoretical. He explained
that the "love that we profess of our people" was related to his "desire that
literature and poetry, breaking the old molds of its narrow and artificial
conventionalism, rise to the category of science."[32] This new science he
called a "*baby* science, called to vindicate the right of the people, until
now unknown, to be considered as an important factor in the culture and
civilization of humanity."[33] The scientific turn of folklore brought with it a
broad field of interest. In the founding principles of the Andalusian folklore society *El Folk-Lore Andaluz*, Machado and his associates agreed that
they aimed to collect

> all of the knowledges of our people in the various branches of
> science (medicine, hygiene, botany, politics, moral [science],
> agriculture, etc.), proverbs, songs, riddles, stories, legends, fables,
> traditions and other poetic and literary forms; local, national, and
> familial habits, customs, ceremonies, spectacles and celebrations;
> rituals, beliefs, superstitions, myths and childhood games in which
> most essentially the vestiges of past civilizations are conserved;
> the expressions, turns of phrase, tongue-twisters, expressions,
> nicknames, idioms, provincialisms, and children's words [*voces
> infantiles*], the names of places and towns, of rocks, animals and
> plants, and in sum, all of the constitutive elements of genius,
> knowledge, and language of the country.[34]

This list would be modified only slightly by de los Reyes when he introduced his own folklore collection.[35]

One of the most important aspects of Spanish folklore was precisely
its regionalism: Spanish folklore was conceived of as a collective project
of relatively autonomous regional centers, each documenting the local
contribution to the heterogeneous Spanish whole. Whereas the English
Folk-Lore Society was structured along national lines and oriented more
to the archaeological and the antiquarian, folklore in Spain was strongly

regional and oriented toward contemporary practices.[36] *El Folk-Lore Espa-ñol* was composed of "as many centers as there are regions that constitute the Spanish nationality [*nacionalidad española*]," including, in addition to eleven peninsular regions, the Balearic Islands, the Canary Islands, Cuba, Puerto Rico, and the Philippines, "all of these regions [being] true members of the *Folk-Lore Español*," in Machado's words.[37] The regional structure for folklore studies in Spain reflected the strong regionalism in the peninsula more generally (a regionalism strongly supported by linguistic diversity, political structures, and political traditions) that distinguished Spain from many of her European neighbors. The Spanish folklore association "was first constituted in order to try to encourage all Spanish regions to carry out their work. Thus this [national] organism will only hold the aim of coordinating the different groups that appear, but never in a centralizing sense."[38] Some of the most important centers and journals of folklore research were specific to a region, such as *El Folk-Lore Andaluz* and *El Folk-Lore Frexnense*, and regional centers were free both to further subdivide themselves or to combine with other regional centers, "because of the homogeneity of their dialect, analogy of customs, geographical conditions, or any other analogous reason."[39] This strong regionalism was also reflected in *Library of Spanish Popular Traditions* (Figure 3.1), an organ of *El Folk-Lore Español*, which contained many articles on the folklore of a particular locale and even deferred to the authority of local languages; while most of its articles were in Castilian, it also published articles and literature in Galician, Catalan, and Portuguese.[40]

The folklore of the Philippines was both part of a larger project of Spanish folklore and its own entity. *El Folk-Lore Filipino* (Figure 3.2) could be seen as part of *El Folk-Lore Español*, in which Andalusian, Frexnense, Extremaduran, and so on also participated, reflecting the structure of the propagandists' strategy of full integration for the Philippines into the Spanish polity. On the other hand, *El Folk-Lore Filipino* also reproduced the multilocal structure of *El Folk-Lore Español* in a way that might suggest it to be the latter's equal, rather than its subsidiary. That is, just as *El Folk-Lore Español* was a composite whole, so was *El Folk-Lore Filipino* (of Tagalog, Ilocano, Bulaqueño, etc.). De los Reyes found in Spanish folklore a useful vehicle—not just a model—for negotiating the relationship between region and nation, between a people (*pueblo*) and the broader groups with which they were in historical or contemporary relation. anish folklore was strongly regional, with a gravitational center

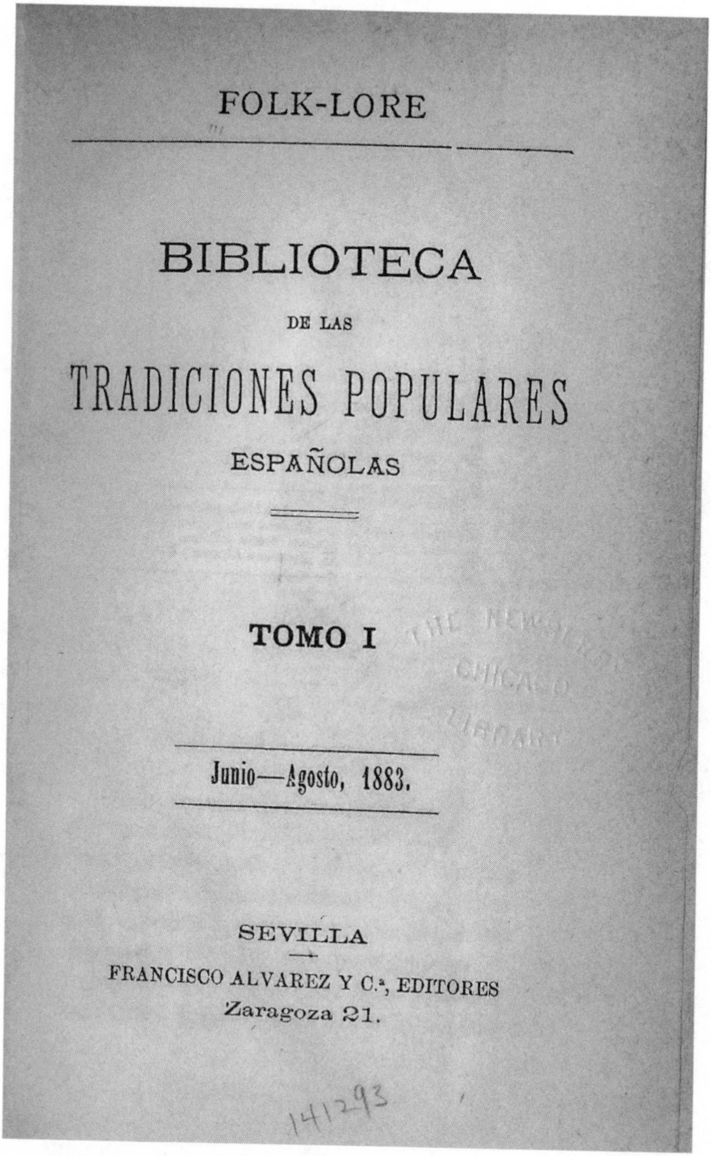

FOLK-LORE

BIBLIOTECA

DE LAS

TRADICIONES POPULARES

ESPAÑOLAS

TOMO I

Junio—Agosto, 1883.

SEVILLA

FRANCISCO ALVAREZ Y C.ª, EDITORES

Zaragoza 21.

Figure 3.1 Title page of the first volume of *El Folk-Lore Español's Library of Spanish Popular Traditions*. "Folk-Lore Español" appears in capital letters on the covers and some title pages of the volumes, so its title is often taken to begin with those words. Its covers' background colors were red and yellow in three horizontal stripes as on the Spanish flag. Photo courtesy of the Newberry Library, Chicago. Call # B 854.3.

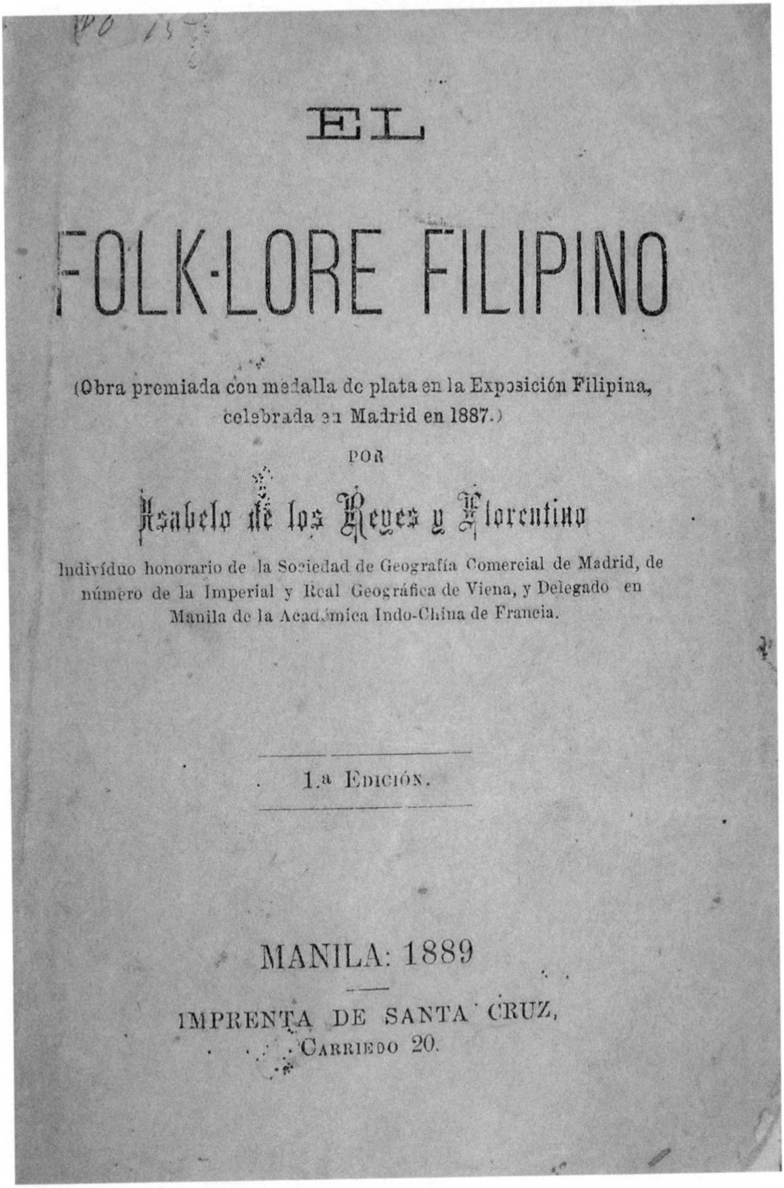

EL

FOLK-LORE FILIPINO

(Obra premiada con medalla de plata en la Exposición Filipina, celebrada en Madrid en 1887.)

POR

Isabelo de los Reyes y Florentino

Individuo honorario de la Sociedad de Geografia Comercial de Madrid, de número de la Imperial y Real Geográfica de Viena, y Delegado en Manila de la Académica Indo-China de Francia.

1.ª EDICIÓN.

MANILA: 1889

IMPRENTA DE SANTA CRUZ,
CARRIEDO 20.

Figure 3.2 Title page of the first volume of the Filipino folklorists' Filipino Folklore; the project was dominated by de los Reyes, and only the second volume contained others' contributions. Photo courtesy of the Newberry Library, Chicago. Call # Ayer 2168 .R45 1889.

in the southern regions of Andalusia and Extremadura, and be
ish folklore was in languages other than Castilian, the Filipino wa₃
equivalent to the peninsular. Machado credited de los Reyes with being the
head of the Filipino folklore association; an *indígena* of the Philippines was
being imagined to be heading a regional Spanish association (though the
association was never formalized beyond the pages of its collections).

Filipino folklore was officially a component of Spanish folklore, but
it is not always clear what "Spanish" meant. Machado himself at times
took a broad view, but he also was ambivalent about the significance of
that classification. On the one hand, he promoted a nationalist vision,
for while he emphasized the autonomous nature and equivalent status of
each regional center, he also phrased the overall aims of the association
in nationalist terms. For example, the society's goal was "to collect, compile and publish all of the knowledges of our people" (not in the plural),
and the data collected was "indispensable for the knowledge and scientific
reconstruction of Spanish history and culture."[41] (This was word for word
what de los Reyes would write in his introduction to *El Folk-Lore Filipino*,
though he would drop the modifier "Spanish.") Elsewhere in the same
document, he wrote that the objective of the society was "the scientific
reconstitution of the national history, language, and culture."[42] Further,
though Machado noted regional differences, he seemed to underplay the
significance of differences more radical than those between his own (Castilian speaking) Andalusia and Castile. The Basque Provinces, Galicia, and
Catalonia, for example, did not so easily share the "national" language, and
indeed folklore studies in these provinces followed a markedly different
lead from Machado's, emphasizing the differences of these peoples from
Castilian-speaking Spain, and employing a more literary-romantic mode
that emphasized the essence of a people to be found in its literature over
the value that popular literature had for a scientific comparison of peoples'
origins and development.[43]

Though Machado's rhetorical moves sometimes erased more radical
regional difference, his understanding of "Spanish" could be surprisingly broad. For example, he published a piece on Spanish popular stories,
comparing them with stories collected elsewhere (primarily Portugal, Sic-
ily, and the Lorraine region). The "Spanish" stories, however, hailed from
Santa Juana, Chile, and, in the peninsula, Seville and Huelva in Andalusia,
and Zafra in Extremadura.[44] Introducing the work, he advised his readers that "I call the stories in [the collection] *Spanish* popular stories . . .

because they are written in the Spanish language, and for no other reason. The vast majority of them, if not all, *are not native to Spain and have a remote ancestry*."[45] Here, though, Machado found himself in something of a bind and again revealed his Castilian-centered sense of the Spanish nation: "notwithstanding this [the stories' foreign origins], as they circulate on the lips of our people or of the nations and lands that speak *our language*, they receive a Spanish stamp, whose historical value it is very important to study and understand."[46] Machado's ambivalence on the question of the Spanish nation, reflected more generally in the structure and internal tensions of *El Folk-Lore Español*, is reflected in the ways that de los Reyes and other practitioners of *El Folk-Lore Filipino* characterized the Philippines both as Spanish and as its own nation.

De los Reyes borrowed much from peninsular folklore. His footnotes and references frequently cite two major peninsular folklore publications that Machado and Guichot likely sent him, *El Folk-Lore Andaluz* and the *Library of Spanish Popular Traditions* of *El Folk-Lore Español*, both of which ran in the early and mid 1880s.[47] *El Folk-Lore Andaluz* carried a number of pieces by Machado that reflected on the practice and meaning of "folklore," including the introductory piece that de los Reyes quoted, and Guichot's work on Andalusian popular superstitions, which de los Reyes used to theorize the Spanish origins of some Filipino traditions. To theorize peninsular origins of Filipino beliefs, de los Reyes also drew from the pages of the *Library of Spanish Popular Traditions*, using the work of Montoto (on Andalusian popular customs and his translation and commentary of a fifteenth-century Dominican's "De los Maleficios y los demonios" [Of Curses and Demons]), Eugenio Olavarria y Huarte (under the pseudonym Luis Giner Arivau, on folklore of Madrid and of Asturias), and José Perez Ballesteros (on Galician superstitions). *El Folk-Lore Español* was also part of an international scientific project of "universal folklore," and though de los Reyes's footnotes and citations suggest a familiarity with scholarship of England, Italy, and France, his sources were likely the peninsular folklorists. For example, de los Reyes refers to Consiglieri Pedroso's *Tradições populares portuguezas* (*Portuguese Popular Traditions*) and Walter Gregor's *Notes on the Folk-Lore of the North-East of Scotland*, and these are also referred to by the *Library of Spanish Popular Traditions*; de los Reyes refers to Eugène Rolland's *Faune populaire de la France* (*Popular Fauna of France*), and this is also referred to by *El Folk-Lore Andaluz*. In this instance, then, the peninsular connection was one that brought with it a relatively cosmopolitan scholarly world, accessible through the Spanish language and peninsular publications.

It is important not to underestimate the debt that de los Reyes, in particular, owed to peninsular folklore, in order to see his own specific contributions and innovations, and the work folklore did for him and other politically minded young Filipinos. In one sense, *El Folk-Lore Filipino* can be seen to be an extension of the federated *El Folk-Lore Español*. Folklore provided an illustration of the place of the Philippines in the Spanish republic, as the propagandists would have it: the Philippines was, properly understood, a fully "Spanish" region, simply located across the seas rather than in the peninsula. While distinct culturally and linguistically from other (peninsular) Spanish provinces, in this it was precisely "Spanish," for Spanish provinces retained their own distinct local traditions and identities, and they were united in Spanish-ness by a history of political association and accompanying sentiment of common patriotism, rather than by any "natural" commonalities among the people.

However, to see Filipino folklore in this light is only part of the picture. The theory and practice of *El Folk-Lore Filipino* diverge from the Spanish model. First, "Filipino" was itself a multicultural, multiprovincial denomination, and so, while Filipino folklore could be considered in some sense to be a subset of Spanish folklore, it was at least as complex a conglomeration as was peninsular Spanish folklore. The regional diversity of Filipino folklore suggested that it might better be seen as a peer to, rather than subset of, Spanish folklore. Within the structures of folklore, comparison with Spain made the Philippines' diversity seem not a liability but, perhaps, an asset. Second, and significantly, Filipino folklore—precisely as part of Spanish folklore—was a project not of peninsulars but of *indígenas*. Here the "natives" of the Philippines were working in tandem with peninsular scientists. Filipino folklorists claimed authority both as natives and as Spaniards, both as subjects and as scientists. These roles were complicated ones to negotiate, and peninsular folklorists did not face the same challenges. An Andalusian folklorist, for example, need not have feared that his status as scholarly expert would be compromised among Spanish readers by his being Andalusian; *indios* of the Philippines did not have the same assurance. As we will see, different authors approached this problem differently, which reveals in part just how fraught, yet central, it was. The narrative voice employed by some practitioners, or gatherers of folklore, claimed an intimacy that was missing from peninsular folklorists', and that positioned them as both colonials and as scientists.

Untangling Origins, Comparing Peoples

As other scholars have argued, *El Folk-Lore Filipino* often worked toward drawing together the disparate peoples of the Philippines through noting similarities as evidence of a common pre-Hispanic origin. Like ethnology, linguistics, and some kinds of history, one aim of these folklore writings was to recover the wreckage of the past of the Philippines and its inhabitants from the shores of Spanish colonization.[48] One of the mysteries was "which [of the peoples of the Philippines] were the aborigines [*aborígenes*] of this archipelago?"[49] De los Reyes concluded that the islands' aborigines were no single contemporary group but instead a common ancestor of various contemporary peoples. He wrote that "[i]nitially I thought that the Ilocanos were of a race [*raza*] distinct from the Tagalogs, because some differences between them exist, such that many times I distinguish the one from the other at first glance by appearance alone. But after having thoroughly studied the customs, superstitions, and traditions of both, I changed my opinion."[50] Thus folklore—a study of the customs, superstitions, and traditions—could reveal a deep commonality among various peoples of the Philippines, one that he conceived of as *racial*, in the ethnological sense, but that might be hidden by both physiological and linguistic differences.[51]

The data of folklore could trace the outlines of that common ancestor. For example, when Rizal found that the folktale of the monkey and the tortoise "is known everywhere in the Philippines, in every island, province, village and dialect," he concluded that "it must be the inheritance of an extinct civilization, common to all the races which ever lived in that region."[52] That common civilization was not necessarily limited to the Philippines. As Rizal suggested in comparing a Tagalog folktale with a Japanese one, the Philippines shared some kind of common ancestry even with Japan. More commonly—and closer to home—Rizal, de los Reyes, Paterno, and T. H. Pardo de Tavera often linked peoples of the Philippines to the greater "Malayan" race and more specifically to peoples of the Malay peninsula. Folklore was one of the ethnological tools that could be used to theorize the relationships between peoples of the Philippines and others.

Typically, however, the writings of *El Folk-Lore Filipino* used folklore as an ethnological tool to show common ancestry among peoples of the

Philippines, rather than to emphasize ties that linked them to others beyond the Philippines' borders. By "collecting folkloristic articles about the Philippines," folklorists were both documenting and publicizing the common inheritance, "in order to tighten the bond that unites all Filipinos [*todos los filipinos*]," as Serrano Laktaw put it.[53] That common inheritance was derived from the ancestral people (or *raza*, or *civilización*) from which all contemporary *indígenas* of the Philippines, in all of their diversity, sprang. That original people's religion remained in bits and pieces in present-day beliefs and practices. Folklore could recover those remnants and use them in the scientific pursuit of the study of mythology, which, as de los Reyes put it, "endeavors to determine whether [the materials folklore has gathered] are native or exotic, to study them in the light of history and in a word, to use them to reconstruct a Religion that is now completely or in part extinct."[54]

Much of de los Reyes's focus was on identifying the elements of this ancestral religion. For example, he told his readers that while traveling with other passengers on a vessel between Ilocos and Manila in 1880, "at the indication of my countrymen [*paisanos*], we knelt together to pray in front of a rock formation in the shape of an oven [*horno*], and they told me that if we did not comply with this obligation, we would have been continuously sick in Manila."[55] De los Reyes interpreted this obligation as a modification of an earlier practice and speculated that "[i]n view of all of this, it should be clear that Ilocanos worshipped in promontories and rock formations."[56] The practices and beliefs of his contemporary *paisanos* (countrymen), then, bore the traces of those of their ancestors, the (ancient) Ilocanos. Similarly, de los Reyes wrote about contemporary Ilocano beliefs—in spirit possession, visits by ghosts of the dead, and "an incorporeal thing called *karkarmá* innate to man," which could be lost and whose loss made one crazy—which all suggested to him that "the ancient Ilocanos [*antíguos ilocanos*] knew a kind of soul."[57] De los Reyes also found in the data of other contributors to *El Folk-Lore Filipino* material that he believed showed that different Filipino peoples shared pre-Hispanic origins. For example, commenting on Mondragón's account of superstitions of Tayabas, he noted, "Many or almost all of these superstitions are also observed in the Folklores of Ilocos, Pampanga, Bulacan and other places of the Philippines, which indicates the community [*comunidad*] of their origin and that of those who harbor [those superstitions]."[58]

Though he built the case that many peoples of the Philippines shared a common ancestral people, de los Reyes cautioned against assuming that all "civilized indigenous [*indígenas civilizados*]" peoples were the same, a habit of other authors who took as a given that Tagalog "qualities and customs" would also be those of the "Bicolanos, Ilocanos, Pangasinans [*pangasinanes*], Kapampangans [*pampangos*], Cagayanos [*cagayanes*], and Zambaleños [*zambales*], [as if] no differences at all existed [among them]."⁵⁹ Instead, he thought that "in those distant provinces [where Ilocanos live] one finds many precious materials for Folk-Lore, as Ilocano customs, practices and beliefs are among the few of the country that are conserved most purely and most similarly to those of the age of the Conquest."⁶⁰ Ilocanos' difference from other peoples was not a result of different origins; rather, it indicated that they were closer to what they had all at one point *shared*, and so their folklore was particularly valuable. Others sometimes complained of de los Reyes's Iloco-centric writings, as Rizal did when he wrote to Blumentritt in 1888: "As I see, many folklorists and future anthropologists are appearing in Ilocos. There is [or such is] a Mr. Deloserre [Isabelo de los Reyes], with whom you correspond. I note one thing: Since most Filipino folklorists are Ilocanos, and because they use the epithet *Ilocano*, anthropologists will designate traditions and customs that are properly Filipino as being Ilocano."⁶¹ Rizal claimed here in one respect just what de los Reyes had written—that Ilocano customs *were* in some way rightly and more broadly "Filipino," though it is probably in part the prominence of de los Reyes's writings about Ilocano folklore in the world of Filipino folklore that made Rizal fear Ilocanos would be unduly prominent in foreign folklorists' eyes. Though de los Reyes and Rizal disagreed about the meaning of the relationship between Ilocano folklore and the folklore of other "Filipinos," they agreed that they shared common origins and ancestry.

For de los Reyes, reconstructing the ancient religion of the Philippines by investigating current beliefs required careful comparison with Catholicism and other beliefs and practices with origins in Spain or elsewhere. Once those foreign impurities were identified, the scientist could remove them to distill the ancient religion of the Philippines, for "without doubt, the superstitious beliefs of today's Ilocanos which were not introduced by the Spanish and Asiatics [*asiáticos*], are inherited from the ancient Ilocanos [*antiguos ilocanos*], their ancestors."⁶² He identified, for example, a pre-Hispanic origin of a now-Christian practice, noting that a belief that one is not to bathe during days around the feast day of San Lorenzo had its origins in "a [certain] time of the year that the primitive Ilocanos [*ilocanos primitivos*] had."[63] But determining which beliefs were from the ancients and which were introduced by others often proved to be difficult.

> Only a few and vague notes about that primitive [*primitiva*] religion are conserved in the annals of the country, and in the memory of the indigenous, indefinable remains enveloped in superstitions and fables [*consejas*], of which some are vitiated with many European beliefs [that have been] introduced, some diminished or mixed with the sacred ideas of Christianity. In order to be able to distinguish the genuine Filipino superstitions [*supersticiones filipinas*], it is necessary to possess profound knowledge of *Universal Folklore*, and of the prehistory of the country. Otherwise we risk accepting as a Filipino belief [*creencia filipina*] one that is of Chinese, Portuguese, Spanish, American, or . . . even German filiation.[64]

To this end, de los Reyes, both in his own writings on folklore and in editorial notes to others' contributions to *El Folk-Lore Filipino*, compared the data of any particular group or locality in the Philippines to folkloric data of other peoples of the Philippines (both past, as was sometimes recorded in early chronicles, and present, as he or other folklorists had gathered) as well to folkloric data of Spain and beyond.

As part of this work, de los Reyes devoted a chapter in his *El Folk-Lore Filipino* to "Ilocano superstitions that are found in Europe," and he introduced the chapter by saying that it was a list "of superstitions that I suppose the Spanish introduced in past centuries" that he had compiled by reading folklore of the peninsula.[65] He traced Ilocano superstitions to Galicia, Castile (including Madrid specifically), Andalusia, Portugal, and Asturias. Elsewhere, too, he pointed out when he thought that an Ilocano belief had Spanish origins or, more specifically, when Jesuit missionaries had introduced it.[66] As others have noted, the comparisons between folklore in the Philippines and folklore in the peninsula, and especially the implication that superstitions of the Philippines originated in the peninsula, poked fun at the Spaniards—and at friars in particular, who held their forbearers' superstitions strongly enough to pass them on to their flocks in the Philippines.[67] This allowed de los Reyes to note that "the most absurd beliefs were in fashion in the [Iberian] Peninsula during the first days of Spanish domination," adding that his "long literary sketch, titled 'The Devil in the Philippines, As Stated in Our Chronicles,'" which he had already published, showed through its readings of early friar accounts that the friars were superstitious and that *they* were likely the origin of many superstitions in the Philippines.[68]

That piece took the form of a story in which two young friends recount to each other passages documenting supernatural phenomena from early friar chronicles. De los Reyes pointedly wrote that in this piece, "no foreign authors speak," just (Spanish) friars of various parts of Luzon and the Visayas; "and I, with my limited knowledge, will speak of the Ilocano territory [*comarca ilocana*], including Abra."[69] To frame the readings of friar chronicles, de los Reyes contrived a story in which two friends at a funeral gathering look for a book in the dead man's library. When one of them becomes worried that the ghost of the deceased might be watching them, the two become engrossed in a debate over whether such things as ghosts exist (in the Philippines), citing evidence from the books in the man's library. The debate itself, and the bulk of the story, is constituted almost exclusively by long quotations from friar chronicles, with brief editorial comments from the two young men, and comments about Ilocano beliefs as related by the narrator.

Ostensibly to prove that ghosts and spirits exist in the Philippines, one friend quotes from a seventeenth-century Franciscan chronicle, which documents that the ghost of a prominent *indio* appeared to a Franciscan. In the Franciscan's account, the man appeared with a heavy chain around his neck, "a sign of his eternal condemnation"; was carried by two "ferocious blacks [*feroces negros*]"; and could only answer the Franciscan's questions "between belches of fire and furious groans."[70] De los Reyes used the chronicles to document the superstitions of their authors—friars—who believed that *Apolaki* (*Apolaqui*, the "god of war") had appeared before people, that people had received messages ("oracles") from the devil during a *maganito* (sacrifice or ceremony), and that an *anitera* (a "priestess" of the pre-Hispanic religion) had been made by the devil to do many things.[71] "The Devil in the Philippines" and *El Folk-Lore Filipino* both point out that peninsular Spaniards' superstitious beliefs—past and present—were on par with the most absurd of the Filipinos', and many Filipinos' superstitions derive from the friars' supposed enlightenment.

De los Reyes described a complicated relationship between peninsular Spanish beliefs and those of contemporary Filipinos; sometimes it was not possible to simply subtract the former from the latter in order to arrive at the "original" Filipino. For example, he found that the *pugót* (a frightening supernatural being), eluded easy categorization. On the one hand, he thought that the *pugót* was native to the Philippines, a version of "one of the *household anitos* [spirits] of antiquity," as evidenced by where he dwelled: "in unoccupied habitations, in houses under construction, or in the ruins of an old building."[72] But if the *pugót* was native to the Philippines, the descendent of an *anito* (spirit) of old, it had become, in some sense, Spanish. De los Reyes noted, for instance, that "some of the Spaniards call him [the *pugót*] *cafre* [Sp., derived from Arabic *kafir* or 'unbeliever,' from whence also the offensive English word],"[73] and that in an old Dominican account, the devil appeared to a (peninsular) friar in forms that were according to de los Reyes "neither more nor less than the *pugót* of the Ilocanos."[74] Though the *pugót* contained important clues about the pre-Hispanic religion, it was itself a hybrid being.

De los Reyes also found that *mangkukulam*, people with magical powers who could harm or heal others, had hybrid origins that he could not completely untangle. In one place, de los Reyes likened the *mangkukulam* to Spanish sorceresses, noting that a Dominican chronicler documented that sorceresses (*hechiceras*), confirmed as such by the ecclesiastical authority, had made the devil appear to a prominent townsman, made a woman sick, and caused other evils.[75] De los Reyes's narrator then asks, "And don't these maleficent [women, *maléficas*] seem like *mangkukulam* . . . ?"[76] But elsewhere he had written that Tagalog *mangkukulam* were "neither more nor less than" the Asturian *brujas* (witches) described by a peninsular folklorist.[77] To further complicate matters, though Tagalog *mangkukulam* were Spanish witches (*brujas*), the Ilocanos called by the name *bruja* a "fabulous being, very similar to the *asuang* [*aswang*, another supernatural being, like a vampire] of other Filipinos, which, like the *bruja* of the Spaniards, has a fear of salt, and roams at night."[78] De los Reyes also noted that the *aswang*'s actions in harming fetuses resembled those of an inquisitorial confessee (*maléfico*, male witch) of fifteenth-century Lausanne.[79] It was impossible to disentangle completely the origins of the *mangkukulam*, *bruja*, and *aswang*; what was clear was that there were relationships among them and that neither *indígenas* nor peninsulars (nor others of Europe), neither friars nor pre-Hispanic Filipinos, were clearly more or less superstitious than the other.

De los Reyes's interest in superstitions as evidenced in friar chronicles was in part about recovering the pre-Hispanic and in part about poking fun at Peninsular friars, but the connections he drew between peninsular and Filipino folklore extended beyond these projects. Both de los Reyes and Mariano Ponce showed interest in detailing syncretic Catholic folklore that was distinctly local. Syncretism in their works produced meaning beyond indicating mixed origins; it indicated contested understandings. De los Reyes, for example, explained that "re-baptism [*rebautizo*]," which he called "this new Hispano-Filipino term," was carried out entirely outside of the structures of the Catholic Church and with reference to *anitos* and gods of "the ancient Ilocanos."[80] Yet knowledge that this practice—called *buniag* in Ilocano—was named for the ancient Ilocano god *Buni*, was the reason, according to de los Reyes, that a church council prohibited the word *buniag* from being used for a Catholic baptism. Thus, even though the practice itself had distinctly pre-Hispanic roots, for de los Reyes, its significance lay partially in its articulation with the Catholic Church.

In Ponce's work, we also see a distinctly indigenous Catholicism described, for biblical and Catholic figures were often found to be the subjects of particularly local lore. The Bible itself became a subject of folklore; or, rather, Ponce found biblical characters and events to be part of the folklore, folk-technologies, and folk-medicine of Bulacan, as when he wrote that "[t]he weapon with which Cain killed his brother Abel, since in those times neither the sword nor any other sharp weapon was known, was a piece of wood of the tree called *sapang*, whose bark is very useful for dying things red, and whose coloring property was due to the blood of Abel. At the same time, a medication for consumptives that are vomiting or spitting blood is giving them an infusion of the bark to drink. The red that is extracted from this plant is 'blessed' [*bendito*], since it is the red of the blood of Abel."[81] Here the Bible was a source for place-specific lore, as Ponce reported its understanding. The medicinal and physical qualities of the bark of a local tree were understood through reference to a biblical tale, its association either untranslatable or without need of translation from the Castilian (*bendito*, blessed).[82] The Bible was thus quietly transported to Philippine soil via association with the *sapang* tree, indigenized through association with the local natural world, and the local was given universal significance through its presence and role in biblical time. Ponce's and especially de los Reyes's attention to syncretic Catholicism in the Philippines can only be partially explained by the project of recovering a pre-Hispanic Philippines.

El Folk-Lore Filipino, as Anderson has noted, refers to beliefs and practices from the peninsula but also beyond, and this broader world of folklore comparisons does two kinds of work: it both contributes to a broader work of "universal folklore" and also suggests equivalences between the peoples of the Philippines and those from other, and particularly from "civilized," countries.[83] Comparisons with mythologies and folklores from beyond either the Philippines or the peninsula abound in *El Folk-Lore Filipino*, especially but not exclusively in de los Reyes's sections and his notes in others'. By noting when the Philippines participated in the universality of folklore, the Philippines and its peoples were brought into the broader picture of knowable and known man. De los Reyes did this work when he speculated that while the *duende* (a mythical creature) seemed to be of peninsular origin, it also "seems to me true, what various authors have said about how in Universal Folk-Lore it is observed that all peoples have an idea of child-demons," proceeding to note the names for "child-demons" in Asturian and Catalan, Irish, Breton, ancient Greek, Ilocano, and Tagalog mythologies.[84] Elsewhere, de los Reyes compared folklore of the Philippines with Nordic mythology, Greek mythology, and the beliefs of ancient and contemporary peoples from around the globe, including Hottentots, Guaranos (of Paraguay), "Californians," Romans, Iroquois, and Chinese.[85] Ponce, in "Bulaqueño Folklore," also noted the similarities between Bulaqueño beliefs and practices and those of other parts of the world. He noted similarities between a practice of Bulaqueño lovers and their counterparts of sixteenth-century Scotland and noted that in France (as documented in one of Émile Zola's novels), as in Bulacan, men influenced the sex of a woman's fetus by arranging the bed in a certain way and surreptitiously hiding sprigs of a certain plant beneath her pillow or bed.[86] Ancient Greek mythology and beliefs about Mount Aetna were compared to a Bulaqueño belief about earthquakes, and a Bulaqueño forest spirit was likened to "Pan and Sylvan ... of mythological times."[87] Such comparisons were drawn in part in the spirit of the comparative and universal study of folklore, which required that similarities be noted, regardless of whether an explanation for those similarities was already known.

Comparison could also be used to highlight the exotic. Paterno's *Ninay* (1885), a novel that self-consciously documented Manila and environs in a *costumbrista* mode, occupied a curious position in this literature, using comparison and compatibility to emphasize the uniqueness of the local.[88] On the one hand, it was addressed to folklorists of Europe; "Europeans who had come there just to study Tagalog customs [*costumbres tagalas*]" appeared in a nonspeaking role as a collective minor character of the novel, part of the audience that listened, along with the narrator, to the story of the heroine's life.[89] Both Ninay's story and the story in which it is contained (the nine-day wake following her death) became occasions to educate the novel's readers about the Philippines, including the customs and beliefs of its peoples (mostly Tagalog), and their history before Spanish colonization. Paterno explained every local reference to the reader, who was clearly presumed to be Spanish (and European), neither familiar with nor from the Philippines. The readers were invited to think of themselves as being there, along with the group of curious Europeans. The guide through this exotic world was the narrator, a highly educated local recently returned from Europe, whose liminal position—as an upperclass, highly educated, and worldly Tagalog—highlighted the exoticism of the local, even while he translated it into terms and frameworks intelligible to the foreign reader.[90]

While *Ninay* addressed European folklorists, however, it departed from folklore scholarship in a number of significant ways. The book contained a story within a story, but neither of these were themselves folklore—they are clearly fictional narratives, not folk narratives. Paterno referred to folklore in the text, but that was one of the many kinds of data about the Philippines that was explained to the reader via footnotes: flowers, trees, fruits, birds, fish, towns, rivers, products, boats, and food of the Philippines were also explained in footnotes, which often quoted extensively from Spanish and foreign published sources—usually contemporary, but sometimes old chronicles. The novel treated folklore as one of the many Philippine subjects about which the reader might be curious, but it did not present itself as a contribution to scientific knowledge, either by presenting data or by engaging in theoretical debates. Like other pieces of Filipino folklore, however, the text performs the authority of the native intellectual, carefully balancing its claim to nativeness with a self-consciously European perspective.

The exoticization of the local that *Ninay* performs has some counterpart in *El Folk-Lore Filipino*, where the Filipino was figured as Oriental via comparisons made between stories and figures of the Philippines and those contained in *The Thousand and One Nights*, better known to English-speakers as *The Arabian Nights*. *The Arabian Nights* stories were wildly popular in nineteenth-century Europe and beyond, as bowdlerized children's stories, bawdy adult literature, and theatrical productions.[91] But the collection was also, significantly, treated as folklore, as Richard Burton's

1885 preface and notes to his translation made clear.[92] Ponce explained that the *tigbalang* (a mythical creature), had a tendency to be enslaved; he likened it to a genie, "similar to those of which *The Thousand and One Nights* speak."[93] When Ponce described being told of a magical cave, which opened only for the folk hero who knew the magic words, he wrote, "With which you can see, dear reader, that we in our province have also had a cave similar to the famous one of Ali Baba, of which *The Thousand and One Nights* speaks, and which like those, could not be opened except under the influence of certain words that would serve as the *open sesame* [*ábrete sésamo*] of the latter."[94] With these notes, Ponce not only tied the glamorous exoticism of the *Arabian Nights* tales to the folklore of the Philippines but also demonstrated his familiarity with current literary fashion and folklore studies. Mondragón also burnished the prestige of folklore of the Philippines by comparing it to the stories of the better-known *Arabian Nights*: "Let the intransigent Orientalists come now and say if through my pale and sparse laconic style, and my awkward and babbling manner of speaking, they cannot make out a picture filled with ostentation [*galas*], vigor, and richness of invention, worthy of 'The Thousand and One Nights.'"[95] As the folklore of a people was supposed to indicate something of their nature, their potential, and their being, Mondragón's writing expressed a challenge to, but also anxiety about, the idea of Filipinos as "laconic" and instead put them on par with an "Oriental" lore that was heralded as full of "vigor" and "richness." At the same time, with his reference to "intransigent Orientalists," he jabbed at the snobbery and exclusivity of the genre.

Comparison could also express anxiety about the status of Filipinos and other peoples. Mondragón began his piece by comparing the peoples of the Philippines with those of Europe, but in a way that belies an anxiety about whether the Philippines and its peoples would be considered civilized. "What people [*pueblo*]," he asked rhetorically, "is free of beliefs [*preocupaciones*]? Education leads us to hold instinctively as false that which is contrary to it. And in the 'brain of the world,' Paris, do not the most enlightened people kill time dressing up as animals, . . . and in the most cultured [*cultísimas*] palmistry and fortune-telling?"[96] In asserting this equivalence and mocking the supposedly sophisticated Parisians, Mondragón nevertheless proceeded from the premise that the Philippines was behind, retrograde, or somehow had regressed. Mondragón began his work with a long list of the reasons why the Philippines was backward, reasons he thought his readers should keep in mind before tackling the question of religious beliefs in the Philippines, writing, "It would offend the intelligence [*ilustración*] of readers if I would proceed to demonstrate that the English used to be Visayan or *pintados* ['painted ones,' referring to conquest-era Visayans, who were tattooed], that the Gauls and Germans, as well as all of Europe in the most distant past, lived like the *Aetas*, in the style of the barbarians of the north."[97] For Mondragón, the Philippines had to be compared to ancient (barbarian) Europe or, better yet, to ancient Greece and Rome, for

> [t]he Tagalog *Bathala* is the supreme Jupiter, the *katalona* a priestess like the vestals, . . . druidesses and sybils; the oracles were the haruspices, diviners, and horoscopes; the nymphs and nereids are the *tianak* and the *taong damó* (forest men) and satyrs, the pygmies: Lastly, the magicians and witches that were banished by Cervantes and immortalized him, are the *aswang* and *mangagaway*; our *galing*, *mutia* and *anting-anting* being the talismans, *patalim* [knife blade], and amulets. In a word, perhaps fewer superstitions exist among the Tagalogs today than among the Europeans five hundred years ago, and among these and those, is there a common origin?[98]

Mondragón's preface suggests that he felt the need to contextualize the beliefs of the Tagalogs that he was about to describe by indicating both that other countries had irrational beliefs and that there were external reasons, not having to do with the Tagalogs' own potential or essential characteristics, that explain why the Tagalogs had the beliefs that they did. Implicitly, the beliefs were seen to be retrograde, but only if out of time—that is, only if they were seen to linger too long in the advance of history, outlasting their use. Thus the fact that a country or people had its superstitions was not in itself a mark of backwardness—if anything, the dandies of Paris were more superstitious—and so to be documenting the superstitions of Tagalogs was not and should not have been seen as indicating the backwardness of Tagalogs as a people.

Authority and Authenticity

It is significant that folklore in the Philippines was not led by a peninsular Spaniard; instead, de los Reyes was indisputably its foremost

representative, with Ponce, Serrano Laktaw, Mondragón, and in a separate venue, Rizal, its contributors. Folklore allowed for a kind of "native
informant" role that each of them took up; at the same time, each invoked
his authority as a folklorist and established the authenticity of his data.
In what follows, I examine how "native" scholars approached the tension
between native informant and analytic scientist or scholar.[99]

These indigenous scientists were in a uniquely privileged position to
gather data that was authentic according to the accepted practices of folkloric science. As we have seen and others have noted, many of the scholarly
patriotic writings of the propagandists and *ilustrados* found opportunities to correct the misunderstandings and misrepresentations of earlier
authors, through their access to language or firsthand knowledge about
material objects, practices, or beliefs.[100] Even when praising Blumentritt's
work, for example, de los Reyes noted its limitations and suggested that
because Blumentritt "has not been here, I could have multiplied [the number of] his terms and corrected some of his definitions and descriptions."[101]
Folklore studies invited an intimate acquaintance with "culture" and thus
validated a "native informant's" position. Though the "native informant"
was distinguished from and subordinate to the person who actually analyzed the data (the true "scientist"), folklore as a practice emphasized
authenticity as a standard, and so the appeals to "native" knowledge that
ilustrados made in other works, too, could be even more strongly wielded
in folkloristic writings. Folklore writings of the Philippines often were
more intimate in tone and less formal than the writings of *ilustrados* in
other genres. While the Filipino folklorist was a scientist and litterateur,
participating in the latest scholarly debates and invoking well-worn literary tropes, he also wrote of his subjects with ambiguous intimacy. The
Filipino folklorists' position as native scholars created opportunities as
well as risks: their proximity to the people was a source of potential scholarly authority, but the closer they were to the irrational people that they
described, the more suspect their status as scientist might appear.

On one side of this complex picture, the Filipino folklorists established
their authority as objective scientists—that is, as equals of European
folklorists. This authority, which might have been easily assumed by
peninsular (or other European) writers of similar educational levels, was
something that these colonial subjects, and especially "natives," could not
so easily assume their readers would grant them. By demonstrating their
familiarity with European folklore and with its scholarly and scientific

conventions, they were not only *doing* folklore, but they were *performing* that work and their roles as folklorists. One of the ways that they both did and performed the work of folklore as a science was by emphasizing the comparative interest of their data in relation to other data of "universal folklore." These Filipino folklorists not only provided the data and served as informants but also analyzed its significance for the broader international scientific community.

Rizal's piece on the folktale of the monkey and the tortoise, published in a scholarly journal of London, *Trübner's Record*, performs this work perhaps more consistently than any other piece of Filipino folklore. More so than fellow Filipino folklorists, Rizal assumed his authority as a scientist, embodying the voice of the universal scholar. Though he might have been identified as a native Tagalog speaker by his mastery of the language and its literature, nowhere in the piece did he identify himself as such. He maintained a distance between himself and the material, referring to "Philippine children," "Tagal literature," and the "Tagal" and "Philippine" tale or version.[102] Rizal's work reveals him to have been confidently within the fold of European authority, and either uninterested in marking his own origins or hesitant to do so. By comparison, other authors worked out more directly the relationships between their material and their own authority to speak of it.

While no one else duplicated the confident ambiguity of Rizal's authorship, other Filipino folklorists established their own authorial voices and the authenticity of their data, in large part drawing on established convention. De los Reyes assumed the role of impartial observer and distanced himself and some other Ilocanos from the beliefs about which he wrote when he described different classes and noted that the *katalonan* (peasants from the countryside) "are almost the only ones that profess the superstitions of which we speak in this book."[103] As others did, he cited the authenticity of his sources, noting that his data came from "a respectable and reliable person (I do not say educated [*ilustrada*])."[104] Resil Mojares has noted of de los Reyes that "[t]he self-assurance of the young colonial is remarkable," and even his writing style demonstrates this, for de los Reyes wrote in a casual tone, simultaneously self-deprecating and confident.[105] Yet moments of self-consciousness quite distinguish de los Reyes's writing from Rizal's. They suggest an awareness of his "outsider" position with regards to the world of European scholars, and they negotiate between his ambivalent positions as insider and outsider, native and scientist.[106]

De los Reyes demonstrated his mastery of the literature of folklore—and, in particular, of the theoretical literature that addressed what the science of folklore was, how it should be practiced, and what it could do—in his introductory chapter to the collection *El Folk-Lore Filipino*. In this piece, part of which was written at the behest of Machado and first published in the *Bulletin of the Free Institution of Teaching* of Madrid, de los Reyes both reviewed current debates about the aims and methods of folklore as a field and suggested revisions and additions based on his own observations and conclusions about folklore in the Philippines. But he also closed this introduction with sentences that called attention to his unusual location as both scientist and native: "Such is my humble opinion. Now show the modest native of the Philippines [*indígena de Filipinas*] if he is in error."[107] On the one hand, the closing reveals his confidence, such that he could boast such a challenge to his readers; on the other, the passage acknowledges his outsider status and how unusual or out of place it might seem for a "native" of the Philippines to speak to such scholarly and theoretical questions. Though he usually referred to Ilocanos as "they," in the third person, he sometimes spoke of Ilocanos as "we" and of Ilocano folklore as what "we" do, believe, or say, what happens to "us" or "our" things.[108] He sometimes invoked his authority as an *indígena* and his access to authentic sources, prefacing some of his data with phrases like "according to my countrymen [*paisanos*]."[109] His *indígena* status was thus both a source of authority as well as a source of authorial anxiety. He bore this contradiction self-consciously, but lightly.

Of the contributors to *El Folk-Lore Filipino*, de los Reyes was not only the most prolific but also the most immersed in contemporary folklore practices and theory. Yet other contributors demonstrated their authority, or their familiarity with the science's method, by using the same techniques that were practiced among folklore gatherers elsewhere. The science of folklore privileged data whose origins were demonstrably old (e.g., oral data from old people or texts that recorded the oral accounts of people no longer living).[110] Filipino folklorists sometimes emphasized the authenticity of their data in these terms. One of the sources that Ponce cited most often, for example, he first described as "a Tagalog manuscript (none could assure me of having seen it) that an educated native [*ilustrado indígena*] of the province, who was one of the first students of the University of Santo Tomás of Manila, had. . . . It is of note that the elders that supply me with these data only know this by tradition, transmitted from generation to generation by their ancestors who have read said manu-script."[111] Ponce's words are those of a folklorist documenting his sources and attentive to the significance of its authenticity for those who told the story as well as those who listened to it. The authority and authenticity of these "data," for both the folklorist as well as his subjects, rested (per-haps tenuously) on a complex set of associations. The data's interest and authority rested in part on its origins in an authoritative ancient text. Even if here the text was itself absent—"none could assure me of having seen it"—it was authoritative both because of its purported age and because of its association with (possession by) one who was *ilustrado,* a student at the university. For the folklorist, what was authoritative was not necessar-ily the text itself, but the shared belief in it by the elders via oral tradition.

Serrano Laktaw, too, established the authenticity of his sources by noting that they came from old people via oral tradition. For example, he identified the source of a story as an old man, "an old octogenarian, as he normally called himself, a man that was in the twilight of life, and who was there to watch over his children and grandchildren who worked in a nearby hacienda."[112] This old man told Serrano Laktaw things that "he [the old man] said that, when he was young, he had been told by an old man who by reputation was the only one that had managed to penetrate the bowels of the enormous mountain" that was the subject of the legend.[113] The authenticity of Serrano Laktaw's data was verified by his having docu-mented the source, a source both oral and of the people. In both examples, the original source of the story is someone *of* the people or province, who is necessarily invested with an exceptional authority: Ponce's *ilustrado* was one of the first students of the university, and Serrano Laktaw's elder had penetrated a different kind of exclusive and powerful space, of the enchanted mountain.

Ponce's and Serrano Laktaw's voices sometimes took on another familiar trope of folklore writing: the storyteller. While the voice of the storyteller was familiar among folklorists elsewhere, the particular dynamics of this narrative voice for Filipino folklorists are worth exploring. First, the sto-ryteller's narrative voices served to heuristically link the folkloric subjects (Filipino peasants) with the audience (educated and worldly, whether Fili-pino, Spanish, or European). The storyteller's ambiguous intimacy with the folkloric subjects, on the one hand, and readership, on the other, simulta-neously secured the author's position in two places at the same time: of the people, and impartially observing them. In this storytelling mode, Ponce's narrator invited his reader to imaginatively enter the world of Bulaqueño folklore, entreating, "If the reader would imagine a tall and skinny man, skin and bones, like a skeleton covered with skin; imagine further that as the ancient Egyptian god Anubis is represented by the body of a man with a dog's head, . . . so [the *tigbalang*] has [the head] of a horse . . . imagine all of this, I repeat, and you will have an idea of the *embodiment* [*personificación*] of this being that we describe."[114] The reader could have been from either the Philippines or Europe, but must have been formally educated in order to follow the lead that Ponce provided when describing the *tigbalang* in terms of Egyptian mythology. Serrano Laktaw's Kapampangan folklore, like Ponce's of Bulacan, took on a familiar, storytelling narrative voice when he told folktales. His narrator often addressed "the reader" in a familiar way, but also referred to the story's protagonist as "our youth" and "our hero" and invited the reader to imagine how the hero must have felt. Serrano Laktaw opened his stories by telling his readers how he came to know them, weaving himself into the narrative. Yet Serrano Laktaw was not technically *of* the people, in the sense that he wrote of Kapampangan folklore but was himself a Tagalog speaker native to Bulacan.

In some respects, then, these folklorists affirmed their data's authenticity by employing the same strategies as those of European folklorists and taking an "objective" approach to their data. In other respects, however, they authenticated their data by emphasizing their more intimate knowledge of the people, highlighting their position as "native" informants. Ponce invoked his authority as a "native," introducing the pieces as a set of observations about "my natal province," referring at times to "my town," and even relating something that happened near "our house."[115] His status as native strengthened his standing not so much because he positioned himself a specimen (i.e., as a Bulaqueño whose own beliefs, customs, and practices were up for review) but because as a Bulaqueño himself he was in a better position to collect from other Bulaqueños data on their beliefs, customs, techniques, and stories. His proximity was both physical—he was there—and also something more social or intellectual than that. Perhaps even more importantly, we are meant to trust what others have said to him because we know him to be one of them—that is, of Bulacan and recognized as such by others of Bulacan. He closed a section of the work, a local story related in storytelling fashion, by writing, "And I end this story saying to you, reader: As they told it to me, I tell it to you," invoking an intimacy not only with the reader but with the source of the story as

well.[116] His reader, whom he addressed in Spanish with the familiar form
for "you" (*tú*), was invited to trust him because he pledged that he related
the story faithfully and because, having established himself as Bulaqueño,
the reader would trust that the story, "as they told it" to him, was as they
would tell it to each other.

At times, Ponce demonstrated his intimacy with the material by noting
how contemporary his information was, as, for example, when he wrote
that "I have here what they say" about what happened "in April of 1885 . . .
in the town of Baliwag."[117] As he proceeded to tell the story, however, he
brought himself closer to it by noting that "a friend of mine" had tried to
determine what was happening.[118] In other words, the "they" here is sud-
denly brought into a close embrace rather than kept at the arm's length
of an objective observer. Ponce's work makes worldly comparisons (Gods
of ancient Egypt and the world of *The Arabian Nights*, for example) that
establish the narrator's familiarity with the world of an educated, well-read
reader; it also draws from the more intimate, local world of Bulaqueño
folklore. This combination works to establish the voice of the narrator—
the folklorist Ponce—as one that is both of the people, a native informant;
and of the audience, a scientist.

Serrano Laktaw, Ponce, and de los Reyes all established a kind of
ambivalent authority, intimate and objective, invoking both conventions
of European folklorists as well as rhetoric that placed them among, if not
completely of, their subjects. The ambiguity of their authoritative claims
is part of what distinguishes their texts from peninsular folklore. While
Rizal's folklore took a more objective and distanced approach and treated
the content as particularly relevant to ethnological questions, Mondragón
distanced himself in a different way from his material, writing consistently in a tone that seemed to disapprove of the very practices about which
he wrote. For instance, in beginning the section headed "Superstitions"
(*Supersticiones*), he wrote that he was "making mention here only of [the
practice of] attributing supernatural importance to purely physical things,
leaving the work of speaking about other erroneous beliefs [*creencias*] for
the articles on 'Preoccupations [*Preocupaciones*]' and 'Useless Practices
[*Prácticas vanas*].'"[119] On the other hand, he later noted more playfully that
though what he was describing might sound odd, "the dear reader should
not think these events . . . are common, since then we would be savages
[*salvajes*]."[120] The apology suggests the anxiety of self-consciousness, even
while protesting that there is no reason for being so.

In comparison with Mondragón, de los Reyes wrote scathingly about superstition and ignorance, though in an entirely different tone. Where Mondragón condemned the beliefs themselves, and so perhaps too the people who held them, de los Reyes condemned the *consequences* of people's beliefs, using folklore to write social commentary and political criticism.

Folk-Lore as Contemporary Critique

De los Reyes used folklore not just to write about the past and its persistence in the present but also to critique the present. Practiced by de los Reyes, folklore analysis was a form of social and political critique; this sort of folklore writing had no equivalent in the peninsula, but it anticipates the kinds of critique prevalent a few years later in the propagandists' *La solidaridad* and in other private and public *ilustrado* writings.[121] Other scholars have noted that de los Reyes's folklore served the purposes of social commentary, whether generally as propaganda critical of Spaniards or the Catholic Church, or as critical commentary on the incredulity and lack of education among his compatriots.[122] I argue here that folklore held particular opportunities that de los Reyes used to comment on institutions of government, both existing and potential. That is, as a method, folklore offered more opportunity for contemporary commentary than did other scholarly forms.

Folklore was especially well suited to this kind of critique because the raw data that it used was gathered from the present. In contrast to ethnology, history, or even linguistics, folklore required no conquest-era chronicles in order to assemble data on the pre-Hispanic Philippines. Though it might refer to those historical texts, its primary data was drawn from contemporary peoples: their stories, their beliefs, and their practices.[123] Because folklore's data were contemporary, it could treat unscrupulous or corrupt practices—for example, de los Reyes decried charlatans who practiced as healers and government officials who abused their positions. Often, the practices that he exposed were those that took advantage of what de los Reyes portrayed as the credulity of the common people. By calling attention to their credulity, de los Reyes portrayed common folk as ignorant and therefore vulnerable to abuse, from which education could protect them.

Among his frequent targets were the charlatans who, he alleged, pretended to have healing skills or powers but in fact simply duped the common people for their own benefit. Usually, these con men and women got material goods from their victim, as did *curanderos* (healers) who pretended to be friends of supernatural beings and then ate the food and drink left for the latter by those who had sought their help.[124] De los Reyes named a series of messianic leaders from the seventeenth to the nineteenth centuries, commending that "as happens in all times and places, there was no lack of ingenious or wicked people who would exploit the credulity of the superstitious" people and who were able to "make business of religion."[125] These contemporary fake healers were hucksters, "scoundrels [*pillos*] that live and enjoy [themselves] at the expense of the ignorance and credulity of those around them," quite unlike the ancient *babailan* and *katalonan* (healers, priests or priestesses, or shamans) who were authentic figures of the ancient religion.[126]

Unscrupulous, inauthentic *curanderos* were not the only targets of his commentary: Church and government practices and officials came under harsh scrutiny. One of the more interesting chapters of his *El Folk-Lore Filipino*, called "The Popular Calendar and Christian Celebrations," began by invoking a presumed contrast between the "backward" ancient religion of the pre-Hispanic Philippines and "enlightened" Catholicism.[127] De los Reyes noted that the previous section had treated "the remains of an uncultured and prehistoric Religion (not extinct), that owing to its great antiquity and the backwardness that it reveals, has descended to the category of Mythology, which is to say, a tall tale or invention, sanctioned by the ignorance of the ancients and by the long stretch of time in which it was believed."[128] Rather than present Christianity as a contrast, however, he wrote of it in similar terms and with sarcasm: "Now, we proceed to speak of Christianity, which today, too, is beginning to seem incompatible with the intellectual progress of the day to those that attempt to monopolize love of the light of intelligence and the liberty of thought."[129] While he voiced this criticism of Catholicism as superstitious and out of time, he also (perhaps strategically) distanced himself from that claim by referring to "those" unnamed others who make it.

The practice of government in the Philippines and its relationship with the Church turn out to be the subjects of the "Popular calendar and Christian celebrations" named in the chapter's title.[130] The vast bulk of what he documented here were practices of the state functionaries that took place on Sunday, practices involving much pomp (processions of various office holders, complete with musical bands) but that also constituted some of the business of government. He described how all the *gobernadorcillos* (lit. "little governor," a position often occupied by members of the "native" elite) along with their retinues processed to the residence of their superior, the provincial head (*jefe*), to receive their orders. Each *gobernadorcillo* then held a meeting (announced with drums and flute) of his subordinates, the *cabezas de barangay* (neighborhood or village head, also members of the native elite) who in turn communicated orders to their subordinates in another meeting. In describing this seemingly absurd series of meetings, de los Reyes ridiculed the ceremony and pomp of governance. He also found opportunity to comment on corruption, noting the graft and abuses of privilege practiced by "[t]he *cabeza de barangay* [who] is in the habit of exploiting his taxpayers [*tributantes*], who help him to construct his house and anytime that there be need for their labor; and they give him hens, fruits, etc., whether spontaneously or no."[131] All these aspects of de los Reyes's critique of government practices are contained within the rubric of comments on "Christian" practices. Very little in this chapter describes anything other than the workings, and performance, of administration. When he did describe Catholic ceremonies or practices, he noted how the Church benefited both financially and in prestige at local people's expense, describing, for example, how the expensive Catholic celebrations were often paid for by individuals rather than the Church and that those expenses included sermon fees. In the coming years, the pages of *La solidaridad* would also complain that the Church benefited from such ceremonies at the expense of the people, both financially and politically.[132]

Another critique of government administration is found in the chapter "Celebrations of the Authorities," which treats the "traditional celebrations [*felicitaciones*] with which the Ilocanos royally entertain the provincial heads [*jefes*] and governors [*alcaldes mayores*]" who were feted on their birthdays by "all the *gobernadorcillos* of the province."[133] The *gobernadorcillos* would arrive at the residence of their superior with their bands of musicians, the "attractive young women [*pollitas*, lit. chicks] (usually the most beautiful of the town)" and the elite [*principalía*], along with lavish gifts of birds, embroidery, deer, sweets, and fruits.[134] He described such officials' birthday parties within the framework of the universal science of folklore, but his editorial voice was clear and critical of the graft, the opulence, and the decadence that they revealed. "On the eve of the celebration," he noted, "the crème de la crème of the province rushes to the *Casa-Real* [Royal House], as the residence of the *alcalde* [governor] is called, in order to greet him" in an event complete with coronation, children's choirs, speeches, and fireworks.[135] Later in the evening, "the *principalía* and the women without daughters retire, leaving the chicks [*pollitas*] with their mothers for the dance that then commences among the [public] employees, functionaries, and other persons."[136] Overall, the picture is one where vacuous flattery and self-serving rule the day, where young women are paraded by their mothers, where dandies try to outdo each other in sycophantic speeches, and where schoolboys make fools of themselves by forgetting the lines of their speeches even though they had asked "I don't know how many weeks of vacation from classes" to prepare for them.[137] Seeming to relish rendering the absurdity of the event, de los Reyes wrote of these orators that "several of them become confused in the performance and often they forget the speech upon arriving at certain periods: they look then to the *gobernadorcillos*, as if they wanted to ask them something; they forget the words, and . . . thus went Troy."[138] De los Reyes related that the absurdity of the event was not lost on the crowd: "*Blunder! Flop!* is heard on all sides, a noisy storm erupts of guffaws and cries of *Out! Out!!*"[139] The veneer of folklore data here is thin; this was pure social critique that reflected badly on government practices and that likely got past the censor's pen because it was located within a work on "folklore."

While folklore had other kinds of value, as de los Reyes had outlined in the prologue to the work, this kind of use of the genre had value for what it could reveal about the nature of Spanish administration, the practice of government, and society's moral state. These kinds of critiques were made in *La solidaridad*, but in *El Folk-Lore Filipino* they were painted vividly, with humor, by portraying administration as it was practiced and showing in a relatively lighthearted way how some aspects of government looked not on paper but in town streets and in the ballrooms of officials' residences.

The section of *El Folk-Lore Filipino* that most clearly operated as a piece of social commentary is titled "Administrative Folklore?"[140] This section may have been included as "folklore" to avoid a censor's close attention, for it is a work of fiction in which a character manipulates the folklore of others in his efforts to escape the corrupt colonial state. The story is about a young man with good intentions and admirable goals who, compelled to accept a low-ranking position of authority in the colonial government, is personally ruined and morally corrupted by the financial obligations of the position and demands of corrupt superiors. The protagonist, Isio (short for Dionisio), begins the story as a conscientious and well-intentioned youth full of promise. As the story unfolds, however, Isio finds himself unable to carry out the supposed obligations of his role. He instead becomes a tool of a corrupt bureaucracy that demands that he perform the very corrupt acts that he despises.

One of the first fixes that the hero finds himself in is the problem of tax collection, an issue that *La solidaridad* repeatedly treated and an issue emblematic of the corruption of the Spanish administration and of the friars who benefited from it. When an official tells Isio that he has been appointed *cabeza de barangay*, Isio replies with words that confirm his moral character and respect for government service: "Sir, I have no objection to serving the State, because I recognize in it the most perfect right to demand of each and every one of its citizens some service, without which, neither would there be a State, but neither would there be society for which we were raised [*criados*], as demonstrated by our natural weakness and the indispensable necessity that we feel for another's aid."[141] Isio adds what seems like a small request of the official who has "honored" him with the position:

In a word, I accept enthusiastically the *cabecería* [the position], . . . but for the peace of my conscience and satisfaction of my honor, I demand as a condition that you surrender the accounts to me clearly; which is to say, that you convince me that those that figure in the register or list of taxpayers [*tributantes*] that you have to hand over to me, truly exist, or that there is the possibility of collecting from them here, because I neither consent that my fortune, acquired at the effort of great works, be lost by paying what those absent owe, nor can I go to look for them in other provinces, nor . . .[142]

At which point, our hero is interrupted by the official who explains that he has no option: Isio has already been appointed, and his personal property and wealth has been made collateral for the financial accounts of the government position.

Here de los Reyes explored in fiction a common subject of *La solidaridad*: how the tax system, manipulated by greedy parish priests, forced *cabezas de barangay* to become either financially ruined or corrupt.[143] Under this system, *cabezas de barangay* were held accountable for the taxes owed by each person on the official list of taxpayers: the *cabeza de barangay* paid the entire sum up front and then collected from taxpayers. Yet many of those whose names appeared on the official list either could or did not pay, did not live in the area, or were not living at all. The discrepancy arose, *La solidaridad* alleged, from the role of the parish priest. The parish priest was paid a percentage of the tax officially collectable according to the list of taxpayers, but it was also he who *determined* the list itself, for it was derived from the parish list. Thus the list was often inflated, and it was the *cabeza de barangay* who had to make up the difference by paying out of his own pocket, rendering him prone to other kinds of graft in order to make up for the deficit.

In de los Reyes's story, Isio consults an ex-*gobernadorcillo* friend about his predicament. Isio's friend tells him that it is possible neither to refuse the post nor to demand that the list of taxpayers be accurate nor to carry out the role with integrity (for that would ruin him financially). The ex-*gobernadorcillo* explains to Isio how he had himself handled the role, by abusing his power over his subordinates such that he could cover his obligations to his superiors. Isio cannot stomach the advice.

Despite his good intentions, Isio falls victim to the corruption inherent in the system. Forced to cover the difference between what he can collect and what he officially owes, Isio is financially ruined. Broke and with broken spirit, Isio turns to drink but still cannot bring himself to abuse his authority as his friend had advised. As a result, he is thrown into jail for his debts, and his properties are auctioned. Here, the narrator intercedes: "My readers will not understand, as I do, the reason for this procedure, common in the provinces; and note that it is not because the provincial authorities arbitrarily arrange it in order to avoid overwhelming files [*expedientes*], aiming that the *cabeza*, even if out of embarrassment, would look for money elsewhere in order to save his accounts; no, it is not arbitrariness, therefore it must be some higher [administrative] order, poorly understood, whose mistaken application has been sanctioned by routine."[144] The narrator's voice is strongly critical of government administration, unusual for a work published from within the colony's censored press. If it were a piece of nonfiction, the words would probably have been more difficult to pass by the censor. But the critique was articulated in the language of fiction, and the story was wrapped within a book on folklore, which might have looked to the censors like a collection of ignorant superstitions of the *indios*. The words might have been subject to less scrutiny because they were contained within these layers that deflected a censor's close attention.

The narrator's political and critical voice is heard repeatedly through-out the piece, often noting how the fictional events compare with the usual practice of politics in the Philippines. At one point in the story, having noted that backstabbing among members of competing parties often happens during the election of the *gobernadorcillo*, the narrator analyzes the reasons for and solution to this problem, citing the authority of the Italian historian of the nineteenth century, Cesare Cantu, whose works on "universal history" constituted the basis of the curriculum for history classes in institutions of higher education in the Philippines: "Cantu has already proven, with the universal history of humanity in his hand, that indolence or indifference is often the effect of tyranny. . . . Concede to them [the people], then, more rights [*derechos*]; do not limit those that they have, and only then can you judge their exaggerated inertia."[145] Using the authority of the text familiar to readers—*indígenas* and Spaniards, insular and peninsular—the narrator makes a direct appeal to political reform, a subject supposedly banned from the pages of Manila's newspapers.

But how does the story relate to folklore? Isio eventually comes up with a plan to get out of his impossible situation when he happens to gaze at the mountains and sees in them a possible refuge. His patron and friend responds to Isio's plan by saying, "[Y]ou cannot imagine the sadness that would be your exile, always in perpetual danger of being surprised by agents of justice or by the cannibals, and without the ability to return to this life in good society [*buena sociedad*]."[146] Isio's reply reveals a dark, bleak view: "'And how good it [society] is!' answered Isio with disdain. 'No, I prefer savagery [*salvajismo*]. Gossip, envy, the oppression of the inferior by the superior, the enmity between rich and poor, in short, the horrors of inequality: are those the enchantments of society? . . . What attractions does it have?"[147] Here Isio shows just how much his bad experience as a government official has changed his earlier well-intentioned and optimistic approach to the idea of government service. He goes on, describing the ideals he once cherished as a woman who can only be "adored" far from the meddlers and distractions of society: "If treating love, is it not better, infinitely more gratifying, to carry to the depths of the forest the object of our affection, and adore her there without obstacles, making jealousies impossible and proclaiming her as queen of brute Nature [*Naturaleza bruta*]?"[148] Hearing him speak in such terms, Isio's alarmed friend "fear[s] that [Isio] is losing his reason."[149] At this moment, Isio receives news that he is being sentenced to labor for his supposed crimes, and flees to the mountains.

There, armed with his magic tricks (courtesy of time he spent in Manila's amusements), Isio becomes one of the charlatans of which de los Reyes has written: he tricks the Igorot tribespeople into believing that he is a spirit of their ancestors, and he rules for some time as a sort of benevolent despot, taking only what he can use, promoting useful knowledges like medicine and agriculture, and managing "to civilize [*civilizar*], relatively, those people [*gente*]; with the liberty and justice that he obtained for his inferiors, they were stimulated to work zealously; with the sincere brotherhood [*fraternidad*], forgetting of grievances, and mutual aid that he preached, he abolished the daily fights of village against village."[150] He is also briefly successful in leading the people to resist the authorities. Eventually, however, Isio's forces are overwhelmed by the Spanish, and as the story ends we are told that they returned to their prior mode of living.

Toward the end of the story—when Spanish authorities learn of Isio's little mountain republic and attack it—the tone of the story shifts. Here, the narrator gives dates of military operations and the name of a Spanish captain, seeming to link the fictional story even more clearly to actual fact. But another voice warns the reader in a footnote: "As the historical truth relating to those names and dates cannot harm [*perjudicar*] the administrative problems that constitute the object of this article, we'll thank our readers not to check it [the historical truth], because it could have been disfigured by the imagination [*loca de cosa*]."[151] This voice simultaneously reinforces that the problems of government are "the object of this article," having just tied the fictional story to concrete places, dates, and names, and yet slyly reminds the reader that the story comes from his imagination—that is, it is fictional. The statement, with its seemingly conflicting messages, simultaneously affirms the story's *basis* in fact, and also its *status* as fiction.

The story about Isio is at one level a story about folklore, for while it is a fictionalized account of how even a well-intentioned and morally upstanding young man might fall prey to ineffectual and corrupt government structures, it is also a fictionalized account of how a messianic leader can come to power among uneducated people by articulating himself and his aims through their folklore. Though the Igorots' lives are improved by Isio's benevolent despotism, Isio ultimately fails to permanently transform their lives. Isio's rule, furthermore, depends on his ability to manipulate the Igorot because he understands their superstitions and beliefs—their religion—and uses this knowledge to gain prestige and to trick them into thinking that he has supernatural powers and abilities. The story calls for

popular education, for unmasking superstition, and for educational progress. At the same time, it marks the failures of colonial government, and the
people's vulnerability to leaders who manipulate their religious beliefs.[152]

This story stands out clearly from the rest of de los Reyes's work for
its manifest political commentary; but, as such, it can help to illuminate
other aspects of de los Reyes's folklore. A few examples will suffice. In
relating beliefs that spirits sometimes threw stones on houses, de los Reyes
wrote that "[r]ecently the same thing happened in Abra, where the house
of a peninsular Spaniard [*español peninsular*] was stoned and despite all
attempts, they were not able to catch or frighten off whoever threw the
stones; . . . [even] taking into account that in the provinces Spaniards are
very respected and feared by the natives [*indígenas*]."[153] The unspoken suggestion, of course, was that if one did not believe in spirits, one would have
to come up with a different explanation for stones having been thrown on
a peninsular Spaniard's house. In a section titled "Meteorological Tales"
(*Consejas Meteorológicas*), de los Reyes recorded the "belief among Ilocanos that fire produced by thunderbolts and strokes of lightning cannot be
put out with water, but only with vinegar," noting that this explains why,
"when the Government House [*Casa-Gobierno*] of Abra burned down, all
of the houses of Bangued suffered a complete lack of vinegar."[154] Did the
people of Bangued give up their vinegar trying to extinguish the fire, or
did they claim to be without this common staple when hearing that it was
the Government House that was burning?

As a final example, consider how de los Reyes explained that "[i]n Ilocos Norte, it is said that lightning is initially a pig or white rooster, and a
tao [man] swears to have seen with his own eyes (?) a white rooster before
an electric spark was released above the courthouse of the town of Sarrat; the rooster, running quickly, changed into a bolt of lightning that later
reduced the said courthouse to ashes."[155] Following procedures outlined
by practitioners of the new science of folklore for collecting its data, de
los Reyes gave a specific example of the belief by citing the account of a
rural peasant (whose status is marked by the use of *tao* [man] instead of
the Spanish *hombre*) and recording the name of the town (Sarrat). But
de los Reyes clearly questioned the man's account, for he inserted a question mark in it and invited his reader to speculate along with him what
really happened, or in his words, "how is this explained?"[156] He began by
exploring how it could have been possible, according to a modern scientific perspective, for a man to have seen what he thought was a rooster

converted into lightning: "Perhaps an electric spark would have burnt the rooster, reduced it to ashes, and made it disappear in a horrific way? Many meteorologists attest that lightning can reduce its victim to embers."[157] But de los Reyes did not give this modern scientific explanation the last word, countering with another Ilocano belief that itself, he implied, had an empirical basis: "Ilocanos say that lighting *absorbs only the brains* of its animal victims, basing this on the fact that those killed by an electric charge have no other lesion than some holes in the head, and have no brains."[158] According to this superstitious but empirically supported belief, lightning could not have consumed the rooster. The *tao's* explanation could not be easily accepted, for de los Reyes's question mark suggests that he doubted whether the man actually saw the white rooster "with his own eyes." The unresolved puzzle might be answered another way, then: We might wonder whether the object that everyone agrees *was* burnt to the ground—the courthouse—was a victim of lightning or whether perhaps the tribunal burnt at the hand of someone else, in which case the *tao's* story of the white rooster might itself be a kind of smoke screen. If the latter were the case, then the peasant used folklore to divert the authorities' attention away from the saboteur. This admittedly speculative cover-up could have functioned regardless of whether the listener shared the epistemology that was being invoked: that is, if a meteorologist heard this story from the *tao*, he might well have doubted whether the lightning began as a rooster, but his belief that peasants had such irrational beliefs might have supported the idea that the town hall was the victim of lightning rather than human action. In other words, beliefs about folklore—or folklore about folklore—might be what were documented in this account.

Conclusion

The complicated relationship of Filipino folklorists to their subjects, on the one hand, and audiences, on the other, calls to mind the tension in some of the ethnological works of the previous chapter between claiming "primitives" as ancestors of, but also distancing them from, contemporary "civilized" Filipinos. Both of these dynamics suggest the difficulty for educated, cosmopolitan Filipinos to link themselves and their contemporaries
st in the intellectual and political climate that emphasized a nat-
ship of power and governance between the modern and the
he civilized and the primitive, the European and the "other."

The methodological aim of ethnology—tracing origins—underlay some interest in folklore in the Philippines, the peninsula, and beyond. As we have seen, Rizal framed his folklore study in these terms quite clearly; de los Reyes employed more varied frames, but the question of racial origins was among them. For de los Reyes, however, the difficulties of tracing the origins of the cultural practices contained in folklore also raised different possibilities and liabilities. The question of descent, when applied to the cultural practices of contemporary Filipinos, led both to Spain and to the pre-Hispanic Philippines. As we have seen, sometimes de los Reyes delicately characterized "superstitions" as alternatively remnants of a pre-Hispanic religion, or Spanish-Catholic imports. Sometimes he emphasized the hybrid nature of beliefs without settling on origins. The hybridity of contemporary practices and lore helped to indigenize Catholicism; this would later become significant for his work on the Philippine Independent Church.

Folklore's subjects and methods, however, also lent it to contemporary critique and to imagining possible future formations. De los Reyes exploited this opportunity presented by folklore's data, and he paid particular attention to administrative formations. In de los Reyes's writings, folklore was something that could be used, for good or ill, by existing and would-be political authorities and leaders. We will see these themes taken up again when we treat in a later chapter de los Reyes's telling of the history of Diego Silang.

Unlike the racial science of ethnology, folklore was well established in the Spanish peninsula. Its particular formation, however—as a strongly regional practice—allowed for its Filipino practitioners to take it up in ways that could support both assimilationist and also more confrontational and revolutionary political visions. Different authors and pieces of Filipino folklore studies treated their subject in quite distinct and sometimes contradictory ways. Mondragón, for example, treated the value of Filipino folklore in its exotic, wondrous, and elaborate nature. Akin to the grand fables of other "Oriental" peoples, folklore was for Mondragón an opportunity to cast Filipino culture in a rich and deeply historical, if exotic, light. He had to distance that folklore from what he characterized as more ignorant superstitions, in which he showed little interest. In quite stark contrast, de los Reyes found precisely in "superstitions" not only evidence of pre-Hispanic religion but also opportunities to critique friar orders, contemporary government, and popular society.

The writings of Filipino folklorists, especially those of de los Reyes, spoke in multiple voices. One voice spoke from the past, recreating the pre-Hispanic Philippines; another spoke in the language of ethnology, tracing racial relationships between the peoples of the Philippines and others; another spoke to the project of "Universal Folklore," which sought to record as accurately as possible folklore data; another spoke critically of the contemporary Philippines, calling out the credulity of the people, the wickedness of those who hoodwinked them, and the corrupt practices and arrangements of government administration, including the Church's roles in it. The criticism that de los Reyes's writings contained was the most original part of his work, and the way in which it departed most strongly from what was in some respects its parent project of *El Folk-Lore Español*. Though this aspect is perhaps the most interesting of de los Reyes's work, we should note, too, just how much of de los Reyes's and other folklorists' work depended on Spanish models. That they did so does not detract from the significance of their work. If they had merely reproduced in the Philippines what had already been done in Spain, their work would nevertheless have a different meaning from that of the peninsular folklorists, and the process of translation is itself creative and rarely straightforward. Their work did not merely reproduce a copy of peninsular folklore, however, and so both the similarities and differences are instructive.

In the following chapter, we will consider how the philological science of linguistics—which we have already seen was used to reconstruct the past—led its practitioners to consider the present in a new way, and to seek to alter it. Linguistics might seem a less likely candidate for political argument than folklore, which was focused on behavior and the contemporary in ways that lent it to commentary on practices of government. But as we will see, linguistic science opened up a quite virulent debate in Manila newspapers. Though de los Reyes successfully printed what we might consider to be straightforward propaganda in Manila under the guise of folklore, the debate that we will see carried out in Manila newspapers over orthography far surpassed any Manila-based printed public debate about government practices that de los Reyes's folklore might have inspired. Part of the reason for this might, as we will see, lay in formal qualities of written language and its function as iconography.

CHAPTER 4

Is "K" a Foreign Agent?

Philology as Anticolonial Politics

From Ethnology to Orthography

In April of 1888, the peninsular journalist Pablo Feced, under the pseudonym Quioquiap, published an article in the *Diario de Manila* (*Manila Daily*) claiming that Tagalog, a "Malayan language [*lengua malaya*]," was "rigid, plain, rudimentary, and inflexible," incapable of innovation.[1] This attack on the Tagalog language—in part through its association with the family of "Malayan" languages more generally—prompted Ferdinand Blumentritt to respond in the press with a defense of the richness, sophistication, and dignity of the language family to which Tagalog and other languages of the Philippines belonged. Blumentritt compared Malayan languages to the languages of Europe derived from local vulgar Latin, noting that "many Malayan dialects have a literature so grand and rich that certain Romance nations [*naciones romanas*] do not possess its equal, like, for example the Romanians (natives of the Romanian kingdom)," referring perhaps pointedly to this marginal and relatively young European kingdom (unified in 1859) that until 1878 had been part of the Ottoman Empire.[2] Continuing, he asked, "How can this ignorant [man] speak with disdain of the Malayan languages [*idiomas malayos*], if he knows (or does he not know . . . ?) that the majority of the branches of the Malayan race [*raza malaya*] had their own alphabets? Where are the Spanish, French, English, or German alphabets? Were not the Malayans superior in this respect to the majority of the European nations that now march *à la tête* [at the head] of civilization?"[3]

Blumentritt chided Feced for his ignorance and prejudice—saying that Feced knew less than his own Bohemian secondary-school pupils did—and cited an international body of distinguished Orientalist and linguistic scholarship on Malayan languages, in German (Wilhelm von Humboldt),

French (Eugène Jacquet, Edouard Dulaurier, the Abbé Pierre Favre, Aristide Marre), Dutch (G. K. Niemann, J. G. F. Riedel, and scientific societies in both Batavia and Holland), and Spanish by "a learned [*sabio*] *filipino*, the distinguished linguist T. H. Pardo de Tavera."[4] The linguistic scholarship of Pardo de Tavera, the only Spanish-language scholarship that Blumentritt saw fit to note, represented a pioneering application of Orientalist methods to analyze the data of the Philippines and was part of the broader scholarly effort of the 1880s to reconstruct the islands' pre-Hispanic past. It also became the basis of an orthographic reform that, as we will see, would come to have political associations far more radical than those embraced by Pardo de Tavera himself.

We saw in an earlier chapter how Pardo de Tavera, who was trained at France's School of Oriental Languages, used philological and linguistic techniques to reconstruct the pre-Hispanic past of the Philippines, first in his work comparing pre-Hispanic alphabets of Philippine languages and subsequently in his *Sanscrito en la Lengua Tagalog* (*Sanskrit in the Tagalog Language*).[5] In the latter study, he identified the Sanskrit roots of many Tagalog words and concluded that there had been an era of Hindu colonization in parts of the Philippines, which had brought with it a higher level of culture.[6] In the same work, he also described transformations brought by Spanish language and culture during the era of Spanish colonization. More particularly, he identified two ways that Spanish influence had changed the Tagalog language. Both of these transformations would become the subject of some contention in the Manila press.

The first result of the colonial interactions of the Spanish and Tagalog languages was what Pardo de Tavera described as effectively the birth of a new language that "has been formed in the Philippines, called 'kitchen Spanish' [*español de la cocina*] in Manila, a language that has a Tagalog grammar and a Spanish vocabulary."[7] This language of street, market, and household, also known as "*parián* Spanish" (*español del Parian*, *parián* referring to part of the city where Chinese were obliged to live, but also meaning simply the market area), was a medium of communication between people of different native tongues.[8] As was commonly the case for pidgin languages, kitchen Spanish was considered vulgar, impure, and inauthentic. For example, it was derided by Pascual Poblete, a native speaker of Tagalog, newspaper writer, editor, and translator, as being "confused gibberish," neither "the sweet and poetic Tagalog language" nor "the rich and sonorous Castilian language."[9] Pardo de Tavera did not place the same premium on purity, for he offered a different way of considering the significance of the language's origin. He noted that kitchen Spanish had emerged in the Philippines "[i]n the same way" that Kawi had in Java, which used a Sanskritic vocabulary within the structures of indigenous grammar.[10] Rather than seeing kitchen Spanish as a decayed version of a purer original or as a corrupted version of either Spanish or Tagalog, Pardo de Tavera compared it to the sacred, classical language of Java, the language on which Humboldt had based his pioneering study *Über die Kawi-Sprache auf der Insel Java* (*On the Kawi Language of the Island of Java*), and the language in which the "most beautiful monuments of the national literature" of Java were written.[11]

The second transformation that Pardo de Tavera noted Spanish influence had brought to the Tagalog language was a form of spelling that "disfigure[d] the physiognomy of many words" and to which he proposed reforms based on principles of comparative linguistics.[12] These proposals sparked a surprisingly heated debate among those who advocated educational reform in the islands and considered themselves patriots of the Tagalog language, of the Philippines, and of Spain. Though adopted and advocated by some, others said the spelling proposals did "nothing but disturb" and degraded the language to the level of the "confused gibberish" of kitchen Spanish.[13] By looking into the origins of the proposed reforms to Tagalog orthography and the work that this orthography performed, we will better understand why it was championed by some and resisted by others. We will also see that this disagreement over the significance of Tagalog orthography was staked on the status of Tagalog and its relationship with Spanish and, in turn, on the problem of finding a possible national language in this multilingual colony. The question of language in the Philippines was central to (but troubling for) the search for pre-Hispanic unity, significant for claims to dignity and refinement, crucial to contemporary political struggles over education in the islands, and loomed as a question and problem in any imaginable political future.

A New Tagalog Orthography

Before we can understand why the new orthography was proposed and what its significance was, it is useful to briefly review a few features of the history and grammar of the Tagalog language. A member of the Austronesian language family, Tagalog has changed very little grammatically since the sixteenth century, but its appearance has changed dramatically.[14] As we have already seen from Pardo de Tavera's study of pre-Hispanic alphabets, Tagalog was one of the languages of the Philippines that had had its own script before the arrival of the Spaniards in the sixteenth century.[15] When the Spanish arrived, they recorded the sounds of Tagalog in the Roman alphabet, using Spanish rules of spelling and pronunciation, and this Spanish, romanized orthography became standard for printed texts while the older, pre-Hispanic alphabet fell into disuse. Thus late nineteenth-century Tagalog was spelled like Spanish languages.

For example, in hispanized Tagalog orthography, the fricative glottal stop (pronounced more or less as "k" is in English) was spelled with either a "c" or "qu" (the former before an "a," "o," or "u" and the latter before an "e" or "i"). The new orthography used by Pardo de Tavera represented this sound always with a "k." A few other regularizations were also part of the proposed reformed orthography. For example, whereas the Spanish hard "g" sound was sometimes spelled "gu" (when preceding "i" or "e," to differentiate it from the soft "g" sound of "gi" and "ge"), Tagalog had only the hard "g" sound, which was represented in the new orthography always with the single letter "g."[16] And the "w" was introduced to represent a consonant sound that had alternatively been represented by "o" or "u" in the old orthography, to distinguish this sound from the proper vowel sounds "o" and "u" in Tagalog.

Though Castilian and many other European languages conjugate verbs by changing their endings, in comparison with them, Tagalog conveys much more of its grammatical information by using prefixes and suffixes as well as infixes (particles that are added in the middle of a root rather than at its beginning or end). The result of the combination of Spanish orthography with Tagalog grammar was a plethora of spelling irregularities. As an example, if we use the letter "k," we can represent the common Tagalog verb root *kain* (to eat) and its relative *kinain* (was eaten) with the same initial letter, the latter being exactly the former with the addition of the infix "in." Using Spanish orthography, the root "cain" had to exchange its first letter to become "*qu*inain" (my emphasis, see Figure 4.1). This was the sort of confusion that led Pardo de Tavera to write that the Spanish orthography "disfigure[d] the physiognomy of many words."[17] The new orthography rationalized and regularized Tagalog spelling in a way that would make it easier to identify the root and the grammatical insertions or appendages of Tagalog words. Though Pardo de Tavera's orthography

Old Hispanized Spelling	New Spelling	(Meaning)
c or qu	k	
cain	kain	(to eat)
cumain	kumain	(ate)
quinain	kinain	(was eaten)
quinacain	kinakain	(is eaten)

Figure 4.1. Spellings of words derived from the root "to eat" in the old and new orthographic systems. Notice that the spelling of the root kain changes with different tenses under the old system.

is now in standard use for Tagalog and many other Filipino languages, we will see in the pages that follow that it received widely differing responses and initially seemed more likely to be a passing experiment than the beginning of the national standard that it became in the twentieth century.

Pardo de Tavera first noticed the difficulties of the hispanized orthography, and considered alternatives to it, while studying the ancient alphabets of the Philippines as part of his 1884 work. He saw in the old syllabic alphabets a way of spelling that more naturally fitted the languages of the Philippines than the hispanized Roman orthography then in use. Reverting to the pre-Hispanic script, however, would have been impractical, whereas the Roman alphabet had clear advantages: it was already in use in typesets in the Philippines (for Castilian and native languages of the islands), was familiar to literate Filipinos, and was the alphabet shared not only with Castilian but with other important European languages. The way forward, then, seemed to be to reform the system for romanizing Tagalog, and so Pardo de Tavera developed a system "with Latin characters that correspond more accurately to the orthography of the word, according to the ancient Tagalog characters, than do the letters now used according to Spanish orthography."[18] Pardo de Tavera publicly introduced his new "more logical, more scientific, and easier" orthographic system in one of the introductory chapters of his Sanskrit in the Tagalog Language.[19]

He used the new orthography throughout this work, offering the new spelling of all Tagalog words in parentheses after the then-standard hispanized spelling (if there was a difference between the two). Each Tagalog word (in both spellings where appropriate) was followed by its Sanskrit root. As the Tagalog words sit side by side with their Sanskrit counterparts

rding to the standard convention), the reader can easily
ularity of the Sanskrit spellings and of the new Tagalog
n compared to the old (Figure 4.2). Both Sanskrit and
̣ ̣ ̣ ̣ been written with syllabic scripts before Europeans encountered the languages.[20] Romanization of Sanskrit was a way of recording
Sanskrit syllables for people familiar with the Roman alphabet but not
with Sanskritic writing systems; likewise, the new romanization of Tagalog
proposed by Pardo de Tavera provided a way of representing Tagalog syllables for those who were not familiar with the original Tagalog script. The
Orientalist science of linguistics allowed Pardo de Tavera to see a new possibility for representing the Tagalog syllabary with the Roman alphabet, in
a process parallel to how Orientalist scholars of Sanskrit had developed a
way to represent the Sanskrit syllabary with Roman characters. Pardo de
Tavera was able to recognize the structure of Tagalog and suggest a new
orthography for it, then, precisely because he studied Tagalog in comparison with other languages. That his spellings originated in his knowledge
of other languages made them, for Pardo de Tavera, no less natural for
Tagalog; instead, because they accorded to the linguistic principle of one
letter for one sound, and followed more closely the ancient alphabet of the
Philippines, they were more accurate or true to Tagalog's internal logic.
He was so confident about the accuracy and logic of the new orthography
that he judged the Spanish romanization to be in "error."[21]

Unbeknownst to Pardo de Tavera, his 1884 book on ancient alphabets of the Philippines had inspired similar study and conclusions by
José Rizal. When Rizal first read the book, he, too, was inspired to work
out and promote a new orthography that would be "more rational and
logical" than that then in use; and, independently of Pardo de Tavera, he
developed some of the same spelling reforms, later writing that "I thought
I was the first to introduce this reform. . . . I was, however, mistaken."[22]
When he found out about the new orthography proposed by Pardo de
Tavera, an orthography "more perfect than" the one he had developed, he
"rejoiced because I saw that I was not the only one with that idea, that
it had appeared almost simultaneously in our minds . . . and because
the authority of Dr. Pardo de Tavera made my aspirations considerably
stronger. The great proof that both attempts emerged independently and
almost simultaneously in our minds, without any consultations or expla-
nations passing between us, is the practice by Dr. Pardo de Tavera of using
the 'w,' which had not occurred to me in my work, a practice that I adopted

26

Mal. *kati*, un peso. Pam. *kati*, peso de veinte onzas. Este pesos muy usado en las islas del Archipiélago indico. *Kati*, que en Sans. significa cantidad fué á significar peso en Tag. ocurriéndole la suerte de *bahala* que significa en Tag. una cantidad cuando en Sans. significa un peso.

Cati (*kati*), diez millones. Sans. *kôti*, diez millones. Mal. *keti*, cien mil. Este es quizás al único ejemplo de un nombre de cantidad que conserva, al pasar al Tag., la misma significación que en el Sans.

Causa (*kausa*), saber dominarse, sufrir. En Sans. *vaca*, deseo, voluntad, poder, potencia. Mal. *kuasa*, potencia, capacidad, capaz. En en Dicc. Pam. veo que *causa* significa «sin cesar» : dudo de la exactitud de esta significación, pero mi poco conocimiento del pampango me impide ser mas afirmativo.

Caui (*kawi*), jerigonza, lenguaje incomprensible. Sans. *kawi*, que canta, sabio, instruido, poeta : nombre de la lengua sagrada de Java. Esto nos demuestra que llegó á Filipinas el Caw. y fué hablado por un número muy limitado de la sociedad, por los sacerdotes y poetas quizás. Mas tarde, este nombre que era el de una lengua misteriosa ó incomprensible para el vulgo, sirvió para calificar cualquiera otra lengua deconocida ó incomprensible : del mismo modo se dice hoy en español « Algarabía » sin pensar, y sin sospechar algunos, que algarabía quiere decir el español que los Arabes de la península hablaron. Mas exacto seria comparar el sentido que los tagalos dan á esta palabra, con el que se dá cuando se dice, por ideas ó frases que no se comprenden, « eso es griego, eso es latin. »

Codyapi, ver **Cudyapi**.

Consi (*kunsi*), cerrojo, candado, cerradura. Del Sans. *kûñchika*, llave, salió también el Mal. *kunchi*, cerradura. La llave se dice en Tag. *susi*.

Copya (*kupya*), casco de hierro. Sans. *kupya*, cualquier

metal que no sea plata ú oro : cobre, hierro, etc., etc. En Pam. *cupya*. Consigno esta derivación bajo toda reserva.

Coryapi, ver **Cudyapi**.

Cosa (*kusa*), ganas, deseos : gratis. Sans. *kôsha*, interior de alguna cosa ; contenido de un vaso. En Pam. *cusa* significa criterio, voluntad : el Dicc., dice : « Calctre ». Todas las significaciones de *loob*, corazon, interior moral, se aplican á *kusa* Tag. [Kern].

Cota (*kuta*), fuerte, fortaleza. Del Sans. *kôta*, fuerte, ciudadela, castillo. Mal. *kuta*. Pam. *cuta*.

Cudyapi (*kudyapi*), una guitarra. Sans. *kachchapi*, laut. Mal. *kachapi*, especie de laut ó lira de cuatro cuerdas, Pam. *cudiapi*, una especie de guitarra.

Cuta, ver **Cota**.

Daga, velar, no dormir. Sans. *djâgr*, velar, estar despierto. La transformación de *dj* inicial en *d* al pasar al Tag. se observa ademas en las siguientes palabras : *dala, dalampasig, dambo, dani, dapa, dati, dayang, dayan*.

Daga, un ídolo. Sans. *dâka*, el que dá, dador de algo. En Tag. la *k* de las palabras Sans. se convierte además en *g* en las palabras siguientes : *dalaga, banyaga, talaga, tumbaga, tingga*.

Dahas, bravura, valentia. Del Sans. *sâhasa*, fuerza, vigor y *dahasa* que proviene de el [Kern].

Dala, atarraya, red para pescar. Sans. *djala*, red. En Mal. *djala* y en Pam. *dala*. Para ejemplos de la transformación del *dj* en *d*, ver **Daga**.

Dala, carga, traer, llebar, cargar. Sans. *dhara*, que tiene, que ha, que lleba. Compuestos Tag : *dalankiya*, que tiene vergüenza; *dalangpoot*, que tiene ódio; *dalangtawo*, que lleba gente, es decir : mujer preñada : *dalabasa*, intérprete, que tiene ó lleba el discurso ó la lectura. Pam. *dala*, carga.

Figure 4.2. Some entries in Pardo de Tavera's Sanskrit in the Tagalog Language. Notice that the Tagalog words beginning with "c" are also spelled phonetically, according to standard Orientalist orthographic practice, with the letters "k" and "w" and that these phonetic spellings closely match the corresponding Sanskrit words—for example, "Cati (kati), Sans. kôti," "Caui (kawi), Sans. kawi," and so on. Photo courtesy of the Newberry Library, Chicago. Call # Ayer PL6059 .P3.

as soon as I saw it, because I understood its perfect utility."[23] For Rizal, the new orthography had a scientific validity that was confirmed by the fact that the same or similar conclusions had been independently reached.

Rizal used the new orthography in 1886 when he translated into Tagalog Friedrich Schiller's *Wilhelm Tell*, introducing the new orthography, with reference to Pardo de Tavera's work, in a note at the end of the work.[24] By translating the German piece into Tagalog using a new orthography, Rizal was responding to a number of needs. The first was for an example that this great work of German literature might provide because of "the relatively small number of Tagalog works [*obras tagalas*]."[25] For Rizal it was important that Tagalog have a literature, even if at first this would be Tagalog translations of other languages' great works. *Wilhelm Tell*'s nationalist themes of resistance to tyranny were, Rizal thought, "translatable" to the context (and language) of the Philippines, as Ramon Guillermo has shown.[26] Rizal's brother Paciano also thought that foreign works could, via translation, provide examples for Tagalog literature. At the same time that Rizal was working on *Guillermo Tell*, Paciano began translating into Tagalog Schiller's *Maria Stuart* about the life and death of the Catholic queen of Scotland.[27] This Tagalog literature was oriented to the young: Rizal wanted children to have a literature in their own language to learn from, to be fascinated by, and to be inspired by. To this end, he also translated the children's stories of Hans Christian Andersen into Tagalog around the same time.[28]

But Tagalog youth needed not only to have works written in Tagalog; they also needed a new way of spelling the language, "more rational and logical, that would be, at the same time, in harmony with the spirit of the language and of its siblings [related languages]."[29] The reform was inspired in part, as he later explained, by "the study that I was making at that time of the primary schools in Saxony where I saw the efforts of the teachers to simplify and facilitate the education of the children."[30] Rizal hoped that his own efforts to develop a simpler orthography would improve children's schooling, because he believed that the future success of the country lay in education. He had admired the educational system and progress of the German nation, where he spent much of 1886 and the first part of 1887, and he hoped Germany's successes could be duplicated in the Philippines.[31]

Rizal first published the new orthography in *Noli me tángere* (1887, the same year as Pardo de Tavera's *Sanskrit in the Tagalog Language*), capturing in this Castilian-language novel, set in the contemporary Philippines, the occasional interruptions of Tagalog into the Castilian spoken by some native Tagalog speakers. Rizal later wrote that he used the new orthography, "hoping that the Filipino public [*público filipino*] would adopt it after a reasonable discussion of its convenience and opportuneness."[32] That Rizal used a new orthography in this novel is often invisible to its students of today; because the spelling that was new at the time has since become standard, its novelty disappears before the eyes of the modern reader.

Rizal introduced his friends and family to his new orthography and encouraged them to adopt it. When he sent his brother Paciano the manuscript of the Tagalog *Guillermo Tell* at the end of 1886—apparently the first time that Paciano had seen the new orthography—Paciano echoed his brother's sense that the orthography was an improvement, but he remained skeptical of its prospects. Paciano wrote, "I dare not do it [use it]. Will one's name be enough to establish it, like the authority of an Academy does? Will it be accepted universally? I doubt it, but if this change can be introduced, now is the time to do so, because Tagalog still lacks good books."[33] Rizal later wrote that by 1887 he had urged his friends to adopt the new orthography, and apparently at least some of them had already done so.[34] We know that in July of 1888 Rizal sent a postcard to Mariano Ponce from London, written in Tagalog and in the new orthography, and in August he wrote again to Ponce that "[t]he new Tagalog orthography that we are using is perfectly in harmony [*de acorde*] with the ancient writing according to what I find out from some books that I find in the British Museum, and according to the Sanskrit origin of many Tagalog words. Adopt it; Pedro Serrano [Laktaw] has already published a pamphlet in this new orthography and a dictionary will be published."[35] Ponce replied to reassure Rizal that he and his family had already adopted the new orthography and that his friends were adopting it as well.[36] Through Rizal's efforts, the new orthography came to be used and advocated by many of the propagandists; and one can see, scattered throughout the pages of *La solidaridad* as well as other propagandist and *ilustrado* texts, remnants of this early effort to reform orthography, in the k's and w's in Tagalog words and those of other indigenous languages.

The New Orthography in Manila Publications

The dictionary that Rizal mentioned to Ponce in 1888 was the Spanish-Tagalog dictionary of the schoolteacher Pedro Serrano Laktaw who, it will be remembered, contributed to Isabelo de los Reyes's *El Folk-Lore Filipino*.

The dictionary's first volume was published in Manila in 1889, the same year that *La solidaridad* appeared in the peninsula (to which Serrano Laktaw contributed articles) and just a couple of years after Rizal's *Noli me tángere* and Pardo de Tavera's *Sanskrit in the Tagalog Language*.[37] Pardo de Tavera later noted that this was the first dictionary to be published using the new orthography, and it was also pathbreaking in that it was the first book ever published in which whole sentences of Tagalog prose appeared in the new orthography, rather than just single words or short phrases.[38] As Pardo de Tavera later wrote, "even the second last name of the author, that was written in a way that is imperfect (Lactao), presented an opportunity to apply the two newly-introduced consonants that he did not pass up."[39] Indeed, the book was by Pedro Serrano "Laktaw" (according to the new orthography, rather than "Lactao" as in the old).[40] It is possible that the pamphlet to which Rizal referred was this work or a part of it; more likely, Serrano Laktaw had already written something else in this orthography (perhaps a clandestine political pamphlet for circulation in the Philippines), which has since been lost.[41]

Serrano Laktaw's dictionary began with preliminary notices to the reader, some in Tagalog and others in Castilian. The last notice to the reader of Castilian announced that the author would employ the new orthography for Tagalog with which "it is easy to distinguish the root and the affixes which compose each word, writing is less complicated, and the spoken word is represented more accurately, which is not true with the orthography which has been used until now."[42] While he mentioned the "accuracy" of the orthography, Serrano Laktaw emphasized that it made reading and writing Tagalog easier and so thus could improve primary education in the Philippines. These themes were echoed in the book's dedications: to Benigno Quiroga L. Ballesteros, who served in Manila under the liberal government as director of the civil administration, and to the "development of education" in the Philippines.[43] These dedications highlight how this dictionary functioned simultaneously as what it purported to be—a dictionary useful to students and teachers—and as a piece of propaganda, in the sense that it was a venue for political opinion and critique to be published in the Philippines, for an insular audience. These propagandistic qualities were echoed in the book's prologue.

Written by Marcelo H. del Pilar y Gatmaytan (formerly del Pilar y Gatmaitan), the prologue emphasized the importance of teaching Castilian to students in the Philippines. Del Pilar (1850–96) was an intensely active propagandist, both in the Philippines and later in the peninsula where he directed *La solidaridad*.[44] Making the link between literacy in Tagalog—which seemed to motivate Serrano Laktaw—and literacy in Spanish, del Pilar wrote that the work was inspired by "the lack of books that teach the Tagalog speaker the equivalent, in his own language, of the Spanish word."[45] Del Pilar praised the "aspirations of the government"—here the liberal administration under which Ballesteros had served—to teach Castilian to all schoolchildren and wrote that he hoped the book would "contribute to the diffusion of Castilian in this archipelago, which [being] a piece of Spain, should be Spanish in its language, just as it is Spanish in its government, Spanish in its religion, in its sentiments, in its habits and in its aspirations."[46] By complimenting the liberal government, del Pilar pointedly showed his support for a specific set of policies and officials whose reforms had been threatened by the new more conservative regime of Governor-General Valeriano Weyler. Thus while del Pilar professed patriotism to Spain and Spanish law, and respect for the Catholic religion (when in its proper sphere, outside of governance), he aligned himself with a liberal and reformist Spanish civil administration. These same strategies he commonly pursued in *La solidaridad*, but here they appeared in the pages of a book published in Manila, whose audience would presumably be schoolteachers and students. Had they appeared in the pages of a newspaper, such comments would likely have fallen victim to the censor's pen.

The new orthography also appeared in another Manila publication of 1889: a new bilingual weekly, *La España oriental* (*Eastern Spain*). *Eastern Spain* printed each of its articles in both Castilian and Tagalog. Other newspapers were printed only in Castilian, with the exception of one other bilingual paper that started six months earlier, *La revista católica de Filipinas* (*The Catholic Review of the Philippines*). Though the *Catholic Review* was the first of the two papers, it was part of a much older tradition of printed Tagalog texts that were almost always religious in character. The secular thrust of *Eastern Spain*, however, was quite unusual for a Tagalog-language publication at this time; in its first issue, it told its readers that it aimed "to transmit to the native people all that which is within the reach of their intelligence and useful to their civil and political state. We shall bring them up to date on all of the governmental and administrative regulations that they need to know. . . . We will give them, in short articles, easy lessons to popularize knowledge of the arts and sciences useful for practical life, concentrating above all on agriculture, industry and commerce, likewise on advice about matters of Medicine and hygiene, and on improvements to their domestic life."[47] The aims of *Eastern Spain*, then, were broadly speaking those of secular education and uplift for natives, and we should not be surprised that its primary editor and writer was Isabelo de los Reyes, who also contributed pseudonymously to *La solidaridad* as well as to many Manila newspapers with fiction, serialized works of history, ethnography and folklore, and political commentary. Both because of its secular, progressivist content and because of its personnel, we should consider *Eastern Spain* to be "propaganda," like *La solidaridad*, but in a different register, in another language, and printed in the colony: it was an effort to propagate enlightenment and education among a class in Manila and its environs that was literate in Tagalog but not necessarily in Castilian.[48]

Unlike the erudite readers of Pardo de Tavera's linguistic works and the relatively elite readers of *La solidaridad*, *Noli me tángere*, and other propagandist and *ilustrado* texts, *Eastern Spain*'s intended audience spanned social classes and educational levels in Manila. The Tagalog-language text of *Eastern Spain* had the task of introducing the new orthography to a readership that was not only encountering it for the first time, but for whom it must have seemed initially exotic and puzzling. The orthography was introduced in a footnote, telling readers that that the paper had decided to use it "because [we] believe that the words of the Tagalog language are thus better composed and represented."[49] The newspaper then demonstrated the advantages of the new orthography with the following example and commentary: "From the root *akó* [*aco*] (meaning 'I'), are formed the words *ak*-IN [*aquin*] (meaning 'my'), by dropping the final 'o' and substituting for it the suffix '*in*,' which is doubled in *ak*-IN-IN [*aquinin*], which converts the root into a verb, meaning 'to appropriate something, to make something one's own, etc.' This clarity and simplicity of composition is not achieved with the use of our 'c,' which we had been using and which produces difficulties for finding the component affixes and roots of a compound word."[50] I have added the old spellings in brackets in order to help demonstrate the utility of the new orthography to those not familiar with the old, but *Eastern Spain* trusted that its readers would be able to immediately recognize *akó*, *akin*, and *akinin* as the words formerly spelled as *aco*, *aquin*, and *aquinin*.[51] Even in this introductory demonstration, the new orthography was thought to be sufficiently transparent and logical that the reader would not need the old

spellings for orientation. The footnote also contained the following dis-
claimer, which acknowledged the fluidity of Tagalog orthography at the
time and anticipated the substance, if not the degree, of the objections
that the spelling changes would encounter: "However, if our readers think
the other orthography more understandable or convenient, we will comply [with their wishes and use the old orthography]."[52]

Both *Eastern Spain* and Serrano Laktaw's dictionary, when they introduced the new orthography, cited as authoritative its origins in the work of
distinguished "Orientalist" scholars, as if its legitimacy and value could be
measured in part by the scholarly credentials of those who had previously employed it. Serrano Laktaw's dictionary read, "We hope to make . . .
a contribution to philology by adopting the orthography employed by the
learned [*sabios*] Orientalists such as the Abbé Favre, D. Manuel Troyano,
Humboldt, Jacquet, Pardo de Tavera, etc., and recently by the M. R. P.
Toribio Minguella, Augustinian Recollect, learned philologist, author of
various works in Tagalog, and to whom we owe the curious and no less
thorough work of *Comparative Studies of Tagalog and Sanskrit*."[53] *Eastern
Spain* similarly introduced the new orthography by noting that it would
"use the orthography recently [*modernamente*] introduced by the learned
Orientalists Humbold [*sic*], Dr. T. H. Pardo de Tavera, Fr. Toribio Minguella, Moyano, and others."[54] The similarity of these citations, and the
fact that the second is an abbreviated version of the first, suggests that
Eastern Spain may have been directly borrowing from Serrano Laktaw's
dictionary without naming him or his work as a source.[55]

Who were these "learned Orientalists," and how had they used and promoted the new orthography for Tagalog? Humboldt's work on languages
was of course broadly influential; the Abbé Favre was Pardo de Tavera's
teacher at the Parisian School of Oriental Languages; and Jacquet, whose
work Pardo de Tavera had studied, was published in one of the leading
Orientalist journals of Europe.[56] All three of these Orientalists used the
"k" when transcribing Sanskrit and Malayan languages using Latin letters, and Jacquet had transliterated the Tagalog letters of the pre-Hispanic
alphabet as "ka" and "wa"; but none had used or promoted a particular
orthography for the contemporary Tagalog language. Neither of the peninsular Spaniards was in remotely the same class as the Prussian and French
Orientalists. Minguella had authored a textbook intended to help teach
Tagalog students the Castilian language, and both he and Manuel Moyano
had written articles about Philippine languages for the Madrid paper *El*

globo, which were republished in a collection commemorating the Philippine Exposition of 1887. Though each wrote specifically about Philippine languages, their use of the new orthography was distinctly limited, and neither merited nor achieved broad recognition as Orientalist or linguistic scholars.[57] In fact, then, Pardo de Tavera was the only scholar named who had used the new orthography in any comprehensive way, and only he had written *about* it and advocated its use.

Why cite these authorities when most of them had used the orthography only marginally for Tagalog if at all? First, these references to Orientalist authority were to those who had used *any* aspect of the orthography, either or both of the letters "k" and "w," in transliterating any of a number of languages related to and including Tagalog (but not necessarily Tagalog itself). While Pardo de Tavera had specifically proposed the orthography for use in Tagalog, the others had employed the orthography for other languages; its use for those languages established the validity of its use for Tagalog. The orthography itself was, in other words, treated as something generally accepted in scholarly circles, with Tagalog being one of the languages that could be written in it. These references to Orientalist authority were probably also attempts to try to introduce the new orthography as being impartial, scientific, and apolitical. For while Pardo de Tavera was cited as an Orientalist scholar who had used and promoted the orthography, Rizal was not—he was already a controversial figure, and his name would not have been permitted by the censors to appear in the press in Manila. Despite the care that its promoters took to introduce it as logical, useful, easy, and politically uncontroversial, the new orthography inspired a reaction from the writers of the *Catholic Review*, who accused it of being precisely the opposite of all of these things.

Is "K" a Foreign Agent?

Soon after this first issue of the bilingual *Eastern Spain* hit the streets of Manila with the new orthography, the *Catholic Review* ran a series of articles attacking the orthography, to which *Eastern Spain* replied with a series of articles in its defense. Pascual Poblete, a key writer for the *Catholic Review*, questioned the credentials of those who developed the new orthography, writing that "I am not a philologist, but I am a Tagalog, by which I mean to say that, with respect to my native language, I can say, without bragging, that I know Tagalog better, simply *much* better than any Orientalist gentleman (whether European or *filipino*, not being pure Tagalog)."⁵⁸ As none of the cited Orientalists were native Tagalog speakers, Poblete called into question their supposed expert authority, arguing that "Tagalog is not learned in any book put together by authorized academics of the language, because up until now it has not occurred to us to form a core of individuals who would [and here he echoed the motto of the Royal Academy of the Spanish Language] 'fix,' 'purify,' and 'give splendor' to our words. Each Tagalog is an academic of his tongue."⁵⁹ For Poblete, the new orthography was imprecise and impractical; if it were implemented, "almost all the Tagalogs" would read the spellings incorrectly, "since they aren't 'Orientalists' even though they may have been born in the East, nor are they learned philologists."⁶⁰

A regular contributor to the *Catholic Review* and one of its Tagalog translators, Father Pablo Tecson, also wrote in his article "Orthography of the Tagalog Language" that the new orthography was imprecise.⁶¹ Furthermore, he wrote, in advocating it, *Eastern Spain* was in effect insulting the Tagalog language and so its speakers. Though Tecson claimed to be "not currently concerned with impugning the Orientalists *Humbold* [*sic*], *Pardo de Tavera, and Moyano*," he in effect dismissed their work by saying that engaging in the debate about the modern orthography that they advocated would amount to "useless polemics."⁶² Instead, he took up a position defending the dignity and integrity of Tagalog against the supposed insults of Orientalist scholars, invoking the authority of a great nineteenth-century Tagalog poet: "[W]e will demonstrate, guided by . . . the inspired Muse of Mr. Francisco Baltazar, that Tagalog, just like the other languages and dialects of the country, is not a toy of caprice or an intellectual aberration, but that its structure and its mode of being, no less than its writing and mode of being written, obey certain rules, that have their interconnections and interdependencies, and the collection of which, methodically ordered, is what we call Orthography."⁶³ Here he invented a charge that the Orientalists had never made: that the rules of Tagalog were capricious and illogical. These scholars understood perfectly well that the "structure and mode of being" of Tagalog obeyed "certain rules, that [had] their interconnections and interdependencies," which, when collected, could be "methodically ordered"—it was exactly such methodical work for which they found the "k" and "w" useful. But Tecson charged that to tamper with the spelling of the language was to tamper with the language itself, that to find fault with the orthography that was commonly used was to accuse the language of being illogical and inferior.

Baltazar's text was the classic text, and his Tagalog, for Tecson, was the authoritative literary language: to tamper with his language was to insult the great poet and all Tagalogs.

Tecson defended Tagalog from insults that the Orientalists had not made, but that others had. Feced's denigration of Tagalog had prompted Blumentritt, it will be recalled, to cite Orientalist scholarship in defense of Tagalog's dignity. In a linguistic world in which rationality and therefore status were often accorded to European languages but less so to languages of other places, a rationalized orthography for Tagalog might highlight what was thought by many linguists of the era, including Pardo de Tavera, to be Tagalog's highly developed state, one that was close to perfection as a language and thought to accompany a comparatively high state of civilization.[64] Tecson, however, either did not see or ignored the acclaim that linguistics had brought Tagalog; instead, he suggested that these Orientalists had attacked the language's dignity and that he was coming to its defense.

Perhaps more significantly, the *Catholic Review* appealed to its readers' patriotism toward the Tagalog language in a way that rendered that patriotism as also directed toward Spain and the Spanish language. The new orthography was both impractical and unpatriotic because Tagalog was, the paper argued, a Spanish language, and so must be spelled accordingly. Certain letters—the "k" and the "w"—were singled out for criticism as being "foreign," specifically, "German." Poblete protested that Tagalogs did not know letters foreign to Castilian and thus would not be able to read their own language when spelled with the "foreign" letters. Not knowing the letter "w," he said, Tagalogs would think that it was either a double "u" sound or like a "u" and a "v" together; and since the Castilian "v" sounds like "b," he ventured that Tagalogs "would read [*karaniwan* as] *karani-u-ban*, [*tawo* as] *ta-u-bo*, [*kagawian* as] *caga-u-bian*, [*giliw* as] *gili-u-u*, [and *wika* as] *u-bica* ... because their first teachers in the reading and writing of the Phoenician alphabet . . . were the Spanish, and not the English or the Germans."[65] The interloping letter "k" became, in the *Catholic Review*, the focus of especially strong criticism. The writers repeatedly claimed that "k" was particularly German and definitely *not* Spanish (and therefore not Tagalog). They gleefully reminded their readers of the supposed German origins of the new orthography, signing one of the articles with a pseudonym *hindí aleman* (not German) and demonstrating a point about the conjugation of Tagalog verbs by using the Castilian word for "German" (*aleman*) as if it were a

Tagalog verb root, coining words for "to do German" (*umale-aleman*), "was made German" (*inaleman*), and "to be made German" (*alemanin*).[66]

Poblete directly appealed to his readers' patriotic feelings both for Tagalog and for Spain:

> Furthermore, Tagalog compatriots: If our religion, our laws, our customs and our entire mode of being are Spanish, why do we have to use some letters that are not genuinely Spanish, and pronounce the syllables *ge* and *gi* like the Germans do and not like our brothers across the seas? Are the letters that have been taught to us not enough for us to express our ideas and thoughts? Then let us invent those that would be necessary: better yet, let us revive our primitive alphabet, before we use a letter of origin foreign to our Mother country.[67]

In Poblete's rendition, his "Tagalog compatriots" were profoundly Spanish, and Tagalog was a Spanish language. This claim was not as absurd as it might seem, as it was made in the context of multilingual Spain. Castilian was the language of the state, but the nation of Spain was multilingual, and so to the list of Castilian, Asturian, Basque, Galician, and Catalan, one might conceivably add Tagalog, just as *El Folk-Lore Español* might include *El Folk-Lore Filipino*.[68]

The *Catholic Review* writers Poblete and Tecson, then, attacked the "foreign"—that is, non-Tagalog and non-Spanish—origins of the new orthography. They claimed the orthography was suspect both because the people who developed it were not authentically Tagalog and because the spellings that it employed—particularly the use of "k"—were "German" and thus traitors to Tagalog and to Spanish. Against this inauthentic, unpatriotic orthography, these writers invoked the authorities of the native speaker and classic poet's text, as well as patriotism toward both Tagalog and Spanish. But the *Catholic Review*'s vitriolic attacks on the new orthography, and more particularly the emphasis on Germany in those attacks, requires a different kind of explanation.

Orthographic Reform as Political Reform

As we already know, Tecson and Poblete were in a sense correct about the foreign origins of the new orthography, for it derived in part from Pardo de Tavera's Orientalist linguistic training. Though that training was itself French, French scholarship in this field was heavily influenced by the pre-eminence of German scholars. It seems doubtful, however, that Pardo de Tavera's linguistic training, or indeed the Orientalists so maligned, could fully account for the intense response of the *Catholic Review*, particularly the vitriol against the supposed German qualities of the orthography.

Most obviously, by labeling the letter "k" as "German," the *Catholic Review* marked it as politically subversive to Spain by appealing to anxieties about the declining status and power of Spain as a global empire in contrast to the ascendant Germany that had recently challenged Spain in the Carolinas. As noted in chapter 2, the Philippine Exposition of 1887 had been inspired by Madrid's anxiety over Germany's colonial appetite. Perhaps linking the orthography to Spain's enemy, Germany, was simply a strategic choice made by those whose real objections to the orthography lay elsewhere.

Accusations of being "German" or under "foreign" influence also carried more particular associations, however. Rizal's associations with Germany were infamous, if often misrepresented. Just around the time of the argument over the orthography, Vicente Barrantes, a Spanish official of the civil administration of the Philippines and a conservative occasional contributor to Manila's press, accused Rizal of having a soul that had been "twisted" by the Germans, in reply to which Rizal wrote in an open letter that if his soul was "twisted" it had happened in the atmosphere of Manila, not Germany.[69] Rizal had compared Germany favorably to both Spain and the Philippines in some respects, and he openly admired the people and progress of the German nation.[70] The writers of the *Catholic Review*, knowing that Rizal was one of those who had used the new orthography, were likely making reference to him with their references to Germany. Either they sought to discredit the orthography by associating it with the controversial Rizal or they attacked the orthography to symbolically attack Rizal himself. *La solidaridad* reported that those who supported Rizal and his family in the controversy over land struggles in Calamba, ongoing during this period, were called "German," and so the orthography controversy might have been a stand-in for this contest over land.[71] Censors would likely have struck Rizal's name, and so Germany and German-ness stood as a ready reference that escaped the censor's cuts.

It is also possible that connections between Isabelo de los Reyes, who edited and wrote much of *Eastern Spain*'s content, and those who were more visible propagandists, including Ponce, Rizal, and Blumentritt, were either known or suspected and that the *Catholic Review* wanted to taint its competition by associating it with the more controversial newspaper *La solidaridad*. In claiming to be simultaneously loyal to Tagalog and to Spain, the writers of the *Catholic Review* invoked *La solidaridad*'s own claims to be motivated by loyalty to Spain and concern about preserving Spanish sovereignty in the Philippines. The *Catholic Review*'s writers echoed *La solidaridad*'s own protestations of Spanish loyalty but also indirectly questioned whether they were genuine.

Pardo de Tavera commented on the coded nature of the references to Germany in a letter printed in *Eastern Spain*. He addressed himself directly to Tecson, writing, "We all know the intention bound up in the label 'German' when used in the Philippines and we know perfectly the system that some adopt, of applying to others disagreeable epithets that they make a show of abhorring, in order to free themselves later from being the object of their application."[72] For Pardo de Tavera, then, what was meant by "German" was transparent; perhaps it was code for *filibustero* (political subversive). To accuse someone of being a *filibustero* would merit the kind of warning that followed in Pardo de Tavera's letter: "Careful, Father: *Proximus ardet Ucalegon!*"[73] Pardo de Tavera, whose own guardian and uncle had been exiled from the Philippines on the basis of suspected complicity in subversive activities, here used a common nineteenth-century warning of impending danger with the phrase from Virgil's *Aeneid*, exclaimed when Troy was sacked and burning, and fire had already engulfed a neighbor's house (lit. "Ucalegon['s house] burns near!").[74] By implication, then, Pardo de Tavera thought Tecson's overzealous accusations of subversion ill behooved someone who might become the victim of the same accusations.

In 1890, a year after the polemical debate in Manila newspapers about the new orthography, Jose Rizal outlined his position, and what he held to be the orthography's significance, in *La solidaridad* in an article titled "On the New Orthography: A Letter to My Countrymen."[75] Rizal explicitly discussed the issues of patriotism that the *Catholic Review*'s Tecson and Poblete had raised. However, while Rizal encouraged his readers to think of the question of orthography as a political question, he steered them to conclusions different from the *Catholic Review*'s. *Eastern Spain* had also responded to the criticisms, but its response had primarily focused on the logic of the new orthography and its utility; *Eastern Spain* did not overtly push the political implications of their position perhaps because of the censorship of the Manila press. Rizal had more room to advocate certain political positions, however, in *La solidaridad*.

Rizal opened his appeal with a picture of a classroom in the Philippines, painted to accentuate problems that he thought were holding back the country:

> When you were attending the town's school to learn your first
> letters, or when you had to teach them to the younger ones, your
> attention must have been drawn, as mine was, to the great difficulty
> that the children encountered when they got to the syllables *ca, ce,
> ci, co, ga, ge, gua, gue, gui*, etc., because they did not understand the
> cause for these irregularities or the reason that the sounds of some
> consonants change. Whips rained down, punishments abounded,
> canes broke when the little hands did not become cracked, the first
> pages fell to pieces, the children cried, and sometimes even the
> *decurions* [head students] had to pay, but these terrible *Thermopy-
> lae* could not be passed.[76]

Emphasizing the futility of the prevailing system—and the brutality of the classroom—he invited his readers to identify both with the suffering boys and with him. He reminded his "countrymen [*mis paisanos*]" that he was a native Tagalog speaker, asserting the authority of authenticity that *Catholic Review* had denied Pardo de Tavera and other Orientalists.[77]

After a long section where he detailed the technical features of the old and new orthographies, he came to the question of patriotism and what spelling had (and had not) to do with it. Again, he invoked his readers' sympathy for their former selves, as boys struggling in the classroom, and for their own sons, actual or imaginary, who would toil continually up this mountain unless a new orthography was adopted:

> Why torture the boys into learning [Spanish syllables] when they
> have to speak nothing other than Tagalog, because Castilian is
> completely forbidden to them? If later they have occasion to learn
> this latter language, then they will study these combinations, as we
> all do when we begin to study French, English, German, Dutch,
> etc. No one in Spain learns from childhood the French or English
> syllabary: Why, then, do the children of the towns have to kill
> themselves in learning the syllabary of a language that they will

never have to speak? The only thing that they can gain is a hatred of
their studies, seeing that they are difficult and useless.[78]

In contrast to del Pilar's claim that the new orthography would help Tagalog speakers learn Castilian, Rizal made it clear that reforms should be
introduced not primarily for the sake of the privileged few who studied
the Spanish language and who went on to study other languages. Instead,
it was for the sake of most Tagalog children, who would likely never
become literate in Castilian. What he proposed, he stressed, was that
Tagalog should be made easier for Tagalog children to learn to read and
write, and learning Tagalog in the Philippines should be more like learning
Castilian in Spain. In other words, Tagalog should be treated as its own
language, rather than as a strange local version of Castilian. Tagalog was
linguistically distinct from, but equal to, Castilian, and the logic of orthography dictated that it follow that distinct nature.

Rizal rebuked the provincialism of Tecson and Poblete, who objected
to the supposed foreignness of the letters "k" and "w," arguing via analogy
the absurdity of basing patriotism for a country on the supposed origin of
a letter:

It is, then, exceedingly childish . . . to reject the use [of the letter "k"]
saying that it is of "German origin" and taking up the issue in order to
make boasts of patriotism, as if patriotism consisted of letters [of the
alphabet]. "We are Spaniards above all!" say its opponents, and with
this they think that they have performed an act of heroism; "We are
Spanish above all! And we reject the 'k' of German origin!" Surely
nine tenths of these patriots of my country's alphabet wear hats that
are authentically German and perhaps authentically German boots,
too! What? Then where is their patriotism? Do Germany's exports
rise when we use the "k," more than when we import and wear
German things? Why not wear a *chambergo* [a broad-rimmed Spanish hat], a *salakot* [a wide Filipino hat worn by peasants, or fancier
versions, by petty officials], or a hat made of *buntal* [palm fibers], if
they are such protectionists? Will the "k" impoverish us? Is the "c" a
product of our country? It is very easy to be a patriot thus.[79]

Mocking the shallowness of his opponents' professed patriotism, Rizal
teased that even the absurd suggestion of a millinery patriotism would

be more logically sound than an alphabetic patriotism—though such patriots might look ridiculous in their unfashionable hats, at least their hats would be material products of Spanish or Philippine manufacture; letters of the alphabet had no such significance. Pardo de Tavera, too, had cuttingly referred to the chauvinism of the *Catholic Review* writers, remarking sarcastically that "I was unaware that the *k* was German national property, though even if it were, I do not see why we would not use it when we need it: in Paris we are hardly friends of Germanisms, but it has occurred to no one, up to now, to wage a war against beer for being of German origin!"[80]

Rizal closed his piece with an invitation to those who were skeptical of the new orthography, inviting them to join those who were interested in "the free sphere of scientific facts."[81] He was confident that "in the end [the reform] will be widespread . . . we are sure that, convinced of its advantages, [the skeptics will] have to consider it to be nothing but the national, rational, and easy writing of our harmonious language."[82]

Although heated exchanges between *Eastern Spain* and the *Catholic Review* continued for several months, in January of the following year (1890), the two papers merged, apparently because neither could afford to continue publishing in competition with the other. This merger represented a failure of the bilingual publications to the extent that the reading public could not support both papers, but it also indicated that, despite the fierce debate in these publications about Tagalog orthography and the differences between the two papers' positions on the role of religion, some of their main goals were similar. Both papers considered themselves advocates of Tagalog education and vehicles for uplifting the Tagalog people. The argument about orthography underscored a deep rift in how they believed these goals could best be achieved, but the fact that they could merge into one bilingual paper is testament to the urgency that both camps felt for the project of having a bilingual paper. Indeed, the staffs of the papers had overlapped with each other, despite the fact that certain members of each had attacked the other so virulently. The new bilingual publication, *La lectura popular* (*The Popular Reader* or *Popular Reading*), was run by de los Reyes, the moving force behind *Eastern Spain* but who had also worked on the *Catholic Review*. The major figures from the *Catholic Review* became contributors to the *Popular Reader* as well.[83] In the pages of the new paper, some of the Tagalog articles used at least some aspect of the new orthography, and some used the old. The inconsistency in its own pages seemed not to trouble the editors.

Whether the fight had been the occasion for personal rivalries that then resolved themselves, whether the respective parties simply tired of polemics, or whether those concerned became focused on other more pressing projects, I do not know. In this brief period, however, the orthography had been introduced and fought over, in terms of its political and patriotic merits. While all of those involved in the debate agreed that there was political significance to orthography, they differed over that significance. Noticeably, however, the new orthography would resurface in the Philippines a few years later as a different kind of symbol, one that was distinctly not German but also and primarily distinctly not Spanish.

"K" for Katipunan

The new orthography was not immediately adopted more broadly; in the months following the controversy described previously, the letter "k" was not consistently used by bilingual periodicals in Manila, not even by papers associated with de los Reyes. By 1892, however, two years after Rizal wrote about the orthography in the pages of *La solidaridad*, the "k" reemerged as a symbol of the secret revolutionary brotherhood, the Katipunan, the organization that began the Philippine Revolution.[84] As early as its first year, official Katipunan documents appear to have been written using "k"; and once the Katipunan got their own press, purchased from de los Reyes, they went to great lengths to acquire enough of the right letters to print Tagalog, including the letter "k."[85] Sometime in 1896, just before the society was discovered by the authorities (a discovery that sparked the revolution), the Katipunan was using membership forms printed with the letter "k." A copy of this form reveals that this letter's typeface is a different typeface from others used—the "k" was apparently not common enough in type sets in Manila to easily produce a page of Tagalog writing using it, and as Teodoro Agoncillo confirms, the Katipunan press had difficulty getting enough of these letters.[86] Apparently, using the then-standard "c" and "q" was not an option! This deliberate and inconvenient use of "k" underscores its significance. Even more telling is the way that the letter "k" itself came to symbolize the Katipunan, which we can see by briefly looking at a few different versions of the flags (Figure 4.3). The Katipunan commonly used as a symbol the initials of the first three words of the

Figure 4.3. Three of the many different Katipunan flag designs. The figure in the middle of the bottom flag is the pre-Hispanic Tagalog script for "ka." (Author's drawings, with help from Robeson Bowmani, based on those in Agoncillo's Revolt of the Masses [1996]. Reprinted with permission from Cambridge University Press.)

name: "Kataastaasan Kagalang-galang Katipunan," or "K.K.K." Not every Katipunan flag used the letter "k," but many did, and notably, on some flags, "k" was the only figure.[87]

The prominence of the letter "k" in Katipunan imagery and documents has at least two important implications. First, while the Katipunan is generally taken to be the movement of the people, or the masses, as opposed to the elite nationalist movement of the propagandists, its orthographic choices suggest a continuity between those who advocated the new orthography in 1889 and those influential in the new society of the Katipunan a few years later.[88] This continuity suggests that the ideology of the Katipunan, at least at the higher levels of the popular but hierarchical organization, was at least in some way quite directly related to the work of the propagandists and *ilustrados*, not divorced from it.[89]

Second, that the Katipunan *did* adopt the letter "k" and that they used it emblematically suggests that the imagery or visual difference from written Spanish might have been part of the reason it was adopted. While the pedagogical benefits of using "k" may well have been embraced by this revolutionary organization, the use of the figure of the "k" as an emblem exploited its symbolic significance. In other words, contrary to the protestations of those who advocated the orthographic shift to the letter "k," in fact the "k" did and does become a sign of difference, a marker that distinguished visually the local language from the language of the colonizers: the Tagalog language, rendered according to Castilian orthography, was filled with "qu" and "c," whereas in the reformed orthography, it is riddled with "k." Even more particularly, however, the shift to the letter "k" not only changed the shape of Tagalog words, but it helped obscure the Spanish origins of some Tagalog words.[90]

A New "National" Language?

As with most languages, the origins of many of Tagalog's root words can be traced to other languages. In addition to the Sanskritic roots that Pardo de Tavera identified, the Tagalog spoken today includes vocabulary borrowed from Malay, Arabic, Chinese (Hokkien and Cantonese), and increasingly English, but the greatest number of Tagalog's exotic roots are Castilian.[91] These are sometimes terms that have no pre-Hispanic Tagalog equivalent (such as *relo* or *relos* for "watch," from the Castilian *reloj*), but newer technological terms were not the only Castilian words that became

Tagalog roots. It is difficult to distinguish visually the Spanish origins of some of the most common words of informal spoken Tagalog, thanks to the eventual success of the new orthography: the Castilian ¿Cómo está? (How are you?) has become kumusta, for example. The Castilian roots in Tagalog would not have been considered by more conservative linguists to be part of the Tagalog language until relatively recently. But as we have seen from references to español de la cocina (kitchen Spanish), the boundaries between these languages were already permeable in the 1880s.

It is instructive to look at how Castilian words were treated in the Tagalog text of Eastern Spain. Many of those for which there were no Tagalog equivalents were printed in italics, which had the effect of marking them as foreign. To take examples from the first page of the first issue, we find prensa (press), Evangelio (gospel), gobierno (government), administración (administration), and ciencia (science). But there were other Castilian words and words of Castilian derivation in the Tagalog column of the same page of text that the translators chose not to italicize: "kastilang" (meaning "Castilian," or more generally "Spanish," from "Castilla"), "arteng" (meaning "arts," from arte), and "industria" (meaning "industry"). In contrast to the italicized words, these Castilian words blend into that text—some of them with suffixes added according to rules of Tagalog grammar—in a way that suggests that they could already be considered to be Tagalog. The first of those examples is the most instructive: the new orthography changed Castilla to kastila.[92] While the new orthography might have made it easier to identify the Tagalog root of a Tagalog word (to paraphrase Pardo de Tavera's characterization of its utility), it did not make it easier to identify the Castilian root of a Tagalog word. Instead, the "k"s worked to mask the Spanish origins of Tagalog words: Spanish roots, rendered with the "k" in the new orthography, no longer looked Spanish. The new orthography accepted Castilian words, but it accepted them as Tagalog words, hiding their Spanish origin. It made it easier for Tagalog, a language that borrowed words from Castilian, to have its own vocabulary, different from the Castilian (in spelling, at least) and equal to it. By severing the very real links between Castilian and Tagalog that had been visible in the shapes of words, the new orthography enacted a separation between the two languages. In this sense, the new orthography was indeed a "traitor" orthography, a traitor to Spain and to the Spanish language.[93]

The writers of the Catholic Review protested that the new orthography was disloyal to Spain; but they never complained about this kind of separation. They complained that under the rules of the new orthography, the language became more like the foreign languages of German, French, or English; but perhaps the bigger threat was that Tagalog itself became a language foreign to Spain—not more like German, French, or English but just less like a Spanish language. Why did the writers of the *Catholic Review*, so loyal to Spain and the Spanish-ness of the Tagalog language and eager to question their competitor's loyalty, not lodge this complaint? Perhaps they simply felt that it would be more devastating to impute German connections to their rivals—those who advocated the new orthography— than simply to call them anti-Spanish.

But a different possibility is worth considering: perhaps it was their patriotism to Tagalog that kept them from calling attention to how the "k" disfigured the Castilian words that were increasingly part of the vocabulary of Tagalog. Though languages are rarely if ever "pure," in the sense of unaffected by other languages, they are often considered so by their speakers. To complain that Spanish words would no longer be recognizable as Spanish would, then, acknowledge that Spanish words were an important part of the Tagalog language. It would be to acknowledge that "pure" Tagalog did not express the range of terms that one would need as an educated person in the advanced and cosmopolitan city of Manila, that Tagalog was no longer "pure," and that it would never again be so in a world of technological change and economic development. The Tagalog so loved by the writers of the *Catholic Review* was the Tagalog of Baltazar's "Florante at Laura." This classical Tagalog was fit for metrical romance poetry but not for describing the new penal code for the Philippines or the latest agricultural techniques. To dwell upon the dehispanization of loan words in Tagalog, then, might be to call attention to the limitations of "pure" or classical Tagalog; if a language was the essence of its speakers, then Tagalogs might also be marked as premodern, simple, or unsophisticated.[94]

Indeed, the purity of Tagalog—and of Spanish—was an explicit concern of Poblete and Tecson, and it is here that we finally return to the question of kitchen Spanish about which Pardo de Tavera had written. Poblete had closed one of his articles against the new orthography with a plea specifically against the "impure" language—like but not quite Tagalog, like but not quite Spanish—that was spoken in the streets of Manila at the time: "And so I invite my countrymen, the Tagalog translators of *Eastern Spain*, to stop introducing innovations that do nothing but disturb, and to endeavor with us to restore in all its primitive richness the poetic and sweet Tagalog language, the language of which half the words have already been forgotten and the language which is soon fated to disappear, a disappearance that will only console us if arriving to replace it completely is the rich and sonorous Castilian language, rather than the confused gibberish that is spoken now."[95]

Poblete's fear seemed to be that this mixed language threatened to replace the real or pure Tagalog. This mixed language was, as Anderson has recently noted, documented by Rizal in his second novel, *El filibusterismo*.[96] Anderson notes that Rizal himself seemed quite aware that Tagalog could not be a national language, for reasons of its own geographic and ethnic limits. While Spanish had the potential to be a national language among peoples of the Philippines, Anderson cites evidence of Rizal's skepticism about the project of promoting it as such in *El filibusterismo*: Simoun dismisses it, and the students organizing for the Spanish language academy in Manila are rendered in terms only occasionally sympathetic. Rizal's skepticism is also reflected in his writing about orthography, for we have seen that he emphasized that Spanish would *never* be truly available to the children in the Philippine countryside. In Anderson's text, it is the street language of Manila, a decidedly unofficial language, that emerges as a possible "kind of Filipino Spanish," almost as a lost opportunity for a truly national language, uncontaminated by the state.[97] Rizal captured in his novel how Filipino Spanish, or creolized Spanish, functioned as a lingua franca, and he knew that this language was studied by European scholars including his friend Blumentritt, but he did not endorse it as a possible national language.[98]

Perhaps most intriguing about Anderson's piece is his suggestion of the missed opportunity—what might have been—of a national language "to which everyone can contribute in her or his own wild way."[99] Anderson suggests that Rizal trumped his own "call for a single pure language"[100] by exhibiting the mixed street language of kitchen Spanish in its cross-ethnic, cross-class, and thoroughly urban use. As Anderson puts it, Rizal "was aware of the possibilities of a domestic lingua franca . . . understood completely by Spaniards and the nationalist elite, as well as the masses, in multiethnic and multilingual colonial Manila."[101] Anderson decades ago described the democratizing role that the language of "Revolutionary Malay" played in Indonesia; the language "could be used across the complications of ethnic and status lines to fulfill the unifying function at the mass level which Dutch [to which we might compare Spanish in the Philippines] had performed among the elite."[102] However, the comparison between market Malay ("Revolutionary Malay") and kitchen Spanish is instructive. Writing about Malay in Indonesia in 1966, Anderson noted that

> *pasar* (market) Malay had long been the lingua franca of the archi-
> pelago, and this became the basis of an essentially *political language*,
> Indonesian (Revolutionary Malay). It was a language simple and flex-
> ible enough to be rapidly developed into a modern political language,
> *analogous* but, as it were, *verso* to Dutch . . . This was all the more pos-
> sible because Malay as an "inter-ethnic" language, or lingua franca,
> had *ipso facto* an almost statusless character, like Esperanto, and was
> tied to no particular regional social structure. It has thus a free, almost
> "democratic" character from the outset, which had its own appeal
> to an intellectual class, which at one level (the desire to be on equal
> terms with the colonial elite) aspired to egalitarian norms.[103]

Market Malay had been in wide use across a broad region as a language of trade, while kitchen Spanish was not regionless in the same way, for its grammatical structure was derived from Tagalog, as were some of its root words. Despite this, the language did function as a lingua franca in Manila and elsewhere among native speakers of different languages. It was free of the preciousness around the supposed purity of language. This is precisely what Poblete found objectionable about it when he wrote that anything would be preferable—even giving Tagalog up completely to adopt Castilian—to the "confused gibberish," or mixed language, that he heard on the streets.[104]

Conclusion: Orientalist Sciences, Decolonizing Practices

We have seen in this chapter how the comparative science of philology, its methods and standard practices, inspired the orthographic reform that would become so politically potent in the years leading up to, and the first years of, the Philippine Revolution. While linguistic science could and did posit a pre-Hispanic unity among indigenous languages of the Philip-pines, and thus among their speakers, the problem of a unifying language in this polyglot, modernizing, and increasingly cosmopolitan archipelago remained. The struggles over Tagalog orthography in the Manila press indi-cate one of the axes on which this problem turned. While some professed a preference for a pure Tagalog against the contamination of foreign letters and the meddling of foreign science, others advocated a new orthography, in the name of science and education, which effectively hid the degree to which Tagalog was already a language contaminated by Spanish words.

In comparison with ethnology and folklore, the science of philology (or linguistics) became entangled in, and a subject of, a political battle fought on multiple fronts. Like folklore, linguistic science was a tool in reconstructing a pre-Hispanic past, but it was also a source of data, and even more particularly a method, for looking toward future progress in the Philippines. The future of the Philippines was also a subtext of *ilustrado* writings about the history of Spanish colonization in the Philippines. In the following chapter, we will see how these works gestured toward possible futures for the Philippines, using the data and methods of linguistics, ethnology, and folklore to challenge Spanish colonial history.

· CHAPTER 5 ·

Lessons in History

The Decline of Spanish Rule, and Revolutionary Strategy

IN 1885, THE SPANISH GOVERNMENT commissioned a painting from Juan Luna, a young Ilocano who had won prizes for earlier canvases in major competitions. The result, *Pacto de sangre* (*Blood Compact*), depicted what was understood to be the founding moment of Spanish sovereignty in the Philippines, in which the indigenous ruler Sikatuna and the Spaniard Miguel López de Legazpi sealed their pledge to mutual aid by ceremonially drinking each other's blood. The painting shows Legazpi in the center (flanked by others of his party), looking at Sikatuna, whose hand holds the raised glass of ceremonial drink, but who faces away from the viewer inviting speculation about his facial expression. Luna's *Blood Compact* is one of many *ilustrado* representations of the subject. Spanish histories took the event to be the glorious inauguration of Spanish sovereignty and tutelage in the islands, and symbolic of the legal basis and moral legitimacy of Spanish rule—moral because won by goodwill and cooperation.[1] *Ilustrados* also cited the blood compact as a founding moment of Spanish sovereignty, but instead of emphasizing a connection between Legazpi and the current institutions of the state, they noted difference. *La solidaridad*, for example, called the *Blood Compact* the "sole legal historical foundation of the Spanish intervention in the Government of the Archipelago of that era," challenging the legality of any Spanish sovereignty that exceeded the terms of that particular contract.[2] José Rizal also used the blood compact to question the strength of Spain's power, noting that to call that early era of Spanish presence "the conquest" inaccurately suggested that Spain overpowered local people and institutions. Writing in his annotations to an early seventeenth-century Spanish account, Rizal deemed that "'Conquest' can only be accepted for a few islands and only in a very broad sense. Cebu [*Sebú*], Panay, Luzon [*Lusón*], Mindoro, etc., can not be called conquered" because they were acquired "by way of pacts, treaties of friendship, and reciprocal alliances," arrangements that by definition suggest two parties of equal status and legitimacy if not power.[3] To stress the reciprocal nature of the agreements, and thus the equivalence between the signatories, Rizal noted that "Legaspi's soldiers fought under Tupas, the ruler [reyezuelo] of Cebu," an arrangement that indicated mutual trust and recognition between Legazpi and the Cebuano sovereign.[4]

In ilustrado hands, then, the blood compact became symbolic not as the foundation of a valid and moral Spanish sovereignty that lived forever after but as a moment of contract between equals in which the sovereignty of the Spanish crown depended on the assent of the indigenous ruler. The blood compact symbolized the status and sovereignty of the islands' natives, and their recognition by early Spanish emissaries. Sikatuna was the sovereign who had conferred some privileges and responsibilities upon Legazpi and so, by extension, upon the Spanish crown. By implication, those privileges could be revoked should Legazpi or the crown fail to fulfill their obligations.

Legazpi's blood compact with Sikatuna was a particularly potent symbol, but it was one of many events documented by Spanish histories of the Philippines that ilustrado and propagandist authors reevaluated. Such historical moments were, as we might expect, ripe for reinterpretation and rewriting in the politicized scholarly writings of propagandists. Elsewhere we have explored the ways that Isabelo de los Reyes, T. H. Pardo de Tavera, Pedro Paterno, and Rizal represent the pre-Hispanic "prehistory" of the Philippines, or its peoples at the moment of first contact. In this chapter, we will consider how de los Reyes, in his Historia de Ilocos, and Rizal, in his notes to the 1609 account of the Spaniard Morga, represented the period of Philippine history that commenced with the arrival of the Spanish.[5]

As scholars have already shown, these authors read earlier versions of the Spanish era of Philippine history critically—versions written for the most part by Spaniards and friars. Propagandists questioned the Spanish and friar authors' honesty, motives, methods, and knowledge. They used these histories to write different versions of the same events, characterizing Spanish presence in the Philippines as having destroyed pre-Hispanic Filipino peoples' knowledge, skills, and culture. Overall, as John Schumacher has written about Rizal's notes to Morga, they "depict[ed] the advanced state of pre-Hispanic Filipino society and portray[ed] the destructive effects of colonization on that society."[6] Propagandists' accounts of Philippine history, however, also employed a different kind of strategy in questioning Spain's accomplishments and emphasizing native agency: they highlighted exceptional examples of admirable Spanish actions in the islands to highlight, by way of contrast, the present era of injustice and hypocrisy. These histories offered, by comparison and example, cautionary and perhaps inspirational tales about the fragility of Spanish sovereignty and the vulnerability of despotic rule. Such cautionary histories—and the veiled threats they contained—appeared, too, in the pages of *La solidaridad*, where, for example, Ferdinand Blumentritt described how Spain lost the Americas.[7] The message was repeated in different ways by different authors and with different characters playing the roles of ruler and people, but the message was consistent: to rule, a power must be *with*, not *against*, the people.[8]

Writing the history of the islands after the arrival of the Spaniards involved a different, though related, project from that of reconstructing pre-Hispanic history. As we have seen, Spanish scholars had for the most part not attempted to study the pre-Hispanic Philippines using Orientalist and anthropological data about the islands' present-day peoples; *ilustrados* stepped into this space, using methods and structures of European (but usually not Spanish) scholarship to do so. In contrast, the history of Spanish presence in the Philippines was thoroughly recorded by both historical and contemporary Spanish sources. Yet *ilustrados* used many of the same methods in both projects—recovering pre-Hispanic history and writing about the era of Spanish rule—and in doing so, they reevaluated the data contained in Spanish sources.

Having reconstructed the state of peoples of the Philippines *before* the Spanish arrived, *ilustrado* authors then critically reinterpreted subsequent history, as recorded in Spanish texts. By referring to the state of affairs before the Spanish had arrived, biases about Spanish-era history could be identified and exposed and data correctly reinterpreted. One way to characterize the method of this *ilustrado* revisioning of Philippine history is, as Schumacher has described Rizal's historical work, "to read once more through Asian eyes the accounts that had come from European pens."[9] In this account of *ilustrados'* method, the Spanish authors' data were to be correctly interpreted in light of their biases and interests.

Yet as we will see, *ilustrados* selectively, not consistently, attended to their sources' interests and biases. *Ilustrados* sometimes translated the terms of political struggle from their sources' eras into their own in quite productive, creative, and perhaps misleading ways. The friar chronicles were products of political struggles of their own times—between different orders, or between Portuguese and Spanish—which were quite remote from the political struggles of the *ilustrados*. This distance made the chronicles' content available for creative appropriation, an opportunity *ilustrados* exploited.

The first part of this chapter explores a widely recognized narrative of pre-Hispanic glory and subsequent decline under Spanish rule, drawing especially on Rizal's notes to Morga's account. I highlight how this narrative (1) draws on key Orientalist tropes of civilizational differentiation, namely law and technology, and (2) critiques contemporary Spanish administration and rule. Propagandists' accounts of Philippine history also employed a different strategy, one less recognized in the historiography of the *ilustrados*. As I show in the second half of the chapter, their accounts also emphasized exceptional examples of noble Spanish actions in the islands, highlighting by way of contrast the present era of injustice and hypocrisy. By painting the era of Spanish sovereignty in the Philippines itself as one of early glory and achievement that had since fallen into a state of decay and decadence, these histories duplicate the contours of Orientalist accounts of the ancient glory, but subsequent fall and decay, of Oriental societies. While such a narrative in some times and places served to legitimate colonial rule, here its political imperatives were more ambiguous. *Ilustrados* were the (Orientalist) moderns who called for the rescue of the glories of the past (whether pre-Hispanic or early Spanish) from the decayed present. These histories walk a fine line between suggesting that this modern renaissance was compatible with Spanish sovereignty—that it could blossom within the parameters of a greater Spain—and suggesting that a change of sovereignty would be required. The final section of the chapter therefore looks at how history was written as a cautionary tale about the contingency and fragility of Spanish sovereignty in the Philippines and focuses on de los Reyes's account of the remarkable rebellion led by Diego Silang, who nearly succeeded in overthrowing Spanish rule.

Notably absent from these histories is attention to the histories of Spanish interactions with rulers of peoples and areas that were recognizably Muslim in the late nineteenth century. Though the works on history shared methods with the works on "prehistory," here lies a significant difference: the works on prehistory (ethnology) emphasized the connections between contemporary Christian Filipinos and their pagan ancestors' contemporary pagan descendents, but the works that treat the era of Spanish history distance Christian Filipinos from some of their ancestors' Muslim polities. This is particularly significant given that rulers of Luzon who appear in early chronicles were Muslim at the moment of the conquest, and those rulers are sometimes represented in *ilustrado* and propagandist histories.[10] The Muslim rulers who had offered significant resistance to the Spanish more recently, in the eighteenth and nineteenth centuries on the peripheries of the archipelago, were left out of the *ilustrados'* rewritings entirely. Here a major limit of Spanish sovereignty throughout the three centuries of Spanish rule went without comment: the persistent ability of many Muslim rulers to either defeat or contain Spanish efforts to claim sovereignty in their states. Propagandists had no investment in forging alliances with Muslim rulers; on the contrary, they were interested in forging alliances with secular but Catholic Spaniards. Even to show interest in the history of Muslim rulers of the Philippines and their success in resisting Spanish sovereignty might be to suggest a willingness to consider Muslims to be eligible for solidarity. In addition, one of the major themes of *La solidaridad* was the service that "Filipino" troops were giving to Spanish military campaigns in the South, campaigns directed against Muslim rulers and peoples.[11] Fighting against the Muslims was one of the qualifications for Spanish-ness that *La solidaridad* touted.

For propagandists and *ilustrados,* the problem of Muslim peoples in the Philippines exceeded the immediate tactical context of Spain's battles in the southern Philippines and Filipino troops' service to the Spanish cause. Moros were, as we have seen in chapter 2, an unsettling presence for an idea of the Filipino people or nation. While pagans could be safely positioned as ancestors or wards, Muslims were evidence of a competing paternity of Filipinos that no *ilustrado* or propagandist was eager to claim, a paternity shared by the most prominent pre-Hispanic states. "Moro" was, alongside "Filipino," a term that could describe unity among peoples. But the terms were used as if they were mutually exclusive.

Spanish Exploitation and Destruction of the Pre-Hispanic Civilization

In earlier chapters, we have seen how *ilustrado* authors reconstructed the features of pre-Hispanic society and history of the Philippines. When Rizal dedicated "to the Filipinos" his reprinting of and notes to Morga's 1609 account of the early years of Spanish presence in the islands, he wrote that he hoped "to awaken in you the consciousness of our past, erased from memory."[12] His notes attempted this awakening by calling attention to the parts of Morga's account that described indigenous society as the Spanish encountered it. Rizal also incorporated data from other sources to describe pre-Hispanic society, including friar chronicles, which he critically and selectively reread "to correct that which has been falsified and slandered."[13] The combination of Morga's text with Rizal's footnotes yields a picture of pre-Hispanic society more positive than that of any earlier Spanish accounts.

Other scholars have analyzed how Rizal used his notes to Morga's text to reconstruct the pre-Hispanic Philippines; and in this respect Rizal's *Morga* can be considered along with the texts treated in chapters 2 and 3.[14] Reconstructing the past and making this past known to fellow Filipinos was a significant goal and accomplishment of Rizal's work, but he also saw it as a means toward another end, for he wrote of the urgent need "to first make the past known, in order to be able to better judge the present and measure the path traversed during three centuries."[15] Knowledge of the pre-Hispanic past, then, was essential to any kind of informed analysis about Spanish accomplishments and failures, as well as those of the Filipinos they ruled. With this base of knowledge of pre-Hispanic society and an informed evaluation of the history of the Philippines under Spanish rule, "we will all be able to dedicate ourselves to studying the future."[16] Bearing in mind the relationship that Rizal drew in his dedication between the study of the pre-Hispanic Philippines and the study of the Spanish era, we will consider here Rizal's notes to Morga's text less for how they reconstruct pre-Hispanic society than for how they compare that society with what followed under Spanish "tutelage." The contrasts that Rizal drew between the pre-Hispanic world and the contemporary Philippines served to critique not only the history of Spain in the Philippines but also the contemporary Philippines under Spain.

The ancient culture that Rizal used Morga to describe had disappeared almost entirely, he wrote, thanks to the avarice of agents of Spanish colonization and their disastrous policies and projects. Contrary to the narrative that the Spanish had brought progress to the backward "people without history" of the Philippines, the narrative of Rizal and other propagandists held instead that Spaniards were the agents of decay.[17] Rizal constructed this narrative of decay by first highlighting and reflecting on achievements of the societies that the Spanish encountered in the Philippines. In his footnotes to Morga's text, Rizal described a pre-Hispanic society with relatively advanced technologies, robust production, and elegant and effective systems of religion, morality, and governance. Overall, as Ambeth Ocampo has put it, "Rizal argued that the pre-Hispanic Filipinos had their own culture before 1521, and thus were not saved from barbarism, and did not require 'civilization' or a new religion from Spain. Rizal insists that the flourishing pre-Hispanic Philippine civilization, obliterated by Spain and the friars, could have developed on its own into something great."[18] In comparison with contemporary Filipino society, Rizal wrote, the pre-Hispanic world seemed in many respects to be more noble, harmonious, and advanced. Through these comparisons, Rizal condemned Spanish colonization as having brought not progress, but decline.

In this section, I note especially how Rizal compared institutions of law in the pre-Hispanic Philippines with those of the Spanish Philippines, as well as the state of technology in both eras. Institutions of law—formal and informal, as Rizal conceived of them—were significant as markers of legitimate states and a favorite subject of Orientalists elsewhere; technology, on the other hand, was often taken to be at home in the advanced countries of Europe, a possession of the modern West.[19] Rizal's claims in these areas both used and disrupted Orientalist tropes.

Ancient Filipino morality, Rizal wrote, constituted a set of practices that performed the work of governmental structures and a legal system. This moral system greased the wheels of society without need of large-scale, complex bureaucratic institutions or the codification of law or doctrine in durable written form. Rizal's notes effectively turned what might be considered a liability into a virtue: the pre-Hispanic Philippines lacked textual documentation or large and complex bureaucratic states and religious institutions typically associated with great ancient "Oriental" societies. Ancient texts, in particular those that were seen as the bases of legal systems, were the subject of significant Orientalist research elsewhere.[20] Rizal's notes attended particularly to how ancient moral systems functioned effectively as law and so addressed what might be seen as a deficiency. He further established the ancient civilization's achievements by comparing its characteristics with those of societies that were generally accepted as dignified and even advanced. In those comparisons, ancient Filipino society at least measured up to those standards and often exceeded them.

Rizal reconstructed indigenous legal structures by drawing on Morga's notes about formal institutions of rule but also by defining governing structures more generally in terms of social morals. When Morga described how the indigenous *principalía*, generally translated as "nobility," might form a confederation and choose its leadership, Rizal noted the resemblance between these arrangements and those of "states of the Middle Ages, with their barons, counts, and dukes who chose the bravest to govern them, or accepted the rule of the most dominant leader."[21] The rules of royal succession in the ancient Philippines were "the same [as those] followed now by royal families of Spain, England, Austria, etc. etc.,"[22] and ancient Filipino society even "outstripped the Europeans" and was "in conformity with natural law" when it came to noblewomen's status; whereas European noblewomen "lose their nobility if they marry with plebeians," their ancient Filipino counterparts did not.[23] Ancient Filipino society had a way of handling robbery that "was like the practices of the Middle Ages" of Europe; but, in terms of divorce laws, it was "more advanced than the modern French and English," for a marriage could be dissolved if "*relatives of both parties* and the *elders*" agreed.[24] If there were children, however, "out of love for them, [the parents] never separate[d]," and Rizal added cattily that children's presence was "something which by the way does not impede divorce in Europe."[25] Similarly, on the topic of moral systems and punishment, when Morga noted that physical injury was more easily forgiven than verbal offense, Rizal exclaimed, "What an elevated idea of moral sensibility the ancient Filipinos must have had: they considered offenses to it more serious than offenses to the body! European civilizations of that time, and even many now, would never give such weight to it, despite all their pretensions of idealism."[26] The morality of the pre-Hispanic system was a consequence of the ancients' religious beliefs, which, Rizal explained, should not be undervalued.[27] Here again, comparison was used to establish the equivalency and even superiority of ancient Filipino morality to European moral and legal systems, both ancient and modern.

Comparison worked not only to establish the achievements of ancient civilization but also to mitigate what appeared to be its barbarous moments. Pre-Hispanic laws and morals did have their imperfections, Rizal acknowledged, but these had been misunderstood and misrepresented. When Morga described sex out of wedlock and between relatives, Rizal noted that while "[it] is not *impossible* that these things may have happened," one had to consider that "similar and even worse cases are recorded in . . . the annals of the great peoples and families of Christian and devout Europe."[28] Yet it was "probably an exaggeration to say 'it was *common*' since even now after more than three centuries, we see Spanish writers saying the most absurd and ridiculous things when it comes to denigrating the Indios."[29] Similarly, in an extended note about the pre-Hispanic system of slavery or indebtedness, Rizal noted that the slavery practiced in the Philippines was different from and more humane than the slaveries of Greece, of Rome, or of Africans in the Americas.[30]

Filipinos' conversion to Catholicism, in Rizal's notes, brought cultural amnesia and self-misunderstanding.[31] That conversion also loosened the moral ties that had so effectively held pre-Hispanic society together. Pre-Hispanic society "had no need" for written wills, for example, because "the memory of parents, so sacred and venerated, and the belief that the spirits of the ancestors came to live among their descendents, punishing or protecting them according to their subsequent behavior," meant that inheritance was easily arranged without risk of selfish contestation.[32] In contrast, "since the missionaries convinced the Indios that most of their ancestors roasted and burned in Purgatory or Hell," such arrangements would require "notaries, official documents [stamped paper], and litigation and scheming, from now on, forever and ever."[33] The ultimate comparison, at which the others also point, is that between the ancient Filipino society and the contemporary one, as produced in part by Spanish intervention.

Rizal contested what was considered "progress," by affirming the radical difference between the pre-Hispanic and the hispanized Philippines but valuing the former over the latter. The contemporary Philippines also suffered in comparison with the pre-Hispanic past in terms of criminal justice. An ancient method for recovering stolen goods "should not have been lost," he wrote, "but rather, as an anti-Filipino observer notes, the Europeans should have imitated it. Between this [so-called] 'barbarian practice' and the 'civilized' [practice] that we have now for investigating stolen goods—by means of electrical machines, whips, clamps, and other inquisitorial tortures—there is a great distance."[34] Further, a pre-Hispanic method of determining guilt or innocence in cases of robbery was "ingenious," a far cry from the methods of the present day: Rizal noted that a friar had recently been consulted in a criminal investigation because he was "known as a diviner," and that "hysterical old women, . . . tricksters, etc." were also routinely consulted, "demonstrating that the intellectual level has fallen greatly: before they reasoned, now they are content with asking and believing. For the enemies of reason, this is called 'progress.'"[35] It is no surprise that Rizal targeted the civil and criminal legal systems of the contemporary Philippines. These were years in which the civil and criminal codes in the Philippines were contested, and propagandists had peninsular Spanish allies who were interested in reforming the administration of justice in the islands.[36] Legal systems had been favorite subjects of Orientalist scholars elsewhere, who appealed to the authority of ancient texts; without comparable textual sources, Rizal reconstructed a picture of a noble, well-functioning, and just pre-Hispanic legal system. Unlike many Orientalists elsewhere, Rizal did not suggest the past systems be institutionalized in the present; instead, he used the past to criticize the present.

Laws, religion, and morality were common areas of attention for Orientalists, and this focus contributed to the European idea of Eastern peoples as contemplative and philosophical. In contrast, however, technology was not a classic area of Orientalist attention. Its practical, applied nature ran counter to an idea of the contemplative, spiritual, and philosophical. Rizal, however, paid particular attention to evidence of technological development in the pre-Hispanic Philippines. By contrasting the pre-Hispanic era (of relative advance) with his current age (of technological backwardness and incompetence), he pointed the finger of technological ineptitude at the colonizing Spaniards.[37] Before the Spanish had arrived, "the Indios eagerly dedicated themselves to gold mines, not only by panning for gold, but also performing the real work of mining," which required relatively sophisticated engineering.[38] Rizal noted other technological and commercial accomplishments of the ancients in carpentry, metallurgy, shipbuilding, trade, medicine, and weapon design and manufacture.[39] Such technological accomplishments belied the "primitive state" in which Spaniards had supposedly found the natives, and their concrete materiality made them more resilient in the face of skepticism than were the moral accomplishments Rizal also lauded.[40]

Rizal argued that the relatively advanced knowledge, technology, and industry of the pre-Hispanic Philippines had been destroyed—along with the healthy economy—in the Spanish era. He noted that Morga described arms that were more beautiful and intricate than those used in his own day, "proof of the backwardness into which present-day Filipinos [*actuales Filipinos*] have fallen in their industries," and added to Morga's account of indigenous knowledge of herbal medicines and poisons that "today's toxicology in the Philippines is very backward."[41]

Perhaps nowhere was the loss of indigenous technology more keenly felt than with shipbuilding. One of La solidaridad's lead stories had covered a current scandal, revealing how friars had interfered in the technological and secular world to disastrous ends for the Philippines.[42] A committee in Manila, composed of both friars and those La solidaridad called "prominent citizens," had solicited donations in order to commission a gunboat from a Hong Kong company to donate to the navy in the Philippines.[43] Unbeknownst to other members of the committee, one of the friars had altered the plans advanced by the Hong Kong engineers, and the resulting ship was too unstable to leave the port of Hong Kong. When the committee demanded a refund, the Hong Kong company refused, saying that the ship had been constructed according to order. When the committee investigated the claim, it found the meddling friar to be the culprit and appealed to the government for help.

Rizal quietly referenced this scandal in a note that he added to a section of Morga that praised the navigational and shipbuilding skills of the ancients. Rizal wrote, "Filipinos . . . , far from progressing, have fallen backwards, since although ships are constructed in the Islands today, we can say that they are almost all of [a] European model. The ships [described by Morga], that contained a hundred oarsmen on each side and thirty combat soldiers, disappeared; the country that once with primitive methods built vessels of almost 2,000 tons now has to run to foreign ports, like Hong Kong, to give gold wrested from the poor in exchange for useless cruisers."[44] Rizal used the comparison to simultaneously highlight the accomplishments of the past and contrast them to the absurdity of the present: "the poor," who were descendents of ancient master shipbuilders, had had their money extorted in order to pay for an imported substitute for their own forbearers' lost technology, but inappropriate and inept friar meddling rendered even that substitute "useless." Rizal again later lamented the same decline, adding a wry comment to Morga's description of skilled carpenters and shipbuilders: "Comparing all of this with the present state of affairs, it is necessary to console oneself with the number of [government] employees and friars who swarm [pululan] in the islands, in order not to feel so keenly the backwardness into which we have fallen."[45] The ancient past, as so often was the case in this work, was a foil that highlighted the sorry state of the present.

Emphasizing law and morality on the one hand and technology on the other, Rizal's comparisons of past with present functioned in two important ways. First, they articulated with common Orientalist themes in unusual ways that ennobled the ancient past, despite its textual lack. Laws, morality, and religion—the subjects of some of the most ancient and ennobling texts elsewhere in the Orient—were figured as having functioned so effectively in practice that written codifications were superfluous. This captured the value of ancient (Oriental) grandeur while eliding the lack of texts (the source of admiration of the ancient Oriental elsewhere). Second, technology—an area usually contrasted in Orientalist scholarship with the more typically "Oriental" accomplishments in the spiritual realms of the philosophical and contemplative—was emphasized as one of the ancient society's strengths. This strength, in contrast with present-day technological weakness, figured Spanish intervention as the source of technological backwardness. These characterizations work to accrue all the positive associations of Orientalism to ancient Filipino society, while displacing negative associations to the Spanish.

However, the picture that Rizal painted of Spanish history in the Philippines was yet more complicated, as we will see shortly. Both Rizal's *Morga* and de los Reyes's *History of Ilocos* painted two quite contrasting pictures of Spanish presence in the Philippines. On the one hand, they described how practices of greedy and cruel Spaniards destroyed pre-Hispanic society. On the other hand, they also praised quite highly the actions and nobility of two of Spain's earliest representatives in the islands: Legazpi and his grandson, Juan de Salcedo. This high praise requires explanation and reveals a more complicated narrative of propagandist history: a narrative that criticized some institutions of Spanish colonization, both religious and secular, but also claimed for itself the mantle of a particular kind of Spanish honor. In a move reminiscent of British Orientalists in South Asia, *ilustrados* painted an earlier glorious Spanish age to which they, not contemporary Spanish institutions, were the heirs.

Villains of Early Spanish Rule:
Encomenderos and Other Exploiters

As we have noted, Rizal acknowledged and contextualized pre-Hispanic systems of slavery and indebtedness. In Rizal's analysis, Spaniards had exacerbated those abuses, rather than ending them as was their mandate.

As Rizal wrote in a footnote that accompanied Morga's text on pre-Hispanic slavery, "[a]fter the conquest, the bad became worse. The Spanish made [people into] slaves without ... pretexts and without the Indios in question being in their jurisdiction, even selling them and removing them from their townships [*pueblos*] and islands."[46] When Morga wrote that the natives had been tyrannically subjugated to the *principalía* before the arrival of the Spanish, Rizal noted that "[w]e have already shown ... that in the change of master [*señor*], the status of Filipino pariahs went from bad to worse" and that those who were supposedly freed from slavery by the Spaniards "were later easily enslaved by the Spanish *encomenderos*."[47] The system of *encomiendas*, along with the galleon trade, was one of the main culprits in what Rizal described as the Spanish-induced economic ruin of the Philippines.

Under the *encomienda* system, common to Spanish possessions in the Americas and the Philippines, the crown granted a Spanish colonist (the *encomendero*) the right to collect tribute (tax) from the locals of a certain area (the *encomienda*) in supposed exchange for their military protection and education in the faith. In effect, the crown subcontracted the authority it had been granted by Rome. Rizal highlighted the extraordinarily coercive and exploitative nature of this arrangement, noting, for example, that the astounding wealth of a man mentioned by Morga "is not strange, because he was an *encomendero*," and that "it is well known how quickly many of those *encomenderos* made themselves extremely rich in few years, leaving colossal fortunes behind upon [their] death."[48] That fortune was accrued from tribute in the form of a combination of cash, kind, and labor, and Rizal quoted from another early chronicle to give a detailed example of such spoils.[49] Exploitation exceeded the bounds of the already exploitative law, for in Rizal's accounts, "some [*encomenderos*] were not content with tributes ..., but used false measures, [and] balances of a weight twice what was marked, demanding tributes in certain kind only and setting the price that pleased them."[50] Rizal wryly concluded that the term *encomienda* "took on an ironic significance" in the Philippines that was almost opposite from the meaning of the verb from which it was derived.[51] Whereas *encomendar* meant "to entrust," Rizal wrote that one might better say that land had "been distributed. ... [because] according to how the *Encomenderos* later behaved themselves, *to entrust* [*encomendar*] *a province* was like saying: to hand it over to someone's pillaging, cruelty, and greed."[52]

De los Reyes similarly attended to "the cruelties, abuses, arbitrary acts and injustices of the *Encomenderos*" as "[t]he most important, momentous, and talked-about question" of the history of the Philippines, in his *History of Ilocos, Volume Two*, which covers the history of the region beginning with the arrival of the Spaniards.[53] Comparing the record of *encomenderos* on both sides of the Pacific, de los Reyes noted that "in forty years, the Spanish with their atrocities killed more than fifteen million American Indians [*indios americanos*]," citing the work of Bartolomé de las Casas as an authority and thus aligning himself with the Spanish Dominican.[54] The natives of the Philippines, however, suffered even more than those of the Americas, for "the Spaniards who came to these islands were the worst"; and, unlike America, which had great mines to attract ambitious men of means, the Philippines became a destination "only [for] criminals that fled persecution by justice, exiles, military deserters, [and] those already dishonored in other parts."[55] He explained that sixteenth-century Spaniards "were short of good sentiments, and they learned cruelties in barracks and in ships of war."[56] In contrast with Rizal, who had a rich sense of the systematic and institutional character of the problem, de los Reyes blamed these individuals' (and their society's) moral failing. He had already mentioned to his reader, however, that he would be able to comment on the problem of the abuses of the *encomenderos* only "as far as official censorship allows."[57]

While *encomenderos* were the primary agents of the Filipinos' impoverishment, they were not the only institutions that had enriched themselves at the expense of the Filipinos and the Philippines. Friar orders, Rizal wrote, had also exploited the peoples and riches of the Philippines for their own advantage.[58] Discussing this, Rizal often made reference to the present, linking his comments to contemporary political struggles to release the grip of the friar orders on the Philippines. Even when the orders were not the subject of Morga's text, Rizal found opportunity to remark in his footnotes that "everywhere and in all religions the office of priest has been profitable [*productivo*]."[59] Rizal noted that Morga's description of how the friars' monasteries were supported showed that "already beginning in the first years, the missionary friars had very few opportunities to suffer for religion."[60] On the contrary, friar orders enriched themselves in shady ways; for example, Augustinians had collected rice ostensibly to support themselves, yet the amount was equivalent to "thirteen times more [per friar] than any Indio" consumed.[61] Those riches were paralleled by the present-day wealth of the orders. Rizal took the opportunity in his notes

to highlight the current real estate wealth of the Dominicans, whose properties included the land that Rizal's family managed and farmed and from
which they and the resident laborers (peasants) were evicted after a con-
tentious lawsuit.[62] Rizal noted that the Dominican order also had many
properties "in Hong-Kong, where it manages its millions, builds houses
continually, conducts business, acquires stocks, etc."[63] The historical abuses and injustices of the friar orders were thus occasions to comment on
contemporary abuses and injustices.

Rizal's notes showed that the legacy of the *encomiendas* and other extrac-
tive institutions was the destruction of pre-Hispanic wealth, industry, and
agriculture of the Philippines. In addition to losing skills and technology,
Filipinos had purposefully abandoned their mines and destroyed their own
industry, seeing that their wealth and goods made them targets for Spanish
avarice.[64] Forced labor was a major mechanism for this destruction, but it
was exacerbated by the forced disarmament of coastal communities, which
left them vulnerable to piracy, and by excessive taxation.[65] The situation
was so appalling, Rizal noted, that a Spaniard had written to his king that
"Indios . . . hung themselves, . . . left their wives and children, and, fed up
[with their situation], fled to the mountains."[66] According to Rizal, even
Philip II had noted similar death and destruction, writing that "many hang
themselves, and are left to die without food, and others drink poisons. And
there were even mothers who killed their children at birth."[67] This radical
depopulation was another feature of Spanish destruction: great towns had
disappeared while, in a contrast that Rizal noted with black humor, the
population of friars had grown considerably.[68]

With such brutal descriptions of Spaniards in the Philippines, it might
seem surprising that Rizal or de los Reyes had any kind words for the
Spanish at all. Yet in both Rizal's and de los Reyes's pieces, the early Spanish figures of Legazpi and Salcedo were portrayed not as dishonorable
scoundrels or even as unwarranted invaders. They were praised as heroic, brave, wise leaders, whose example ought to be emulated. Rizal also
praised some governmental structures of the early years of Spanish presence, and contrasted them with the much less desirable structures of the
present day. These sections painted a different kind of picture of the Spanish history in the Philippines, one in which early moments of worth and
reason were replaced by later greed, corruption, and incompetence. This
early golden era was a legacy that propagandists themselves could claim
to rescue from the decadent present-day Spaniards. Though present-day

Spaniards were in some sense descendents of those earlier noble men, they had betrayed their legacy.

Heroes of Early Spanish Rule: A Golden Age of Spanish Presence

Several propagandist texts painted a picture in which an early era of Spanish valor and dignity in the Philippines had been followed by decay. Though Spaniards were far from perfect in those early years, they were portrayed as having demonstrated at least some integrity that was absent from more recent Spanish administrations, and some were even written of as heroes. The Legazpi of the blood compact was claimed as the valid ancestor not so much of the modern Spanish state but of those seeking moral and respectful Spanish administration in the Philippines. Here, the propagandists appealed to an idea of a noble Spanish history of which they posed themselves as the legitimate heirs, and they called upon the current Spanish administration to live up to the honor of these early rulers.[69] While emissaries of the crown such as Legazpi had contracted treaties in the earlier years of Spanish presence in the islands, later state agents had not honored them. As Rizal lamented, "If only [the Spaniards] had always conducted themselves according to the letter of those contracts!"[70]

Juan de Salcedo was one of these early Spanish heroes singled out for particular praise by both de los Reyes and Rizal. Born in New Spain, Salcedo arrived in the Philippines in 1567 as a youth of eighteen. De los Reyes wrote that Salcedo had "been distinguished from the beginning by his heroic deeds," including campaigns in the Visayas (Panay and Mindoro) and Luzon (Zambales, Pangasinan, Batangas, Laguna, Cagayan, and Ilocos).[71] Of particular note, he had, in de los Reyes's words, secured a "treaty of alliance" with the Ilocanos after difficult battles and negotiations; helped lay a diplomatic foundation with local rulers for the founding of Manila in 1571; and had, in Rizal's words, "saved Manila from Li Mahong [*Limahón*]," a Chinese pirate who challenged Spanish sovereignty in Luzon for several months beginning in November of 1574.[72] Over a tenth of de los Reyes's *History of Ilocos, Volume Two* is dedicated to Salcedo's brief but glorious career in the Philippines, which ended with his death in 1576 at twenty-seven years of age.[73] De los Reyes's words tended toward the hagiographic when he noted that Salcedo had been a dashing young figure whose accomplishments, bravery, and fairness were unequaled: "Salcedo was lenient with captives and with the natives in general for whom he professed true affection;

extremely patient in calling for peace, but valiant and forceful in war; his extreme prudence and good tact contrasted greatly with his youthful age."[74] De los Reyes did not hesitate to call Salcedo the "discoverer" (*descubridor*) of Ilocos as well as of other places in the Philippines, a term that would seem to valorize the Spanish role in first contact, rather than examine it critically.[75] But this characterization makes sense when we consider the particular respect de los Reyes showed for Salcedo and the special relationship of mutual admiration that he claimed this conquistador had with the Ilocano people. De los Reyes wrote that Salcedo, "by his valor, unselfishness, generosity and love of the Ilocanos, was almost deified by them," and after his death and burial, locals had disinterred his skull, "certainly not as a trophy, but instead because of the great estimation in which they held such a magnanimous and generous man, as they were accustomed to doing in ancient times with notable men."[76] Salcedo's magnanimity was evidenced by his having left his inheritance in part to "the natives of his *encomienda* in Vigan," as both de los Reyes and Rizal noted, Rizal adding that he was "the only one we know of" who had done such a thing.[77] Rizal called Salcedo a "hero" who "was truly the intelligent arm of Legaspi, [and who] completely won the sympathies of the Filipinos, conquered enemies, and inclined them towards peace and friendship of the Spaniards, by [way of] his cunning, his excellent qualities, his talent and personal valor."[78] Salcedo was in both propagandists' accounts a heroic example of Spanish integrity, in contrast with which contemporaries' venality became more visible.

While a few early Spaniards were treated as heroic individuals in propagandist histories, more generally, those texts emphasized that the early years of Spanish rule had better institutional structures than later years did: governors were held accountable for their actions through procedures that were later abandoned. By emphasizing the relative impartiality of those early structures, they drew a contrast with the present day in which government posts were opportunities for personal enrichment, with little risk of being held accountable so long as one stayed on the right side of the powerful friar orders. When Morga described how officials had been annually reviewed by the high court as a matter of practice, Rizal noted that "[t]his good custom has been completely lost."[79] In the early days of Spanish colonization, even governors-general were not immune: at the end of their term they, too, were subject to a review called the *residencia* and were held responsible for their actions if they were judged to have abused their powers. Rizal told his readers to "[o]bserve how strictly governors were held accountable then. Some were imprisoned in Manila, one of whom . . . spent five years [imprisoned] in Fort Santiago."[80] In contrast, "this sacred *Residencia* [formal review] has [now] been lost; now no one is held strictly accountable for their conduct."[81] Juxtaposed to present-day arbitrary rule, the *residencia* of early years was a model of Spanish accountability.

Propagandist histories also favorably contrasted other policies and practices of early Spanish administration with those of the present day. Rizal gave examples of such lost practices: military service was often considered grounds for exemption from tribute; Cebu was founded "with all the rights and privileges of Spanish political cities and communities"; and a Jesuit had been sent to Spain to represent the Philippines whose mission "was similar to that of a deputy today, having, however, more importance, since he went on to be a kind of Advisor or representative close to the absolute Monarch of that era. Why was it possible to have a representative of the Philippines in that age and not now?"[82] In the early days of Spanish colonization, Rizal noted, Morga described elections in which every married native could vote, whereas "now, no longer do all Natives [*Naturales*] vote. . . . The resident [*vecino*] has lost his right to elect his leader."[83] Here, Rizal invoked the struggles of propagandists in Madrid to win representation and other citizenship rights for Filipinos, citing precedent in the history of Spanish administration. In short, Rizal took every opportunity to note the passages of Morga's text that described a government practice of the early years of Spanish administration that was better than current practices, especially noting when he found precedent for the rights and privileges for Filipinos that the propagandists advocated.

These narratives that praised early Spanish actions in the Philippines may seem counter to the harsh criticism that we have already considered of the Spanish era as a whole and of *encomenderos* in particular. We can see that they worked complementarily, however, if we keep in mind their function as *propaganda*, in the best sense: to enlighten, to motivate, to educate. Such historical narratives might speak simultaneously to Spaniard and Filipino, calling on each to take up the cause of right and reason in the contemporary Philippines, a cause that claimed both indigenous and Spanish patrimony.

Instructive and Cautionary History

When *ilustrado* histories lauded what Filipinos had accomplished despite Spanish incompetence and greed, they functioned not only to inspire

Filipinos to revere their own past but also to serve as a kind of cautionary history. The Spanish era, according to this history, had an age of
earlier glory, but had since fallen. In this view, the laws and lessons of
history—both "universal history" as well as the history of the Philippines
specifically—dictated that such an era of decline was unlikely to survive.
The Spanish era was not doomed by fate in the sense that Paterno's Ita
had been doomed to extinction by their belonging to an earlier era; it was
destined to be either wholly transformed or superseded because a weak,
decadent, decrepit state was vulnerable to outside forces as well as internal
ones. Scholars of propagandist accounts of Philippine history have long
discussed how propagandists used history to warn Spain of the inevitability of Philippine independence should Spain not reform.[84] We can see
evidence of two different kinds of historical narratives, which have conflicting logics but sometimes coexist in the pages of these texts. The first
of these narratives had Orientalist contours: it claimed a golden era of
the past (in this case, either the pre-Hispanic era or that of early Spanish
heroes) that required rescue from a decayed and decadent present, toward
a revived future. We have seen this narrative at work in both British Orientalist accounts of India and Indian nationalist appropriations of them.
Distinct from and to an extent running counter to this Orientalist shape of
history, these texts also emphasized that the history of Spanish domination
in the Philippines was one of *perpetual* contingency; this contingency suggested not the inevitability of the arc of golden era, decline, and renewal
but instead a continuing vulnerability of Spanish hegemony in the islands.

Both de los Reyes's *Historia de Ilocos* and Rizal's *Morga* can be read as
histories that were—with exceptions previously noted—generally skeptical about Spanish successes and accomplishments in the Philippines,
and quick to point out successes and accomplishments of Filipinos. In de
los Reyes's rendering, the history of the Spanish presence in Ilocos was
a history of mixed success at best. While he duly recorded certain mile-
stones of the spread of Spanish sovereignty in the province—much of the
work consists of notes about when townships were established and when
representatives of the Spanish administrations arrived, for example—he
repeatedly noted the failures of Spanish administration. This history was
filled with deception, conflict between clergy and civil authorities, failed
efforts to convert the highlander Igorot, and fruitless expeditions (subsi-
dized financially and militarily by locals) to find Igorot gold mines. At the
same time, and in spite of the general Spanish incompetence that these

events belied, the hardworking Ilocanos were shown to have sustained a healthy economy.

Spanish vulnerability and Filipino strength were underlined by both Rizal and de los Reyes when they noted that impressive "Spanish" military forces were often not, strictly speaking, Spanish. Where Morga mentioned how the Spanish monarchy had discovered and conquered remote parts of the world with Spanish *armadas* [navies] and people, Rizal included a note reminding the reader, "And we can add Portuguese, Italian, French, Greek, and even African and Oceanian, since the expeditions captained by Columbus and Magellan (the one Genoese and the other Portuguese), and others after them, though they were Spanish *armadas*, were nevertheless composed of different nationalities, and among them there were Blacks, Malukans and even people from the Philippines and Marianas."[85] Rizal found similar opportunities in Morga's references to Spanish victories in the Philippines, pointing out in one case that though Morga referred to a force of nine hundred "Spaniards," that force must have consisted in part of Filipinos.[86] De los Reyes, too, pointed out that the "Spanish" victories relied on native strength. Always the Ilocano patriot, he noted that while historians rightly gave credit to Salcedo for having saved Manila from Li-Mahong, that credit belonged not exclusively to him: "undoubtedly Ilocanos also have a share in the glory of having saved the city of Manila," for Salcedo fought with Ilocano soldiers.[87] Such praise for native soldiers' military contributions to Spain's campaigns in the islands echoed claims being made in *La solidaridad* that Filipino soldiers were demonstrating their patriotism in military campaigns in the south.[88] These claims implied that Spanish sovereignty in the islands was conditional and dependent: if it was Filipinos who gained and held the islands for Spain, then without their cooperation the islands might be lost.

Some of the most notable examples of cautionary history come in Rizal's *Morga*. As we have seen, when Rizal wrote about pre-Hispanic slavery, he generally mitigated what he thought was likely to be an overly negative perception of it by comparing it favorably with other kinds of slavery and with the *encomiendas* that the Spanish brought. But in one section, he wrote quite strikingly of this slavery in terms of it being a burdensome "yoke" and "tyranny":

Thanks to the social condition and number [of slaves] in that time, Spanish domination encountered such little resistance, and the *principales filipinos* [Filipino nobility or elite] easily lost their independence and liberty: the people, accustomed to the yoke, neither went to defend them from the invader nor went to fight for liberties that they had never enjoyed; for the people, it was a change of masters; the nobles, accustomed to tyrannizing by force, were obliged to accept the foreign tyranny, when it appeared more powerful than theirs, and finding neither love nor feelings of rebellion among the enslaved masses, they found themselves without arms and without strength.[89]

The bloodless victories of the Spanish, Rizal argued, were a result of neither benevolent terms offered by the Spanish nor a lack of valor, pride, or military capability among Filipinos. Instead, Spanish victories were uncontested because pre-Hispanic Filipino masses were oppressed by their rulers and so not inclined to fight against their rulers' enemies. Rizal more commonly extolled the virtues of pre-Hispanic society than he dwelt on its injustices. He pointed to this history of injustice and overthrow, however, as a displaced cautionary tale for contemporary tyrannical rulers: you may keep the Philippines with the consent of Filipinos, but if the masses turn against you under the leadership of another you will lose the islands. The same cautionary tale might have another message for those under the tyrant's rule: this tyrant may fall to a challenger if you withhold your support, but beware the tyrant that follows.

Rizal underscored the contingency of Spanish sovereignty and the inevitability of the destiny that awaited it should it continue down the path of injustice, continuing:

Between a people with a tyrannical aristocracy and another with an unbridled democracy, there are well-balanced peoples. The one and the other easily fall under the domination of the first foreign invader, the first because of weakness and the second because of anarchy. Many of the colonies that are retained thanks to a systematic brutalization of the inhabitants by one class, caste, or race that surrounds itself with glittery, substance-less prestige, and that to maintain itself, has to defend itself absurdly in order to be consistent with a false principle, will without doubt end somewhat like the tyrannized peoples, like Persia, India, etc., succumbing before the first foreigner.[90]

Rizal prophesied the end of unjust colonial rule not because of the particular strength of the Filipino people who would rise up against it but because tyranny was inherently weak, vulnerable to another's usurpation. Such rule would, "like Persia, India, etc." be overthrown by another empire's challenge; the Spanish Philippines had become like a decadent Oriental despotism. In his notes to Morga's text, then, Rizal implied that history predicted Spain's likely fall should she continue to obstruct rather than assist the Philippines in the path of progress.

In contrast, de los Reyes's *Historia de Ilocos* presented a cautionary history that focused on how the institutions of the Spanish state were vulnerable to those supposedly ruled by it, rather than vulnerable to foreign powers. The most remarkable section of the work, and perhaps the most remarkable example of cautionary history in propagandist writings, is a long and vivid story of the rise and fall of Diego Silang.[91] In de los Reyes's account, Silang was a politically astute, strategically deft, and courageous leader who took advantage of the crisis of authority surrounding the British attack on Spanish sovereignty in the Philippines in 1762, part of the worldwide conflagration that was to usher in the era of British ascendancy.[92] In de los Reyes's telling, Silang was a patriot both of Ilocos and of the Philippines, more broadly, who had two overarching objectives. First, he aimed to drive both British and Spanish forces from the archipelago by playing each off the other and uniting the people. No less ambitiously, he also aimed to bring about a full-scale class revolution in the Philippines, liberating the lower classes from their *principalía*. For de los Reyes, this was neither a simple premodern peasant insurrection, nor an effort to restore traditional authority from invading usurpers, nor the work of a power-hungry messianic leader; it was nothing short of a complete modern and anticolonial revolution, grounded in principles of freedom and liberty.

In presenting de los Reyes's account, my point, as elsewhere, is neither to affirm nor to dispute its veracity but to show what kinds of political meanings it produced. Why might de los Reyes have dwelt on the revolt led by Silang? First and foremost, it was a story of rebellion against Spanish sovereignty in the modern age that was, at least in de los Reyes's telling, reasonably close to being successful. This rebellion was made possible by English aggression, and so the story served as an instructive lesson in how two European powers—one the established sovereign and the other the aggressor—could be played off each other by a local leader. Second, as Silang reminded his forces and de los Reyes reminded his reader, Spanish

sovereignty depended on the peoples' cooperation, and "if we unite ourselves as brothers, the Spanish could do nothing against us."[93] Third, while
the rebellion ultimately faltered because of what de los Reyes called Ilocanos' "fanatical" Catholicism and respect for the Church, de los Reyes
emphasized the initial success that Silang had in mobilizing his rebel
forces *against* the parish priests and church authorities.[94] Fourth, similar to
how Silang managed to rally forces that were fervently Catholic against the
Catholic authorities, Silang also successfully usurped Spanish government
authorities while claiming to defend the Spanish cause.

De los Reyes's telling of these events highlighted the conditions that
favored the rebellion: the numerical superiority of the Ilocanos united
against the Spanish and the power of appeals to freedom and justice among
people living in a condition that resembled serfdom. At the same time,
de los Reyes emphasized Silang's ability both to exploit those advantages
and strategically to overcome his disadvantages: his forces in this struggle
against Spain were drawn from among people whose zealous faith had
led them to hold the clergy and church officials in high regard, while the
Spanish and English forces had the considerable weight of well-established
military states behind them. Overall, the story presented not just a series
of illustrative lessons in political strategy but an exercise for the political
imagination in which the reader was invited to imagine the possibilities of
what had been, what might have been, and what might yet be.

Briefly and broadly, the story's events as de los Reyes related them can
be outlined thus: In 1762, when British forces had seized Manila from the
Spanish, Diego Silang called for the people of Vigan to gather together to
defend the Catholic faith and Spanish sovereignty *against* local Spanish
civil authorities who, he claimed, were ready to surrender to the British.
The British, meanwhile, sought local support by promising tax relief to
peasants. Silang successfully scared off the local civil authority, demanding two things of the Catholic authority (the prelate) in return for handing
him power: (1) that he proclaim his support for Silang's supporters' actions
(against the Spanish civil authorities) and (2) that he concede the tax relief
that the British had promised those who would rebel against the Spanish.
When the prelate refused, Silang's supporters moved against the clergy as
a whole, still *in the name of defending the Spanish cause and faith* against the
threatening English. This set off a confrontation between men mobilized
by Silang and others mobilized by a Catholic authority (the provisor), in
which the latter eventually prevailed but only after the former had briefly

effectively taken over Vigan, raised more forces by appealing to the down-trodden to rise against their oppressors, and for a while maintained an effective defense against the Catholic authorities' forces. Silang had also appealed to the British for aid, from whence arose accusations that he had acted against the Spanish and in the aid of the British.

De los Reyes began his telling of Silang's story by putting it in the context of English attacks on Spanish sovereignty in the Philippines and what he judged to be the feeble response of many Spanish officials. De los Reyes noted that when the British attacked Manila, "the *indios* demonstrated heroism," such that the English, recognizing that *indios* "were the most formidable defenders of the Spanish cause," sought to curry favor with them.[95] The Spanish, on the other hand, were not so patriotic or valiant. Pointedly quoting the Spanish Jesuit source, de los Reyes noted that, "as Father Baranera says," Spanish leaders, who "were in collusion with the English, ordered the *indios* who had fought so valorously [to go back] to their townships."[96] Having sent the valorous *indios* away from their defense of Manila, Spanish authorities were not to be trusted in defending the Spanish cause, for "history demonstrates that many Spanish leaders did not act very loyally towards their own *patria* during the English invasion, which made the English think that the Spaniards they encountered in the Philippines *were not Spaniards from Spain*," an assessment de los Reyes attributed to Spanish author Sinibaldo de Mas.[97]

In this context, de los Reyes told his readers, Silang presented himself as the true defender of Spain, against the governor (*alcalde*) of Vigan who Silang claimed was planning to surrender to the English. And though the governor never got the chance to prove or disprove this assertion, because Silang seized power, de los Reyes noted that once the governor ceded power to Silang, he "fled the province."[98] Against this background of Spanish cowardice, de los Reyes wrote, it became understandable that Silang could portray himself "as a defender of the Spanish cause."[99] However, Silang's true goal was not to defend Spain, nor to work for the English, as he at one time claimed and as many Spanish authors adjudged; rather, for de los Reyes, Silang was an *autonomista* [autonomist] who wanted "the independence of Ilocos," or, as he later and more broadly asserted, "to throw the English and Spanish out of the Philippines."[100] And while de los Reyes marked these aims as Silang's, he also conjured the specter of such a movement being repeated. Silang and the purported bid for independence stood as an example, perhaps not to be emulated, but at least to be contemplated.

De los Reyes's telling of the story focused on the actions of Silang, making a full and admirable character out of a rather thin historical record. Silang was a heroic individual, "on the whole, one of the most important figures that stand out in Philippine records," a "gigantic figure," "intelligent, educated, courageous."[101] No *individual* ever effectively challenged Silang. Instead, it was the weight of the combined forces against him, aided by fortune, which led to his downfall. Silang

> had a great talent and singular political sagacity. The [Catholic] Religion was professed almost to the point of fanaticism by the Ilocanos and proof of this was that they did not dare to kill the parish priest, and because of excommunication they finally lost their enthusiasm for serving Silang; and notwithstanding, the latter had succeeded in taking the Bishop and the parish priests prisoner. The same Silang knew that the Ilocanos feared the Spanish government very much, and were enemies of risks and change; however, the rebel leader succeeded in shaking off the yoke of the Spaniards, initially using the leverage of the most influential Spaniards themselves. . . .
>
> The great Filipino politician succeeded in mastering his most fearful and powerful enemies: the fanaticism and timidity of the locals . . . and the influence of the Religious and the Spanish.[102]

Thus the power of the Spanish was not due to Spanish forces or the clergy but the "fanatical" Catholic faith of the Ilocanos. The true battle was between Silang, the sole individual historical agent, and the influence that European institutions had on the Ilocanos. This challenge Silang met with ingenious skill of manipulation: in de los Reyes's description, Silang skillfully used the people's faith against both Spanish state and church forces.

In de los Reyes's telling, however, Silang also aimed at a total political and social revolution, because he struggled against "the power of the *principales*."[103] Silang's true goals, de los Reyes speculated, probably included that of "liberating . . . the plebe from the hateful tyranny of the *babaknáng* (indigenous *principales*)."[104] Silang conducted his campaign for a revolution, understanding "that the social constitution had to be completely transformed," and he endeavored "to raise the *kailanes* (the lower class) against the *babaknáng* (*principales*)."[105] This complete social revolution required not only military prowess on the part of Silang but also the ability to educate the people so that they would see their own true position in the social order.

Part of Silang's brilliance, in de los Reyes's telling, is that he was able to prepare the minds of the people for this true revolution, educating the people and calling them to action at the same time; he was, in this sense, a true propagandist. To this end, "[t]he envoys of Silang preached democratic ideas, and they said that the *principales* enriched themselves at the expense of the poor whom they oppressed with illegal levies, usurious loans and fraud, which was true."[106] Silang issued a decree in which he promised "to liberate . . . the people from the heavy yoke of the *principales*, . . . firmly telling the *principales* that the death knell had sounded for their privileges and abuses. . . . And finally, he invited the disenfranchised people [*pueblo bajo*] to appoint a local leader from among the common class [*clase popular*], that would guarantee their liberties."[107] In evaluating the overall successes of Silang, despite his eventual fall, de los Reyes noted that "[t]he indigenous *principales* always, even now (and moreso, earlier), have held the inferior classes as slaves; and notwithstanding, Silang, accomplishing earlier what would be repeated much later in the great French Revolution, succeeded in raising the people against their oppressors: the indigenous *principalía*."[108] Silang was a liberator ahead of his time; and, according to de los Reyes, "his deeds seem to be inspired by the theories of Voltaire, Rousseau, Diderot and other philosophers [*filósofos*] that later would produce the events of the Paris Commune."[109]

According to de los Reyes, then, in this hero's aims were entwined nothing less than anticolonial revolution and class revolution, anticipating both American and French revolutions. Silang's biggest obstacles were the peoples' attachment to the very forms of influence that he was trying to dislodge—the Spanish and the *principalía*—and their fervent faith, which prevented them from acting against agents of the Catholic Church. In other words, as de los Reyes judged it, the radical aims of Silang were ultimately frustrated by the people's lack of ideological preparation, a preparation that de los Reyes himself, with his writings, sought to provide.[110] Silang's story, then, was illustrative and enlightening both as a lesson in what needed to be done (prepare the minds of the people) and as a lesson in how a leader might strategically accomplish his own aims, with the aid of the people whom he rallied despite their antagonisms to his true aims. Leadership, in other words, might require strategic duplicity. This extraordinary story was told in the pages of a book on history. It is perhaps the boldest example of cautionary history in propagandist writings.

Conclusion: Nationalism and Exclusive History

Historians and ethnologists drew textual data about pre-Hispanic culture and history in the Philippines from sixteenth- and seventeenth-century accounts, many produced by or based on reports of missionaries. These accounts were often written for a royal or papal audience—that is, they were written to report back to ecclesiastic and royal officials who would determine the policy of church and crown in the East. Though *ilustrados* often emphasized the bias *against* Philippine *indígenas* in these accounts, Scott has suggested that "missionary reports intended for European audiences are often distorted by the desire to prevent converts from appearing like naked savages."[111] Some of these chronicle sources were produced in political circumstances and for political ends that shaped the content of their message; that content then became available and useful for authors who centuries later had a different kind of political interest in the subject. As Joan-Pau Rubiés has argued, these accounts were produced under some "peculiar" conditions.[112] These particular conditions were partially responsible for the contours that would make the accounts attractive sources for *ilustrado* rewritings of Spanish history.

Rubiés shows that most of the chronicle sources were produced during a period of intensified political conflicts among Spanish and Catholic forces in Asia and that those struggles in turn shaped the chronicles' narratives. For example, Dominicans and Franciscans challenged Jesuit missionary monopoly in China and Japan; this conflict shaped what is referred to as the "Chinese rights controversy," which pitted Jesuits against their Dominican and Franciscan adversaries who claimed they were too tolerant of local heretical Chinese practices.[113] That controversy was political as much as it was theological. The resulting accounts shaped by those controversies "could at times be well informed . . . , but violent theological polemics totally unbalanced the image of China they transmitted to Spain and Europe."[114] A related and complicating political factor around the same period was that the Castilian and Portuguese crowns were temporarily joined (1580–1640), though their imperial institutions remained distinct. Distrust, enmities, and contestation between Castilian and Portuguese dominions and agents complicated analyses of "Spanish" and Catholic projects in the

Philippines and elsewhere in the region.[115] Not coincidentally, the same period—the late sixteenth through mid-seventeenth centuries—brought the earliest major European-language textual sources for studying pre-Hispanic and contact-era societies in the Philippines.

Those early sources, then, were produced of and through political contestations, and their accounts of the early years of Spanish presence in the Philippines were necessarily colored by their authors' structural positions: whether they were members of one of the competing church institutions of the Jesuits, Dominicans, or Franciscans, or whether they were of the competing institutions of the Spanish or Portuguese crowns (who might in turn be either allied with or opposed to the Jesuits, Dominicans, or Franciscans on any given policy or project). In these circumstances, the significant political antagonisms were not thought to be Spanish versus Filipino or Catholic versus pagan, but instead Castilian versus Portuguese, Jesuit versus Dominican, or Jesuit versus Franciscan.[116] With these the axes of contestation, a text's subtext could be about the Jesuits, in comparison to the work of the Dominicans or Franciscans, for example; or it could be a comment on the success of Castilian-based institutional efforts, in comparison with Portuguese-based ones.

Ilustrado histories largely obscured the particular conditions under which these early sources were produced, and that work of obscuring produced more powerful meaning. In other words, though *ilustrado* histories are revisions of earlier (Spanish) royal and (Catholic) ecclesiastical accounts, the revisions do not simply challenge the veracity of those early Spanish accounts or mine them for data that could be stripped of bias. They do both of these things, but they also make use of the value judgments contained in those works that were more complementary to native society and critical of friar orders. Positive value judgments became all the more notable in *ilustrado* accounts precisely because *ilustrado* authors could presume that their own readers will think that the "Spanish" or "Catholic" chroniclers would be predisposed to view native society critically. Conversely, critical comments about any of the specific friar orders were taken as general evidence of friar orders' greed and corruption, rather than as artifacts of an intra-Church squabble.

Such appropriations were productive, exactly because they avoided specifying *what* kind of history was being appropriated. The complexities of the political struggles that produced friar chronicles—complexities of which the *ilustrados* were likely at least aware, given contemporary intra-Church struggles in the Philippines—melted away in their accounts, but the language left behind, language of judgment (whether praise or condemnation), became redeployed with different political actors. While history's textual sources were available in this particular way for propagandist work, selective recontextualization of textual sources was hardly specific to history in particular as a genre. The bulk of this chapter has focused not on the unique methods or data of the discipline of history but instead on how the propagandists' historical writings relied on the kinds of methods, data, and presumptions that we have seen at work in ethnology, folklore, and linguistics.

As we have seen, *ilustrado* and propagandist histories focused on narratives that emphasized two eras of the distant past as models of an ethical social state, models that needed updating but whose intrinsic values needed to be recognized by the present in order to reinvigorate and renew its future: a pre-Hispanic era, on the one hand, and an early Spanish-Catholic era, on the other. The pre-Hispanic era was constructed in part with the aid of Orientalist and anthropological methods, as earlier chapters have considered. The account of the early Spanish-Catholic era, however, employed Orientalism in a different sense: it reproduced the contours of some Orientalist accounts of great ancient pasts in need of rescue from lesser present-day descendents. In the case of de los Reyes's Silang, a more recent historical event was rendered as fully modern and, despite ambiguous evidence, as a movement that aimed for complete political independence from Spain. Silang presented a model of a modern, rational leader who strategically used his knowledge of the peoples' less-rational loyalties and proclivities to pursue his aims, including their liberation. In de los Reyes's hands, in particular, history became (again) an opportunity to critique the present.

These propagandist histories, then, were based on varied models and pointed toward quite distinct possible futures. They articulated future possibilities that would reclaim the ethical glories of pasts. If in many of those futures Spanish sovereignty remained possible, it was always figured as insecure, reinforcing the message that Spanish presence in the islands continued by the grace of the people.

Politics and the Methods
of Scholarly Disciplines

I N THE PRECEDING CHAPTERS, WE have seen how young intellectuals of the Philippines took up "modern" forms of knowledge. The
cosmopolitan scholarly modernity of which the young intellectuals of the
Philippines partook rarely belonged to their colonizers in any particular
recognizable way, as they were well aware. They put modern knowledges
to use to recover the undocumented precolonial past of the Philippines
but also to critique the colonial present and provide a foundation for the
future. More specifically, this work has attended to how scholarly techniques associated with Orientalism and anthropology had political lives
much more varied than their standard histories suggest. Particular genres,
modes, disciplines, foci, languages, terminologies, and concepts had their
own possibilities, exploited (unevenly) by Filipino authors.

Ethnology, especially, but also the related practices of ethnography,
philology, and even folklore, offered, via the language of "race" (considered
as both biological and cultural), a naturalized basis for conceiving of different ethnolinguistic groups of the Philippines as all comprising a unified
people. This move had two appealing features. First, race was the language
of what was called "prehistory," or the history of human collectivities
without written record. Those "prehistorical" histories were of migration, conflict, contest, mingling, adoption, and adaptation; sometimes
bellicose, sometimes peaceful, but regardless the peoples *acted*—not as
individuals, but as peoples (or races). The language of race invited a kind
of historical imagination in which the inhabitants of the islands before
the arrival of the Spaniards were collective protagonists and actors, rather
than occupants of an ahistorical pagan world that would only be brought
into history by Catholicism's arrival. As we have seen, such a narrative did
not always dislodge Catholicism from history's apex, but it allowed for
indigenous and popular historical agency.

ound, the language of ethnology, with its stories of peopling and descent, articulated a narrative of natural history that enacted exclusions similar to those of Catholicism, but based on "science" rather than religion. The naturalized ancient *people* of the Philippines, the ancients from whom the *indígenas* of the Spanish Philippines descended, were conceived of in different ways. Some thought of them as one branch of a larger Malayan family, others as the product of Malay-Negrito mixing. Either way, they were taken to be distinguishable, whether by physical, linguistic, or other markers, from the supposed ancestors of the Muslim peoples to the south and west, and from the ancestors of the highland animists with whom they might nevertheless share some common ancestry. Ethnology, then, reproduced Catholicism's borders, marking highland peoples as outside of this people in the present but potential members in the future, and excluding contemporary Muslims entirely.

Ethnography, ethnology, folklore, and linguistics offered techniques to identify and value specific qualities of pre-Hispanic societies—now conceived of as part of a unified ancestral people. Pre-Hispanic people had not just acted or spoken; they had a religion, morals, industry, technology, and medicine. The accomplishments of ancestral society were recovered and reconceived in secular terms afforded by ethnological science rather than according to how closely they approximated Catholicism. Folklore was part of the material from which "prehistory" could be reconstructed. But it had more particular uses as well: Folklore's data—contemporary practices—allowed it to be a venue not just for finding clues about the past but also for critiquing the present. The data and methods of linguistics suggested a new way to spell old languages, which emphasized their difference from Spanish. This controversial move became a subject of public debate in which the status of the local's relationship to Spain and to the wider world was at issue. Though not the explicit subject of debate, the new spelling in fact hid Spanish roots incorporated into modern languages. History (of the Spanish era) offered the opportunity to criticize the contemporary Spanish state and the state of society under it, via contrast with both pre-Hispanic society (as established via ethnology, folklore, and linguistics) and early, more noble Spanish administration in the islands. History also was an opportunity to present scenarios of the fragility of Spanish sovereignty, safely historically displaced. Finally, a particularly Orientalist trope of history allowed Filipinos to claim the patrimony of the earlier more noble Spanish history for themselves.

Each of the forms of study around which the preceding chapters are based—ethnology, folklore, linguistics, and history—had different constellations of origins. I say "constellations" because none of these practices can be said to have a single beginning point without unduly and misleadingly prioritizing some influences, causes, and conditions of possibility over others. While the methods and terms of many of these studies "originated"—though even here it is difficult to use such language—in the German-, French-, and English-language scholarly worlds, these studies were transformed into Filipino knowledges.[1] That transformation from European model to Filipino product was not just the result of local content being injected into a European mold. The models themselves were put to Filipino uses and defined by local political contexts and projects (always connected to the global). Nonetheless, the specific work the models performed depended on who was wielding them, in what place, for what purposes, and in conversation and contestation with what other struggles.

These young men responded to certain Spanish and Catholic discourses about the Philippines, its peoples, and its government. Not all of them set out to lay the scholarly foundations for a Filipino "nation" as such, and the different texts and their authors did not always speak in unison. They often differed on who the Filipino people comprised and on what basis, what their roots were, what problems and possibilities they faced in the present, and what their future was or should be. Despite these differences, when taken as a whole (and only when taken as a whole), the writings made it possible to think with certainty and a sense of inevitability of "Filipinos" as a distinct ethnic people with ancient roots, an emerging modernity, and a political future. Collectively, they enabled thinking about "Filipino" as an ethnicity in ways that would become useful for nationalist politics, even though the "nation" as such is rarely invoked in these writings.

Others have studied the lives of scholarly disciplines in colonial contexts. In the Philippines, as elsewhere, disciplines were translated and renegotiated, producing themselves as hybrid discourses. Accounts of modern scholarly disciplines in colonial India, in particular, are organized around an actual or imagined confrontation between "Western" (modern) and "traditional" (Indian) knowledge, even when the opposition is resolved.[2] But in the Philippines, unlike in colonial Bengal, scientific disciplines were not so clearly brought by and in the terms of the colonizers, only available to the colonized when they "spilled over their colonial embankments."[3] The colonized of the Philippines sometimes encountered scholarly disciplines via flows of knowledge and ideas in which their colonizers were only tangential. Further, the scholarly disciplines taken up by these "natives" of the Philippines were not the instruments of colonial rule. Their use as instruments of colonial rule was being developed by other Europeans elsewhere, but not significantly by the Spanish in the Philippines.

In the Philippines, then, the same questions of what we might call "translation" do not apply as they do in India. When de los Reyes challenged the Church, for example, he did so not as an adherent of native religion—despite how deeply he cared about and valued what he could recover of native religion—but as a rational critic of Church obscurantism and abuses. That this was so makes his critique no less native. So long as we try to classify their knowledge production in terms of "Western" versus "native," we will miss its meaning. Even if conceived of as a matter of hybridity and interaction (transculturation), models of the appropriation of "Western" knowledge generally presume too clear a break between indigenous and foreign knowledge to be helpful in thinking about the late nineteenth-century Philippines.[4]

There is likely no *standard* model of modern scholarly knowledges' adoption and adaptation in the colonial world. Here, as elsewhere, the politics of scholarly knowledge depend on the political associations of that knowledge, its implementation in techniques of governing, and the field of social formations in which it is articulated. Indian intellectual history presents a particularly interesting and rich case, but not necessarily an exemplary one, for here a particularly formidable set of (indigenous) scholarly interpretive traditions met with a set of modern scholarly knowledges that were both *of* the colonizer and highly instrumentalized by the colonial state. In the Philippines, the modern scholarly knowledges (not clearly of the colonizer) were challenging predominantly (Spanish) Catholic ones and were strikingly absent from the state's repertoire. It may be more helpful, instead, to conceive of the "Western," knowledges themselves as collections of contested moments and variegated discourses, products of various kinds of hybridizing processes, and to look at their arrival in the colony as only one of many moments of transformation and translation.

In studying the histories of knowledges, then, perhaps too much emphasis is placed on large-scale transformations and dramatic confrontations rather than smaller-scale adaptations. Following Michel Foucault, histories of scholarly disciplines sometimes tend toward marking major shifts and discontinuity, in particular the rupture between early modern and modern.[5] More specifically, the history of anthropology, as the science of man and of the origins of his physical and cultural diversity, is often dated to the eighteenth century.[6]

As we have seen in these pages, however, major shifts are unevenly felt and older discourses not entirely displaced, a point Ann Stoler attributes to Foucault himself in a lecture on race.[7] In the Philippines, an older, early modern (Catholic) civilizational mode of thinking about peoples and difference overlapped with a newer one conceived in terms of "races." Further, this case highlights that it is in the smaller-scale transformations that some of the most salient political allegiances of scholarship are defined. Scholarly innovation, even as significant as Darwin's, could be put to use in a variety of different ways politically.[8] Histories of scholarly disciplines may be too quick to attribute political outcomes to abstract concepts without attending to how variously those concepts are actually used.

Further, this case shows that while the data, methods, and presumptions of some modern disciplines are established by the late nineteenth century, we need to attend carefully to the continuities among and differences between those times and the present. Assuming too close a continuity between contemporary disciplines and their late nineteenth-century counterparts may incur some of the same dangers as those John Christie identifies with presuming continuity between modern and early modern knowledges: "terms such as psychology and sociology are names of [contemporary] disciplines which possess coherent intellectual and institutional identities, . . . it is therefore misguided to think in terms of entities such as '18th-century psychology and sociology,' if neither the names nor the requisite disciplinary identities exist as such."[9] By the same token, we ought to recognize the anachronism in presuming contemporary anthropology to be a direct descendent of nineteenth-century linguistics, archeology, cultural and physical anthropology. The term "anthropology" was not always and consistently thought of as encompassing subfields as it is today; "cultural" and "physical" anthropology were not established as such as fields, and in the mix of practices and genres related to cultural and physical anthropology one would find, besides the practices that fit more comfortably into either of those today like ethnology, ethnography, folklore, physiognomy, and natural history, also fields like ethology, zoology, (popular) psychology, popular literature, and sociology.[10] The solution here is neither to dismiss continuities between these nineteenth-century sciences and contemporary anthropology nor to overstate them. Instead,

POLITICS AND THE METHODS OF SCHOLARLY DISCIPLINES

the aim is to indicate "potentially continuous or generative histories, or, to put it in slightly more up-to-date terms, [to indicate] real lines of genealogical descent for the fully formed disciplinary identities which emerge" in the twentieth century.[11]

In pursuing such genealogical work, one must attend precisely to the references to authors that are marginal and forgotten, as well as the more familiar and canonical, in order to appreciate how contingent was the world of intellectual and scholarly engagement. Major works and authorities were marked as such, to be sure, and their authority conscripted when useful. But these practices partook of fields whose boundaries were not clearly defined, such that no single authority monopolized model or method, and instead a broad variety of studies, data, ideas, and speculations could collectively constitute one of any number of possible paths to be followed. Further, the political lives of scholarly ideas, principles, and methods are worked out as much by minor figures as major ones.

Though some practitioners of the emerging human sciences held institutionally secure positions, the world of practitioners that we have encountered was variously professional and amateur. So it was not just the absence of Spanish scholarship in these areas that encouraged Filipinos to step in; the relative fluidity between amateur and scholarly authority—a fluidity enabled in part by the prior exclusions of class—was a medium through which Filipinos could pass from insular to universal, or from *indio* to scholar.

Nineteenth-century Indian nationalists imagined their nation's history as one of decline from ancient greatness in part because this narrative had been established in modern scholarly terms by (especially British and German) Orientalists. Such an imagined history of decline was not preconstructed for *ilustrados* and propagandists of the Philippines, for they were thought to belong to a "people without history" and had no surviving "original" texts to which they could appeal.[12] As we have seen, however, they worked to establish a similar narrative, using ethnographic, ethnological, folkloric, and linguistic techniques to reconstruct the pre-Hispanic past, often in terms that emphasized its accomplishments and contested inaccurate and defamatory existing accounts. Another significant opportunity that Orientalism presented Filipinos, in particular and in distinction from their Indian counterparts, was the fact that no Jones, Müller, or Anquetil had made the ancient or contemporary Philippines a central subject of study; and, though it was a site of interest to current

questions of German anthropology, the most imposing intellectual figures of the day were not doing original research on the Philippines. This
is another reason why the Filipinos could with such confidence enter
into debates and research in modern sciences with relatively little self-
consciousness about their marginal status: they were not competing, as
were the Indians, with a strongly supported and relatively distinguished
record of European scholarship about their own history.

Outside of South Asia, the most salient comparisons—in particular
for the connections between Orientalism and emerging anthropological
thought—may be with German and other European nationalist movements, many of which did, like the Philippines, emerge from under
crumbling empires. German Romantics found in Orientalism opportunities to identify and theorize the unique properties and position of the
German nation as a direct descendent of the ancient conquering forefa-
thers of both Europe and Asia.[13] The great ancient Oriental civilization(s)
played a role in the aggrandizement of the modern German nation, for
through association the latter partook in the greatness of the former
without the stigma of association with their fallen present-day Asian
descendents.[14] In contradistinction to (the Enlightenment of) Napoleonic France, German Romantics asserted particular national genius and
quality and sought its substance in the remnants of a glorious past. Those
remnants were available (in translation) in ancient Indian civilization, as
found in surviving texts, and in the cultural survivals of ancient Germany,
as found in the *Volk*'s stories, songs, language, and poetry. Here the work of
the brothers Grimm and Herder comes to mind. In the hands of Grimm,
comparative philology—linguistic science—turned into a method of particular use for defining the nation (through language) and codifying its
form (in the dictionary). Such linguistic work had its parallels—as well as
complicated associations, which themselves became liabilities—in some
of the linguistic work of the *ilustrados* and propagandists. In both Germany and the Philippines, linguistic work "helped to unify spelling, [was]
used to purify the language of foreign (and as such, resented) intrusions
and to spread a unified standard form among all its speakers"; and in these
battles, in both places, the "k" had a particular symbolic role to play.[15]

Empire was a condition of possibility for German nationalism—both
aging, shrinking Austro-Hungary, on the one hand, and Napoleon's imperial "Greater France," on the other—but within Europe, these empires
were not themselves focused on racial typologies. Race was, however, a

salient category for the nationalists opposed to Napoleonic empire, for it was through race that Germany and Germans could be conceived of as a transhistorical category, independent of the political institutions that had either encompassed or divided German peoples through the preceding centuries. In similar ways, race operated to unite "Filipinos" across linguistic divisions and yet separate them from the wider world of "Malayan" peoples in Southeast Asia as well as from "others" living in the Philippines.

The German Romantics preceded later ethno-nationalisms across Europe of the nineteenth century, which were especially apparent along old empires' frayed edges. In the nineteenth century, new nations were emerging from the former subject peoples—not just peoples subject to the Austro-Hungarian throne but also those subject to the Ottoman and Russian empires.[16] These nationalisms adapted many of the techniques of the German Romantics without feeling the need to claim a similar connection with ancient Oriental civilization. New in these nationalisms, however—of Greece and the Balkans, for example—was a complicated appeal to the nation's place in historical time.[17] On the one hand, the nation was always conceived of as ancient—predating the empire from whose belly it was emerging—and yet it was also understood to be emerging from the antiquated and into the modern. This national modern was one that used cosmopolitan science toward the ends of national development and regeneration, developing national orthographies in the service of both documenting the fading traditional stories of the elders and educating the youth for a literate, learned, and modern future citizenry.[18]

The nineteenth century also brought a different kind of national modern transformation. While the empires of England and France were just hitting their stride, the decaying empires' hearts—in Turkey, Russia, and, we might add, Spain—were fitting themselves, often uncomfortably and awkwardly, in national clothes.[19] In these transformations, declining empire used some of the same tools of linguistic and folkloric sciences employed to build emerging nations. As we have seen, folklore in Spain was simultaneously about preserving remnants of the past at the same time that its study was understood to be important for promoting practical, modern knowledge among the populace.

Each of these decaying empires transforming themselves into modern nations—Turkey, Russia, and Spain—had their own particular and fraught relationship with Orientalism, however. If the Ottoman Empire was the quintessential Oriental empire in decay, then the emerging modern

Turkish nation had to contend with its Oriental (perhaps despotic) history.[20] Russia's Orientalism was part of its bid to be a modern *European* nation, for like other modern European nations (France, England), it could be shown to have its own subject Orientals in its empire.[21] Spain's Orientalist anxieties were different ones. Spain had been on the southwestern "Oriental" periphery of Europe (especially protestant Europe) for some time, in a position in some respects similar to Russia's on the Eastern "Oriental" periphery. Spain's status as premodern was cemented in part through its own dubiously "Oriental" past—its Moorish and Jewish history. Part of Spain's becoming a modern nation in the nineteenth century was through its study of its own "Oriental" past. Thus Orientalism in Spain was largely focused on its own history and on its immediate neighbors and relations in the Mediterranean world, more than on its remote Eastern possessions.[22]

Nineteenth-century scholarly nationalisms were of necessity articulated in languages of Orientalism and emerging anthropological practices, not just because those were the matrices in which peoples could be understood to be related to each other, but because they were the languages in which one could even speak of peoples or identify them with histories. What is more notable is the variety of things that those languages could be made to say. This work has traced how Orientalist and emerging anthropological methods, presumptions, and narratives were employed in the context of the late colonial Philippines and how the narratives that resulted had potential political uses—uses in some respects quite contrary to others to which similar narratives were put. To understand what a text does, Quentin Skinner tells us, is to understand how it both engages in, but also pushes, the "ideological conventions" of which it partakes.[23] All the texts we have considered engage in, but also push on and against, ideas from various kinds of discursive formations—ethnological theory, liberal political principles, nineteenth-century Spanish republican propaganda, and Catholic classical history. Further, each of these discursive formations in some sense traveled from other historical, political, and geographical contexts to arrive in the late nineteenth-century Spanish Philippines. It may be the case that the terms of any of these discursive formations were made more malleable both by the combination of multiple discursive formations and by the travels from one context to another in which they were made to be meaningful.

Too easily, if we seek to localize intellectual thought and scholarly disciplines, we think of linguistic boundaries in national terms. When differences between French or German intellectual history are noted, for example, sometimes unclear is whether the comparison is being made between the scholarly literatures of France and Germany (the nation-states) or of French and German (the languages). The fact that nation-states are historically novel means that intellectual history of the early modern or premodern is less likely to fall into this trap. And intellectual histories of empires are, too, less likely to frame their subject in national terms.[24] *Ilustrado* writings show some obvious difficulties with quick "national" categorization because, though they are rightly seen as an originary moment of Philippine (and Filipino) studies, they are examples of Spanish-language scholarship and sometimes (but only sometimes) locate themselves "within" a Spanish national context. *Ilustrado* writings remind us that intellectual moments, or schools, are shaped by local contexts (not any single local context) and that any local context is complexly entwined with others in global relationships. Any intellectual history, whether of the colonial or colonizing world, ought to approach its subject with attention to how different local contexts have global links, without assuming the nation-state to be the most relevant unit of analysis.

This book has aimed not so much to present the works of *ilustrados* and propagandists as forming a coherent whole but instead to look at the range of meanings that they employ and deploy. These works themselves sometimes exploit the internal contradictions of the discourses in which they engage. To borrow James Tully's language, "[a]n ideologist changes one part of an ideology by holding another part fast; by appealing to and so reinforcing convention."[25] It would be a mistake to assume coherence, whether in the works of canonical authors or lesser-known thinkers, in part because the search for coherence "gives the thoughts . . . a coherence, and an air generally of a closed system, which they may never have attained or even meant to attain."[26] The political possibilities of the *ilustrados*' and propagandists' writings were far more flexible than the events of subsequent history might lead us to believe.

Notes

Introduction. Worldly Colonials

1. The Spanish text reads, "en Madrid se decia que 'la causa principal de la insurrecion en Filipinas eran los Padres jesuitas por dar á los jóvenes del Archipiélago [...] una instruccion cosmopolita [...] y no española [...] como la de otras Ordenes religiosas.'" The letter was later published in Madrid: Miguel Saderra Mata, "La enseñanza en el Ateneo Municipal de Manila," *El siglo futuro*, December 10, 1896. Unless otherwise noted, all translations are mine, done with significant assistance from Thomas Genova and Cora Gorman Malone. To keep the text of the book to an acceptable length, I have preserved the original foreign-language quotations only when the original text is particularly rare, when the original language is particularly resonant, or when my translation might be controversial. Many of these texts were very rare until recently; electronic sources such as Google Books and the University of Michigan Library have made facsimile electronic versions more widely accessible, though they can be difficult to locate when catalogued irregularly. The original quotations include many typos, spelling irregularities, and orthographical marks which are either simply incorrect, or reflect outdated orthographical practices. All of these oddities have been preserved insofar as possible, with only the most unusual marked with [*sic*].

2. The Spanish phrases are "capaces de ser enseñadas en todo el mundo" and "para obtener uno de los fines que presidieron á la fundacion del Ateneo, esto es, que no vayan al extranjero los filipinos (lo cual me parece poco cosmopolita)." Ibid.

3. "Consta que bastantes alumnos han dejado la Universidad por disgustos con los profesores ... y han ido á estudiar fuera de Filipinas, donde aprendieron las ideas disolventes." Ibid.

4. In the original, "(Rizal, vg.)." Ibid. Countless biographical accounts of Rizal are available; I rely on León Ma. Guerrero, *The First Filipino* (Pasig: Anvil, 1998).

5. The document is preserved as "Exposición del provincial de dominicos al gobiernos español para defender a las ordenes religiosas" in Folletos, tomo 42, no. 11 of the Archives of the University of Santo Tomás, Manila. The original phrases read, "*Notas* al Morga y sus artículos y folletos [...] tan gran ilusión causaron entre muchos de los ilustrados del país [...] los cuales escritos no eran más que preparación consciente para lograr la independencia del archipiélago."

6. "[P]onderando la antigua civilización tagalog, propagó las mismas ideas que Rizal en sus notas al Morga, y quiso demostrar lo poquísimo que los habitantes de estas islas debían á España y á la Iglesia." Alvaréz, "Exposición."

7. The original phrase reads, "verdaderos causantes de la revolución filipina." Ibid.

8. The original phrases read, "Influidos por esa culta Europa, y halagados por varios de nuestros hombres de ciencia y por conspicuos políticos de Madrid," "esa culta pero desquiciada Europa," "tratando de *abrirles los ojos y de iniciarles en el progreso y moderna cultura*," and "se ha conservado durante tres siglos pacífico y próspero, sin soñar en utópicas independencias, ni en los llamados derechos individuales ni en sufragios políticos, ni en libertades redentoras, ni en que fueran iguales á los europeos." Ibid.

9. This approach to *ilustrado* writings has become conventional; until recently, however, little attention had been paid to the content of many of their scholarly writings. A brief discussion of this literature can be found in the "*Ilustrados*, Propagandistas, and Philippine Historiography" section of the introduction. Resil Mojares's work on Paterno, Pardo de Tavera, and de los Reyes has set a new standard; readers will find references to it throughout the book. Resil Mojares, *Brains of the Nation: Pedro Paterno, T. H. Pardo de Tavera, Isabelo de los Reyes and the Production of Modern Knowledge* (Quezon City: Ateneo de Manila University Press, 2006).

10. Partha Chatterjee, *Nationalist Thought and the Colonial World: A Derivative Discourse?* (Minneapolis: University of Minnesota Press, 1986).

11. Paul A. Kramer, *The Blood of Government: Race, Empire, the United States, and the Philippines* (Chapel Hill: University of North Carolina Press, 2006); Filomeno V. Aguilar Jr., "Tracing Origins: *Ilustrado* Nationalism and the Racial Science of Migration Waves," *Journal of Asian Studies* 64, no. 3 (2005): 605–37; Mojares, *Brains of the Nation*; Benedict R. O'G. Anderson, *Under Three Flags: Anarchism and the Anti-Colonial Imagination* (London: Verso, 2005).

12. José Rizal, "Sobre la nueva ortografía de la lengua tagalog (carta á mis paisanos)," *La solidaridad*, April 15, 1890, 92. *La solidaridad* was published first in Barcelona and then in Madrid. The entire run (1889–95) has been reprinted, with English translation by Guadalupe Fores Ganzon and Luis Mañeru (Pasig City: Fundación Santiago, 1996). I have referred to but sometimes modified their translations.

13. Benedict R. O'G. Anderson, *Imagined Communities: Reflections on the Origin and Spread of Nationalism*, rev. ed. (London: Verso, 1991), esp. 71, 75. Throughout this work, my approach to nationalist thought is indebted to Anderson.

14. The relationship between Orientalism and anthropology will be the subject of chapter 1. These disciplines are studied as colonial practices in Edward Said, *Orientalism* (New York: Vintage, 1979); Bernard S. Cohn, *Colonialism and Its Forms of Knowledge: The British in India* (Princeton, N.J.: Princeton University Press, 1996); Talal Asad, ed., *Anthropology and the Colonial Encounter* (London: Ithaca Press, 1973); Frederick Cooper and Laura Ann Stoler, eds., *Tensions of Empire: Colonial Cultures in a Bourgeois World* (Berkeley: University of California Press, 1997); Nicholas Thomas, *Colonialism's Culture: Anthropology, Travel, and Government* (Princeton, N.J.: Princeton University Press, 1994); Nicholas B.

Dirks, *Colonialism and Culture* (Ann Arbor: University of Michi
and *Castes of Mind: Colonialism and the Making of Modern India* (
Princeton University Press, 2001); Peter Pels and Oscar Salemin
Subjects: Essays on the Practical History of Anthropology (Ann A
of Michigan Press, 1999); George W. Stocking, ed., *Colonial Situations: Essays on the Contextualization of Ethnographic Knowledge* (Madison: University of Wisconsin Press, 1991); Lloyd I. Rudolph and Susanne Hoeber Rudolph, "Reversing the Gaze: The Diarist as Reflexive 'Native' Ethnographer," in *Reversing the Gaze: Amar Singh's Diary, a Colonial Subject's Narrative of Imperial India*, ed. Rudolph and Rudolph, and Mohan Singh Kanota (Boulder, Colo.: Westview, 2002), 39–43; Daniel R. Brower and Edward J. Lazzerini, *Russia's Orient: Imperial Borderlands and Peoples, 1700–1917* (Bloomington: Indiana University Press, 1997); and Carol A. Breckenridge, ed., *Orientalism and the Postcolonial Predicament: Perspectives on South Asia* (Philadelphia: University of Pennsylvania Press, 1993).

15. Chatterjee, *Nationalist Thought.*

16. On nineteenth-century transformations, see Alfred McCoy and Ed. C. de Jesus, eds., *Philippine Social History: Global Trade and Local Transformations* (Quezon City: Ateneo de Manila University Press, 1982); and Michael Cullinane, "'Ilustrados' and Filipino Elites in the Nineteenth Century," in *Ilustrado Politics: Filipino Elite Responses to American Rule, 1898–1908* (Quezon City: Ateneo de Manila University Press, 2003), 8–94.

17. I use "native" for *indio*, a legal designation, originally deriving from the *indios* of the Americas, that had assumed a derogatory taint. On the changing meanings that these designations had, see Eliodoro Robles, *The Philippines in the Nineteenth Century* (Quezon City: Malaya Books, 1969); Edgar Wickberg, *The Chinese in Philippine Life: 1850–1898* (New Haven, Conn.: Yale University Press, 1965).

18. Vicente Rafael, *The Promise of the Foreign: Nationalism and the Technics of Translation in the Spanish Philippines* (Durham, N.C.: Duke University Press, 2005). I later return to Rafael's work on Castilian and its significance for these figures.

19. John D. Blanco and Resil Mojares have each approached *ilustrado/ilustración* as "enlightened"/"enlightenment" in the nineteenth century, with different scopes and subjects. John Blanco, *Frontier Constitutions: Christianity and Colonial Empire in the Nineteenth-Century Philippines* (Berkeley: University of California, 2009), 158–82; Mojares, *Brains of the Nation*, 381–418. Cullinane ("'Ilustrados' and Filipino Elites in the Nineteenth Century") uses the term to designate a broader grouping within elite society. Just as Cullinane distinguishes between political-economic elites with reference to whether their influence was mainly urban, provincial, or municipal, it is useful to distinguish between different kinds of *ilustrados*. Most graduates of the institutions of higher education in the islands, though "enlightened" and educated, could not be said to be scholarly— producing research that traveled intellectually and geographically—in the same

ense as were the narrower group of authors that are my subjects. Likewise, de los Reyes's self-education in the field of folklore, for example, is not equivalent to Pardo de Tavera's formal training in Oriental languages.

20. The standard works on this movement are John N. Schumacher's *The Propaganda Movement, 1880–1895: The Creation of a Filipino Consciousness, the Making of the Revolution*, rev. ed. (Quezon City: Ateneo de Manila University Press, 1997) and *The Making of a Nation: Essays on Nineteenth-Century Filipino Nationalism* (Quezon City: Ateneo de Manila University Press, 1991). Recent important scholarship includes Rafael, *Promise of the Foreign*; Anderson, *Under Three Flags*; Kramer, *Blood of Government*; and Mojares, *Brains of the Nation*.

21. Megan C. Thomas, "Isabelo de los Reyes and the Philippine Contemporaries of *La Solidaridad*," *Philippine Studies* 54, no. 3 (2006): 381–411.

22. Rizal capitalized *Indio* here and often elsewhere, though the word was not generally capitalized in Spanish; this and other similar capitalization inconsistencies will be discussed in chapter 2. José Rizal, "Diferencias," *La solidaridad*, September 15, 1889, 167. Note also that "Igorot" is a generic term to describe any number of highland peoples (though not "Negritos" who are held to be distinct—see chapter 2 of this book) and is often considered to be offensive today both because it has a history of being a derogatory term of the colonizer, and because it is generally preferable to refer to a more specific people—(e.g. Bontoc, Itneg, Kalinga, etc.) when possible. I follow the usage of the authors I treat.

23. Anderson, *Under Three Flags*, 56–57.

24. José Montero y Vidal, *Historia general de filipinas desde el descubrimiento de dichas islas hasta nuestros días*, vol. 3 (Madrid: M. Tello, 1895), 543.

25. This period of history is reviewed in, and my account largely derived from, Mojares, *Brains of the Nation*, 7–8, 441–45; Anderson, *Under Three Flags*, 56–58; and Guerrero, *The First Filipino*, 9–14.

26. Many articles in *La solidaridad*, as well as Del Pilar's *Frialocracía filipina* and *Soberanía monacal en Filipinas*, develop these arguments and are treated in Schumacher, *Propaganda Movement*.

27. Anderson, *Under Three Flags*.

28. As Reynaldo C. Ileto's transformational work on the Revolution made clear, rank-and-file *Katipuneros* were neither fighting clearly against Spanish sovereignty nor to win independence for a "Filipino" nation. Reynaldo C. Ileto, *Pasyon and Revolution: Popular Movements in the Philippines, 1840–1910* (Quezon City: Ateneo de Manila University Press, 1979).

29. Reynaldo C. Ileto, *Filipinos and Their Revolution: Event, Discourse, and Historiography* (Quezon City: Ateneo de Manila University Press, 1998), 70.

30. Portia L. Reyes, "Fighting over a Nation: Theorizing a Filipino Historiography," *Postcolonial Studies* 11, no. 3 (2008): 241–58.

31. Ileto, *Filipinos and Their Revolution*, 70. Questions of connections (or divisions) between elite and popular endure in Philippine historiography, particularly of the revolution. Ileto's own work on the Katipunan (*Pasyon and Revolution*) is key in this discussion.

32. Teodoro A. Agoncillo, *The Revolt of the Masses: The Story of Bonifacio and the Katipunan* (Quezon City: University of the Philippines Press, 1996), 18–44, 282–86.

33. Renato Constantino, *The Philippines: A Past Revisited* (Quezon City: Tala, 1975), esp. 146–53, 162–66, 180, 213–14.

34. Schumacher, *Propaganda Movement* (originally published 1973, Manila: Solidaridad).

35. Ibid., 299.

36. Ibid., 301.

37. Schumacher concludes "that united as the real leaders of the Propaganda Movement might be on the goal of eventual independence from Spain, they were irrevocably separated on the strategy to be used" (ibid., viii). In Schumacher's work, for example, Pardo de Tavera plays a small role because he was only marginally part of the propagandists' political efforts, and de los Reyes's Manila-produced work is left to the side because Schumacher locates the propagandists' work primarily in Europe. Schumacher focuses on del Pilar as the bearer of a broader propaganda committee's efforts between Manila and peninsular cities.

38. Mojares, *Brains of the Nation*.

39. Anderson, *Under Three Flags*.

40. Kramer, *Blood of Government*; Aguilar, "Tracing Origins"; Mojares, *Brains of the Nation*; Anderson, *Under Three Flags*.

41. Anderson established this emphasis in *Imagined Communities*. His own more recent work develops this theme, as does other scholars', for example, Rebecca Karl, *Staging the World: Chinese Nationalism at the Turn of the Twentieth Century* (Durham, N.C.: Duke University Press, 2002).

42. Rafael, *Promise of the Foreign*.

43. Ibid., 43.

44. Ibid., 13.

45. Chatterjee, *Nationalist Thought*; Frantz Fanon, *The Wretched of the Earth*, trans. Constance Farrington (New York: Grove Press, 1963), 148–205.

46. Chapter 2 develops and modifies previous iterations of this argument.

47. On India, see Sanjay Seth, *Subject Lessons: The Western Education of Colonial India* (Durham, N.C.: Duke University Press, 2007). For Southeast Asia claim, see Anderson, *Under Three Flags*, 23; Mojares, *Brains of the Nation*.

48. Mojares, *Brains of the Nation*, 459–62.

49. José Rizal, *Sucesos de las islas Filipinas por el doctor Antonio de Morga, obra publicada en Méjico el año de 1609 nuevamente sacada a luz y anotada por José Rizal y*

precedida de un prólogo del prof. Fernando Blumentritt (Manila: Instituto Histórico Nacional, 1991), v–vi.

50. Andrew Sartori, *Bengal in Global Concept History: Culturalism in the Age of Capital* (Chicago: University of Chicago Press, 2008), 5.

51. In this respect, Quentin Skinner and the Cambridge School are instructive. I am more comfortable with and committed to making connections between concepts across historical time, but do so to try to defamiliarize contemporary conceptions (such as "race" or "nation"). See James Tully, *Meaning and Context: Quentin Skinner and His Critics* (Princeton, N.J.: Princeton University Press, 1988). I am indebted to both Kirstie McClure and Kenneth McIntyre for calling my attention to the parallels between my attempts to wrestle with the challenges of my material and the Cambridge School's approach to dealing with the past.

1. Locating Orientalism and the Anthropological Sciences

1. Raymond Schwab, *The Oriental Renaissance: Europe's Rediscovery of India and the East, 1680–1880*, trans. Gene Patterson-Black and Victor Reinking (New York: Columbia University Press, 1984), 53. Here Schwab refers specifically to 1790s Germany; I use the phrase to describe the "renaissance" as a whole that his book treats. Schwab's work has been criticized by Martin Bernal (and Said) for emphasizing the mind-opening qualities of Orientalism without comparable attention to how it "narrow[ed] . . . the imagination and intensified feelings of the innate and categorical superiority of European civilization," Martin Bernal, *Black Athena: The Afroasiatic Roots of Classical Civilization*, vol. 1, *The Fabrication of Ancient Greece 1785–1985* (New Brunswick, N.J.: Rutgers University Press, 1987), 236; see also Edward Said, *Orientalism* (New York: Vintage, 1979).

2. Schwab, *Oriental Renaissance*, 17.

3. Hugo, as quoted by Schwab in ibid., 11–12.

4. Schwab, *Oriental Renaissance*, 16.

5. I make this argument with reference to Jones, Schlegel, and Müller in my "Orientalism and Comparative Political Theory," *Review of Politics* 72 (2010), 653–77.

6. On the anthropological sciences, see note 45 in this chapter.

7. Gopal Balakrishnan, "Machiavelli and the Reawakening of History," in *Antagonistics: Capitalism and Power in an Age of War* (London: Verso, 2009), 265–79; Schwab, *Oriental Renaissance*; Thomas, "Orientalism and Comparative Political Theory."

8. See, for example, Sir William Jones, "The Third Anniversary Discourse, Delivered 2 February, 1786," in *Sir William Jones: A Reader*, ed. Satya S. Pachori (Delhi: Oxford University Press, 1993), 172–78; Carl [Karl] Wilhelm Friedrich Schlegel, "On the Language and Wisdom of the Indians," in *The Aesthetic and*

Miscellaneous Works of Frederick von Schlegel, trans. E. J. Millington (London: Henry G. Bohn, 1849), 425–526.

9. Johann Gottfried Herder, "This Too a Philosophy of History for the Formation of Humanity," in *Johann Gottfried von Herder: Philosophical Writings*, ed. Michael N. Forster (Cambridge: Cambridge University Press, 2002), 273–99, esp. 278–97.

10. G. W. F. Hegel, *Lectures on the Philosophy of World History: Introduction*, trans. H. B. Nisbet (Cambridge: Cambridge University Press, 1975). Herder strenuously objected to Hegel's use of his historic framework; see Sankar Muthu, *Enlightenment Against Empire* (Princeton, N.J.: Princeton University Press, 2003), 227.

11. F. Max Müller, *India: What Can It Teach Us?* (New York: Funk & Wagnalls, 1883), 116, 118.

12. Ibid., 122.

13. Said, *Orientalism*. Drawing from Said, sometimes critically, are Bernal, *Black Athena*; Partha Chatterjee, *Nationalist Thought and the Colonial World: A Derivative Discourse?* (Minneapolis: University of Minnesota Press, 1986); Lisa Lowe, *Critical Terrains: French and British Orientalisms* (Ithaca, N.Y.: Cornell University Press, 1991); and Vasant Kaiwar, "The Aryan Model of History and the Oriental Renaissance: The Politics of Identity in an Age of Revolutions, Colonialism, and Nationalism," in *Antinomies of Modernity: Essays on Race, Orient, Nation*, ed. Vasant Kaiwar and Sucheta Mazumdar (Durham, N.C.: Duke University Press, 2003), 13–51. More critical of Said are Aijaz Ahmad, *In Theory: Classes, Nations, Literatures* (London: Verso, 1992), chap. 5; Robert Irwin, *Dangerous Knowledge: Orientalism and Its Discontents* (Woodstock, N.Y.: Overlook, 2006); James Clifford, *The Predicament of Culture: Twentieth-Century Ethnography, Literature, and Art* (Cambridge, Mass.: Harvard University Press, 1988), chap. 11; Lloyd I. Rudolph and Susanne Hoeber Rudolph, "Occidentalism and Orientalism: Perspectives on Legal Pluralism," in *Cultures of Scholarship*, ed. Sarah C. Humphreys, (Ann Arbor: University of Michigan Press, 1997), 219–51; and Robert Young, *White Mythologies: Writing History and the West* (London: Routledge, 2004), chap. 7.

14. See note 13; also Schwab, *Oriental Renaissance*, and Bernard S. Cohn, *Colonialism and Its Forms of Knowledge: The British in India* (Princeton, N.J.: Princeton University Press, 1996).

15. Cohn, *Colonialism and Its Forms of Knowledge*, chap. 2; Arif Dirlik, "Chinese History and the Question of Orientalism," *History and Theory* 35, no. 4 (1996): 96–118; Mohamad Tavakoli-Targhi, *Refashioning Iran: Orientalism, Occidentalism, and Historiography* (New York: Palgrave, 2001), esp. chap. 2.

16. Chatterjee, *Nationalist Thought*.

17. Homi K. Bhabha, "Of Mimicry and Man," in *The Location of Culture* (London and New York: Routledge, 1994), 90.

18. Dipesh Chakrabarty, "Postcoloniality and the Artifice of History," in *Provincializing Europe: Postcolonial Thought and Historical Difference* (Princeton, N.J.: Princeton University Press, 2000), 27–46.

19. Chakrabarty, "Radical Histories and the Question of Enlightenment Rationalism: Some Recent Critiques of Subaltern Studies," in *Mapping Subaltern Studies and the Postcolonial,* ed. Vinayak Chaturvedi (London: Verso, 2000), 268.

20. Bhabha, "Of Mimicry and Man"; Chatterjee, *Nationalist Thought*; Chakrabarty, "Postcoloniality and the Artifice of History"; Said, *Orientalism*; Frantz Fanon, *Black Skin White Masks,* trans. Charles Lam Markmann (New York: Grove, 1967; reprint, October 1991); and Fanon *The Wretched of the Earth,* trans. Constance Farrington (New York: Grove, 1963).

21. Fanon, *Wretched of the Earth.*

22. On Haiti, see C. L. R. James, *The Black Jacobins: Toussaint L'Ouverture and the San Domingo Revolution* (New York: Vintage, 1963); Laurent Dubois, *Avengers of the New World: The Story of the Haitian Revolution* (Cambridge, Mass.: Belknap Press of Harvard University Press, 2004); and Susan Buck-Morss, "Hegel and Haiti," *Critical Inquiry* 26, no. 4 (2000): 281–65. On Bolívar, see Anthony Pagden, *Spanish Imperialism and the Political Imagination: Studies in European and Spanish-American Social and Political Theory 1513–1830* (New Haven, Conn.: Yale University Press, 1990). On Martí and other Cubans, see Ada Ferrer, *Insurgent Cuba: Race, Nation, and Revolution, 1868–1898* (Chapel Hill: University of North Carolina Press, 1999).

23. Ferrer, *Insurgent Cuba,* 137.

24. Andrew Sartori, *Bengal in Global Concept History: Culturalism in the Age of Capital* (Chicago: University of Chicago Press, 2008), 19.

25. Chatterjee, *Nationalist Thought,* 38.

26. Gyan Prakash, "Writing Post-Orientalist Histories of the Third World: Perspectives from Indian Historiography," in *Mapping Subaltern Studies and the Postcolonial,* ed. Chaturvedi, 168.

27. Chatterjee, *Nationalist Thought,* 42, 50. Similarly, on "legacies of the European Enlightenment," see Chakrabarty, "Radical Histories and the Question of Enlightenment Rationalism," 257, 269; and on the "post-Enlightenment ideology of Reason," see Prakash, "Writing Post-Orientalist Histories of the Third World," 183. Sumit Sarkar critiques Chatterjee and Chakrabarty on this point in "Orientalism Revisited: Saidian Frameworks in the Writing of Modern Indian History," in *Mapping Subaltern Studies and the Postcolonial,* ed. Chaturvedi, 244–45.

28. Sarkar, "Orientalism Revisited."

29. Sartori, *Bengal in Global Concept History,* 150.

30. Chakrabarty, "Radical Histories," 259–65.

31. Resil Mojares notes many of the important distinctions that complicate the Indian-Philippine comparison but generally frames *ilustrado* thought as deriving

from and challenging colonizer/colonizing knowledges. Resil Mojares, *Brains of the Nation: Pedro Paterno, T.H. Pardo de Tavera, Isabelo de los Reyes and the Production of Modern Knowledge* (Quezon City: Ateneo de Manila University Press, 2006).

32. Sarkar, "Orientalism Revisited."

33. Tapan Raychaudhuri, *Europe Reconsidered: Perceptions of the West in Nineteenth Century Bengal* (Delhi, New York: Oxford University Press, 1990), 7. On this "Bengal Renaissance" see also Vasant Kaiwar and Sucheta Mazumdar, "The Coordinates of Orientalism," paper presented at the Roundtable at Maison des Sciences de l'Homme, Paris, November 21, 2005; and Chatterjee, *Nationalist Thought*. For analyses of similar material, critical of the "renaissance" conception, see Sartori, *Bengal in Global Concept History*, 7; and Sarkar, "Orientalism Revisited."

34. Raychaudhuri, *Europe Reconsidered*, 3.

35. Prakash, "Writing Post-Orientalist Histories," 168.

36. M. K. Gandhi, *Hind Swaraj and Other Writings*, ed. and trans. Anthony Parel (Cambridge: Cambridge University Press, 1997), 122, 123. Gandhi quotes "Mr. Alfred Webb's valuable collection" (121). The quotations derive from Müller, *India*, 24; Schlegel, "Language and Wisdom," 471–72; and Schlegel, *Lectures on the History of Literature, Ancient and Modern* (London: George Bell and Sons, 1896), 125.

37. Rudolph and Rudolph ("Occidentalism and Orientalism") also show how Orientalist (as opposed to Anglicist) scholarship and administration imagined themselves to be local (against the imperial), which lent them to later anticolonial use.

38. For example, Anquetil, as quoted in Wilhelm Halbfass, *India and Europe: An Essay in Understanding* (Albany: State University of New York Press, 1988), 66; or Sir William Jones, "Preface to the Institutes of Hindu Law: Or, the Ordinances of Menu, According to the Gloss of Culluca Comprising the Indian System of Duties, Religious and Civil," in *Sir William Jones: A Reader*, ed. Satya S. Pachori (Delhi: Oxford University Press, 1993), 199–203; see also Bernard S. Cohn, *Colonialism and Its Forms of Knowledge: The British in India* (Princeton, N.J.: Princeton University Press, 1996), chap. 3. See also Thomas, "Orientalism and Comparative Political Theory"; and for a more sympathetic view of Orientalist skepticism toward indigenous authorities, Rudolph and Rudolph, "Occidentalism and Orientalism."

39. Schlegel, "Language and Wisdom." See also Kaiwar, "Aryan Model of History"; and Thomas R. Trautmann, "Constructing the Racial Theory of Indian Civilization," in *The Aryan Debate*, ed. Trautmann (Oxford: Oxford University Press, 2005), 84–105.

40. Raychaudhuri, *Europe Reconsidered*, 9; Sanjay Seth, *Subject Lessons: The Western Education of Colonial India* (Durham, N.C.: Duke University Press, 2007), 12; Chatterjee, *Nationalist Thought*, 77–79.

41. Prakash, "Writing Post-Orientalist Histories," 169; Sartori, *Bengal in Global Concept History*, 208–10; Kaiwar, "Aryan Model of History."

42. David Anthony Brading, *The First America: The Spanish Monarchy, Creole Patriots, and the Liberal State 1492–1867* (Cambridge: Cambridge University Press, 1991); Pagden, *Spanish Imperialism and the Political Imagination.*

43. Trinidad Hermenegildo Pardo de Tavera, *El sanscrito en la lengua tagalog* (Paris: Faculté de Médicine, A. Davy, 1887), 8–9.

44. On Orientalist philology, see Schwab, *Oriental Renaissance*; Maurice Olender, *The Languages of Paradise: Aryans and Semites, a Match Made in Heaven* (Cambridge, Mass.: Harvard University Press, 1992); Bernal, *Black Athena*; and Halbfass, *India and Europe.*

45. Many scholars have written about the emergence of the "sciences of man," ethnology, or anthropology. My interest is, in particular, with nineteenth-century methods, data, and presumptions. In chapter 2, I generally follow Robert Bernasconi, ed., *Race and Anthropology*, 9 vols. (Bristol: Thoemmes, 2003); Robert Young, *Colonial Desire: Hybridity in Theory, Culture, and Race* (London and New York: Routledge, 1995), chap. 2; George W. Stocking, *The Ethnographer's Magic and Other Essays in the History of Anthropology* (Madison: University of Wisconsin Press, 1992), chap. 8; Stocking, *Victorian Anthropology* (New York: MacMillan, 1987); Stocking, *Race, Culture, and Evolution: Essays in the History of Anthropology* (Chicago: University of Chicago Press, 1982), 2–6; Andrew Zimmerman, *Anthropology and Antihumanism in Imperial Germany* (Chicago: University of Chicago Press, 2001); and Peter Pels, "From Texts to Bodies: Brian Houghton Hodgson and the Emergence of Ethnology in India," in *Anthropology and Colonialism in Asia and Oceania*, ed. Jan van Bremen and Akitoshi Shimizu (Richmond, Surrey: Curzon, 1999), 65–92. The important literature on the pre-nineteenth-century genealogy of anthropology is somewhat less relevant for my emphasis on the nineteenth century. This includes Anthony Pagden, *The Fall of Natural Man: The American Indian and the Origins of Comparative Ethnology* (Cambridge: Cambridge University Press, 1982); Michel Foucault, *The Order of Things: An Archaeology of the Human Sciences* (New York: Vintage Books, 1973); Christopher Fox, Roy Porter, and Robert Wokler, eds., *Inventing Human Science: Eighteenth-Century Domains* (Berkeley: University of California Press, 1995); John Christie, "The Human Sciences: Origins and Histories," *History of the Human Sciences* 6, no. 1 (1993): 1–12; and John H. Zammito, *Kant, Herder, and the Birth of Anthropology* (Chicago: University of Chicago Press, 2002).

46. Stocking, *Ethnographer's Magic*, 347.

47. Ibid.

48. On comparison, with reference to Orientalism and nationalism, see especially Schwab, *Oriental Renaissance*; and Benedict R. O'G. Anderson, *The Spectre of Comparisons: Nationalism, Southeast Asia, and the World* (London: Verso, 1998).

49. Stocking, *Ethnographer's Magic*, 18–20. Ethnography may not have held such a subordinate status in the German tradition, however; see Zammito, *Kant, Herder, and the Birth of Anthropology*, 236, 345.

50. Blumentritt, as quoted by Cesáreo Blanco y Sierra, "Prólogo," in Isabelo de los Reyes y Florentino, *Filipinas: Artículos varios de Isabelo de los Reyes y Florentino sobre etnografía, historia y costumbres del país* (Manila: J. A. Ramos, 1887), ii.

51. For the Indian context, see Raychaudhuri, *Europe Reconsidered*, 16–19.

52. For example, Schlegel, "Language and Wisdom"; and F. Max Müller, "Lecture on the Vedas, or the Sacred Books of the Brahmans (1865)," in *The Essential Max Müller*, ed. Jon R. Stone (New York: Palgrave, 2002), 43–67. Theorizing the model are Kaiwar, "Aryan Model of History"; Bernal, *Black Athena*, 224–46; and Trautmann, "Constructing the Racial Theory of Indian Civilization."

53. Kaiwar, "Aryan Model of History."

54. Zammito's formulation in *Kant, Herder, and the Birth of Anthropology* (12), which he uses for eighteenth-century material, also applies to this much later moment.

55. Cohn, *Colonialism and Its Forms of Knowledge*, chap. 3; Tavakoli-Targhi, *Refashioning Iran*, chap. 2; Seth, *Subject Lessons*.

56. Seth, *Subject Lessons*, 2ff.

57. Satishchandra Muckerjee writing in 1898, as quoted in Mukherjee and Mukherjee, *The Origins of the National Education Movement*, as quoted in Seth, *Subject Lessons*, 161, 228n14.

58. Raychaudhuri, *Europe Reconsidered*, 3.

59. On assimilationist politics, see the introduction of this book.

60. Raychaudhuri, *Europe Reconsidered*, 3.

61. Ibid.

62. See this book's introduction, note 40. Most obviously, I differ from these scholars in my reading of folklore as exceptional. Kramer most forcefully emphasizes the political use of this scholarly mastery; see the end of this chapter.

63. The original Spanish phrases read, "desconocidas unas y poco cultivadas otras en mi querida patria" and "me pareció vergonzoso el que hubiésemos de acudir á las [universidades] extranjeras para estudiar una de las lenguas más relacionadas con nuestra historia y literatura." Francisco García Ayuso, *Gramática árabe segun el método de Ollendorf* (Madrid: Imprenta y Estereotipia de M. Rivadeneyra, 1871), iii.

64. The original phrases read, "los diversos y sublimes fines," "*nueva ciencia,*" and "*importantísima ciencia.*" Ibid., iii. His earlier work is García Ayuso, *El estudio de la filología en su relacion con el sanskrit* (Madrid: Imprenta y Estereotipia de M. Rivadeneyra, 1871).

65. The original phrases read, "de estudio puramente *humanístico*, se ha elevado á *ciencia*, y ocupa hoy un lugar distinguido en los círculos científico-literarios. Genios sobre-salientes, como *Herder, L. Hervas, G. de Humbult* [*sic*], *Schlegel, Bopp, Grimm y Burnouf*," "glorioso resultado," and "la *filología general y comparada*." García Ayuso, *Estudio de la filología*, vii.

66. The original phrases read, "las universidades de la culta Europa" and "favorecidos por la mayor parte de los gobiernos europeos," ibid.

67. "Si con esta obrita contribuyo á avivar entre los jóvenes literatos de mi querida patria el amor á los estudios filológicos y del bellísimo idioma de la India, daré mi tiempo y trabajo por bien empleados," García Ayuso, *Estudio de la filología*, vii.

68. Francisco García Ayuso, *Ensayo crítico de gramática comparada de los idiomas indo-europeos, sanskrit, zend, latin, griego, antiguo eslavo, litanico, godo, antiguo aleman y armenio* (Madrid: Aribau y Ca., 1877), 1–8.

69. His masterwork comparative grammar (*Ensayo crítico de gramática comparada*) relied heavily on Bopp's foundational six-volume work (with a very similar title). Ibid.

70. So suggests the catalogue of the Biblioteca Nacional de España, http://catalogo.bne.es.

71. The original reads, "el completo desconocimiento de todo lo que al Archipiélago filipino se refiere; ignorancia que domina, no sólo en la opinión pública, sino en las regiones oficiales [. . .] [es] más conocido en el extranjero que en nuestro propio país." Segismundo Moret y Prendergast, decree issued October 4, 1870, as quoted in D. José Montero y Vidal, *Historia general de Filipinas desde el descubrimiento de dichas islas hasta nuestros días*, vol. 3 (Madrid: M. Tello, 1895), 537.

72. The original text reads, "la descripción, historia é instituciones de las Islas, medios de desarrollar su colonización y examen de las instituciones y sistemas empleados para el régimen de las posesiones de Inglaterra y de Holanda en la India." Montero's words, not Moret's, in Montero, *Historia general de Filipinas*, vol. 3, 537.

73. The original phrase is "la vulgarización de los conocimientos necesarios y la difusión de libros que á este fin contribuyan," Moret, decree issued October 4, 1870, as quoted in Montero, *Historia general de Filipinas*, vol. 3, 538.

74. The original text lists "la lengua tagala y sus principales dialectos.[. . .] historia y civilización de las posesiones inglesas y holandesas del Asia y Oceanía, costumbres, usos, religión, literatura, instituciones políticas, religiosas etc., etc., de sus pueblos indígenas; instituciones europeas bajo todos sus aspectos, y examen crítico de las mismas.[. . .] Historia y civilización de las Islas Filipinas, costumbres, usos; instituciones religiosas, políticas, etc., de los pueblos indígenas; legislación é instituciones españolas; su examen y crítica," Moret as quoted in Montero, *Historia general de Filipinas*, vol. 3, 537.

75. "El último alemán sabe más de Filipinas que muchos de nosotros; y no se crea que nos referimos sólo á los indoctos, sino también á personas cuya ilustración es notoria." Montero y Vidal, *El archipiélago filipino y las islas Marianas, Carolinas y Palaos: su historia, geografía y estadística* (Madrid: M. Tello, 1886), v.

76. Paul A. Kramer, *The Blood of Government: Race, Empire, the United States, and the Philippines* (Chapel Hill: University of North Carolina Press, 2006), 51.

77. Trinidad Hermenegildo Pardo de Tavera, *Contribución para el estudio de los antiguos alfabetos filipinos* (Losana: Juanin Hermanos, 1884), 5–6.

78. Harry Sichrovsky, *Ferdinand Blumentritt: An Austrian Life for the Philippines: The Story of José Rizal's Closest Friend and Companion* (Manila: National Historical Institute, 1987), 4–5.

79. On nineteenth-century German anthropology, see Zimmerman, *Anthropology and Antihumanism in Imperial Germany*; H. Glenn Penny and Matti Bunzl, eds., *Worldly Provincialism: German Anthropology in the Age of Empire* (Ann Arbor: University of Michigan Press, 2003); and George W. Stocking, *Volksgeist as Method and Ethic: Essays on Boasian Ethnography and the German Anthropological Tradition* (Madison: University of Wisconsin Press, 1996).

80. Both Meyer and Schadenberg's writings are translated and introduced by William Henry Scott (ed.) in his *German Travelers on the Cordillera (1860–1890)* (Manila: Filipiniana Book Guild, 1975). Meyer's record describes (proudly) how he begged, borrowed, and stole to get his "ethnographic artifacts."

81. The original German text reads, "Der Gelehrte sagte mir scherzend, er möchte mich *ethnographisch* studieren . . . *ja* aus wissenschaftlichen Liebe und versprach noch ein anders Exemplar (mein Landsmann) mitzubringen." Letter from Rizal to Blumentritt, January 12, 1887, in José Rizal and Ferdinand Blumentritt, *The Rizal-Blumentritt Correspondence*, vol. 1 (Manila: National Historical Institute, 1992), unnumbered leaves between pp. 34 and 37. I have only slightly modified Encarnación Alzona's translation, which appears on p. 39. I am grateful for Gabriela Andrea Frank's help with these translations.

82. "[Y]o mismo en 1881 puse mucho cuidado en recogerlas [mis noticias] con la exactitud posible en Abra, donde mejor que en algunas rancherías de Ilocos creo que se conservan los caracteres del primitivo tinguian." Isabelo de los Reyes y Florentino, "El tinguian," in *Filipinas: Artículos varios de Isabelo de los Reyes y Florentino sobre etnografía, historia y costumbres del país* (Manila: J. A. Ramos, 1887), 4.

83. On Spanish anthropology, see Luis Ángel Sánchez Gómez, "La etnografía de Filipinas desde la administración colonial española," *Revista de Indias* 47, no. 179 (1987): 157–85; Sánchez Gómez, *Un imperio en la vitrina: El colonialismo español en el Pacífico y la exposición de Filipinas de 1887* (Madrid: Consejo Superior de Investigaciones Científicas Instituto de Historia, 2003); and Kramer, *Blood of Government*.

84. The original phrases are, "ocupación predilecta ha sido el relato de los sucesos político-religiosos" and "cargadas de sucesos maravillosos y de relatos de castigos divinos." Pardo de Tavera, *Contribución*, 5–6.

85. Kramer, *Blood of Government*.

2. The Uses of Ethnology

1. Evaristo Aguirre (Cauit, pseud.), letter dated June 14, 1887, in José Rizal, *Epistolario Rizalino*, vol. 1, ed. Teodoro M. Kalaw, (Manila: Bureau of Printing, 1930), 280.

2. Ibid., italics original.

3. Pedro Alejandrino Paterno, *La antigua civilización tagálog* (Madrid: Manuel G. Hernández, Impresor de la Real Casa, 1887).

4. "Was dem Werke meines Landsmann P.A. Paterno . . . betrifft, so sage ich Ihnen, denken Sie nicht daran; P. A. Paterno ist ein so . . . ich finde kein Wort dazu, nur ein Zeichen so. . . ." Letter dated March 29, 1887, in José Rizal and Ferdinand Blumentritt, *The Rizal-Blumentritt Correspondence*, vol. 1 (Manila: National Historical Institute, 1992), unnumbered pp. between 66 and 67, translation on p. 70. On Paterno's image among his compatriots, see Resil Mojares, *Brains of the Nation: Pedro Paterno, T.H. Pardo de Tavera, Isabelo de los Reyes and the Production of Modern Knowledge* (Quezon City: Ateneo de Manila University Press, 2006), 15.

5. Paterno participated in the exposition's planning; see Mojares, *Brains of the Nation*, 13. The quotation is from the title page (Figure 2.2) of Paterno, *La antigua civilización tagálog*.

6. The display of people from the Philippines in the exposition reflects the somewhat schizophrenic nature of Spanish colonial ideology at the time: on the one hand, it included Igorots, Moros, and Negritos, members of groups that represented Catholic Spain's *failure* (more specifically, their failure to convert these groups to Catholicism); on the other hand, weavers and tobacco workers from Catholic areas (in Luzon and the Visayas) were shown at work (and their products—as well as those of the builders—were displays of industry, both "traditional" and "modern"), yet their "civilization" seems not to have been much touted. Instead, the closing ceremony featured "transformed" Igorot, as if the aspiration were being dramatized against the background of failure. On the exposition, see Luis Ángel Sánchez Gómez, *Un imperio en la vitrina: El colonialismo español en el Pacífico y la exposición de Filipinas de 1887* (Madrid: Consejo Superior de Investigaciones Científicas Instituto de Historia, 2003), 57–63, 76–81, 154.

7. On the exposition and *ilustrado* reactions to it, I have followed Paul A. Kramer, *The Blood of Government: Race, Empire, the United States, and the Philippines* (Chapel Hill: University of North Carolina Press, 2006); John N. Schumacher, *The Propaganda Movement, 1880–1895: The Creation of a Filipino Consciousness, the Making of the Revolution*, revised ed. (Quezon City: Ateneo de Manila University Press, 1997); and Filomeno V. Aguilar, Jr., "Tracing Origins: *Ilustrado* Nationalism and the Racial Science of Migration Waves," *Journal of Asian Studies* 64, no. 3 (2005): 605–37.

8. Graciano López Jaena, *Discursos y artículos varios* (Manila: Bureau of Printing, 1951), 151–66. "Civilization" and "civilized peoples" are specifically referred to on pp. 151 and 156.

9. See also Rizal's letters to Blumentritt Oct. 1886–June 1887, in Rizal and Blumentritt, *The Rizal-Blumentritt Correspondence*, vol. 1, 15–100 (leading up to and during the exposition), which reveal his intense interest in anthropology, including his work on a translation of Waitz.

10. For a striking illustration of how Madrileño perceptions were perceived by one of the *ilustrados*, see Vicente Rafael's analysis of some of Antonio Luna's fascinating fiction writing that appeared in *La solidaridad*, in Rafael, *The Promise of the Foreign: Nationalism and the Technics of Translation in the Spanish Philippines* (Durham, N.C.: Duke University Press, 2005), 31–35.

11. Joep Leerssen, *National Thought in Europe* (Amsterdam: Amsterdam University Press, 2006), 119–36.

12. See chapter 1 of this book.

13. Isabelo de los Reyes y Florentino, *Historia de Ilocos*, 2nd ed., vol. 1, *Parte prehistórica* (Manila: Establecimiento tipográfico La Opinión, 1890).

14. Michel Foucault, *Society Must Be Defended: Lectures at the Collège de France, 1975–76*, trans. David Macey (New York: Picador, 2003), 76. Foucault refers specifically to "race struggle," but I find the formulation helpful for thinking about race discourse more generally.

15. Anthony Milner, *The Invention of Politics in Colonial Malaya: Contesting Nationalism and the Expansion of the Public Sphere* (Cambridge: Cambridge University Press, 1994), 52.

16. Ibid., 53.

17. I build on others' work here; see note 21.

18. A succinct account of these categories is in Benedict R. O'G. Anderson, *Why Counting Counts: A Study of Forms of Consciousness and Problems of Language in Noli Me Tangere and El Filibusterismo* (Quezon City: Ateneo de Manila University Press, 2008), 3–4.

19. This "metropolitan" sense follows ibid., 34–36, which in turn revises Schumacher, *The Propaganda Movement*.

20. Anderson, *Counting Counts*, 48.

21. Reading "Filipino" as in its origins here simultaneously ethnic and political, deriving in part from ethnological science, I depart from scholars who either treat the term as a teleological necessity or see it as a post-Cavite formation. (Mojares's *Brains of the Nation* treats this question broadly. More particularly on the shift from "Filipino" creole to something more inclusive, see Mojares, *Brains of the Nation*, 202; Kramer, *Blood of Government*, 65–67; Anderson, *Counting Counts*, 4–5; and Aguilar, "Tracing Origins.") Some of these authors have recently treated anthropology or ethnology and *ilustrado* writings: Aguilar traces the ethnological origins of

"Filipino" in migration wave theory, emphasizing its racial exclusions; as readers will see in chapter 3, those exclusions were established in somewhat different terms by the authors I treat and drew on different methods. Mojares (*Brains of the Nation,* esp. 83–88, 298–300) treats the same texts in similar and detailed ways; I emphasize that the ethnological sense of "Filipino" emerges first in these writings collectively, and offer different readings on more distinct points. Kramer (*Blood of Government,* 51–73) shows that mastering anthropology was politically useful for *ilustrados;* I have taken this insight to delve into material he does not treat. In my argument, "race" has ambiguous political uses, and its appearance in these writings is less a matter of importation, adaptation, translation, or coproduction than it is of the sometimes cacophonous reverberations of concepts traveling to and from different contexts.

22. "Ich habe in meinem Dominguez' Wörterbuch nach dem Namen Raza gesehen, und ich glaube dass diese Bedeutung für Stamm nicht passt." Letter dated December 30, 1886, in Rizal and Blumentritt, *Rizal-Blumentritt Correspondence,* vol. 1, facsimile on unnumbered pages between 32 and 33.

23. "Wir nennen *Razas* die *Caucásica, Mongola, Americana, Malaya,* und *Negra.*" Ibid.

24. On conceptions of distinct races, see the introductory essays of Robert Bernasconi, ed., *Race and Anthropology,* 9 vols. (Bristol: Thoemmes, 2003); see also the other works in chapter 1, note 45, of this book. Readers must note that always in this book, "Malay" and "Malayan" refer to the idea of a "people" or "race" with its attendant language (group) or to the geographic peninsula. The word never refers to the then still distant future nation-state of "Malaysia."

25. "Negrito" is still used, though it is a general term that refers generically to any number of peoples and nowadays one would generally refer to a more specific people's name when applicable. In this book, I follow the lead of the authors I treat, and therefore often use "Negrito," but also sometimes the more specific "Aeta" or "Ita" (who are "Negritos" of northern Luzon).

26. "[W]eiter geben wir diesen Namen den Völkern, welche bedeutend gross sind wie etwa ½ Millionen, was Sie *Nationen* heisen [*sic*] nur, wir nennen nicht *Nationen* die Völker die nicht unabhängig sind, z.B. raza tagala, visaya etc. aber nicht *nacion tagala, visaya,* im Gegenteil, *raza* und *nacion* española etc." Rizal and Blumentritt, *Rizal-Blumentritt Correspondence,* vol. 1, facsimile on unnumbered pages between 32 and 33.

27. Yet in contrast with physiological data, particular "cultural" traits of *Völker* were thought to be vehicles for a more emotive and conscious kind of bond between humans than that generated by biology alone; they were more particular instantiations of a more general and universal idea of "culture" as humans' overcoming of nature. See Andrew Sartori, *Bengal in Global Concept History: Culturalism in the Age of Capital* (Chicago: University of Chicago Press, 2008), 26–40.

28. "*Tribu* ist kleiner wie *raza,* und bedeutet so wie eine Abteilung der raza: z.B.

la raza judia, la tribu de Juda, de Levi etc. . . . und Sie geben diesen Namen immer in Beziehung zu einem *Tronco* aus welchem die Tribus stämmen: z.B. Tribu de Juda, de Levi, de Dan in Beziehung zum Vater Jacob etc." Rizal and Blumentritt, *Rizal-Blumentritt Correspondence*, vol. 1, facsimile on unnumbered pages between 32 and 33.

29. "Tribu ist der gebräulichste Name welchen die Spanier den Völker geben, die weder keine grosse Menge bilden, noch Regierung haben, noch grosse Bedeutung." Ibid.

30. "*Clan* wird schon in Spanisch angenommen, aber nur in seiner ersten und ursprünglichen Bedeutung, wie eine Zusammenstellung mehreren Familien in Schottland. *Casta* scheint mir mehr politisch als ethnographisch, und in dieser Hinsicht gebe ich dem Namen kein grosses [*sic*] Werth. . . . Augenblicklich finde ich in meinem Kopf keinen anderen Ausdruck für Stamm." Ibid.

31. Anderson shows that this meaning was extant in José Rizal's 1887 novel, *Noli me Tángere*, though he does not use these terms to characterize it. Anderson, *Counting Counts*, 15.

32. See the 1869 and 1884 definitions of "civilización" in the *Dictionary of the Spanish Royal Academy*. Real Academia Española, *Diccionario de la lengua española*, http://buscon.rae.es/draeI.

33. Christina Rojas shows that "civilization" had meaning for creole Colombian elites in part precisely for its "universal" quality (though here there was also a possible plurality seeping in), as some societies could be called "civilizations" but others could not, in *Civilization and Violence: Regimes of Representation in Nineteenth-Century Colombia* (Minneapolis: University of Minnesota Press, 2002), chap. 2. Sartori writes about the overlap between "culture" and "civilization" in *Bengal in Global Concept History*, 26–40. Robert Young has written about "civilization," "race," and "culture" in his *Colonial Desire: Hybridity in Theory, Culture, and Race* (London and New York: Routledge, 1995), chap. 2.

34. The entry for *cultura* remained the same from 1884 until 1983 in the Real Academia Española, *Diccionario de la lengua española*.

35. For the overlap of these terms, see Sartori, *Bengal in Global Concept History*, 26–40. The German *Kultur* was both honorific—some peoples had it, but the primitives did not—but also plural. On *Kultur* in relation to anthropology and politics of mid to late nineteenth-century Germany, see Andrew Zimmerman, *Anthropology and Antihumanism in Imperial Germany* (Chicago: University of Chicago Press, 2001), chap. 2.

36. Ferdinand Blumentritt, *Attempt at Writing a Philippine Ethnography*, trans. Marcelino N. Maceda (Marawi City: University Research Center, Mindanao State University, 1980), originally *Versuch einer Ethnographie der Philippinen*, Petermann's Mittheilungen, Ergänzungsheft No. 67 (Gotha: Justus Perthes, 1882). My reading depends on the Maceda translation, though occasionally I have indicated the

original German when that seems particularly relevant. Blumentritt's theory and its place in *ilustrado* thought are particularly well treated in Aguilar, "Tracing Origins."

37. Aguilar, "Tracing Origins."

38. P. Francisco X. Baranera, *Compendio de la historia de Filipinas* (Manila: M. Perez, hijo, 1884), viii. I have been unable to locate a copy of the 1878 edition, which we will later see cited by Paterno, but it has the same number of pages as this edition, which suggests it might have been identical. Smita Lahiri has shown that this narrative was adopted in friar writings at least as early as 1874; see her "Rhetorical *Indios*: Propagandists and Their Publics in the Spanish Philippines," *Comparative Studies in Society and History* 49, no. 2 (2007): 243–75, esp. 262.

39. J. Montano, "Rapport à M. le ministre de l'Instruction publique sur une mission aux îles Philippines et en Malaisie (1879–1881)," *Archives des missions scientifiques et littéraires, 3e serie* XI (1885): 307–08.

40. Anderson, *Counting Counts*, 37.

41. Zimmerman, *Anthropology and Antihumanism in Imperial Germany*, 162n54. Zimmerman explains that bone measurements were preferable to other types of bodily measurement thought to be too variable to changes in diet, climate, and activity (such as skin tone, tissue size and shape, etc.).

42. Luis Ángel Sánchez Gómez, "La etnografía de Filipinas desde la administración colonial española," *Revista de Indias* 47, no. 179 (1987): esp. 165–66; also see his *Un imperio en la vitrina*.

43. *Exposición general de las Islas Filipinas*, (Madrid: Manuel Tello, 1886), 29–33; José María Ruíz, in Exposicion General de las Islas Filipinas en Madrid, *Memoria complementaria de la sección 2a del programa: Pobladores aborígenes, razas existentes y sus variedades: Religion, usos y costumbres de los habitantes de Filipinas* (Manila: Imprenta del Colegio de Santo Tomás, 1887). "Anthropology" (*antropología*) as such was relegated to the section of the exposition that pertained to "nature" (*naturaleza*) and consisted in particular of the display of human skulls. Here anthropology is the physical data, whereas the more theoretical work, of classifying peoples into racial groups and theorizing their relationship with each other and of documenting other kinds of ethnological data such as habits and customs, was separate.

44. Ruíz, in Exposicion General de las Islas Filipinas en Madrid, *Memoria*, i.

45. The original phrases are "los usos, costumbres, ritos" and "carácter." Ibid., i–ii.

46. "Al intentar describir la variedad de costumbres que presentan las extensas islas del Archipiélago en sus diversas razas y múltiples cruzamientos que de ellas han surgido, seguirémos los estudios etnográficos que mas recientemente se han hecho." Ibid., 61.

47. Ramón Jordana y Morera, *Bosquejo geográfico e histórico-natural del archipiélago filipino* (Madrid: Moreno y Rojas, 1885). Interestingly, Ruíz also solicited data

from Isabelo de los Reyes, who contributed summaries of traditional stories, in Exposicion General de las Islas Filipinas en Madrid, *Memoria*, 315–16.

48. "Etnología clasifica, describe y localiza las razas; la Etología ... religión, usos y costumbres." Exposicion General de las Islas Filipinas en Madrid, *Memoria*, 3. As Ruíz credits Sánchez on page i with the first section, this is likely Sánchez's writing. "Ethology" today refers to the study of animal behavior, so this report is a document that predates a disciplinary split between the study of human and animal behavior.

49. From the section headings, "Seccion 1.A Usos y costumbres etc. de las tribus infieles de estas islas" and "Seccion 2.A Pueblos cristianos." Ibid., 61, 211. The section on "Moros" (193–210) comprises just one-sixth of the subsection "Infidels of the Malayan Race" (99–210) and one-eighth of the pages devoted to "infidels" generally (63–210).

50. "Aunque hay notable diferencia en los usos y costumbres de las diferentes tribus de infieles de la raza Malaya, todas con poca diferencia convienen entre sí en su modo de vivir, que si bien no siempre puede llamarse enteramente salvaje, tampoco merece el nombre de racional y civilizado." Ibid., 99.

51. "Descritos los caracteres de las diferentes razas y tribus infieles que pueblan el Archipiélago filipino, pasamos á señalar las de los pueblos reducidos á la vida social y política, ó séan los cristianos, sometidos al Gobierno de España."

"Se denominan comunmente *indios filipinos*, y se hallan distribuidos en las costas y llanuras, distinguiéndose entre sí por algunas ligeras diferencias en sus trajes, usos y costumbres segun las provincias en que habitan y el dialecto que les es peculiar." Ibid., 211. The Spanish *reducido* (reduced) has a wider variety of signification than the English suggests; for its significance for Spanish colonization and the sense that it connotes something more productive than destructive, see Vicente Rafael, *Contracting Colonialism: Translation and Christian Conversion in Tagalog Society under Early Spanish Rule* (Ithaca, N.Y.: Cornell University Press, 1988), esp. 7, 29–30, 91.

52. Very brief references to particular peoples are given in Exposicion General de las Islas Filipinas en Madrid, *Memoria*, 211–13.

53. Ruíz does not generally capitalize *"indio"* (or *"filipino"*), though as section headings the categories are *"Clases sociales," "Indios de sementera," "Indios plebeyos," "Clase media," "Indios acomodados," "Mestizos," "El chino,"* and *"Españoles."* Ibid., 247, 249, 258, 262, 271, 275 (misnumbered as 245), 276, 283.

54. Ibid., 276–83.

55. See Mojares's biographical overview in *Brains of the Nation*, 121–29.

56. Trinidad Hermenegildo Pardo de Tavera, *Contribución para el estudio de los antiguos alfabetos filipinos* (Losana: Imprenta de Juanin Hermanos, 1884); Pardo de Tavera, *El sanscrito en la lengua tagalog* (Paris: Imprimerie de la Faculté

de Médicine, A. Davy, 1887). Mojares treats similar themes in Pardo de Tavera's *Contribución* in *Brains of the Nation*, 165–68, 208.

57. Pardo de Tavera, *Sanscrito*, 9.

58. Pardo de Tavera, *Contribución*, 5.

59. Ibid.

60. Ibid., 6.

61. Ibid., 11–12.

62. Ibid., 13.

63. Ibid.

64. For "Filipinos" referring to people, see ibid., 13, 19, 22, 23, 26.

65. Ibid., 29.

66. Ibid.

67. Ibid., 13.

68. Ibid., 11–12.

69. Ibid., 18.

70. On Pardo de Tavera's *Sanscrito*, see also Mojares, *Brains of the Nation*, 168–69.

71. Pardo de Tavera, *Sanscrito*, 10. He notes no conflict between what he had theorized as the proto-Filipino alphabet's distinct resemblance to Pali (a creolized form of Sanskrit), associated with Ashoka (Buddhist), and the Sanskritic and Hindu origins that he theorized in this work. I thank Rosalind Morris for calling my attention to the significant difference between the two.

72. Ibid., 9–10.

73. Ibid., 9.

74. Ibid.

75. Ibid., 6.

76. Ibid., 7.

77. Ibid., 6.

78. This biographical sketch is drawn from Mojares, *Brains of the Nation*, 3–12.

79. Pedro Alejandrino Paterno, *Los Itas* (Madrid: los Sucesores de Cuesta, 1890); Paterno, *Antigua civilización*.

80. Paterno, *Itas*, 64.

81. Ibid., 65. Though the more secular "Universal History" was still deeply Christian (e.g., Hegel or Herder), the Church was hostile to it.

82. Ibid., 2–3.

83. On Paterno's *Itas*, see also Mojares, *Brains of the Nation*, 56–59. I will follow Paterno and use the term "Ita" in this chapter.

84. Paterno, *Itas*.

85. These are listed originally under the headings referring to the three epochs: "La de los aborígenes," "La de la civilización tagala,"and "La de la civilización católica." Paterno, *Antigua civilización*, 2.

86. More on the French emphasis on civilization as a mark of progress or advance is given later in this chapter, though a quick example may help here: the secretary general of the (French) Society of Anthropology from 1887 to 1902 had a chair in the history of civilizations. Linda L. Clark, *Social Darwinism in France* (University, Ala.: University of Alabama Press, 1984), 140.

87. In another work, for example, he referred to the Bagobos, an animist people who lived on the slopes of Mount Apo in Mindanao, as "Tagalogs of Mindanao (*tagálos de Mindanao*)." Pedro Alejandrino Paterno, "El cristianismo el la antigua civilización tagalog (continuación)," *La solidaridad*, September 15, 1892, 803.

88. Paterno, *Antigua civilización*, 77, 53.

89. Ibid., 35, 41, 67–68, 72, 143–45, 147–48.

90. Ibid., 145–51.

91. The original reads, "con las armas en la mano, nos han hecho conocer al verdadero Dios." Ibid., 31.

92. Paterno cited the example of Father Tachard, a seventeenth-century French Jesuit in Siam who had sought to convert the Siamese court (and thus the Thai people). His source is Luis de Estrada, *Cuadro geografico, histórico, administrativo y político de la India en 1858* (Madrid: Imprenta y Estereotipia de M. Rivadeneyra, 1858). Writing in the wake of news of the "Sepoy Mutiny" (Indian uprising, rebellion, revolt, or revolution, in 1857–58), Estrada stressed how little had been published in Spanish about India. On the Jesuits in India and China and the "Chinese rites" controversy, see Lewis A. Maverick, *China, a Model for Europe* (San Antonio, Tex.: Paul Anderson, 1946); Jonathan Spence, *The Question of Hu* (New York: Vintage, 1989); Joan-Pau Rubiés, "The Spanish Contribution to the Ethnology of Asia in the Sixteenth and Seventeenth Centuries," *Renaissance Studies* 17, no. 3 (2003): 418–48. Du Halde was the major source of Jesuit texts for a broader European audience including both Montesquieu and Voltaire. Voltaire, *The Philosophy of History* (New York: Philosophical Library, 1965); Montesquieu, *Spirit of the Laws*, trans. Thomas Nugent (New York: MacMillan, 1949).

93. Paterno, Antigua civilización, 53–81, 152–68, 175–76, 182–206.

94. The original phrases are, "los *Aetas, Etas, ó Itas*, ó como los llaman los españoles, los *Negritos*," "las diversas razas que en el Archipiélago se encuentran,"and "los primeros pobladores del país." Ibid., 3. Paterno quoted here (without specific attribution but with a footnote) the prologue of the Jesuit text for secondary education. Baranera, *Compendio*.

95. Paterno follows most closely Montano's formulation of three racially distinct successive waves: Negrito, Indonesian, and Malay. Paterno, *Itas*, 27; cf. Montano, "Rapport," 308 (see note 39 for J. Montano, "Rapport à M. le ministre de l'Instrucion publique....").

96. Paterno, *Itas*, 225.

97. Ibid., 226.

98. Ibid., 227.

99. Ibid.

100. The original language is "Vencida por invasores de complexión más robusta, y dotados de un más alto grado de cultura." Paterno, *Antigua civilización*, 4, taken verbatim from Baranera, *Compendio*, VIII. Paterno closely followed especially the prologue of the textbook, which he would have read as a student of the Jesuit's secondary school in Manila. Baranera's Spanish-Jesuit story had used a racial-civilizational rubric (of successive migration waves as advancement) to posit Spanish-Catholic civilization as the culmination of Philippine history; in Paterno's modification, the Tagalog people were both the ancient apex and those destined to bring a new height to Filipino-Catholic civilization. See my brief introduction to Baranera's *Compendio* in the section titled "Race and Civilization in Philippine Ethnography."

101. Paterno, *Itas*, 228.

102. Ibid.

103. "[R]epugnando la unión ó mezcla con otras, consume su existencia en el más degenerador [*sic*] aislamiento." Paterno, *Antigua civilización*, 3. Paterno likely borrowed from Montano the idea that the Ita were racially pure; Montano had noted that some Negrito, having successfully fled from the invading races, had conserved their pure blood. Montano, "Rapport," 310. See my brief account of Montano's report in the section titled "Race and Civilization in Philippine Ethnography" above. Elsewhere Paterno borrows nearly verbatim from J. Montano, *Voyage aux Philippines et en Malaisie* (Paris: Librairie Hachette et Cie., 1886), 310.

104. Paterno, *Itas*, 229.

105. Ibid., 63.

106. Ibid., 46–47.

107. Clark, *Social Darwinism in France*, esp. 138.

108. Lapouge, as quoted in ibid., 145. Lapouge, champion of Gobineau's theories, articulated his ideas in the *Revue d'anthropologie* (in which he reviewed Darwin's cousin's 1883 book, which coined the term "eugenics") and in his lectures on anthropology at the Montpellier Faculty of Sciences, published the following year (the same year as Paterno's *Antigua Civilización*). See Clark, *Social Darwinism in France*, 39, 44–45 (on Lapouge), and 38 (on Lamarckism).

109. Guyot, a classical economist and republican radical, found in evolutionary ideas bases for laissez-faire economic principles but not for imperialism. Also in 1887, French anthropologists attacked some of Lapouge's ideas in *l'Homme*, a journal whose relationship to the *Revue d'anthropologie* reflected a schism among French anthropologists who adopted evolutionary and racial frameworks. A later example of French evolutionary-anthropological race-thinking was articulated in 1900 by Paul Topinard, a prominent French anthropologist during the 1870s and 1880s who "stated explicitly that Jews were not a separate race and called the

'French race' a mixture of three 'peoples.'" By this time, the Dreyfus affair had dramatically brought these issues into the mainstream French political discourse. Clark, *Social Darwinism in France*, 62–64, 159, 165 (on Guyot), 39, 44–45 (on Lapouge), 47–51 (on anxieties about race of Frenchmen), 38–40, 52 (on *l'Homme* and criticism of Lapouge), and 40 (on Topinard).

110. "Sabido es que las razas que no se mezclan, degeneran en el trascurso del tiempo, y luego desaparecen; al contrario, las que se mezclan, las *mestizas*, como son la española, la francesa, la alemana, la inglesa; en general, *las de los países occidentales de Europa, que . . . se hallan tan entremezcladas, que ninguna puede reclamar una genealogía auténtica, viven robustas y poderosas.*" Paterno, *Antigua civilización*, 3–4. Paterno quotes here from Yves Guyot, "Préface," in Paul Mougeolle, *Les problèmes de l'histoire*, (Paris: C. Reinwald, 1886), XI.

111. My translation derives from Paterno: "Los órganos más complicados se perfeccionan por la acumulación de innumerables variaciones, aunque ligeras; lo mismo sucede en los organismos sociales. La heterogeneidad es una de las causas de la fuerza de Francia, y los hombres que trabajan por destruirla, no sólo emprenden una tarea imposible, sino también una obra retrógrada; aspiran, sin duda, á llevarnos á las civilizaciones estacionarias del Asia. Es una desgracia para los chinos, los árabes y las sectas que pueblan el Indostán, haber conservado su hegemonía." Guyot, "Préface," XI, as quoted in Paterno, *Antigua civilización*, 4.

112. The second edition of Gobineau's *Essai* had just appeared in 1884. Clark, *Social Darwinism in France*, 148; Michael D. Biddiss, *Father of Racist Ideology: The Social and Political Thought of Count Gobineau* (New York: Weybright and Talley, 1970), 112–31.

113. Guyot, "Préface," X–XI. Though he refers directly to Gobineau, his language suggests he was arguing particularly with Lapouge.

114. On Paterno's *Antigua civilización*, see also Mojares, *Brains of the Nation*, 46–52.

115. Paterno, *Itas*, 5–6.

116. Ibid., 65.

117. Ibid., 5.

118. Ibid., 5–6.

119. Ibid., 59.

120. Ibid., 58.

121. Ibid., 59, 58.

122. Ibid., 4.

123. Ibid., 3–4, emphasis original.

124. Ibid., 4, 3.

125. Ibid., 4.

126. cf. Bankimchandra's conception of Hindu culture as valuable but also mutable: Partha Chatterjee, *Nationalist Thought and the Colonial World: A Derivative Discourse?* (Minneapolis: University of Minnesota Press, 1986), 57, 62, 64–66.

127. The only document with a racial designation in the National Archives indicates that he was *mestizo sangley* (Chinese mestizo). National Archives of the Philippines, "Reyes, Isabelo de los," in *Varios personajes*, book 8. Manila. This brief biographical account is drawn from Benedict R. O'G. Anderson, *Under Three Flags: Anarchism and the Anti-Colonial Imagination* (London: Verso, 2005), 9–11; William Henry Scott, *Cracks in the Parchment Curtain* (Quezon City: New Day, 1982), 245n2; and Mojares, *Brains of the Nation*, 255–63.

128. For more about his journalistic work, see my "Isabelo de los Reyes and the Philippine Contemporaries of *La Solidaridad*," *Philippine Studies* 54, no. 3 (2006): 381–411.

129. On de los Reyes's "Tinguian," see Mojares, *Brains of the Nation*, 291–93; and, on his prehistory, see ibid., 295–303; and Scott, *Cracks in the Parchment Curtain*, 274–76.

130. De los Reyes y Florentino, *Historia de Ilocos*, vol. 1; de los Reyes y Florentino, *Las islas Visayas en la época de la conquista* (Manila: Tipo-Litogr. de Chofré y ca, 1889); and de los Reyes y Florentino, *Historia de Filipinas* (Manila: Impr. de D. Esteban Balbás, 1889).

131. For example, de los Reyes writes about "the Malay type of the Ilocanos and others (*El tipo malayo de los ilocanos y otros*)," in his *Historia de Ilocos*, vol. 1, p. 20; but "the Malay type of the Filipinos (*El tipo malayo de los filipinos*)" in his *Islas Visayas*, 61 and his *Historia de Filipinas*, 4. Another example is that he writes about "the Filipinos (*los filipinos*)," in his *Historia de Ilocos*, vol. 1, 23, and his *Historia de Filipinas*, 5; but "the Visayans (*los visayas*)," in his *Islas Visayas*, 63.

132. "[N]o hay país que se denomina 'Indonesia.' . . . Esta división etnográfica esta fundada en datos nuevos y aun no bien averiguados. No está adoptada por la mayor[í]a de los etnógrafos, y ent[r]e sus mismos sostenedores no hay unanimidad sob[r]e qué razas [d]eben pertenecer a los indonesianos." De los Reyes, *Historia de Ilocos*, vol. 1, 35–36.

133. The original phrases are "malayos puros" and "los indonesianos." Ibid., 35.

134. The original phrases are "los malayos," "[l]os negritos ó 'aetas,'" and "los aborígenes." Ibid., 18.

135. Isabelo de los Reyes y Florentino, *El folk-lore filipino* (Manila: Chofré y Ca, 1889), 19. He uses the phrase "huraño, misàntropo y nómada" in his *Historia de Ilocos*, vol. 1, 18.

136. One of de los Reyes's newspaper colleagues (José Felipe del Pan) held that anywhere the Malay race appeared it was in fact the result of a mix between Chinese invaders and pre-Sinitic Negritos. De los Reyes, *Historia de Ilocos*, vol. 1, 28–29.

137. "[S]e hallan confirmadas por respetables etnólogos modernos." Ibid., 26. De los Reyes cites James Cowles Prichard, the early nineteenth-century English ethnologist; the peninsular anthropologist Manuel Anton; Karl (or Carl)

Semper, German zoologist and ethnologist who in the mid-nineteenth century traveled in and wrote about peoples of the Philippines; and Alfred Russel Wallace, nineteenth-century British ethnologist who sought to delineate Malay from Papuan. On these figures, see George W. Stocking, *Victorian Anthropology* (New York: MacMillan, 1987); and William Henry Scott, ed., *German Travelers on the Cordillera (1860–1890)* (Manila: Filipiniana Book Guild, 1975).

138. "Malayos puros relativeamente, pues el tipo malayo en Filipinas en realidad está desfigurada por cruzamientos. A estos pertenecen los ilocanos, casi todos los tinguianes, los igorrotes sometidos y los 'alzados' de Abra." De los Reyes, *Historia de Ilocos*, vol. 1, 36.

139. "Mestizos marcadamente de malayo y chino, como son los mestizos sangleyes de Vigan, los igorrotes y tinguianes del SE. de Ilocos Sur que tienen ojos achinados. "Mestizos marcadamente de malayo y negrito. . . . no solo entre los vecinos inmediatos de los negritos, sino entre los ilocanos, especialmente del Norte." Ibid.

140. "Negritos, ni mas ni menos que los de Mariveles." Ibid.

141. "Conocido el carácter avaro y egoista de los chinos, mal podía ser que lo hayan abandonado." Ibid., 33.

142. "Los ilocanos son de un mismo orígen que los tagalogs, bícoles y otros filipinos civilizados y creo que son malayos con sangre negrita." Ibid., 38.

143. "Los autores llaman tagalogs solo à los que pueblan las costas del centro de Luzón; pero para estos tal denominación es común á todos los malayos filipinos, incluso los ilocanos, bìcoles etc. Y á la verdad sería más propia esta denominación que la de 'indios' (porque no son de la India), 'indígenas' (porque esta palabra significa naturales y es aplicable á cualquier hijo de vecino); y 'filipinos' (porque este vocablo no distingue las razas y se puede dar lo mismo al hijo de europeos nacido en Filipinas, que á un aeta de Ilocos." Ibid., 26.

144. "Los tinguianes é igorrotes de Ilocos . . . se acercan mucho más á los ilocanos que á otra raza, y por consiguiente, son de un mismo orígen." Ibid., 37.

145. Isabelo de los Reyes y Florentino, "El Tinguian," in *Filipinas: Artículos varios de Isabelo de los Reyes y Florentino sobre etnografía, historia y costumbres del país* (Manila: J. A. Ramos, 1887), 1–37, quotation on p. 7.

146. Ibid., 7. De los Reyes refers the reader to his *Islas Visayas* for this evidence.

147. De los Reyes, *Historia de Ilocos*, vol. 1, 214–15.

148. Here, as elsewhere, he does not capitalize "tinguian" in the original. De los Reyes, "Tinguian," 14.

149. Ibid.

150. Ibid., 10.

151. "Las insignificantes diferencias que existen entre el ilocano civilizado relativamente; el tinguian que ya viste de pantalón y chaqueta; el igorrote sometido, que aunque desnudo todavía, ya perdió su caràcter huraño y cruel; y el alzado de usos canibalísticos; estas diferencias son efectos de los lugares que ocupan y se ve

que son civilizados ó salvajes según que estén cerca ó lejos de los sitios frecuentados por los españoles ó de los ilocanos civilizados. Aún entre estos últimos, que ya han adquirido un grado considerable de cultura, a veces se practican sacrificios humanos . . . ,y en un principio eran ni mas ni menos que los caníbales del Abra." de los Reyes, *Historia de Ilocos*, vol. 1, 37.

152. Ferdinand Blumentritt, "Las razas indígenas de Filipinas," *Boletín de la Sociedad Geográfica* 28 (1890): 7–41, quotation on p. 7.

153. Ibid., 10, emphasis original.

154. Blumentritt also included entries for names that were not of peoples but might be mistaken for such (e.g., languages, towns, or social titles, which ethnographers, finding in other texts, might mistake for a people) and cross-listed entries for alternate spellings and names. Ibid.

155. Ibid., 10. Blummentritt, following Spanish convention, capitalized no ethnic or national terms. I therefore keep *moro* as it was used by Blumentritt (lowercase), though it has since come to have an ethnonational sense, which is hinted at by Blumentritt in much the same ambiguous and uneven way that "Filipino" had an ethnic sense in de los Reyes's or Pardo de Tavera's writings (comparable to Blumentritt's "*indio*"). This transformation never happened for "infidel"; though "indigenous" is taken as a general type of ethnicity and sometimes a legal category, it is not an ethnicity in itself.

156. For example, "indios infieles" (ibid., 17), "indios salvajes" (ibid., 11, 12, 21, 36); cf. "infieles salvajes" (savage infidels), which he used in reference to a group whose racial origin he was unsure of (either Malay or Malay-Negrito mestizo) (ibid., 23).

157. On Blumentritt's *Versuch*, see also Mojares, *Brains of the Nation*, 89–90; and Aguilar, "Tracing Origins."

158. Patricio N. Abinales, *Making Mindanao: Cotabato and Davao in the Formation of the Philippine Nation-State* (Quezon City: Ateneo de Manila University Press, 2000).

159. Johannes Fabian, *Time and the Other: How Anthropology Makes Its Object* (New York: Columbia University Press, 1983).

160. For an example of an article that challenged racist conceptions, see "Crónica," *La solidaridad*, November 15, 1891.

161. Mojares, *Brains of the Nation*, 125, 30–32.

162. Ibid., 17.

163. Ibid., 258, 62–63

3. Practicing Folklore

1. The original phrase is "progreso, que tiende á nivelar todas las razas con sus vapores, ferro-carriles, actividad comercial y el telégrafo." Blumentritt, as quoted

in Isabelo de los Reyes y Florentino, *Historia de Ilocos*, 2nd ed., vol. 1, *Parte prehistórica* (Manila: Establecimiento tipográfico La Opinión, 1890), 39.

2. The original phrases are "la ciencia folk-lórica," "los pueblos civilizados y salvajes," and "progreso." Blumentritt, as quoted in ibid.

3. Here, as elsewhere, de los Reyes does not capitalize "filipino" in the Spanish original. Isabelo de los Reyes y Florentino, *El folk-lore filipino* (Manila: Tipo-Litografía de Chofré, 1889), 170. The publisher "Imprenta de Santa Cruz" is also given and correct for this same volume and edition. For explanation, see W. E. Retana, *Aparato bibliográfico de la historia general de Filipinas*, vol. 3 (Madrid: Imprenta de la Sucesora de M. Minuesa de los Ríos, 1906), 1145 (entry 2788). I refer to and translate from this edition, though I also consulted the reprinted version with an English translation by Salud C. Dizon and Maria Elinora P. Imson (Diliman, Quezon City: University of the Philippines Press, 1994).

4. Ibid., 10–11.

5. Benedict R. O'G. Anderson, *Under Three Flags: Anarchism and the Anti-Colonial Imagination* (London: Verso, 2005), chap. 1; Resil Mojares, *Brains of the Nation: Pedro Paterno, T.H. Pardo de Tavera, Isabelo de los Reyes and the Production of Modern Knowledge* (Quezon City: Ateneo de Manila University Press, 2006), esp. pp. 304–13. Anderson and Mojares both have built on William Henry Scott, *Cracks in the Parchment Curtain* (Quezon City: New Day, 1982), 245–65. I follow these scholars in reading de los Reyes's folklore as reconstructing the pre-Hispanic Philippines and as a vehicle for social commentary, but I treat why folklore as a genre was particularly conducive to social commentary and how folklore is related to the ethnological sciences that were the subject of the last chapter. In looking at de los Reyes's folklore in comparison with peninsular folklore, I see more commonalities than have others.

6. Isabelo de los Reyes y Florentino, *El folk-lore filipino: Colección comentada y publicada bajo la dirección de D. Isabelo de los Reyes*, vol. 2 (Manila: Imprenta de Santa Cruz, 1889). Contemporary Spanish-language conventions require no capitalization after the initial word of a title; I follow this convention in citations. However, de los Reyes, as well as peninsular folklorists during the late nineteenth century, usually capitalized both elements of "Folk-Lore," and also capitalized the adjectives of folklore titles, as in *Folk-Lore Filipino*, *Folk-Lore Español*, or *Folk-Lore Andaluz*. For this reason, and because de los Reyes's work is well-known as *El Folk-Lore Filipino*, I capitalize all elements of this and other nineteenth-century Spanish-language folkore titles when I refer to them in the main text.

7. Serrano Laktaw later became involved in masonry. See John N. Schumacher, *The Propaganda Movement, 1880–1895: The Creation of a Filipino Consciousness, the Making of the Revolution*, rev. ed. (Quezon City: Ateneo de Manila University Press, 1997), 123, 125, 126n, 137; and E. Arsenio Manuel, "Serrano Laktaw, Pedro," in

Dictionary of Philippine Biography, ed. Manuel (Quezon City: Filipiniana, 1970), 360–62.

8. Schumacher, *Propaganda Movement,* 128–30 and passim; *La solidaridad* (Barcelona and Madrid: 1889–1895). Anderson also writes about Ponce's later work as a diplomat for the Revolution in *Under Three Flags,* 201–3.

9. [Pedro] Alejandr[in]o Paterno, *Nínay (costumbres filipinas)* (Madrid: Fortanet, 1885); José Rizal, "Two Eastern Fables," *Trübner's Record,* no. 245, third series, vol. 1, no. 3 (1889): 71–74.

10. Anderson, *Under Three Flags,* chap. 1.

11. Here my account differs sharply from Anderson's. Ibid., 12–14.

12. De los Reyes, *Folk-lore filipino,* 12. In direct quotations, I will preserve the capitalization and spelling of the forms of the word "folklore" that appear in my sources, even when those forms appear antiquated, to ensure consistency and preserve the novelty of the term for de los Reyes and other nineteenth-century Spanish-language folklorists. In this note and notes following, references to de los Reyes, *Folk-lore filipino* refer to the first volume (see note 3, above) unless "vol. 2" is specified (see note 6).

13. The original phrases read, "donde todo es sombra y superstición" and "muchos cuentos fabulosos y supersticiosos y creía en ellos como dogmas de fé." De los Reyes, *Historia de Ilocos,* vol. 1, 180.

14. The original text is "presentar una lista de supersticiones mas larga aún que juntas todas las de mis rivales." Ibid.; Scott, *Cracks in the Parchment Curtain,* 249–50.

15. De los Reyes includes her work in his collection in *Folk-lore filipino,* and it was subsequently anthologized in an international collection of women's works. De los Reyes, *Folk-lore filipino,* 157.

16. Ibid., 12. Baltanás makes the case that Spanish folklore was on par with folklore elsewhere in Europe, though his study elides divisions, noted by others, among Spanish folklorists. Enrique Baltanás, "Los orígenes de la Escuela Popular de Sabiduría Superior: la idea de *pueblo* en Antonio Machado y Álvarez," *Hoy es siempre todavía: Curso internacional sobre Antonio Machado* (2006): 11–64. Machado's international orientation and early adaptation of folklore as scientific rather than literary pursuit is treated by Joan Prat, "Historia: Estudio introductorio," and Encarnación Aguilar Criado, "Antropología y folklore en Andalucía (1850–1922)," both in *Antropología de los pueblos de España,* ed. Joan Prat et al. (Madrid: Taurus, 1991), 13–32, 58–76.

17. For example, George Laurence Gomme, *Ethnology in Folklore* (London: Kegan Paul, Trench, Trübner, 1892). On European folklore, both eighteenth-century roots and nineteenth-century practices, see Roger D. Abrahams, "Phantoms of Romantic Nationalism in Folkloristics," *Journal of American Folklore* 106, no. 419 (1993): 3–37; Regina Bendix, *In Search of Authenticity: The Formation of Folklore Studies*

(Madison: University of Wisconsin Press, 1997), 16–17, 34–67; George W. Stocking, ed., *Romantic Motives: Essays on Anthropological Sensibility* (Madison: University of Wisconsin Press, 1989), 86–95; Stocking, *Victorian Anthropology* (New York: Mac-Millan, 1987), 53–56; John H. Zammito, *Kant, Herder, and the Birth of Anthropology* (Chicago: University of Chicago Press, 2002), 342–45; Karl J. Fink, "Storm and Stress Anthropology," *History of the Human Sciences* 6, no. 1 (1993): 51–71; Andrew Sartori, *Bengal in Global Concept History: Culturalism in the Age of Capital* (Chicago: University of Chicago Press, 2008), 35–36; and Susan Stewart, "Notes on Distressed Genres," *Journal of American Folklore* 104, no. 411 (1991): 5–31.

18. "Inmediatamente se puso en relación con el señor Gomme, el secretario general de ella, y resolvió pensar en la instauración como asociación del *Folklore en España.*" Alejandro Guichot y Sierra, *Noticia histórica del folklore; Orígenes en todos los países hasta 1890; Desarrollo en España hasta 1921* (Sevilla: Hijos de G. Alvarez, 1922), 163.

19. Aguilar Criado, "Antropología y folklore en Andalucía," 67–68.

20. Information from Machado, as quoted in José Blas Vega and Eugenio Cobo, "Estudio preliminar," in *El folk-lore andaluz,* (Madrid: Tres-Catorce-Diesisiete, 1981), XVII–XVIII. This 1981 volume is a reproduction, with this new preface added, of the first volume of the periodical *El folk-lore andaluz,* which was published originally in Sevilla from March 1882 until February 1883.

21. "[L]a emancipación del pensamiento en literatura es la aurora de la independencia y el síntoma más expresivo de la nacionalidad." Machado, probably quoting Durán, as quoted in Blas Vega and Cobo, "Estudio preliminar," XIII.

22. "[E]studia al pueblo, que, sin gramática y sin retórica, habla mejor que tú, porque expresa por entero su pensamiento, sin adulteraciones ni trampantojos; y canta mejor que tú, porque dice lo que siente. El pueblo, no las academias, es el verdadero conservador del lenguaje y el verdadero poeta nacional." Montoto y Rautenstrauch, as quoted in ibid., XIX.

23. Aguilar Criado, "Antropología y folklore en Andalucía"; Prat, "Historia: Estudio introductorio."

24. Here I follow John Blanco, who identifies this feature in the writings of Spanish *costumbrismo*'s most significant figures, Mariano José de Larra and Mesonero Romanos. John D. Blanco, *Frontier Constitutions: Christianity and Colonial Empire in the Nineteenth-Century Philippines* (Berkeley: University of California, 2009), 163.

25. Larra exemplifies this, though Mesonero Romanos does not. Ibid., 164.

26. See Blanco's reading of the work of two peninsular Spanish newspapermen in Manila: Ricardo de Puga's *La ilustración filipina* (1859–60) and Federico Casedemunt's serialized pseudo-autobiography. Blanco, *Frontier Constitutions,* 160–82. Puga's periodical is not to be confused with the later *Ilustración filipina,* behind which stood Isabelo de los Reyes; see my "Isabelo de los Reyes and the Philippine Contemporaries of *La Solidaridad,*" *Philippine Studies* 54, no. 3 (2006):

381–411. Blanco argues that the significant difference between Spanish-peninsular and Spanish-colonial *costumbrismos* is that in the latter, a "*racial* division" emerges "between Spanish colonialists and travelers, on the one hand, and native subjects, on the other, which consistently displaces the polarization between 'enlightened' and 'unenlightened' sectors of the public." Blanco, *Frontier Constitutions*, 164.

27. Prat, "Historia: Estudio introductorio," 21; Aguilar Criado, "Antropología y folklore en Andalucía," 70.

28. Juan López-Morillas distinguishes between Krausism properly speaking and romanticism but also shows the links between Krausism and German philosophers such as Herder, Fichte, Shelling, and Hegel in *The Krausist Movement and Ideological Change in Spain, 1854–1874*, trans. Frances M. López-Morillas (Cambridge: Cambridge University Press, 1981), esp. 71. The Herderian strand was important for Machado: Folk poetry was the natural expression of the particular genius of a people whose common language indicated a common genius and role to play in the grand drama of humanity. Thus from its inception the study of the lore of the *Volk* was rooted in ideas of the nation as a natural, organic, language-based grouping of people.

29. De los Reyes, *Folk-lore filipino*, 10, italics original.

30. *Boletín de la Institución Libre de Enseñanza* (Madrid: 1877). Carmelo Lisón, "Madrid: Una gran encuesta de 1901–1902 (notas para la historia de la antropología social en España)," in *Antropología de los pueblos de España*, ed. Joan Prat et al. (Madrid: Taurus, 1991), 48–52. On Krausism's adaptation of both positivism and romanticism, and its significance for anthropological and folklore studies in Spain, see Aguilar Criado, "Antropología y folklore en Andalucía," 65–73; and Prat, "Historia: Estudio introductorio," 18. For Krausism and battles over educational institutions in Spain, see López-Morillas, *Krausist Movement*, 54–57, 114–24.

31. Thomas, "Isabelo de los Reyes and the Philippine Contemporaries of *La Solidaridad*."

32. The original phrases read, "El amor que profesamos a nuestro pueblo" and "el deseo de que la literatura y la poesía, rompiendo los antiguos moldes de su convencionalismo estrecho y artificial, se levante a la categoría de ciencia." Machado as quoted in Blas Vega and Cobo, "Estudio preliminar," XXI.

33. The original reads, "esa ciencia *niña* llamada a reivindicar el derecho del pueblo, hasta aquí desconocido, a ser considerado como un factor importante en la cultura y civilización de la humanidad." Machado as quoted in ibid.

34. The final phrase reads, "todos los elementos constitutivos del genio, del saber y del idioma patrios." Antonio Machado y Álvarez (Demófilo, pseud.), *El folk-lore andaluz* (Madrid: Tres-Catorce-Diesisiete, 1981), 501. About this volume, see note 20.

35. De los Reyes, *Folk-lore filipino*, 9.

36. Aguilar Criado, "Antropología y folklore en Andalucía," 69. According to John Ashton, the centralization (and theoretical orientation) of the Folk-Lore Society of London did not represent the bulk of folklore collecting in late nineteenth-century England, which in his description is more regional, field based, and less theoretical; see "Beyond Survivalism: Regional Folkloristics in Late-Victorian England," *Folklore* 108 (1997): 19–23. The regionalism of Spanish and Filipino folklore, and perhaps England's, too, resembles the productive tensions between the local and national noted by Michael Herzfeld in "Localism and the Logic of Nationalistic Folklore: Cretan Reflections," *Comparative Studies in Society and History* 45, no. 2 (2003): 281–310.

37. Machado (Demófilo, pseud.), *Folk-lore andaluz*, 501.

38. "[S]e constituye primero . . . para ver de animar a todas las regiones españolas a que realicen su labor. Así este organismo sólo tendrá la misión de coordinar los diferentes grupos que vayan apareciendo, pero nunca con un sentido centralizador." Blas Vega and Cobo, "Estudio preliminar," XXIV.

39. Machado (Demófilo, pseud.), *Folk-lore andaluz*, 502.

40. Antonio Machado y Álvarez and Alejandro Guichot y Sierra y Compañía, eds., *Biblioteca de las tradiciones populares españolas*, 11 vols. (Sevilla: 1883–86).

41. Machado (Demófilo, pseud.), *Folk-lore andaluz*, 501.

42. Ibid., 502.

43. Prat, "Historia: Estudio introductorio"; Llorenç Prats, "Cataluña: Los Precedentes de los estudios etnológicos en Cataluña, folklore y etnografía (1853–1859)," in *Antropología de los pueblos de España*, ed. Joan Prat et al. (Madrid: Taurus, 1991), 77–80.

44. Antonio Machado y Álvarez, "Cuentos populares españoles anotados y comparados con los de otras colecciones de Portugal, Italia y Francia," in Machado and Guichot, eds., *Biblioteca de las tradiciones populares españolas*, vol. 1 (1883), 101–99. The work does not pretend to represent all regions of Spain; nevertheless, it is notable that the peninsula and even its dominant language (Castilian) are represented by southern regions rather than Castile.

45. Emphasis added in my translation. "Llamo cuentos populares *españoles* á los contenidos en ella . . . porque están escritos en idioma español; y no por otra causa. La inmensa mayoría de ellos, si no todos, no son oriundos de España y tienen un remoto abolengo." Ibid., 107.

46. Emphasis added. "Esto no obstante, al circular en los labios de nuestro pueblo ó de las naciones y tierras que hablan nuestro idioma, reciben un sello español, cuyo valor histórico importa mucho estudiar y conocer." Ibid.

47. On these publications, see notes 20 and 40.

48. This feature of de los Reyes's folklore has been nicely illuminated by Anderson (*Under Three Flags*) and also Mojares (*Brains of the Nation*).

49. De los Reyes, *Folk-lore filipino*, 11.

50. Here, as elsewhere, de los Reyes capitalized neither "ilocanos" nor "tagalos," according to Spanish convention. Ibid.

51. That is, race, physiology, and ethnology overlapped but were not identical for de los Reyes; here what he perceived as physiological *difference* had initially obscured what he found later to be underlying ethnographic similarities.

52. Rizal, "Two Eastern Fables," 74.

53. Pedro Serrano [Laktaw], "Folk-lore pampango," in *Folk-lore filipino*, vol. 2, ed. de los Reyes, 81–109; the quotation is found on page 81.

54. De los Reyes, *Folk-lore filipino*, 27, capitalization original.

55. Ibid., 41.

56. Ibid.

57. Ibid., 45, 46.

58. De los Reyes, *Folk-lore filipino*, vol. 2, 137n1.

59. De los Reyes, *Folk-lore filipino*, 109.

60. Ibid., 110, capitalization original.

61. Letter dated April 30, 1888, in José Rizal and Ferdinand Blumentritt, *The Rizal-Blumentritt Correspondence*, vol. 1, trans. Encarnación Alzona (Manila: National Historical Institute, 1992), 167. I have slightly modified Alzona's translation. The original text reads (unnumbered pages between pp. 165 and 167), "Wie ich sehe, viele Folkloristen oder Zukunftige [*sic*] Anthropologen tauchen in Ilokos auf. Da ist ein Herr Delosserre, mit dem Sie verkehren. Ich bemerke eine Sache: Da die meisten philippinischen Folkloristen Ilokaner sind, und weil diese das Epithet *Ilokanisch* gebrauche, werden die Anthropologen nach her angeben für ilocanische Gebräuchen und Sitten was richtig Philippinisch sind; aber es ist unsere Schuld." Notice that Rizal sometimes spells "Ilocos" and variants with a "c" but usually with a "k"—more on this in chapter 4. Rizal's letter to Blumentritt prefigured one of the points of conflict between Rizal and de los Reyes. Anderson has noted Rizal's hypocrisy here: "while Rizal called his first novel '*novela tagala*,' and evidently understood Ilocano not at all, this was fine, while poor Isabelo was criticized for using Ilocano to stand in for Filipino, and for not fully mastering Tagalog!" (*Under Three Flags*, 95). De los Reyes—an Ilocano living in Manila, to which Ilocanos were not native but where many worked as household servants— was as much a patriot of Ilocos as of the broader abstraction "the Philippines," quick to point out Tagalog centeredness of his compatriots, and generally more attentive to the multiplicity of "Filipino." Scott, Anderson, and Mojares emphasize de los Reyes's claims to brotherhood with highland peoples, whereas Aguilar reminds that de los Reyes was not as magnanimous toward peoples thought to be among the first- and second-wave migrants. Filomeno V. Aguilar Jr., "Tracing Origins: *Ilustrado* Nationalism and the Racial Science of Migration Waves," *Journal of Asian Studies* 64, no. 3 (2005): 605–37; Mojares, *Brains of the Nation*, 341–45, 49– 50; Scott, *Cracks in the Parchment Curtain*; Anderson, *Under Three Flags*, chap. 1.

62. De los Reyes, *Folk-lore filipino*, 46.

63. Ibid., 101.

64. Ibid., 258, ellipsis original.

65. The quotation is from ibid., 74; the chapter is on 74–81.

66. Ibid., 41, 31n2.

67. Anderson, *Under Three Flags*, 18–20; Mojares, *Brains of the Nation*, 354.

68. De los Reyes, *Folk-lore filipino*, 74, 75. As published in his 1887 collection, the title of his piece referred to *the* not *our* chronicles. Isabelo de los Reyes y Florentino, "El diablo en Filipinas; según rezan las crónicas," in *Filipinas: Artículos varios de Isabelo de los Reyes y Florentino sobre etnografía, historia y costumbres del país* (Manila: J. A. Ramos, 1887), 115–38. On this piece see also Mojares, *Brains of the Nation*, 295. De los Reyes's piece was written in part to supplement the peninsular piece which translates and comments on a fifteenth-century Dominican's piece: José María Montoto, "De los maleficios y los demonios," in Machado and Guichot, eds., *Biblioteca de las tradiciones populares españolas*, vol. 2 (1884), 197–289; vol. 3 (1884), 211–98; vol. 4 (1884), 173–280.

69. De los Reyes, "Diablo en Filipinas," 116. De los Reyes used four main sources: the Dominicans of Cagayan, Pangasinan, and Bataan are from Diego de Aduarte's account of Dominican missions in the Philippines, China, and Japan, published in 1693; the Jesuit of Moron is Francisco Colín, whose account of the Jesuit missions of the Philippines was published in 1663; the Augustinian of the Visayas and Manila was Gaspar de San Agustín, whose account of the conquest was published in 1698; and the Franciscan of Camarines was Juan Francisco de San Antonio, whose account was published in three volumes between 1738 and 1744.

70. San Antonio as quoted in de los Reyes, "Diablo en Filipinas," 118–19.

71. Quotations from ibid., 120, 122.

72. De los Reyes, *Folk-lore filipino*, 40, emphasis original.

73. Ibid.

74. De los Reyes, "Diablo en Filipinas," 133.

75. Ibid., 119–20.

76. Ibid., 120.

77. De los Reyes, *Folk-lore filipino*, 81. The work he referred to was Louis Giner Arivau (pseudonym for Eugenio Olavarría y Huarte), "Folk-lore de Praoza," in Machado and Guichot, eds., *Biblioteca de las tradiciones populares españolas, vol. 8* (1886), 101–310. Machado identified the pseudonym in *Biblioteca de las tradiciones populares españolas*, vol. 1 (1883), 207.

78. De los Reyes, *Folk-lore filipino*, 81.

79. De los Reyes, "Diablo en Filipinas," 127.

80. De los Reyes, *Folk-lore filipino*, 121, 122.

81. Mariano Ponce, "El folk-lore bulaqueño," in *Folk-lore filipino*, vol. 2, ed. de los Reyes, 80, emphasis original.

82. On meanings produced in the translation (or its impossibility) of key concepts between Castilian or Catholicism and Tagalog, see Vicente Rafael, *Contracting Colonialism: Translation and Christian Conversion in Tagalog Society under Early Spanish Rule* (Ithaca, N.Y.: Cornell University Press, 1988).

83. Anderson, *Under Three Flags*, 9–25. De los Reyes's comparative notes, however, also in a sense add an Ilocano chapter to the peninsular piece on folklore about serpents; see Alejandro Guichot y Sierra, "Lo maravilloso popular. El basilisco, datos y materiales recogidos y ordenados, para el estudio del mito," in Machado and Guichot, eds., *Biblioteca de las tradiciones populares españolas*, vol. 3 (1884), 5–83.

84. De los Reyes, *Folk-lore filipino*, 82, capitalization original.

85. Ibid., on Nordic mythology (Odin and Bore), see 52; for Greek, 29; Hottentots, Guaranos, and Californians, 131; Romans (Nero's palace), 37; Iroquois, 42; and Chinese, 43, 54, 64.

86. Ponce, "Folk-lore bulaqueño," 45–46.

87. Ibid., 74n, 53

88. Paterno, *Nínay (costumbres filipinas)*.

89. Ibid., 16–17.

90. Anderson describes a similar role for the narrator of José Rizal's 1887 novel, *Noli me Tángere* in Benedict R. O'G. Anderson, *Why Counting Counts: A Study of Forms of Consciousness and Problems of Language in Noli Me Tangere and El Filibusterismo* (Quezon City: Ateneo de Manila University Press, 2008). In this respect Paterno occupied a role that Rafael describes *ilustrados* more generally performing—the mediating role between local and Spanish. Vicente Rafael, *The Promise of the Foreign: Nationalism and the Technics of Translation in the Spanish Philippines* (Durham, N.C.: Duke University Press, 2005).

91. For a fascinating account of how the stories traveled, see Matthew Isaac Cohen, *The Komedie Stamboel: Popular Theater in Colonial Indonesia, 1891–1903* (Leiden: Koninklijk Instituut voor Taal-, Land- en Volkenkunde, 2006).

92. Burton's translation (1885–88) was contemporary with Spanish and Filipino folklore collections. I have consulted Burton's preface and notes in *The Arabian Nights: Tales from a Thousand and One Nights*, trans. Richard Burton (New York: Random House, 2004).

93. Ponce, "Folk-lore bulaqueño," 68.

94. Ibid., 75.

95. Mondragón's style is anything but sparse; here is the original language: "Vengan ahora los intransigentes orientalistas y digan si al travez de mi pálido y escueto laconismo y mi torpe y balbuciente decir, no adivinan un cuadro lleno de galas, vigor y riqueza de inventiva, digno de «Las mil y una noches»." Pío Mondragón, "Folk-lore tayabeño," in *Folk-lore filipino*, vol. 2, ed. de los Reyes, 147–48.

96. Ibid., 112.

97. Ibid., 113, italics (though not capitalization) original.

98. It is worth quoting the original, given the relative obscurity of the terms: "El *Bathala* tagalog es el Júpiter supremo, la *katalona* una sacerdotisa como las vestales . . . druidisas y sibilas; los oráculos eran los arúspices, zahories y horóscopos; la ninfas y nereidas son los *tianak* y *tauong damó* (hombres silvestres) y sátiros los pigmeos. Por último, los encantadores y brujas que fueron desterrados por Cervantes y lo inmortalizaron, son los *asuang* y *mangagauay*, siendo nuestro *galing*, *mutia* y *anting-anting* los talismanes, patalim y amuletos. En una palabra acaso existan menos preocupaciones entre los tagalos de hoy que entre los europeos hace 500 años, y entre las de unos y otros ¿hay comunidad de origen?" Ibid.

99. Both Mojares (*Brains of the Nation*) and Anderson (*Under Three Flags*) have addressed how de los Reyes in particular (and other authors) used local knowledge in the face of peninsular and, even more broadly, European authority. Rafael (*Promise of the Foreign*) offers a different theorization of how *ilustrados* challenged Spanish—and in particular friar—authority. Smita Lahiri has examined how friar literature, in the same period, evoked "native" authority in "Rhetorical *Indios*: Propagandists and Their Publics in the Spanish Philippines," *Comparative Studies in Society and History* 49, no. 2 (2007): 243–75. Leela Prasad examines authority and colonial folklore in "The Authorial Other in Folktale Collections in Colonial India," *Cultural Dynamics* 15, no. 1 (2003): 5–39. I am indebted to all of these works and particularly to Smita Lahiri for help in thinking about the mutual articulations of authority, authenticity, and authorial voice.

100. This theme is also treated in chapters 2, 4 and 5 of this book; as well as by by Mojares throughout *Brains of the Nation*, but in particular see 292 and 295.

101. De los Reyes, *Folk-lore filipino*, 253.

102. Rizal, "Two Eastern Fables."

103. De los Reyes, *Folk-lore filipino*, 116.

104. Ibid., 56.

105. Mojares, *Brains of the Nation*, 312.

106. In this respect, my assessment differs from Mojares's that de los Reyes "shows no consciousness that his was a subaltern voice." Ibid.

107. De los Reyes, *Folk-lore filipino*, 23. The Spanish that I translate as "show" is *enseñad* which could also be translated as "teach."

108. Ibid., 46, 48–51, 56, 58, 65, 110. Anderson has noted the various "tonalities" of de los Reyes's writing and its significance. Anderson, *Under Three Flags*, 20.

109. De los Reyes, *Folk-lore filipino*, 56.

110. Bendix, *In Search of Authenticity: The Formation of Folklore Studies*, 59, 66; Abrahams, "Phantoms of Romantic Nationalism in Folkloristics," 9, 19; Stewart, "Notes on Distressed Genres," 17–21.

111. Ponce, "Folk-lore bulaqueño," 60.

112. Serrano [Laktaw], "Folk-lore pampango," 82.

113. The elegant and complex original reads, "dice que se lo había contado, cuando era mozo, un viejo, que según fama, era el único que consiguió penetrar hasta las entrañas de aquella enorme mole." Ibid., 83.

114. Ponce, "Folk-lore bulaqueño," 66.

115. The original phrases are "mi provincia natal" (41), "mi pueblo" (46n2, 63), and "nuestra casa" (64). Ibid. Ponce's intimate voice when writing on Bulaqueño literature contrasts with his more distant voice when writing on Catalonian folklore. Ponce's writings on Catalonian folklore were published in de los Reyes's bilingual Manila paper *La lectura popular*, vol. 1 (1890), under the pseudonyms Calipulaco and Si Lapulapu, titled "Tradiciones monserratinas/Mañga sali,t, saling sabi bagay sa Monserrat" (nos. 6, 7, 18, 20, 36), "Una tradición manresana/Isang sabisabi bagay sa manresana" (no. 38), and "La torre de la miñona sa Cardona/Ang torre nang miñona sa Cardona" (no. 41).

116. Ponce, "Folk-lore bulaqueño," 78.

117. Ibid., 61.

118. Ibid.

119. Mondragón, "Folk-lore tayabeño," 132.

120. Ibid., 125.

121. It may have had no equivalent anywhere at the time.

122. Mojares, *Brains of the Nation*, 312; Scott, *Cracks in the Parchment Curtain*, 248, 256; Anderson, *Under Three Flags*, 18–20.

123. Some folklore writings referred to early chronicles in order to establish (or refute) the longevity of certain practices; folklore used those early chronicles more rarely, however, than did ethnology, linguistics, or history. We have already seen one way that de los Reyes used chronicles in his "The Devil in the Philippines" in the previous section of this chapter, "Untangling Origins, Comparing Peoples."

124. De los Reyes, *Folk-lore filipino*, 30, 32.

125. Ibid., 260.

126. Ibid., 266, see also pp. 265–66.

127. Ibid., 83.

128. The original reads, "los restos de una Religión inculta y prehistórica (no extinguida), que por la gran antigüedad y el atraso que revela, ha descendido á la categoría de Mitología, es decir, patraña ó invención, sancionada por la ignorancia de los antiguos y por el tiempo más ó menos largo en que fué creida." Ibid., 83–84.

129. Ibid., 84.

130. Ibid., 83–87.

131. Ibid., 86.

132. Ibid., 88, 91, 93–95, 101–102, cf. the following articles (published under pseudonyms) in *La solidaridad*: Guitna, "Cartas íntimas," August 15, 1890; V. M.

Yeser, "La cruz de mayo," September 15, 1890; and Barit, "El arzobispo de Manila," April 15, 1891.

133. De los Reyes, *Folk-lore filipino*, 140.

134. Ibid.

135. Ibid.

136. Ibid., 141.

137. Ibid., 142.

138. Ibid., ellipsis original.

139. Ibid.

140. "¿Folk-lore administrativo?" Ibid., 297–338. For others' mentions of this piece, see Scott, *Cracks in the Parchment Curtain*, 258; and Mojares, *Brains of the Nation*, 312–13.

141. Could *criados* be a misprint for *creados* ("for which we were created")? De los Reyes, *Folk-lore filipino*, 304.

142. Ibid., last ellipsis original.

143. For example, see, both from *La solidaridad*, 1889: "Sistema de recaudación," May 31; "Un Voto de gracias," November 15.

144. De los Reyes, *Folk-lore filipino*, 314. Government *expedientes* (lit. "files") contained the red tape of bureaucracy: reports, investigations, and the like.

145. Ibid., 323.

146. Ibid., 330.

147. Ibid.

148. Ibid.

149. Ibid.

150. Ibid., 335–36.

151. Ibid., 338n.

152. Compare with the character of Simoun in José Rizal's second novel, *El filibusterismo (novela filipina)* (Quezon City: R. Martínez & Sons, 1958).

153. De los Reyes, *Artículos varios*, 131.

154. De los Reyes, *Folk-lore filipino*, 57.

155. Ibid., 56, question mark original.

156. Ibid.

157. Ibid.

158. Ibid., 56–57, emphasis original.

4. Is "K" a Foreign Agent?

1. Quioquiap [Feced] as quoted in Ferdinand Blumentritt, "Un aniversario," *La solidaridad*, April 30, 1889, 64.

2. The original reads, "muchos dialectos malayos tienen una literatura tan grande y tan rica como tal no poseen ciertas naciones romanas, como á ejemplo

los romaníos (naturales del Reino Romanía)." Ferdinand Blumentritt, "Un aniversario," *La solidaridad*, April 30, 1889, 64.

3. Ibid., ellipsis original.

4. Blumentritt used *filipino* here in the older sense of a person Spanish descent born in the Philippines. Ibid. Blumentritt also mentions "the chronicle of the sultans of Tidore and Ternate, published by the Dutchman Dozy," though it is unclear to what this refers. Reinhart Dozy was a prominent Dutch Orientalist scholar of Arabic Spain and the Arabic language, but published no work on the Malay world as far as I know; on the other hand, there was such a chronicle in F. S. A. de Clercq's *Bijdragen tot de kennis der residentie Ternate* (Leiden: Brill, 1890). Could Blumentritt have been aware of this, in advance of its publication, but recorded the wrong author? See Paul Michael Taylor, "Introduction," in F. S. A. de Clercq, *Ternate: The Residency and its Sultanate* (Washington, D.C.: Smithsonian Institution Libraries, 2001), viii.

5. Trinidad Hermenegildo Pardo de Tavera, *Contribución para el estudio de los antiguos alfabetos filipinos* (Laussane: Imprenta de Juanin Hermanos, 1884); Pardo de Tavera, *El sanscrito en la lengua tagalog* (Paris: Imprimerie de la Faculté de Médicine, A. Davy, 1887).

6. See chapter 2 of this book.

7. Pardo de Tavera, *Sanscrito*, 8.

8. Benedict R. O'G. Anderson, *Why Counting Counts: A Study of Forms of Consciousness and Problems of Language in Noli Me Tangere and El Filibusterismo* (Quezon City: Ateneo de Manila University Press, 2008), 72. See *parián* in Wenceslao E. Retana, *Diccionario de filipinismos con la revisión de lo que al respecto lleva publicado la Real Academia Española* (Madrid: Imprenta de la casa editorial Bailly-Baillière, 1921), 147.

9. The original phrases are "la confusa jerga," "el poético y dulcísimo lenguaje tagalo," and "la rica y sonora lengua castellana." Pascual Poblete, "Un tercero en discordia," *Revista católica de Filipinas*, July 28, 1889. Poblete is an interesting figure from whom we will hear more later; a writer in his own right, he often collaborated with Isabelo de los Reyes. He was also the first translator of both the Bible and Rizal's *Noli me tángere* into Tagalog. Greg Bankoff has written about an interesting episode in his later work on labor: "'These Brothers of Ours': Poblete's *Obreros* and the Road to Baguio 1903–1905," *Journal of Social History* (2005): 1047–71.

10. Pardo de Tavera, *Sanscrito*, 8.

11. Ibid.

12. Ibid., 12.

13. In the original, the first phrase reads, "no conducen mas que á trastornar." Poblete, "Un tercero en discordia."

14. Wolff tells us that despite the dramatic number of Spanish—and more recently English—loan words that have displaced older Tagalog roots, "the

language itself . . . has remained remarkably stable over the past four centuries." John U. Wolff, "The Influence of Spanish on Tagalog," in *Lo propio y lo ajeno en las lenguas austronésicas y amerindias: Procesos interculturales en el contacto de lenguas indígenas con el español en el Pacífico e Hispanoamérica*, ed. Klaus Zimmerman and Thomas Stolz (Madrid: Iberoamericana, 2001), 235.

15. See chapter 2 of this book.

16. Thus "ge" and "gi" in the new orthography had the same hard "g" sound as the Spanish *guerra* and *guitarra*, rather than the soft Spanish "ge" and "gi" of *gente* and *ginebra*.

17. Pardo de Tavera, *Sanscrito*, 12. On Pardo de Tavera's linguistic writings and orthographic reform, see Resil Mojares, *Brains of the Nation: Pedro Paterno, T.H. Pardo de Tavera, Isabelo de los Reyes and the Production of Modern Knowledge* (Quezon City: Ateneo de Manila University Press, 2006), 166–69, 205–6.

18. Pardo de Tavera, *Sanscrito*, 13.

19. Ibid. The original reads, "Más lógico, mas científico y mas fácil." Trinidad Hermenegildo Pardo de Tavera, "La k y la w/Ang k at ang w," *La España oriental* I, no. 19 (1889), 138. I am indebted to Mojares's work (*Brains of the Nation*, 206) for calling my attention to this article.

20. More accurately, the strictly oral language of Sanskrit has been written in one of a number of scripts. I thank Betty Nguyen for clarification on this point. Devanagari was the script most commonly used to record Sanskrit among texts of interest to nineteenth-century Orientalists, and also was the script that Pardo de Tavera used.

21. Pardo de Tavera, "La k y la w," 137.

22. José Rizal, "Sobre la nueva ortografía de la lengua tagalog (Carta á mis paisanos)," *La solidaridad*, April 15, 1890, 88.

23. Ibid., 88–89.

24. On *Guillermo Tell*, see Ramon Guillermo's *Translation and Revolution: A Study of Jose Rizal's Guillermo Tell* (Quezon City: Ateneo de Manila University Press, 2009), esp. chap. 1. A reproduction of Rizal's note is on page 19. Rizal's *Guillermo Tell* itself is published in José Rizal, *Escritos varios por José Rizal*, vol. 8, part 2 (Manila: Comisión Nacional del Centenario de José Rizal, 1961), 475–575.

25. Rizal, "Ortografía," 88.

26. Guillermo, *Translation and Revolution*, chap. 1.

27. From a letter to José Rizal from his brother Paciano, July 18, 1886. Rizal, *Epistolario Rizalino*, ed. Teodoro M. Kalaw, vol. 1 (Manila: Bureau of Printing, 1930), 183. According to the catalogue of the national library of Spain, both of Schiller's works had appeared in Spanish translation (possibly for the first time) as *Guillermo Tell* and *María Estuardo* in an 1881 edition published in Barcelona.

28. José Rizal and Ferdinand Blumentritt, *The Rizal-Blumentritt Correspondence*, vol. 1 (Manila: National Historical Institute, 1992), 15, 21; Rizal, "Ortografía," 88.

29. The original reads, "más racional y más lógica, que esté á la vez en armonía con el espíritu del idioma y el de sus hermanos." Rizal, "Ortografía," 88.

30. Ibid.

31. Rizal in Germany wrote much of *Noli me tángere*. For examples of Rizal's admiration of Germany and things German see the letter to him from his brother Paciano (June 16, 1885) and the letters from him to his sister Trinidad (March 11, 1886) and to José María Basa (September 21, 1889) in *Epistolario Rizalino*, ed. Teodoro M. Kalaw, vols. 1–2 (Manila: Bureau of Printing, 1930–31). See also his letters to Blumentritt (January 12, April 13, April 24, June 6, and July 20, 1887) in Rizal and Blumentritt, *Rizal-Blumentritt Correspondence*, vol. 1. Rizal's first novel began with a quotation from Schiller and was originally published in Berlin in 1887. The novel features a young hero who admires certain advances that Germany has made and the educational system it provides for its youth. José Rizal, *Noli me tángere: Novela tagala* (Quezon City: R. Martínez & Sons, 1958).

32. Rizal, "Ortografía," 88.

33. From a letter to José Rizal from his brother Paciano (original in Tagalog and Spanish), dated December 8, 1886. In this letter Paciano used the old orthography when he wrote in Tagalog. Rizal, *Epistolario Rizalino*, vol. 1, 217.

34. Rizal, "Ortografía," 88.

35. The postcard is from Laong Laan (José Rizal) to Mariano Ponce, July 1888, in Rizal, *Epistolario Rizalino*, vol. 2, 31–32. The quotation is from a letter from Rizal to Mariano Ponce, dateline London, August 18, 1888, in Rizal, *Epistolario Rizalino*, vol. 2, 46.

36. Letter from Mariano Ponce to Rizal, dateline Barcelona, August 25, 1888. Ibid., 47.

37. Pedro Serrano Laktaw, *Diccionario hispano-tagalog*, vol. 1 (Manila: Estab. tipográfico "La Opinión" á cargo de G. Bautista, 1889).

38. Trinidad Hermenegildo Pardo de Tavera, "Biblioteca filipina ó sea catálogo razonado de todos los impresos, tanto insulares como extranjeros, relativos á la historia, la etnografía, la lingüistica, la botánica, la fauna, la flora, la geología, la hidrografía, la geografía, la legislación, etc., de las islas Filipinas, de Joló y Marianas," in *Bibliography of the Philippine Islands* (Manila: National Historical Institute, 1994), 406.

39. Ibid.

40. Though the title page identifies the author as "Pedro Serrano Laktaw," his signature on the dedication page reads "Pedro Serrano Lactao." He had been "Pedro Serrano Lactao" or simply "Pedro Serrano"; he later adopted the new orthography for his name.

41. On clandestine pamphlets see John N. Schumacher, *The Propaganda Movement, 1880–1895: The Creation of a Filipino Consciousness, the Making of the Revolution*, rev. ed. (Quezon City: Ateneo de Manila University Press, 1997), 125–27; and Mojares, *Brains of the Nation*, 454–57.

42. The original reads, "fácil es distinguir la raiz y los afijos componentes de cada vocablo, se presenta la escritura menos complicada, y la palabra oral se representa con màs exactitud, lo que no sucede con la ortografia hasta ahora empleada." Serrano Laktaw, *Diccionario hispano-tagalog*, n.p.

43. The original text reads, "el desarrollo de la instrucción." Ibid.

44. Schumacher, *Propaganda Movement*, esp. chap. 6; Benedict R. O'G. Anderson, *Under Three Flags: Anarchism and the Anti-Colonial Imagination* (London: Verso, 2005), 96–104; Paul A. Kramer, *The Blood of Government: Race, Empire, the United States, and the Philippines* (Chapel Hill: University of North Carolina Press, 2006), 48–52.

45. The original Spanish reads, "la deficiencia de libros que enseñen al tagálog la equivalencia en su dialecto del vocablo español." Marcelo H. del Pilar y Gatmaytan, "Prólogo," in Serrano Laktaw, *Diccionario hispano-tagálog*, n.p.

46. In the original phrasing, the second quotation is, "contribuir á la difusión del castellano en este archipiélago, que siendo un pedazo de España, debiera ser español en su idioma, como español en su gobierno, español en su religión, en sus sentimientos, en sus hábitos y en sus aspiraciones." Ibid. This assimiliationist position was parodied by Rizal in his second novel, *El filibusterismo*; see Anderson, *Under Three Flags*, 110.

47. The original text reads, "trasmitir al pueblo indígena todo aquello que esté al alcance de su inteligencia y en las conveniencias de su estado civil y político.

"Procurarémos ponerles al tanto de todas las disposiciones gubernativas y administrativas que necesiten conocer. . . . Darémos en cortos artículos fáciles lecciones para popularizar el conocimiento de las ciencias y artes útiles á la vida práctica, fijándonos sobre todo en la agricultura, industria y comercio, asi como en consejos de Medicina é higiene y perfeccionamientos en su vida doméstica." "Nuestros propósitos," *La España oriental*, July 4, 1889.

48. I demonstrate the extent of de los Reyes's work in the newspapers during this period and argue that his Manila newspapers be considered to be an insular branch of the propaganda movement, in "Isabelo de los Reyes and the Philippine Contemporaries of *La Solidaridad*," *Philippine Studies* 54, no. 3 (2006): 381–411.

49. The original phrasing is, "por creer que se componen y se representan mejor así las palabras del dialecto tagálog [sa pagsang itô ang lalong mabuting paraan nang pagsulat nang wíkang (*sic*) tagalog.]." "Nuestros propósitos," n1. I give the Spanish version first (from which my translations derive) and the Tagalog version in brackets afterward.

50. In the original, "de la raiz *akó* (yo) se forman las palabras *ak*-IN (mio, mia), quitando la última letra *o*, y sustituyéndolo [*sic*] por el sufijo *in*, el cual duplicado en *ak*-IN-IN, convierte la raiz en verbo, significando (*apropiarse, hacérselo suyo etc.*); claridad y sencillez de composición que no se consigue con el empleo de nuestra *c*, que veníamos usando y que produce dificultades para hallar los afijos y raices componentes de una palabra compuesta. [sa raiz *akó* (yo) hináhangô ang

salitang *ak*-IN (mio, mia) na inalisán nang pandulong *o*, at hinalinhan nang sufijo *in*, na kung dublihin sa *ak*-IN-IN, ang raiz ay pagíging verbo, at ang kahuluga'y (*apropiarse, hacérsele, suyo*, etc.), línaw at kadaglián nang pagaakmá ng̃ salitâ na hindî mátamo sa paggamit nang ating *c* na nagpápahírap ng̃ pagkita nang *afijos* at *raices* na taglay nang isáng salitâ.]" Ibid.

51. Note that the Tagalog-language version gives the meaning of *akó, akin*, and *akinin* in parentheses in Castilian (as if readers of Tagalog would not know these Tagalog words!), probably because it was hastily translated from Castilian to Tagalog without much fuss about how the content of the explanation itself required translation. Most if not all of the newspapers' content was written first in Castilian, as is clear from this article and others.

52. "No obstante; si nuestros lectores creen más inteligible ö conveniente la otra ortografía, estamos dispuestos á complacerles. [Gayon man, kung sa akálâ nang mang̃á magsísibasa sa amin ay lálong malínaw ó dápat yaong isáng ortografía, gayak naming pagbigyang loob silá.]" Ibid. The bold letter k's are in the original, a consequence of typesets having insufficient numbers of k's to satisfy the requirements of Tagalog prose. *Revista católica* would take advantage of this opportunity to mock the new orthography for its inconveniences.

53. "Creemos hacer . . . un servicio á la filología, adoptando la ortografía empleada por sabios orientalistas, tales como el Ab. Favre, don Manuel Troyano, Humboldt, Jacquet, Pardo de Tavera, etc., y, últimamente, por el M. R. P. Toribio Minguella, de la Merced, agustino recoleto, sabio filólogo, autor de varias obras en tagálog, y á quien debemos el curioso cuanto concienzudo trabajo de *Los estudios comparativos entre el tagálog y el Sanscrito*." Serrano Laktaw, *Diccionario hispano-tagalog*, n.p.

54. "Usarémos de la ortografía modernamente introducida por los sábios orientalistas Humbold [*sic*], Dr. T. H. Pardo de Tavera, Fr. Toribio Minguella, Moyano y otros. [Aming gágamitin ang bagong ortografía nang pahám na mang̃á *Orientalista* Humbold, Dr. T. H. Pardo de Tavera, Fr. Toribio Minguella, Moyano at ibá pa.]" "Nuestros propósitos," n1.

55. Both works appeared in the same year; and, while I do not know which was published first, it seems likely that de los Reyes had at hand Serrano Laktaw's *Dictionary*, whether in manuscript or printed form. That de los Reyes and Serrano Laktaw would have each others' publications at hand is hardly surprising; both contributed to *La solidaridad*.

56. E[ugène] Jacquet *Considérations sur les alphabets des Philippines* ([Paris, 1831?]), a reprinted version of his "Notice sur l'alphabet Yloc ou Ylog," *Nouveau journal asiatique de Paris* VIII (1831) : 3–30. On Pardo de Tavera's ties to Favre, see Mojares, *Brains of the Nation*, 129.

57. Minguella's *El globo* article on Sanskrit origins of Tagalog ordinals (taken from a longer manuscript, whether published I do not know) transcribed both

Sanskrit and Tagalog with "k," but did not use the "w" for Tagalog and sometimes used a "c" for Visayan. Toribio Minguella y Arnedo, "Estudios comparativos entre el tagalo (Filipinas) y el sanscrito," in *Exposición de Filipinas; Colección de artículos publicados en El globo, diario ilustrado político, científico y literario* (Madrid: J. Salgado de Trigo, 1887), 128. Minguella's textbook had used the old orthography exclusively. Toribio Minguella, *Método práctico para que los niños y niñas de las provincias tagalas aprendan á hablar castellano* (Manila: Tipo-lit. de Chofré, 1886). Moyano's article on different "dialects" in the Philippines focused in fact on Tagalog and Visayan, giving in a very few pages a general overview of grammatical structure, alphabets, and so on. He only used the new orthography to illustrate how the syllable *ki* of the ancient alphabet was pronounced; he wrote no Tagalog words with it. Manuel Moyano, "Dialectos del archipiélago," in *Exposición de Filipinas*.

58. "No soy filólogo, pero soy tagalo, con lo cual quiero significar que, con respecto á mi lenguaje nativo, puedo decir, sin jactancia, que lo poseo mejor, pero muchísimo mejor que ningun señor orientalista (europeo ó filipino no siendo tagalo puro)." Poblete, "Un tercero en discordia." Here *filipino* is comparable to "European" (i.e., "of the Philippines"), neither equivalent to a contemporary and particularly ethno-political sense of Filipino, nor equivalent to the older sense of Spanish creole.

59. "El tagalo no se aprende en ningun libro hecho por autorizados académicos de la leng[ua?], porque hasta ahora no se nos ha ocurrido formar un núcleo de individuos que *fije, limpie* y *dé esplendor* á nuestras palabras. Cada tagalo es un académico de su lengua." Ibid.

60. "[C]asi todos los tagalos como no son *orientalistas* por más que hayan nacido en el Oriente, ni sábios filólogos." Ibid.

61. P. Tecson y Santiago, "Ortografía del idioma tagalog," *Revista católica de Filipinas*, July 14, 1889. Tecson is himself a prominent historical figure; he became secretary of the Revolutionary Congress in Malolos at the end of 1898. Teodoro A. Agoncillo, *Malolos: The Crisis of the Republic* (Quezon City: University of the Philippines Press, 1997).

62. "No tratamos ahora de impugnar á los orientalistas Humbold [*sic*], Pardo de Tavera y Moyano . . . porque no somos amigos de polémicas inútiles." Tecson y Santiago, "Ortografía."

63. "[D]emostrarémos, guiados de . . . la inspirado [*sic*] Musa de D. Francisco Baltasar, que el tagalo, así como los demás idiomas y dialectos del país, no es juguete del capricho ó aberración intelectual, sino que su estructura y modo de ser no ménos que su escritura ó modo de escribirse, obedecen á ciertas reglas, que tienen su conexión y dependencia las unas de las otras, y cuya colección, metódicamente ordenada, es á la que llamamos Ortografía." Ibid. Francisco Baltazar (also known by the name Balagtas) was author of the epic poem "Florante at Laura," the first widely printed piece of literary Tagalog. See Bienvenido L. Lumbera, *Tagalog*

,/0–1898: Tradition and Influences in Its Development (Quezon City: Ateneo
Manila University Press, 1986); Mojares, *Brains of the Nation*, 407–10; Vicente
Rafael, *The Promise of the Foreign: Nationalism and the Technics of Translation in the
Spanish Philippines* (Durham, N.C.: Duke University Press, 2005), 126–58.

64. Pardo de Tavera, *Sanscrito*, 9–10. See also note 94.

65. "[L]eerían [*karaniwan* as] *karini-u-ban*, [*tawo* as] *ta-u-bo*, [*kagawian* as]
caga-u-bian, [*giliw* as] *gili-u-u*, [and *wika* as] *u-bica* . . . pues sus primeros maestros
en la lectura y en la escritura del alfabeto fenicio . . . fueron los españoles, y no los
ingleses ni los alemanes." Poblete, "Un tercero en discordia."

66. Hindî Alemán (pseudonym), "Un parentesis á la ortografía del idioma
tagalo," *Revista católica de Filipinas*, July 28, 1889.

67. "Además, paisanos tagalos: Si nuestra religión, nuestras leyes, nuestras costumbres y todo nuestro modo de ser son españoles, ¿por qué habrémos de usar
unas letras que no son propias y genuinamente españolas, y pronunciar las sílabas
ge y *gi* como los alemanes y no como nuestros hermanos de allende los mares? ¿Es
que con las letras del alfabeto que nos han enseñado no tenemos suficiente para
emitir nuestras ideas y nuestros pensamientos? Pues inventemos las que sean pre-
cisas: mejor aun; resucitemos el alfabeto primitivo nuestro, antes que utilizar una
letra siquiera de procedencia extraña á nuestra Madre pátria." Poblete, "Un tercero
en discordia."

68. See chapter 3 of this book.

69. José Rizal, "Al excmo. señor don Vicente Barrantes," *La solidaridad*, February 15, 1890, 32.

70. See note 31.

71. "Picadillo," *La solidaridad*, December 31, 1891. The place was always
"Kalamba," rather than "Calamba," in *La solidaridad*.

72. "Sabemos todos la intención que encierra el calificativo de alemán lanzado
en Filipinas y conocemos perfectamente el sistema que adoptan algunos de apli-
car á otros, epítetos desagradables que hacen alarde de repugnar, para librarse
luego de ser objeto de su aplicación." Pardo de Tavera, "La k y la w," 140.

73. "Cuidado Padre; *Proximus ardet Ucalegon!*" Ibid.

74. On Pardo's family, see the beginning of the section "Distinguished by
Ancient Colonization: Pardo de Tavera's Filipinos" in chapter 2 of this book.

75. Rizal, "Ortografía."

76. Rizal's lovely prose is worth quoting in full: "Cuando frecuentaban Vds. la
escuela del pueblo para aprender las primeras letras, ó cuando las tenían que ense-
ñar á otros más pequeños, les habrá, sin duda, llamado la atención, como á mí, la
gran dificultad que encontraban los niños al llegar á las sílabas, *ca, ce, ci, co, ga, ge,
gua, gue, gui*, etc., etcétera, por no comprender la razón de estas irregularidades
y el por qué de los cambios de valor en los sonidos de algunas consonantes. Los
azotes llovían, los castigos menudeaban, se rompían las palmetas cuando no se

agrietaban las manecitas, caían en pedazos las primeras páginas, los niños lloraban y hasta los *decuriones* lo tenían que pagar á veces, pero no se pasaba de estas terribles Termópylas." Ibid., 88.

77. Quotation from the subtitle of the article. Ibid.

78. "¿[Á] qué atormentar á los niños á que las aprendan cuando no han de hablar más que el tagalog, porque el castellano les está totalmente vedado? Si más tarde tienen ocasión de aprender este último idioma, ya estudiarán estas combinaciones, como hacemos todos cuando principiamos el estudio del francés, inglés, alemán, holandés, etc. Nadie en España aprende desde niño el silabario francés, ni inglés; ¿para qué, pues, han de matarse los niños de los pueblos en aprender el silabario de un idioma que jamás han de hablar? Lo único que pueden sacar de bueno es cobrar odio á los estudios, viendo lo difíciles é inútiles que son." Ibid., 91.

79. "Es pues, sobrado pueril... rechazar su uso diciendo que es de *origen alemán* y tomándolo por motivo para hacer alardes de patriotismo, como si el patriotismo consistiera en las letras. «*¡Somos españoles ante todo!*» dicen sus adversarios, y con esto creen haber hecho un acto heroico; «*¡somos españoles ante todo!* y rechazamos la K de *origen alemán!*» De seguro que nueve por diez de estos patriotas de abecedario de mi país, usan sombreros genuinamente alemanes y quizás botas genuinamente alemanas también! Qué? ¿donde está el patriotismo? ¿Aumenta la exportación de Alemania, usando nosotros la *K*, más que cuando importamos y usamos artículos alemanes? ¿Porqué no usar chambergo, *salakot* ó sombrero de *buntal*, si son tan proteccionistas? ¿Nos ha de empobrecer la *K*? ¿Es la *C* producto del país? Así es muy fácil ser patriota." Ibid., 90.

80. "Yo ignoraba que la *k* era una propiedad nacional alemana, pero aunque así fuera, no veo porque no la utilizariamos en el momento que la necesitaremos [*sic*]: somos en París muy poco amigos de germanismos, pero á nadie se le ha ocurrido, hasta ahora, hacer la guerra á la cerbeza por ser de orígen aleman!" Pardo de Tavera, "La k y la w," 138.

81. Rizal, "Ortografía," 92.

82. "[A]l fin llegue á generalizarse... estamos seguros de que, convencidos de sus ventajas, la han de considerar como la escritura nacional, razonada y fácil de nuestro armonioso idioma." Ibid.

83. Thomas, "Isabelo de los Reyes and the Philippine Contemporaries of *La Solidaridad*."

84. This section relies on and draws examples from Teodoro A. Agoncillo, *The Revolt of the Masses: The Story of Bonifacio and the Katipunan* (Quezon City: University of the Philippines Press, 1996). The book reproduces many of the manuscripts and documents to which Agoncillo refers, including many in which the use of the "k" is clearly illustrated. I thank Sherwin Mendoza for reminding me to see this as a "k" case. The name itself is significant: Ileto notes that there

were other "organizations" (*katipunan* means "organization") besides the revolutionary Katipunan; but, in the names of those others, the word is spelled, tellingly, with a "c" as in *catipunan*. See Reynaldo C. Ileto, *Pasyon and Revolution: Popular Movements in the Philippines, 1840–1910* (Quezon City: Ateneo de Manila University Press, 1979), 81.

85. Agoncillo, *Revolt of the Masses*, 81–85.

86. Ibid., 59–60, 81. The pages of *Eastern Spain* had similar features; see note 52.

87. These and other flags are described and depicted in ibid. Particularly interesting is one (of the Magdalo faction of Cavite), which used the character of the ancient Tagalog script that corresponds to the letter "k." Almost no one was familiar with the pre-Hispanic script during this period. Its appearance on the flag suggests both that it functioned primarily to signify difference from Spanish (and Spain) and that connections existed between those following *ilustrado* linguistic studies and the Caviteño Katipuneros.

88. Both Agoncillo (ibid.) and Ileto (*Pasyon and Revolution*), in perhaps the most important books on the revolution, characterize the Katipunan as a movement of the masses as opposed to the elite nationalist movement of the propagandists. Glenn May (*Battle for Batangas* [New Haven, Conn.: Yale University Press, 1991]) disputes this, using evidence from Batangas to assert that support for the Revolution was strong among local elites and that the evidence is unclear about enthusiasm from below. Anderson (*Under Three Flags*) emphasizes the distinction between Katipunan and *ilustrado* projects, though he notes evidence that might be helpful in tracing connections between them.

89. The fact that the Katipunan adopted the "k" requires explanation, since the letter had only recently been introduced and had quickly disappeared from public use. Though further research is needed to confirm this, my best guess is that Deodato Arellano, one of the Katipunan's founding members, was one of the links between the elite project of orthographic reform and the plebian society. Arellano, in whose house the first Katipunan meeting took place, was also a member of the *Liga Filipina* (an organization formed by Jose Rizal), the brother-in-law of del Pilar (editor of *La solidaridad*), and part of the propagandist network of supporters in the Philippines. Arellano had been initiated into masonry by Lopez Jaena in 1890. See Agoncillo, *Revolt of the Masses*, 37–48; Reynold S. Fajardo, *The Brethren: Masons in the Struggle for Philippine Independence* (Hong Kong: Enrique L. Locsin and the Grand Lodge of Free and Accepted Masons of the Philippines, 1998), 93–94; and Schumacher, *Propaganda Movement*, 123–24.

90. I thank Ben Anderson for drawing my attention to this aspect of the orthography.

91. Wolff, "The Influence of Spanish on Tagalog."

92. "Kastilang" today takes the more general meaning of "Spanish."

93. Similar work is performed by "k" in other postcolonial orthographies; see my "K Is for De-Kolonization: Anti-Colonial Nationalism and Orthographic Reform," *Comparative Studies in Society and History* 49, no. 4 (2007): 938–67.

94. Compare with Judith T. Irvine and Susan Gal, "Language Ideology and Linguistic Differentiation," in *Regimes of Language: Ideologies, Polities, and Identities,* ed. Paul V. Kroskrity (Santa Fe, N. Mex.: School of the Americas Research Press, 2000), 55. *Catholic Review* writers probably anticipated jabs from some of Manila's more obnoxious and racist Spanish journalists.

95. "Invito, pues á mis paisanos los traductores tagalos de *La España oriental,* á que se dejen de innovaciones que no conducen mas que á trastornar, y procuren con nosotros restaurar en su primitiva riqueza el poético y dulcísimo lenguaje tagalo, del que mas de la mitad de sus términos se han olvidado y está llamado á desaparecer dentro de breve tiempo, desaparición que solo nos consolaría si viniera á reemplazarle por completo la rica y sonora lengua castellana, en vez de la confusa jerga que hoy se habla." Poblete, "Un tercero en discordia."

96. José Rizal, *El filibusterismo (novela filipina)* (Quezon City: R. Martínez & Sons, 1958); Anderson, *Counting Counts,* 70–79. We might also note that Evaristo Aguirre wrote a postcard to Rizal in this Spanish-Tagalog language when Rizal was living in Germany (postcard is dated May 15, 1887, in Rizal, *Epistolario Rizalino, vol. 1*).

97. Anderson, *Counting Counts,* 87.

98. Ferdinand Blumentritt, "Die Spanische Sprache in den Doltsschulen den Philippinen," *Globus* 45, no. 14 (1884). Also see reference to Schuhardt's *Über das Malaiospanische der Philippinen* in Rizal's December 24, 1886 letter to Blumentritt, in Rizal and Blumentritt, *Rizal-Blumentritt Correspondence,* vol. 1.

99. Anderson, *Counting Counts,* 87.

100. Ibid.

101. Ibid., 86–87.

102. Benedict R. O'G. Anderson, "The Languages of Indonesian Politics," *Indonesia* 1 (1966): 103–4.

103. Ibid.

104. Poblete, "Un tercero en discordia."

5. Lessons in History

1. Others have theorized this moment and its significance in the 1880s and beyond; particularly helpful for my purposes are Blanco's and Rafael's readings. John D. Blanco, "The Blood Compact: International Law and the State of Exception in the 1896 Filipino Revolution and the U.S. Takeover of the Philippines," *Postcolonial Studies* 7, no. 1 (2004): 27–48; Blanco, *Frontier Constitutions: Christianity and Colonial Empire in the Nineteenth-Century Philippines* (Berkeley: University

of California, 2009), chap. 7; Vicente Rafael, *The Promise of the Foreign: Nationalism and the Technics of Translation in the Spanish Philippines* (Durham, N.C.: Duke University Press, 2005), 173–82; John N. Schumacher, *The Propaganda Movement, 1880–1895: The Creation of a Filipino Consciousness, the Making of the Revolution,* rev. ed. (Quezon City: Ateneo de Manila University Press, 1997), 228–30.

2. Capitalization original. "Diputado por Filipinas," *La solidaridad,* June 15, 1889, 94.

3. José Rizal, *Sucesos de las Islas Filipinas por el doctor Antonio de Morga, obra publicada en Méjico el año de 1609 nuevamente sacada a luz y anotada por José Rizal y precedida de un prólogo del prof. Fernando Blumentritt* (hereafter, simply *Morga*) (Manila: Instituto Histórico Nacional, 1991), xxxiiin3, xxxiiin1.

4. Ibid., xxxiiin1. Here as elsewhere, Rizal followed the older spelling of "Legaspi."

5. Ibid.; Isabelo de los Reyes y Florentino, *Historia de Ilocos,* vol. 2, *Parte histórica* (Manila: Establecimiento tip. La Opinion, 1890).

6. John N. Schumacher, *The Making of a Nation: Essays on Nineteenth-Century Filipino Nationalism* (Quezon City: Ateneo de Manila University Press, 1991), 110. Thus far, my reading of propagandists' view of Philippine history follows that well established by previous scholars on whose work I draw: Zeus A. Salazar, "A Legacy of the Propaganda: The Tripartite View of Philippine History," in *The Ethnic Dimension: Papers on Philippine Culture, History, and Psychology,* ed. Zeus A. Salazar (Cologne: Caritas Association for the City of Cologne, 1983), 107–26; Ambeth Ocampo, "Rizal's Morga and Views of Philippine History," *Philippine Studies* 46, no. 2 (1998): 184–214; Schumacher, *Propaganda Movement,* 212–44. This reading of propagandists' view of Philippine history, which has antecedents both in the original texts as well as in early commentators and biographers such as Retana, has become standard. See Wenceslao E. Retana, *Vida y escritos del Dr. José Rizal* (Quezon City: R. Martinez & Sons, 1960), 172–78; León Ma. Guerrero, *The First Filipino* (Pasig: Anvil, 1998), 207–20.

7. Ferdinand Blumentritt, "La separación de las colonias españolas de la America continental, reflexiones y consideraciones," *La solidaridad,* November 30, December 15 (1892); January 15, January 31, February 15, February 28, March 15, March 31, April 30, May 15, June 30, August 15 (1893); January 31, April 30, May 15, May 31 (1894); August 15 (1895).

8. Marcelo H. del Pilar, "¡Ojalá!," *La solidaridad,* January 31, 1891; M[arcelo]. H. del Pilar Gatmaytan, "El presupuesto de la paz," *La solidaridad,* December 15, 1892.

9. Schumacher, *Making of a Nation,* 108.

10. Isabelo de los Reyes y Florentino, "Los regulos de Manila," in *Filipinas: Artículos varios de Isabelo de los Reyes y Florentino sobre etnografía, historia y costumbres del país* (Manila: J. A. Ramos, 1887), 87–111; Ferdinand Blumentritt, "De

los estados indígenas existentes en Filipinas, en tiempo de la conquista española," *Revista contemporánea* (Madrid) vol. 61 (1886); no. 253, 468–82; no. 254, 615–27; no. 255, 14–25. Blumentritt's piece was also published in *Boletín de la Sociedad Geográfica* (Madrid) 21 (1886): 200–236. Blumentritt gave more attention to this than de los Reyes did.

11. All from *La solidaridad*: Marcelo H. del Pilar, "Revista de la quincena," February 28, 1892; "Picadillo," October 15, 1891; "Discursos pronununciados en el banquete dado por la Asociación Hispano-Filipina el 23 de Diciembre último en honor del señor Becerra," February 28, 1891.

12. Rizal, *Morga*, v–vi. The first phrase of the dedication is written in all capital letters: "Á LOS FILIPINOS."

13. Ibid., vi.

14. See note 6, especially the works of Ocampo, "Rizal's Morga," and Schumacher, *Making of a Nation*, chap. 7.

15. Rizal, *Morga*, v.

16. Ibid., vi.

17. The phrase "pueblo sin historia" is quoted in Enrique, "¿Quieren historia?" *La solidaridad*, August 15, 1892, 780. As I have already noted, the propagandists' rewriting of Spanish history in the Philippines as decline rather than progress has been well treated by other scholars (see note 6).

18. Ocampo, "Rizal's Morga," 196.

19. Michael Adas, *Machines as the Measure of Men: Science, Technology, and Ideologies of Western Dominance* (Ithaca, N.Y.: Cornell University Press, 1989).

20. For example, Sir William Jones, "Preface to the Institutes of Hindu Law: Or, the Ordinances of Menu, According to the Gloss of Culluca Comprising the Indian System of Duties, *Religious and Civil*," in *Sir William Jones: A Reader*, ed. Satya S. Pachori (Delhi: Oxford University Press, 1993), 199–203.

21. Rizal, *Morga*, 294n4.

22. Ibid., 304n1.

23. The original phrases are, "adelantado á los Europeos," "en conformidad con las leyes naturales," and "pierden su nobleza si se casan con plebeyos." Ibid., 294n2.

24. Emphasis original. For "Middle Ages," see ibid., 306n; otherwise, ibid., 302n2.

25. Ibid., 302n2.

26. Ibid., 307n1.

27. For Rizal on pre-Hispanic religion, see ibid., 272n1, 310n2, 311n4.

28. Ibid., 307n2, emphasis added.

29. Ibid., emphasis added. Here Rizal capitalized "Indios"; I follow his capitalization practices in my translations.

30. Ibid., 299–300n3, 301n1.

31. See, for example, ibid., 259n1. This rupture and cultural amnesia is also suggested by Rizal's preface.

32. Ibid., 303–4n3.

33. Capitalization original. The quoted text ends with the phrase evocative of religious language, "por siglos de los siglos." Ibid., 304n (continued from 303n3).

34. The original text reads, "no debió haberse perdido, sino, como hace observar un escritor anti-filipino, debieron haberla imitado los Europeos. Entre esta *práctica de bárbaros* y la *civilizada* que tenemos ahora de averiguar el hurto á fuerza de máquinas eléctricas, azotes, cepo, y otras torturas inquisitoriales, hay bastante distancia." Ibid., 306n.

35. Ibid, 306–7n.

36. For changes in the criminal code and its application, see Greg Bankoff, *Crime, Society and the State in the Nineteenth-Century Philippines* (Quezon City: Ateneo de Manila University Press, 1996). See also my "Isabelo de los Reyes and the Philippine Contemporaries of *La Solidaridad*," *Philippine Studies* 54, no. 3 (2006): 381–411.

37. In this respect, Rizal and the propagandists offer a strikingly different model from that of Indian nationalist thought provided by Partha Chatterjee in *Nationalist Thought and the Colonial World: A Derivative Discourse?* (Minneapolis: University of Minnesota Press, 1986).

38. Capitalization original. Rizal, *Morga*, 285n3.

39. Ibid., 265n3.

40. Ocampo describes both Rizal's claims to pre-Hispanic Filipinos' technological advance (canon making and ship building, in particular) and the interesting question of how these claims were later challenged. Ocampo, "Rizal's Morga," 196–200.

41. Rizal, *Morga*, 265n3, 276n3.

42. "Una plancha," *La solidaridad*, September 15, 1889.

43. Ibid.

44. "Filipinos" is capitalized as the second word in the original sentence. Rizal, *Morga*, 267n.

45. Ibid., 289n2.

46. Both "Españoles" and "Indios" appear capitalized in the original. Ibid., 295n3.

47. Here, "parias filipinos" contains no capitalization, while "Españoles encomenderos" does. Ibid., 334n2–3.

48. Ibid., 51n2; 336n1.

49. Ibid., 12–13n4.

50. Ibid., 336n1.

51. Ibid., 12n1.

52. Here, *Encomenderos* is capitalized. Ibid.

53. The original phrases read, "las crueldades, abusos, arbitrariedades é injusticias de los Encomenderos" and "[l]a cuestión mas principal, trascendental y ruidosa." De los Reyes, *Historia de Ilocos*, vol. 2, 46–47.

54. "[E]n 40 años, los españoles con sus crueldades mataron á más de quince millones de indios americanos." Ibid., 49. De las Casas's writings might have been no less politically motivated; on las Casas see Patricia Seed, "'Are These Not Also Men?' The Indians' Humanity and Capacity for Spanish Civilisation," *Journal of Latin American Studies* 25, no. 3 (1993).

55. The original phrases read, "los españoles que venían á estas islas eran los peores" and "solo . . . los criminales que huían de la persecución de la justicia, los desterrados, los soldados desertores, los ya deshonrados en otras partes." De los Reyes, *Historia de Ilocos*, vol. 2, 49.

56. "[E]ran escasos de buenos sentimientos y aprendían crueldades en los cuarteles y en los buques de guerra." Ibid., 47.

57. The original phrase reads, "lo que nos permita la Censura oficial." Ibid., 47.

58. For examples of Rizal's commenting on the Spanish state's exploitation, beyond the *encomenderos*, see Rizal, *Morga*, 26n, 341n2. Criticisms of the friar orders in Rizal's and other propagandists' writings are well explored elsewhere; Salazar has paid particular attention to this in propagandists' writings on Philippine history in his "Legacy of the Propaganda." Ocampo has also noted the anti-friar qualities of Rizal's *Morga* and in particular his challenge to friar chronicles in his "Rizal's Morga," 193–94. This quality of Rizal's (and de los Reyes's) history is particularly interesting in light of how each author also invoked the narrative of decline and redemption, an Orientalist narrative but also a Catholic one, as I explore in the section "Heroes of Early Spanish Rule: A Golden Age of Spanish Presence."

59. Rizal, *Morga*, 313n (continued from 312n2).

60. Ibid., 347n1.

61. Ibid., 333n2, capitalization original.

62. On the Calamba affair, see "Boletin oficial de la Asociación Hispano-Filipina," *La solidaridad*, January 15, 1892.

63. Rizal, *Morga*, 346n2.

64. Ibid., 289n1, 337n2.

65. Ibid., xxxiin3, 142–43n2, 201n1.

66. "[L]os Indios . . . se ahorcaron,..los . . . dejaron á sus mujeres y hijos, y se huyeron aburridos á los montes." Fernando de los Ríos as quoted in Ibid., 295–96n3.

67. "[M]uchos se ahorcan, y se dejan morir sin comer, y otros toman hierbas venenosas. Y que hay madres que matan á sus hijos en pariéndolos." Gaspar de San Agustín, as quoted in Rizal, *Morga*, 295–96n3.

68. Rizal, *Morga*, 284n1, 285n4, 289n1–2, 295–96n3, 327n2, 337–38n2.

69. This aspect of propagandists' view of Philippine history is suggested by Salazar's reading of del Pilar ("Legacy of the Propaganda," 113–15), though Salazar does

not pursue the same kind of reading of Rizal, as he focuses on Rizal's "Filipinas dentro de cien años," which does not develop the story of Spain's early conquerors as glorious. Schumacher also notes del Pilar's move to credit early *conquistadores*, rather than friars, with the "civilization" of Filipinos (*Propaganda Movement*, 153).

70. Rizal, *Morga*, 304n4.

71. "Desde un principio se distinguiò por sus hazañas." De los Reyes, *Historia de Ilocos*, vol. 2, 35; see also 35–37.

72. The original of the first phrase reads "tratado de alianza." De los Reyes, *Historia de Ilocos*, vol. 2, 18; Rizal, *Morga*, 12n3.

73. De los Reyes, *Historia de Ilocos*, vol. 2, 8–24, 28–38. His death is dated on p. 33.

74. "Salcedo era indulgente con los cautivos y con los indígenas en general á quienes profesaba verdadero cariño; pacienzudo en requerir la paz; pero valeroso y enèrgico en la guerra; su extremada prudencia y buen tacto contrastaban grandemente con su poca edad." Ibid., 37.

75. Ibid., 8.

76. The original phrases read, "por su valor, desinterès, generosidad y amor á los ilocanos, fuè casi deificado por estos," and "seguramente no como trofeo, sino por la gran estimación en que tenían á hombre tan magnánimo y generoso, como acostumbraban antiguamente con los hombres notables." Ibid., 34, 33.

77. De los Reyes's original phrase is "los indígenas de su encomienda en Vigan." Ibid, 33. Rizal, *Morga*, 12n3.

78. The original has capitalized "Filipinos" and "Españoles." Rizal, *Morga*, 12n3.

79. Ibid., 363n2.

80. Ibid., 16n.

81. Ibid., 343n3.

82. Ibid., 10n5; 12n2; 24n2.

83. Capitalization original. *Naturales* would also correctly be "native born." Ibid., 335n2.

84. See esp. Salazar's discussion ("Legacy of the Propaganda") of this strategy with reference to del Pilar, Lopez Jaena, and Rizal's "Filipinas dentro de cien años."

85. It is strange to render in contemporary language the various ways Rizal identifies kinds of people, since in contemporary terms "Molukans" and "Blacks" would not be the same kind of category, nor would "Greek" and "Oceanian" (which might be roughly equivalent to "Pacific Islander"); here are the original categories as Rizal wrote them: "Y podemos añadir Portuguesas, Italianas, Francesas, Griegas y hasta Africanas y Oceánicas, pues las expediciones que capitanearon Colón y Magallanes, Genovés el uno y Portugués el otro, y las otras posteriores, si bien eran armadas españolas, estaban, sin embargo, compuestas de diferentes nacionalidades, y en ellas iban Negros, Malucos y hasta gente de Filipinas y Marianas." Rizal, *Morga*, xxxin2.

86. Morga used the word "Spaniards," to which Rizal added: "Filipinos must also have gone, since [another chronicler of the event] Gaspar de San Agustín speaks of Indios martyred and captured by the Chinese. Also, it was customary to always take a thousand or more archers, the crew of the ship being almost always entirely Filipino [*filipina*], the majority Visayan [*bisaya*]." Ibid., 29n2. The first "Filipinos" is capitalized in the original though not the first word of the sentence; the adjectival "filipina" and "bisaya," in feminine, form appropriate to modify *tripulación* (crew) could be translated as "of the Philippines" and "of the Visayas" as opposed to "Filipino" and "Visayan," but the adjectives here derive from nominal forms that stand for a people, not a place. Other examples of Rizal pointing out how Filipino soldiers fought for Spanish military campaigns can be found in ibid., xxxivn1, 10n5, 13n1, 19n (continued from 18n2), 32n1, 51n5. Rizal usually used the word "Filipino" or its derivatives and generally only used "Indio" when making a direct reference to or quoting from a chronicle that used that word. He also used *naturales* and the more specific *Sebuanos* (Cebuanos).

87. "Es indudable que tambièn á los ilocanos toca parte de la gloria de haber salvado la ciudad de Manila." De los Reyes, *Historia de Ilocos*, vol. 2, 30.

88. See note 11 above.

89. Rizal, *Morga*, 299–300n3.

90. Ibid., 300n3 (continued from preceding page).

91. De los Reyes, *Historia de Ilocos*, vol. 2, 171–90.

92. For a different example of the writing of this history, see José Montero y Vidal, *Historia géneral de Filipinas desde el descubrimiento de dichas islas hasta nuestros días*, vol. 2 (Madrid: Manuel Tello, 1895), 83–114.

93. "[S]i nos unimos como hermanos, nada pueden los españoles contra nosotros." De los Reyes, *Historia de Ilocos*, vol. 2, 182. De los Reyes had just a few pages earlier written nearly the same words but not in the first person plural: "los pocos españoles no podían nada contra los indios reunidos [the few Spaniards can do nothing against the united *indios*]." Ibid., 175.

94. De los Reyes referred to the "fanaticism" of Ilocanos' Catholicism. Ibid., 188, 189.

95. "Los indios dieron muestras de heroismo," and "eran los más temibles defensores de la causa española." Ibid., 172.

96. The original phrases read, "dice el P. Baranera" (ibid.) and "con el inglès estaban en inteligencia, mandaron á sus pueblos á los indios que tan valerosamente peleaban" (Baranera as quoted in Ibid.). On Baranera, see the section "'Race' and 'Civilization' in Philippine Ethnology" in chapter 2 of this book.

97. "[L]a historia demuestra que muchoos [*sic*] jefes españoles no se portaron muy fieles con su misma pátria, en la invasión inglesa, haciendo decir por esto

á los ingleses que los españoles que habían encontrado en Filipinas, no *eran los españoles de España.*" De los Reyes, *Historia de Ilocos,* vol. 2, 172.

98. "[H]uyó de la provincia." Ibid., 175.

99. The original reads, "como defensor de la causa española." Ibid.

100. The original phrases are, "la independencia de Ilocos" (ibid., 173) and "echar á los ingleses y españoles de Filipinas" (ibid., 183).

101. The original phrases read, "una de las más importantes figuras que destacan en los anales filipinos en general" (ibid., 173), "la gigantesca figura" (ibid., 189), and "inteligente, instruido, valiente" (ibid., 173).

102. "[T]enía gran talento y singular sagacidad política. La Religión era profesada hasta el fanatismo por los ilocanos y prueba de ello fuè que no se atrevieron á matar á los sacerdotes y por la excomunión perdíeron por fin su entusiasmo en servir á Silang; y sin embargo, éste había logrado tener presos al Obispo y á los sacerdotes. El mismo Silang conocía que los ilocanos temían mucho al gobierno español y que eran enemigos de aventuras y novedades; sin embargo, el jefe revoltoso logró sacudir el yugo de los españoles, sirviêndose [*sic*] al principio por palanca de los mismos españoles más influyentes. . . .

"El gran polítìco filipino consiguiò domeñar á sus mas temibles y poderosos enemigos: el fanatismo y timidez de los naturales . . . y la influencia de los Religiosos y de los españoles." Ibid., 188–89.

103. The original reads, "el poder de los principales." Ibid., 189.

104. The original is "libertando . . . á la plebe de la odiosa tiranía de los *babaknáng* (principales indígenas)." Ibid., 173.

105. The original phrases are "se debía renovar completamente la constituciòn social" and "levantar á los *kailanes* (la clase baja) contra los *babaknáng* (principales)." Ibid., 178.

106. "Los enviados de Silang predicaban ideas democráticas y decían que los principales se enriquecían á costa de los pobres á quienes oprimían con exacciones ilegales, prèstamos usurarios y engaños, como era cierto." Ibid.

107. The original reads, "al pueblo . . . libertarle del pesado yugo de los principales. . . . á los principales, les decía enérgicamente que ya había sonado la hora de la muerte de los privilegios y de los abusos. . . . Y por último, invitaba al pueblo bajo á que nombrase un jefe local de entre la clase popular, que garantizase sus libertades." Ibid., 179. De los Reyes's terms here are more than intriguing. Like the subaltern, the *pueblo bajo* (lit. "low people" or "under people," which I have translated as "disenfranchised people") here have agency, but de los Reyes had trouble claiming to know definitively what they actually thought or felt. He did, however, express that he thought the biggest obstacle to Silang was their adherence to traditional authority.

108. "Los principales indígenas siempre, hasta ahora, (y más antes), han tenido esclavizadas á las clases inferiores; y sin embargo, Silang, anticipándose á hacer

lo que mucho más tarde se repitiera en la gran Revoluciòn Francesa, consiguió levantar al pueblo contra sus opresores: la principalía indígena." Ibid., 188.

109. "[S]us hazañas parecen estar inspiradas en las teorías de Voltaire, Rouseau [*sic*], Diderot y otros filósofos que más tarde produjeran [*sic*] los sucesos de la *Comunne* [*sic*] de París." Ibid., 173.

110. The comparison with Gramsci's conception of the war of maneuver is intriguing in part because, like de los Reyes, Gramsci was interested in folklore as a mode of popular education. Antonio Gramsci, *Selections from the Prison Notebooks* (New York: International Publishers, 1971); Gramsci, *Selections from Cultural Writings* (Cambridge, Mass.: Harvard University Press, 1985).

111. William Henry Scott, *Barangay: Sixteenth-Century Philippine Culture and Society* (Quezon City: Ateneo de Manila University Press, 1994), 3.

112. Joan-Pau Rubiés, "The Spanish Contribution to the Ethnology of Asia in the Sixteenth and Seventeenth Centuries," *Renaissance Studies* 17, no. 3 (2003): 418–48. Rubiés's illuminating article refers somewhat anachronistically to "Filipino Indians," though this translation is more consistent with the vocabulary of his subjects than our contemporary sense of "Filipino." See also Scott, *Barangay*, 6.

113. Rubiés, "Spanish Contribution to the Ethnology of Asia," 430. For more on the Chinese rights controversy, see chapter 2 of this book, note 92.

114. Rubiés, 430.

115. Ibid., 422–25.

116. Ibid.

Conclusion. Politics and the Methods of Scholarly Disciplines

1. Perhaps this is the converse of some European Orientalisms being the result of the appropriation of Asian forms of knowledge. See Bernard S. Cohn, *Colonialism and Its Forms of Knowledge: The British in India* (Princeton, N.J.: Princeton University Press, 1996), chap. 2; and Mohamad Tavakoli-Targhi, *Refashioning Iran: Orientalism, Occidentalism, and Historiography* (New York: Palgrave, 2001), chap.

2. Resil Mojares has written about this era of scholarship as the birth of Philippine studies, and the Filipinization of European knowledge, in his *Brains of the Nation: Pedro Paterno, T.H. Pardo de Tavera, Isabelo de los Reyes and the Production of Modern Knowledge* (Quezon City: Ateneo de Manila University Press, 2006); see especially the chapter "The Filipino Enlightenment."

2. Partha Chatterjee, "The Disciplines in Colonial Bengal," in *Texts of Power: Emerging Disciplines in Colonial Bengal*, ed. Partha Chatterjee (Minneapolis: University of Minnesota Press, 1995), 20–21; Sanjay Seth, *Subject Lessons: The Western Education of Colonial India* (Durham, N.C.: Duke University Press, 2

3. Chatterjee, "The Disciplines in Colonial Bengal," 8.

4. On "transculturation," see Arif Dirlik, "Chinese History and the Question of Orientalism," *History and Theory* 35, no. 4 (1996): 96–118.

5. John Christie, "The Human Sciences: Origins and Histories," *History of the Human Sciences* 6, no. 1 (1993): 1–12; Michel Foucault, *The Order of Things: An Archaeology of the Human Sciences* (New York: Vintage Books, 1973).

6. Karl J. Fink, "Storm and Stress Anthropology," *History of the Human Sciences* 6, no. 1 (1993): 51–71; John H. Zammito, *Kant, Herder, and the Birth of Anthropology* (Chicago: University of Chicago Press, 2002).

7. Ann Laura Stoler, *Carnal Knowledge and Imperial Power* (Berkeley: University of California Press, 2002), chap. 6; Michel Foucault, *Society Must Be Defended: Lectures at the Collège de France, 1975–76*, trans. David Macey (New York: Picador, 2003).

8. Linda L. Clark, *Social Darwinism in France* (University, Alabama: University of Alabama Press, 1984).

9. Christie, "The Human Sciences," 3.

10. For fascinating accounts of some such discipline-bending nineteenth-century research, see Hugh Raffles, *Insectopedia* (New York: Pantheon Books, 2010).

11. Christie, "The Human Sciences," 4. Here I again transpose Christie's concern over the presumed break between eighteenth and nineteenth centuries, with my own much narrower focus on transformations since the late nineteenth century.

12. The phrase "pueblo sin historia" is quoted in Enrique, "¿Quieren historia?," *La solidaridad*, August 15, 1892, 780.

13. Vasant Kaiwar, "The Aryan Model of History and the Oriental Renaissance: The Politics of Identity in an Age of Revolutions, Colonialism, and Nationalism," in *Antinomies of Modernity: Essays on Race, Orient, Nation*, ed. Vasant Kaiwar and Sucheta Mazumdar (Durham, N.C.: Duke University Press, 2003), 13–51; Raymond Schwab, *The Oriental Renaissance: Europe's Rediscovery of India and the East, 1680–1880*, trans. Gene Patterson-Black and Victor Reinking (New York: Columbia University Press, 1984). Perhaps the most exquisite formulation of this narrative is in Carl [Karl] Wilhelm Friedrich Schlegel, "On the Language and Wisdom of the Indians," in *The Aesthetic and Miscellaneous Works of Frederick von Schlegel* (London: Henry G. Bohn, 1849), 425–526.

14. Kaiwar, "Aryan Model of History."

15. Joep Leerssen, *National Thought in Europe* (Amsterdam: Amsterdam University Press, 2006), 200. For more comparative examples of the letter "k" in later anticolonial orthographies, see my "'K' Is for De-Kolonization: Anti-Colonial Nationalism and Orthographic Reform," *Comparative Studies in Society and History* 49 (2007): 938–67.

16. Leerssen, *National Thought in Europe*, 195–99.

17. Maria Todorova asserts that Balkan and anti-Ottoman nationalisms emerged before those of Western Europe; she theorizes the particular significance of temporality for Eastern Europe in ways useful here ("The Trap of Backwardness: Modernity, Temporality, and the Study of Eastern European Nationalism," *Slavic Review* 64, no. 1 [2005]: 140–64).

18. Thomas, "'K' Is for De-Kolonization."

19. Benedict R. O'G. Anderson, *Imagined Communities: Reflections on the Origin and Spread of Nationalism*, rev. ed. (London: Verso, 1991).

20. See, for example, feminist and nationalist treatments of the idea and practice of the harem, a quintessentially "Oriental" arrangement, in Reina Lewis, *Rethinking Orientalism: Women, Travel, and the Ottoman Harem* (New Brunswick, N.J.: Rutgers University Press, 2004).

21. Daniel R. Brower and Edward J. Lazzerini, *Russia's Orient: Imperial Borderlands and Peoples, 1700–1917* (Bloomington: Indiana University Press, 1997); Robert P. Geraci, *Window on the East: National and Imperial Identities in Late Tsarist Russia* (Ithaca, N.Y.: Cornell University Press, 2001); Susan Layton, *Russian Literature and Empire: Conquest of the Caucasus from Pushkin to Tolstoy* (Cambridge: Cambridge University Press, 1994).

22. G. Fernández Parilla and M. C. Feria García, eds., *Orientalismo, exotismo y traducción* (Cuenca: Ediciones de la Universidad de Castilla-La Mancha, 2000); Aurora Rivière Gómez, *Orientalismo y nacionalismo español: Estudios árabes y hebreos en la Universidad de Madrid, 1843–1868* (Madrid: Biblioteca del Instituto Antonio de Nebrija de estudios sobre la universidad : Dykinson, 2000).

23. James Tully, *Meaning and Context: Quentin Skinner and His Critics* (Princeton, N.J.: Princeton University Press, 1988), 10.

24. Pagden's accounts always attend to particularities of religious orders, for example, and Tavakoli-Targhi employs a careful account of "Persianate" to describe Mughal scholarship, reducible neither to "Indian," "Iranian," nor even "Persian." Anthony Pagden, *The Fall of Natural Man: The American Indian and the Origins of Comparative Ethnology* (Cambridge: Cambridge University Press, 1982); Pagden, *Spanish Imperialism and the Political Imagination: Studies in European and Spanish-American Social and Political Theory 1513–1830* (New Haven, Conn.: Yale University Press, 1990); Tavakoli-Targhi, *Refashioning Iran*, chap. 2.

25. Tully, *Meaning and Context: Quentin Skinner and His Critics*, 14.

26. Ibid., 39.

Index

Note: Page numbers followed by an *f* or a *t* indicate figures and tables, respectively.

Megan C. Thomas is associate professor at the University of California, Santa Cruz, where she teaches political theory. Her work has been published in *The Review of Politics*, *Comparative Studies in Society and History*, and *Philippine Studies*.